THE LIFE AND ART OF ANNE EISNER

Art direction and cover
Paola Gallerani

Layout
Elisabetta Mancini

Editor
Wendy Keebler

Color separation
Premani s.r.l., Pantigliate (Milano)

Printed by
Esperia, Lavis (TN)

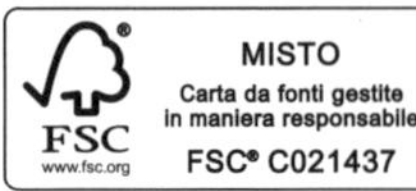

Officina Libraria
Via dei Villini 10
00161 Roma
Italy

ISBN: 978-88-3367-100-0

Printed in Italy

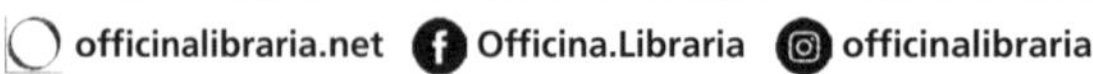

Christie McDonald

The Life and Art of

ANNE EISNER

An American Artist between Cultures

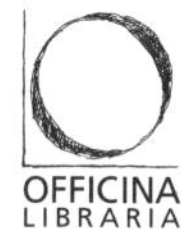

Men, it seemed to me in those days, were uniquely honored by the stories that erupted in their lives, whereas women were more likely to be smothered by theirs.

Carol Shields, *The Stone Diaries*

Memory is not a mere passive receptacle; it is rather a creative faculty. Let it play upon the lives that are no longer sensibly present, and thus maintain the connection with them.

Felix Adler, *An Ethical Philosophy of Life*

Contents

Preface

You might ask why would I spend time over decades poring over the archive of my aunt and writing a biographical narrative about her. What is it in the life of a person that can speak beyond relatives and friends to a generational context in artistic, political, and cultural flux? What can we understand about the globalized world of today (often experienced between cultures) from the perspective of a life lived and art created in the first half of the twentieth century? I hope to have raised these and many other issues in narrating the astounding life and artistic work of Anne Eisner.

The Life and Art of Anne Eisner (1911-1967): An American Artist between Cultures traces Eisner's early years and artistic career in New York, through living at the edge of the Ituri Forest in the ex–Belgian Congo (now Democratic Republic of Congo), to her return to New York. Anne Eisner came of age in the 1930s and 1940s, during the struggle among artists and intellectuals to combat fascism and create a better world. Leaving behind a successful career as a painter, Anne followed Patrick Putnam, with whom she had fallen passionately in love, to Epulu, a multicultural community he had founded in the 1920s. As an American woman and painter, Anne's focus on cultural and aesthetic values and her belief in freedom and equality brought an eccentric perspective to the colonial context. Unanticipated challenges forced her to think about who she was, as she agreed to marry under unfamiliar conditions, became one of the mothers in the community, hosted researchers and tourists, and attempted to care for Putnam in his tragic decline. This book follows Anne's story, based on letters, journals, and documents that reveal her experience of living between several cultures. That her art sustained her throughout her life as a discipline (sketching, drawing, painting) reveals to what extent, despite great challenges and heartache at certain moments, she was able to express joy in creativity; the beauty of her art testifies to its transformative power. In her later work, she continued to explore how cultural transition and memory nourished her art.

I came to the idea of writing a book about Anne Eisner over thirty-five years ago. My sense of her as a warm, feisty, and generous person dates way back to the years in New York City during the mid-1950s and the first half of the 1960s, when she part of the rich fabric of my life. But without her extant art and the archive of her papers, I would never have begun the research for the book. In 1986, my father, John McDonald, gave me Anne's papers, paintings, drawings, and memorabilia as he was donating the papers of her husband, Patrick Tracy Lowell Putnam, to Houghton Library at Harvard University; at the time, Pat being a graduate of Harvard College made his papers of interest but not Anne's. Miffed by rejection of her archive, I took on what I thought was a minor archivist endeavor, which then turned into a passionate project for me. Sifting through Anne's papers, I wanted to find out what it was I didn't know (because before my time, I wasn't there) or what one cannot see (in the public face) of another person's life. I learned that the ideal of her life that I had carried with me—that her years in Africa during the 1940s and 1950s were seamlessly the happiest years of her life—was a fiction. I learned how her narrative had been rewritten by a ghostwriter—even as she published under her married name, Anne Eisner Putnam—in *Madami: My Eight Years of Adventure with the Congo Pigmies*. I learned, most important, how she was then erased from the history of a time and place of which she had been an integral part. That was it! I was hooked. The lessons of Anne's life are, of course, not only hers but apply to many women before and during the first half of the twentieth century: artists, intellectuals, activists, and every other stripe of female contributor to human society. In teasing out the narrative of her unique story from the archive, I realized how important it is (as with all reading) to decipher and interpret different kinds of documents, from letters to family (weekly, sending "all that was fit to print" from Africa) to journal entries, photographs, artwork, and more. Anne's grit as a person and her commitment as an artist (later ethnographer and writer) emerged from my reading of her archive and inspired me to write this book.

I gave Anne's archive to Houghton Library in 1994, the year I was appointed as a faculty member in the Department of Romance Languages and Literatures at Harvard University. The library subsequently acquired artistic works of art by her, as other institutions have—the American Museum of Natural History, New York Historical Society and Museum, the Peabody Essex Museum, and Musée du Quai Branly.

In 2005, I published *Images of Congo: Anne Eisner's Art and Ethnography, 1946–1958* with several colleagues to situate her life and work in the context of colonial Africa and the Western tradition of art, including a preface by Abiola Irele and comments from painters Louis Finkelstein and (my late sister) Joan McD Miller. The writers in this volume analyzed many aspects of Anne Eisner's work as a painter, ethnographer, and writer: modernism and ethnology in understanding differing views of the Mbuti Pygmies (Enid Schildkrout), the dialogue between Mbuti bark cloth and Anne Eisner's painting in mapping the Ituri Forest (Suzanne Blier), the way in which stereotypes and clichés figured in the ghostwriting of *Madami* (Christraud Geary), the music of the forest through art (Kay Shelemay), and "Drawing on the Forest" (Rosanna Warren). The rich plates mostly include art from and about Africa.

Prior to working on *Images of Congo*, I conceived of and wrote a first version of this book which was never finished. I am publishing it now in an expanded and completely revised form to give voice to central questions I asked from the beginning: how did Anne make sense of her life as a woman and an artist who reinvented herself across cultures, and how does historical distance help us to understand her life and work now? This new book delves back into the period in which Anne grew up, came of age, and began her career as an artist. The years growing up in New York, alarm about the rise of fascism, and the political involvement among artists and intellectuals on the left all prepared Anne to live and work across boundaries and cultures.

Unconventional in the colonial context, Anne created a role that few could comprehend. No less offbeat with regard to her American contemporaries, she only disclosed to them a partial version of herself and her life at Epulu. She recreated her life after she left New York, yet in her letters and her book, she wasn't willing to say just how much. I have written in a part of what was silenced, searching for the ways in which one woman can serve as a model for another--through achievements and strengths, certainly, but also through her struggles and mistakes. It is this personal and historical memory that compelled me to write what follows. I was also looking for some explanation of what her life meant to mine. Anne had given me something precious when I was young: a sense of the importance of knowing more than one perspective, not allowing any one set of norms and stereotypes to limit life.

In writing a book whose goal is to better understand the past, I recognize that much has necessarily changed in the way we speak today about that same past. I have nevertheless dealt with the changes in terminology between then and now in the following manner. Throughout the book, I have chosen to remain generally faithful to the vocabulary of the 1940s and 1950s in the colonialist context because it comes from the archive following the conventions of the era: the Epulu villagers are referred to as "boys" when they worked for the hotel or for individuals; the term "Negro" respectfully designates the villagers, as different from the Pygmies, while the term "black" refers to a complex coding of color difference between Africans and those associated with the colonialist hierarchy. The names of the cities and towns are those of the 1950s as well: what I refer to as Stanleyville is now Kisangani; Léopoldville is Kinshasa.

I have probed into much that Anne did not, trying to pull away the protective silence meant to hide the irregularities of life and its pain. I wanted to find the story that she didn't acknowledge—and that others wouldn't, either. This book narrates that story.

Cambridge, Mass., March 2020

Acknowledgments

Bringing this book to light has been collaborative from the very beginning of the project: from the creation of the archive out of Anne Eisner's papers, to interviews with people who knew her in New York or visited in the then–Belgian Congo (now Democratic Republic of Congo) during the 1940s and 1950s, to generous discussions about history, politics, and art over the years with many people and generous readings of the manuscript in different stages.

For early discussion about Anne Eisner and research on her life, I want to acknowledge the role of my late sister, Joan McD Miller, who shared a great deal from personal memories and visual acumen as a painter. My father, the late John McDonald, contributed the archives he inherited from Anne Eisner (his sister-in-law): first, the Patrick Tracy Lowell Putnam papers to Houghton Library, Harvard University, and the Anne Eisner Putnam papers to me; I later donated them to Houghton Library. Special thanks go to Schuyler Jones and Francis Chapman for sharing their memories (as well as visual materials) of Anne Eisner, Patrick Putnam, and the people of Epulu from their respective stays there in 1952 and 1954. In 1990, I exchanged letters with the late Colin Turnbull, who gave me permission to publish his letters and photographs of Anne Eisner. The late Louis Finkelstein's contribution through an extended interview with me in 1992, reviewing Anne Eisner's entire artistic body of work, has been invaluable.

Over the years, Carol Kahn has focused my thoughts with her sharp eye both critically and visually in many phases of this project. Katherine Lasky gave wonderful encouragement and read a very early version of the manuscript, for which I am grateful. For his knowledge and generous response about the politics of the 1930s and 1940s, I thank Alan Wald. For opening the Margaret De Silver archive to me, I thank Susan De Silver. Thanks to Susan Suleiman for a visit to Martha's Vineyard retracing the places Anne Eisner lived and worked and for all the conversations over many years. For permission to publish from the letters of his father, Monroe Mather Stearns, I thank Michael Stearns. I am grateful to Tense Banks for sharing her knowledge of

Linville Falls and the family ranch in Oregon. To Martha Campbell, Hermine Ford, Holly Hartley, and Helen Tworkov, I am grateful for sharing memories of Anne Eisner in New York City and on Cranberry Island.

With grateful appreciation, I acknowledge the insights that have come in many different ways over the years, be they in conversations directly or indirectly related to this project, letter and email exchanges, or early manuscript readings concerning Anne Eisner's life and work: from Alicia Anstead, Suzanne Blier, Jay Bochner, Sally Bochner, Mary Ann Caws, Terence Cave, Penny Chapman, Yves Couvreur and Madame Jacques Couvreur, Helen E. Treganza Crofts, Peter Davis, the late Christian Delacampagne , Edite Denroys, Diane Elam, Johannes Fabian, Sideo and Nora Speyer Fromboluti, Salah M. Hassan, Christread Geary, Nancy Greyson, Richard Grinker, Katherine Hart, Dieudo Hamadi, Michael Herzfeld, Nancy Hunt, John and Terese Hart, the late Carolyn Heilbrun, Marianne Hirsch, Rachel Jacoff, Bogomil Jewsiewicki, Eileen Julian, Sidney Kasfir, Frank L. Lambrecht, the late Michel F. Lechat, Yvette Maertens Lenain, Tom Kahn, Margaret Lock, Richard Lock, the late Fritze Manuel, Joan Mark, Christopher L. Miller, Lucas Miller, Tom Miller, Nancy K. Miller, the late Richard Miller, Stephen Mitchell, Jan and the late Fred Moss, Rosalind Pace, Michael Putnam, Esther Rosengarten, Sarah Rosengarten, Jen Sale, Enid Schildkrout, Kay Kaufman Shelemay, Ellen Handler Spitz, Leo Spitzer, the late Mary Steedly, Allan and Sandy Thomas, Anna Lowell Thomlinson, Ellen Mazur Thomson, Adam Vance, Jacob Vance, Rosanna Warren, the late Sarah Westphal. I thank those who helped early on as assistants with the project in different phases: Benoît Dugas, Grodya Dhechuvi, Ruth Kerkham, Marie-Pierre Maybon, Yannick Portebois, Kelly Patterson, Renée-Claude Lorimier, Olga Nikolova, and Elizabeth Schwartz. For recent work on the revised manuscript, Nathaniel Liberman assisted in research on the 1930s and 1940s. I am indebted to the work of Caleb Shelburne and Emma Zitzow-Childs for their editorial acumen in assisting with this manuscript.

I would like particularly to thank the curators and staff, current and former, of Houghton Library, Harvard University: Leslie Morris, who immediately wanted Anne Eisner's entire archive to come to Houghton Library and with whom I curated the exhibition "Images of Congo" in 2006. I thank Elizabeth Falsey, Mary C. Haegert, Susan Halpert, Tom Ford, Bonnie Salt, and Emily Walhout for their generous help in dealing with a myriad of archival and photographic problems. This project has also benefited over the years from the resources at the American Museum of Natural History (where the collections of African artifacts from Anne Eisner and Patrick Putnam reside, as well as drawings by Anne Eisner); the Joseph Towles Collection of the Avery Research Center for African American History and Culture, College of Charleston (also location of the Colin Turnbull archive); the Kislak Center for Special Collections, Rare Books and Manuscripts, University of Pennsylvania, and New York University Special Collections. I wish also to thank Debra Bach, Margi Hofer, and Wendy Ikemoto of the New York Historical Society Museum; Austen Barron Bailly, formerly of the Peabody Essex Museum; Sabine Bompuku Eyenga Cornelis of the Musée Royal de l'Afrique Centrale, Tervuren, Belgium; and Sarah Ligner of the Musée du Quai Branly, Paris.

I am indebted to Marco Jellinek for his remarkable artistic and editorial expertise in the making of this book.

Finally, with his photographic and technical expertise, his love, patience, and constant support, Michael Rosengarten has helped to make this book come about in more ways than can be enumerated. Thanks do not begin to express the extent of my gratitude.

For permission to reproduce photographs by Aaron Siskind, I thank the Aaron Siskind Foundation; for the Walker Evans photographic portrait of Anne Eisner, I thank the Metropolitan Museum of Art. My heartfelt thanks go to John T. Hill for his photography of Anne Eisner's art included in the plates.

The Canada Council awarded an Arts Award in Non-Fiction and support from the Université de Montréal in 1992 to begin work on the archive and the writing of this project at its inception. The book is being published with the support of the Anne and Jim Rothenberg Fund for Humanities Research and the Potter Fund of the Department of Romance Languages and Literatures at Harvard University. I have also received support from the Faculty of Arts and Sciences. For all of this generous support, I am most grateful.

Part I

NEW YORK

CHAPTER ONE

The Early Years (1911–1944)

Coming into One's Own

Anne Eisner (fig. 1) grew up surrounded by a strong sense of culture through social and political change for women during the early part of the twentieth century. Her older sister, Dorothy, won children's drawing prizes and decided to be an artist for life; their dignified mother, Florine (whom everyone called Fluff), marched in the suffragette parade down Fifth Avenue in 1917, when Anne was six. The fight for voting rights marked a radical transition in women's role in American society. Anne came of age with the stock-market crash of 1929, followed by the Great Depression and the struggle among artists and intellectuals in New York City to combat fascism and find a better world. She immersed herself in the study

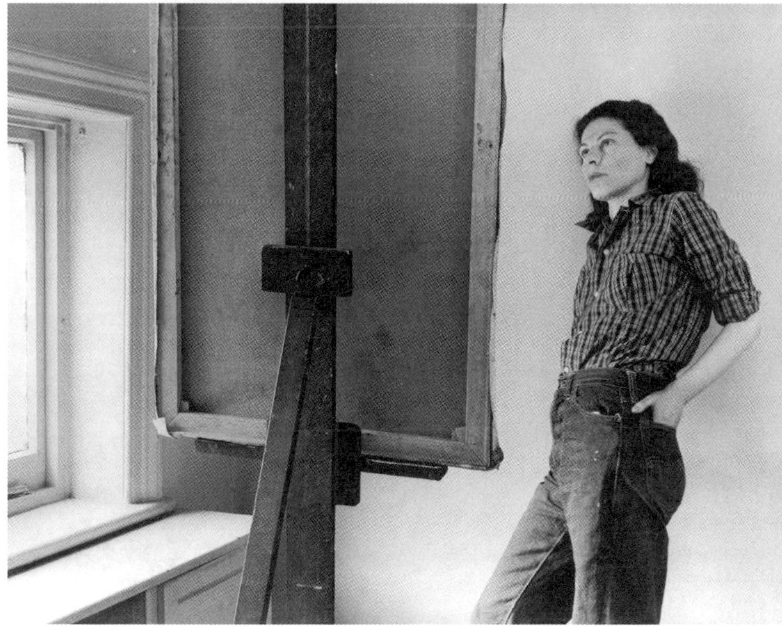

Fig. 1
Aaron Siskind (?) portrait photograph of Anne Eisner, c. 1941. Houghton Library, Harvard University.

of art and found her way through periods of transition—social, political, and artistic—in turbulent times. If the context of one's childhood tells a lot about the values one adheres to or resists, it does not determine the choices any of us make.

Anne Eisner was born on April 13, 1911, to William J. Eisner (1881–1975) and Florine "Fluff" Eisner (1884–1974). They were a second-generation Jewish family from Bohemia, long steeped in European culture. Anne's maternal grandfather, Moritz Eisner (1852–1938), cut an elegant figure as the patriarch of the Eisner family. He had grown up in a quite well-to-do, bourgeois family, until his father, Joseph, a toll keeper, lost almost everything when the Austro-Prussian War began in 1866. His older brother Leopold went into the army, while Moritz was apprenticed to an apothecary in Vienna. Blessed with an excellent memory, as he writes in his brief, unpublished autobiography, Moritz studied physics and chemistry at the University of Vienna, but he spent as much time as possible backstage at the city's Berg Theater; he loved everything to do with theater. At seventeen, Moritz decided to "try [his] fortune in the New World" and set out after two uncles, Meyer and Heinrich (Henry), who had settled in New York around the time of the 1848

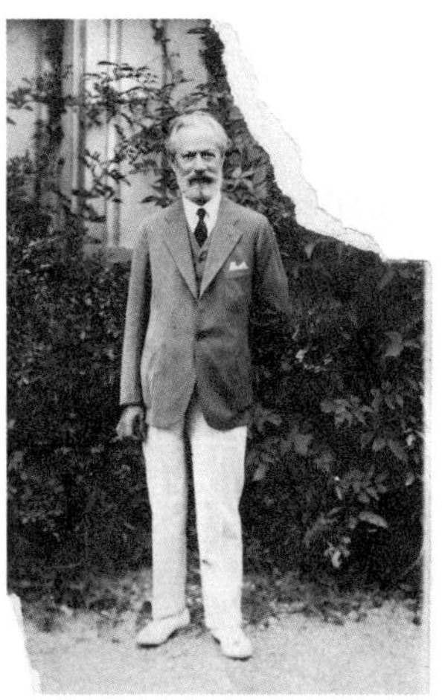
a

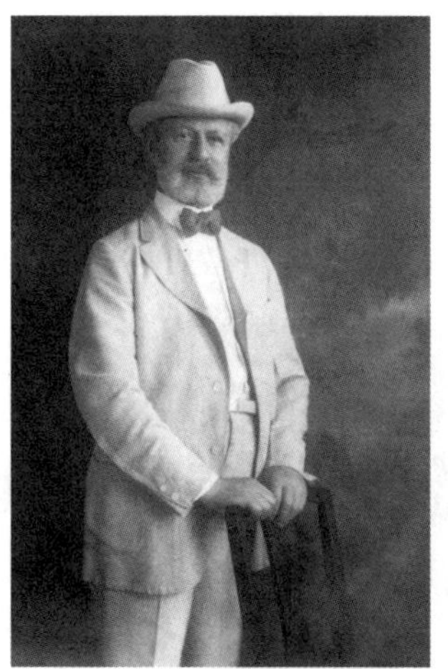
b

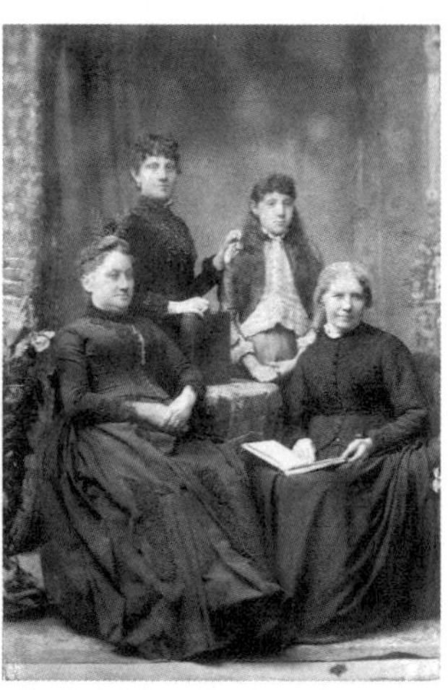
c

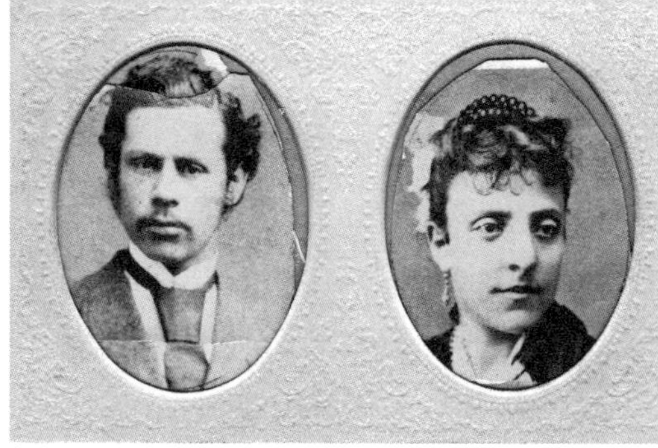
d

Fig. 2a-d
a-b: Moritz Eisner, c. 1920s;
c from top left: Anna Zeitz Eisner; daughter Julia Eisner (?); Julia Haas Eisner, Anna's mother; lower left, unknown, c. 1886;
d: Leopold and Jamie Eisner, c. 1880s.
Christie McDonald archive.

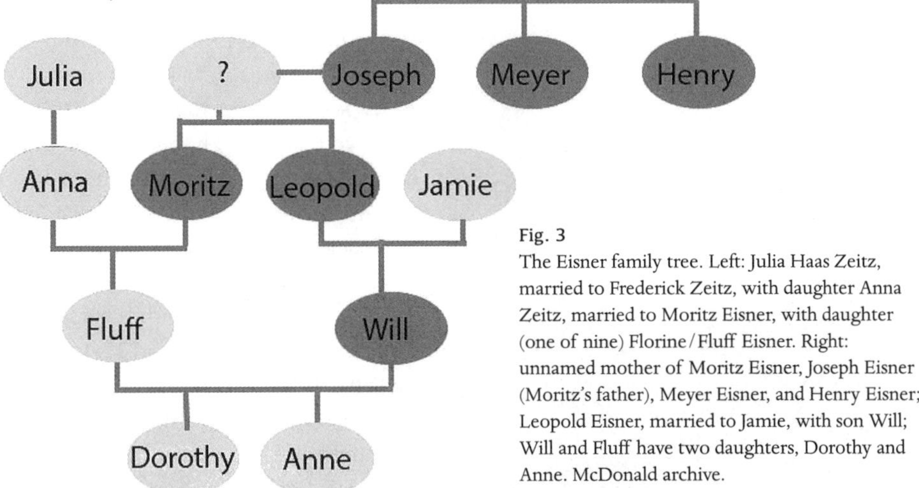

Fig. 3
The Eisner family tree. Left: Julia Haas Zeitz, married to Frederick Zeitz, with daughter Anna Zeitz, married to Moritz Eisner, with daughter (one of nine) Florine / Fluff Eisner. Right: unnamed mother of Moritz Eisner, Joseph Eisner (Moritz's father), Meyer Eisner, and Henry Eisner; Leopold Eisner, married to Jamie, with son Will; Will and Fluff have two daughters, Dorothy and Anne. McDonald archive.

revolution in Austria. Moritz, steeped in the theatrical culture of Vienna, moved to Philadelphia, where he organized a dramatic club, many of whose members were of German descent. There he met Anna Zeitz (1852–1922), a Christian, who played the piano for one of the productions. They fell deeply in love. But Moritz, who was flamboyant and generous, with a deep sense of family, had to delay marriage because he sent all his savings to a widowed sister who wished to come to the States. Once Moritz was able to make a living as a pharmacist, he and Anna married and had nine children, one of whom was Anne's mother, Fluff.

Once established, Moritz helped his older brother Leopold (1850–1892) emigrate from Austria. Leopold went on to settle in San Antonio, Texas. Leopold's son, Will Eisner, who would be Anne's father, spent his childhood there, until he was orphaned at age eleven when his mother died and Leopold committed suicide over a gambling debt. Moritz adopted his young nephew Will and brought him to live with his family. Will left school to go to work when he was thirteen. Later, after Moritz founded the Newark Paraffin and Parchment Paper Company in 1903, Will became president and, with his younger cousin Stanley Eisner, made it into a successful business; they were some of the first manufacturers of waxed paper in the United States. Lore had it that Will and his cousin Fluff had fallen in love during adolescence, although they did not marry until 1905, when he was twenty-four and she was nineteen. They became a legendary couple whose marriage lasted sixty-nine years. A redhead with a Texas-tinted New Jersey accent and a hot temper, Will was a toughie; he had to be. He learned how to take care of himself and then how to take care of everyone around him. He went on to become chairman of the Waxed Paper Industry on the War Service Board during World War I, president of the Waxed Paper Association, and director

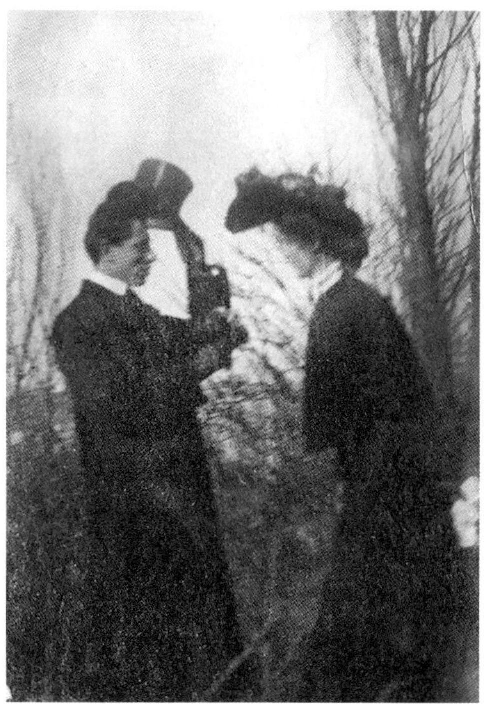

Fig. 4 Will and Florine "Fluff" Eisner, c. 1905. McDonald archive.

of the American Pulp and Paper Association from 1918 to 1919. (See figs. 2a-d and 3 for family photos and a family tree.)

As second-generation Jews, Will and Fluff were faced with the question of how much they could or would want to assimilate into an increasingly exclusionist American society. With a sense of cultural rather than religious heritage from Europe, they became involved with the Society for Ethical Culture, which had been founded by Felix Adler in 1876. Adler's philosophy grounded the relationship between people and society in experience and living rather than belief; it focused on the individual and ethical principles within democracy that could address inequities between the privileged and the poor. "Ethical Culture," as Adler called it, offered a third way, between Christianity and Judaism, in which Jewish heritage was remembered without religious ritual. His philosophy, going back to Immanuel Kant and the Enlightenment, continued the move toward secularization of Charles Darwin, Karl Marx, and Sigmund Freud—Adler's contemporary—to find the definition of a moral life without theology. The premise was that ethics could be both central to life and separate from any metaphysical system. What was most radical about the Ethical Culture movement was its positive emphasis on religious diversity and the coexistence of theists, deists, agnostics, and secularists, all in the same fellowship. It was a profoundly eclectic and tolerant view of life, and the curriculum of the Ethical Culture School, founded by Adler, was based on the equality of races, freedom, and social justice. Will and Fluff inscribed a copy of Adler's book, *An Ethical Philosophy of Life*, published in 1918: "this is what we believe and have always tried to live by." (Will and Fluff are shown in fig. 4.)

For the first ten years of her life, Anne grew up in Woodmere on Long Island. The family then moved to New York City, though she left the city to spend summers in remote areas of New England at camps with such promising names as Kearsage and Walden. Anne, the younger of the two children, was tempestuous and emotional, with a bouncy and often self-deprecating sense of humor. Like her father, she was feisty. Father and daughter got along by competing with each other combatively. Anne was more adventurous and vulnerable than Dorothy, who accommodated herself to the needs of others and avoided confrontations with her father whenever

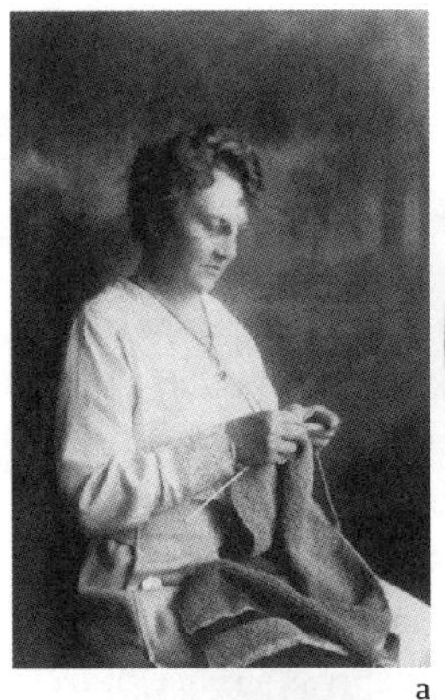

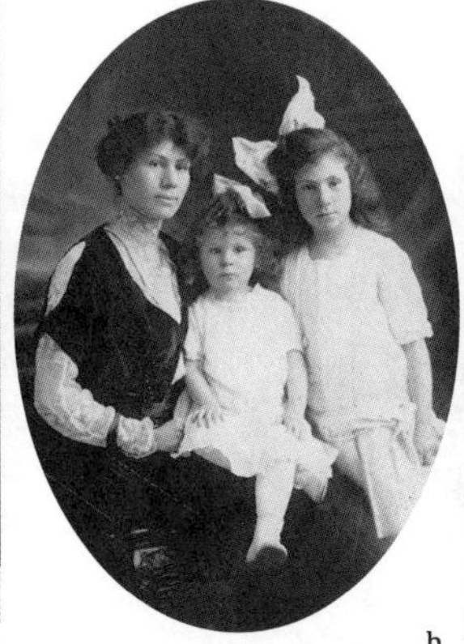

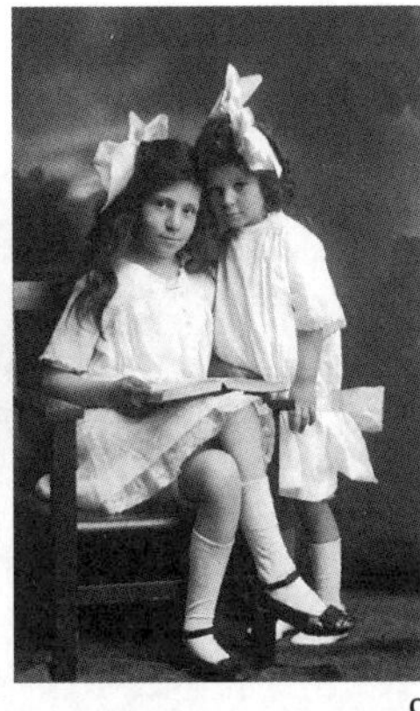

Fig. 5a-c
a: Anna Zeitz Eisner, unknown date.
b: Florine, Anne, and Dorothy Eisner, c. 1913.
c: Dorothy and Anne Eisner, c. 1915.
McDonald archive.

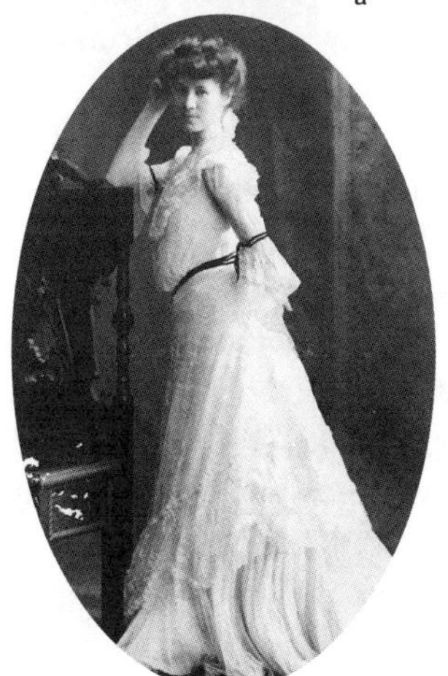

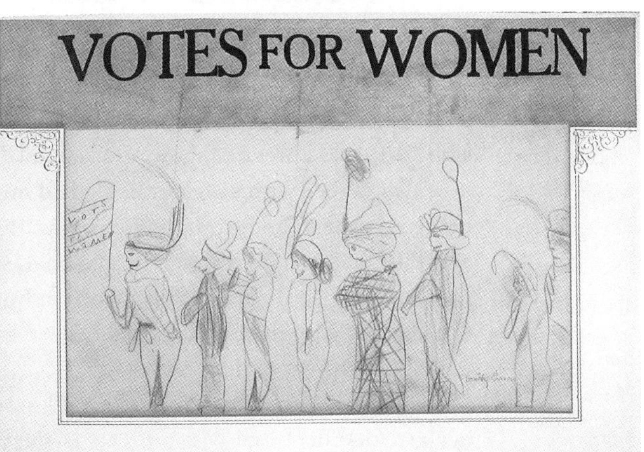

Fig. 6
Florine "Fluff" Eisner, c. 1902. McDonald archive.

Fig. 7
Dorothy Eisner, *Votes for Women*, collage, 1917. New-York Historical Society Museum.

possible; she resembled her mother in this respect. (See family photos in fig. 5a-c.) Their cousin Bob Roland reflected that "Dorothy was about sixty percent conventional, and Anne was zero! Both were extremely artistic and imaginative." As a ballet dancer and teacher of dance (and, later, a photographer), Bob Roland identified more with Anne. He remembered how impulsive and rambunctious she could be, getting herself into a jam when they were young by trying to get a dent out of a ping-pong ball: "She held the ball over a lighted match, and of course, the ball exploded."

The generational change during the first part of the twentieth century, from Fluff's "Victorian" youth to Anne and Dorothy's feminist-minded milieu, was striking. Anne was six and Dorothy eleven when they went with their mother to the suffragette parade for the vote in 1917 (see figs. 6 and 7). Later, as young women in the 1920s, Anne and Dorothy presented themselves as wild spirits rebelling against the Victorian rules of decorum for women. They bobbed their hair in the unisex hairstyle that, it was said, had begun early in the century in Greenwich Village among escaped intellectual revolutionary Russian women, who disguised themselves as men

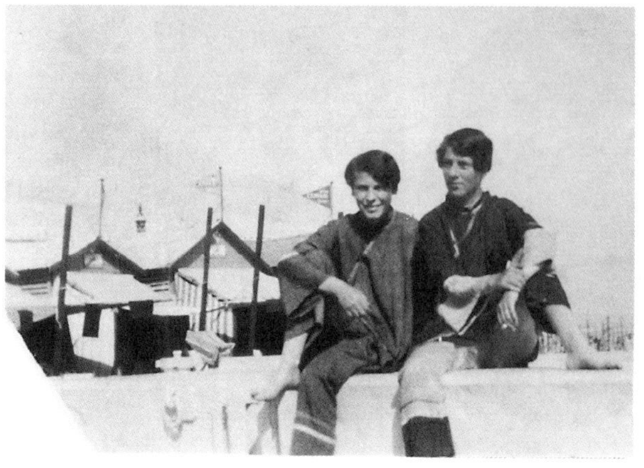

to avoid police surveillance. By 1920, the bob was wildly popular among women, exhibiting a rebellious sense of independence and gender equality. The Eisner sisters also took on the flat-chested androgynous look in their clothing. Wearing pants and dressing as flappers (especially Dorothy), both went on to express a sense of freedom by smoking, drinking, and having affairs with men. (See fig. 8.)

Fig. 8 Anne and Dorothy on Monhegan Island, c. 1931. McDonald archive.

To the Eisner parents, the behavior of their daughters felt dangerously out of control, and they attempted to keep the girls as close to home as possible. Will was known to show up at school dances, ordering Dorothy home if he caught her with a cigarette. He had moved away from the fragility of being an orphan and from the immigrant life of his father and uncle. Will and Fluff had achieved welcome personal, social, and financial security as the world reeled through World War I in Europe. Anne and Dorothy could not identify with their parents' need for stability. They wanted to move out and discover lives of their own.

Anne grew up with a sense of art all around her as Dorothy developed her artistic talent and passion, and as she grew older, Anne would often serve as a model for Dorothy. In 1927, the *New York American* ran an article titled "Painter-Model Combination of Sisters Scores" about the talented young Dorothy and her model, Anne (see fig. 9).

As close as the sisters were, and as inspired as Anne was by Dorothy and Dorothy's close friend, Tess Slesinger, they came into young adulthood at different moments. In the mid- to late 1920s, when Anne was in her early teens, Dorothy and Tess, in their twenties, felt a passionate sense of the importance of their creative work: Tess wanted to be a writer, Dorothy a painter. They felt themselves to be modern women, although they put a distance between themselves and the splits in feminist activism that emerged after the vote was granted in 1920. They combined a flapper style (condemned as frivolous and apolitical by older feminists of all stripes)[1] with a passionate sense of work. Upon receiving a rejection for something she wrote, Tess exclaimed, "You know, its [*sic*] absolutely incredible to me that anything we could do and send out into the world, could be ignored. But its [*sic*] happened to me, and I'm stunned from the shock."[2] Tess got it right: she wasn't to be ignored, later writing the biting satire, *The Unpossessed*, about the political world around her. Anne felt herself to be in the shadow of these exuberant women exercising their freedom. It didn't help when Dorothy and Tess shut her out—literally when they wanted to talk or a beau would visit and figuratively as the younger sibling.

When Anne turned sixteen, she worried that "there is not a single thing I can do well." "I always have the feeling that I'm not wanted or that I'm quite unnecessary. . . . I wonder whether the majority of people feel that way or not. Not that it matters to me whether they do or not." She blamed herself: "I have developed the greatest dislike for myself, and to think that I once had confidence in myself. It is really terrible. I get so bitter I could weep." She understood that these feelings came from standards imposed on young women in a society bound by strictures to which she couldn't adhere and sensed that her difference from others was fundamentally something positive, but she still seethed with anger at the inability she perceived in herself to stand strong: "To think that I should develop an inferiority complex when I know that I'm so God damn much better than most of the people." Anne resisted giving in to silence, but she paid the price by becoming a loner.

Beyond teenage dissatisfaction, there was a more profound longing: a need to do something, to accomplish and be accomplished. "What have I done in all of these years?" she asked herself. At the age of eighteen, Anne made the decision that she could change what was around her: "I've decided to change in a very big way this winter. . . . I've decided not to sit back and wait for it but to go out after things. It's going to be hard as hell, but I've found out that if you take a back seat, you have a backseat time, so—." Anne began attending art school on Saturdays, the beginning of a quest that would last a lifetime. She noted jauntily: "Last Saturday morning our young heroine started art school." But no sooner had she noted the beginning of her heroine's pursuit than she put it down: "And man was she dumb." As further punishment for her lack of success, or rather perhaps for wanting it so much, she cautioned her imaginary reader: "So far our young heroine hasn't met her young and gallant hero."[3]

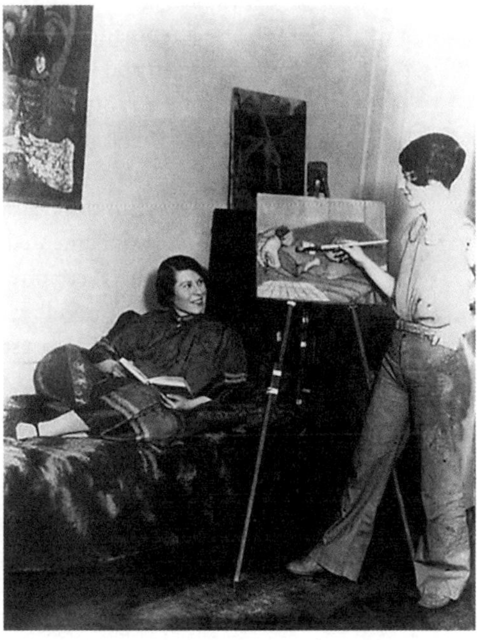

Fig. 9
Anne Eisner modeling for Dorothy Eisner, photograph in the *New York American*, 1927. Anne Eisner Putnam papers, Houghton Library, Harvard University.

Between 1927 and 1930, Anne traveled with Dorothy to France on three separate trips, where they flirted with young men and looked at European paintings (see fig. 10). Although both absorbed lessons from the works of Paul Cézanne and Henri Matisse, neither was tempted by life as an expatriate in Paris.

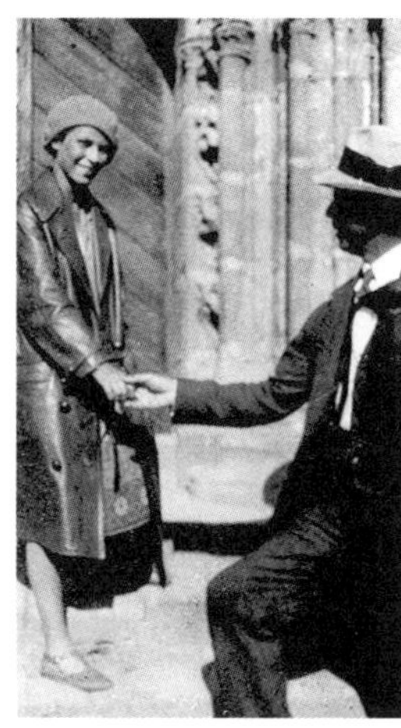

Fig. 10 Anne Eisner and unidentified person in Europe, c. 1927–1930. McDonald archive.

Anne trained as an artist in the tradition of Realist Revival, within the broader American Scene movement of the 1930s. She studied with George Grosz and lithographer George Picken at the Arts Students League, and attended classes at the New York School of Fine and Applied Art, later renamed the Parsons School of Design. Grosz was a painter, draftsman, and illustrator from Germany, who was primarily an Expressionist. He had created William Hogarth–like satirical caricatures of urban scenes depicting moral depravity in post–World War I Germany. Grosz pessimistically characterized the Germany of the 1920s through a sense of class disparity. With the rise of the Nazis, he looked to the United States, where he came as a visiting professor to the Art Students League in 1932 and stayed until the late 1950s. In the United States, his work turned apolitical and focused on gentler caricatures of city scenes and landscapes. Under Grosz's influence, Anne explored lifestyles in everyday activities, working, as other artists on the East Coast in the 1920s and 1930s did, with scenes of the middle and lower class in a kind of American "genre" art. She evoked slices of life as quasi cartoons in both oil and watercolor:[4] street scenes (see pl. 1), women in fitting rooms (see pls. 2a and 2b), and almost anything she might see in the city.

On 14th Street, women experimented with combinations the fashion industry had not dictated. In the dominant style, everything from shoes to suit, gloves, and hat had to match. Anne shopped there in the 1930s, not only for things to wear but also for subjects to draw, such as women trying on clothes at Klein's (see fig. 11). Anne's early watercolors, like the *New Yorker* cartoons of imperfect women sympathetically drawn by Helen Hokinson, evoked a sense of women and their foibles in the life of the city. Kenneth Hays Miller, a teacher at the Art Students League, had focused on shoppers, documenting downtown life in New York with old masters as his models (some called him "the Titian of 14th Street") and Ben Shahn (1898–1969) photographed 14th Street and Klein's in the 1930s.[5] Anne went in a different direction. Gestures and moods were documented in schematized spaces, though often with irony, as a kind of social commentary with Honoré Daumier, Honoré de Balzac, and Émile Zola providing the precedent.

Harnessing herself into a strict discipline of work, Anne focused on practical as well as studio art. She studied costume design and illustration at the New York School of Fine and Applied Art, and at the Gloucester School of the Little Theater she worked on applied art and production. At the age of twenty, she left her family's home on Central Park West to live in a studio apartment in Greenwich Village; it was an important step in separating from her hovering parents. Anne began to exhibit wherever she could and became a regular at the annual open-air festival in Washington Square where anyone could set out their work (see fig. 12).

During the 1930s, Anne's work alternated between city scenes crafted in the winter and country landscapes captured during stays on Monhegan Island in Maine, Cape Cod, Linville Falls in North Carolina, and later Martha's Vineyard for several years. In these communities, Anne connected with a network of artists and friends. Among them was Sarah Freedman McPherson (1894–1978), whom Anne met on Monhegan in 1931 and later in 1939, a fine painter so unassuming as a person that it was a surprise for her friends to learn that Man Ray had photographed her in the 1920s in Paris and that Marcel Duchamp had given her a sketch of a "Nude Descending a Staircase," which she had lost. Anne and Sarah exhibited side by side in a number of New York Society of Women Artists exhibitions. The McPhersons spent winters in their apartment on West 4th Street and summers on Monhegan Island, where Sarah stayed from 1928 on. Sarah had known great poverty, and her early friends in Greenwich Village in New York included John Reed, Rockwell Kent, and Eugene O'Neill (who apparently called her "the Kid"). Dorothy Eisner reflected on how hard life was for Sarah, how much she was admired by painters, and how her work should have been "a sensation." Dorothy was quoted as saying, "It's amazing the people who make it and the people who don't. You can't figure it out."[6] Sarah was a woman who yielded ambition to her husband, John ("Mac") McPherson, a painter and architect, with whom Anne also studied. Among the artists on Monhegan was Anne's teacher Emil Holzhauer (1887–1986) (see fig. 13), a German

Fig. 11
Anne Eisner, *Klein's Inner Sanctum*, lithograph, 11 ½ x 15 in., P.M. Graphic Competition, MOMA, 1939 (photograph by Michael Rosengarten), McDonald collection.

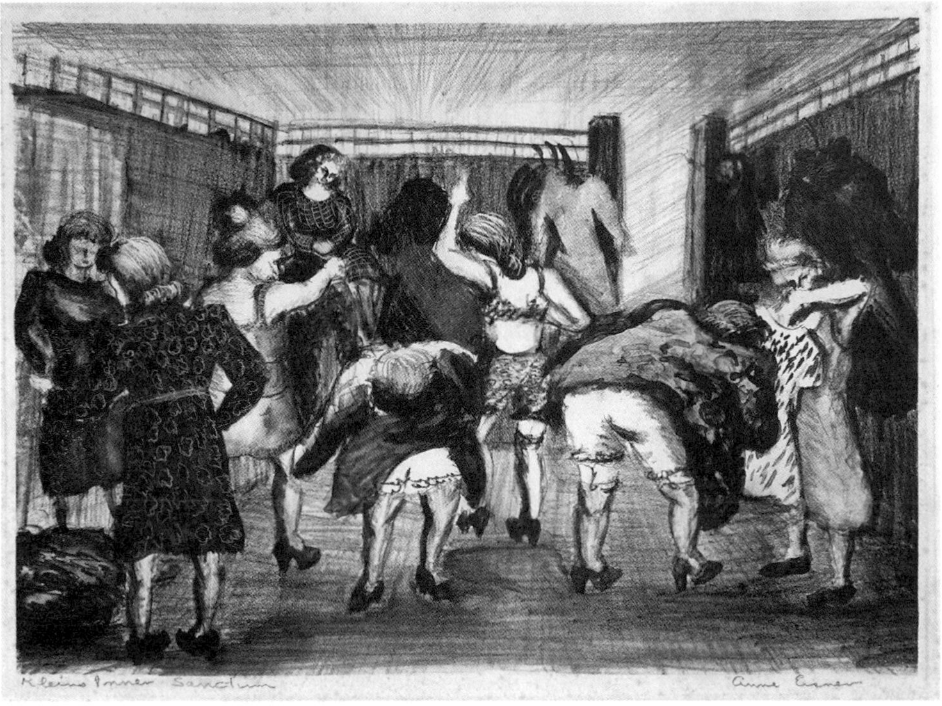

émigré who came to the United States during the early part of the twentieth century and studied in New York with urban realist Robert Henri, a leader of the Ashcan School. Holzhauer became Anne's mentor in watercolor, one of her strengths. Anne's early landscape work from her time on Monhegan reflected the kind of painting encouraged by the American Scene (see pl. 3).

The American Scene movement responded to a need to document life in America realistically, even before the crash of 1929 and the government work projects for artists begun in the early 1930s. It projected a sense of the strength of American art relative to the long history of European art, with the idea of painting America as a nationalistic project. There were two groups: Regionalists and Social Realists. "Regionalists" was a title given to writers Allan Tate, John Crowe Ransom, and Robert Penn Warren in the 1920s and 1930s, with Thomas Hart Benton being perhaps the best-known artist of the movement. Ben Shahn was known among the Social Realists. Despite much debate and a diversity of styles, the two groups shared common values about art in society. American Scene artists were interested in social relevance, anecdotes, and life in local communities. The movement looked toward the future as much as the past in an optimistic way. It was democratic in the sense that artists, as members of their communities, reached out to make art recognizable in style and content; the journal *Art*

Fig. 12
Anne Eisner at Washington Square outdoor exhibition, c. 1935 (photographer unknown). Anne Eisner Putnam papers, Houghton Library, Harvard University.

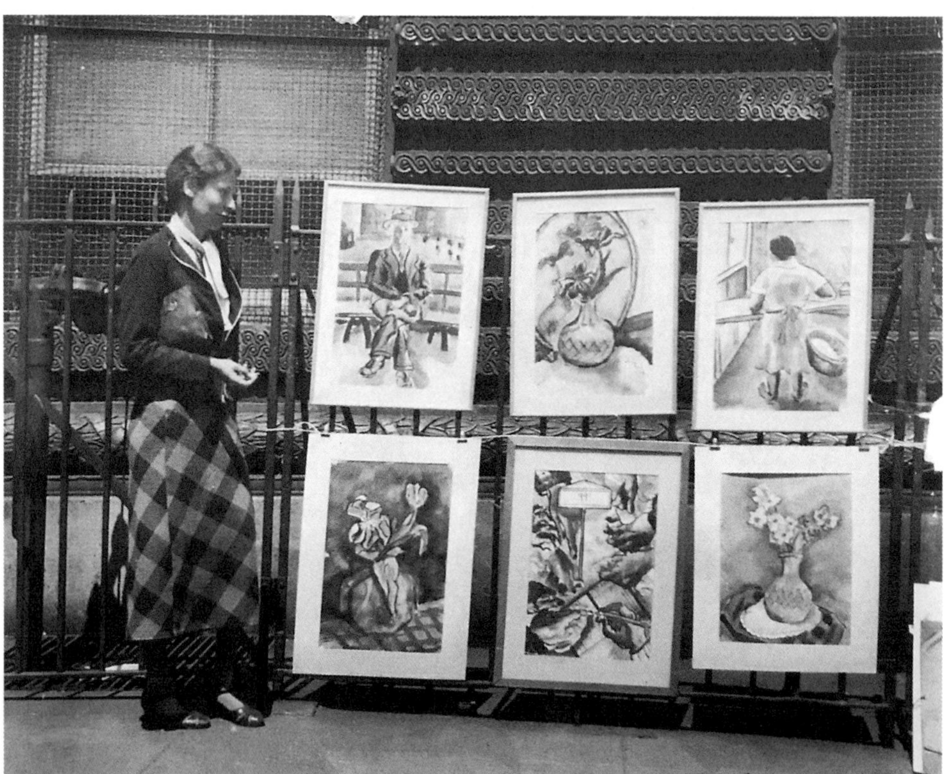

Digest praised artists painting in this vein. They were also interested in work under the New Deal government programs of the Works Progress Administration (WPA) Federal Art Project (1935–1943) that brought a sense of community to the artists and their subjects. Author and critic Thomas Craven, a friend of George Grosz and Thomas Hart Benton, had given three reasons for the importance of the American Scene movement: the European movements had become, according to them, exhausted (they were not, as we know); modern art in Europe shunned art as a means of communication, looking instead to technique; and the American public would not be receptive to philosophical speculation and theories based on abstract notions. The positive aspects of this American Renaissance were themes consistent with the artist in his or her environment throughout the 1930s, based not on individual genius but on a more egalitarian sense of art spreading throughout the country. Benton returned from Europe paradoxically under the influence of Hippolyte Taine's work, which constituted an important theoretical base for the American Scene, situating the artist in his or her social and intellectual milieu.

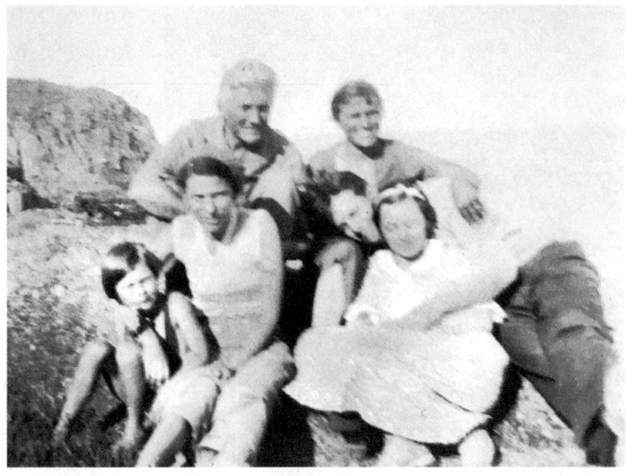

Fig. 13
Emil Holzhauer, Sarah McPherson, an unidentified couple, and Anne Eisner with an unidentified child, Monhegan Island. McDonald archive.

At the beginning of the 1930s, the American Scene was the "most popular movement in American art."[7] The Public Works of Art Project (PWAP), a temporary program, came into existence for a year, supporting thousands of artists and allowing free expression, guided by the American Scene ethos. Social Realist painter and muralist George Biddle appealed to President Franklin D. Roosevelt in 1933, referring to the Mexican model of mural painting, which he called "the greatest national school . . . since the Italian Renaissance,"[8] to create a federal program of support for artists. The Metropolitan Museum of Art held a large exhibition of Mexican art in 1930, and the Museum of Modern Art put on a retrospective Diego Rivera exhibition in 1931. Boardman Robinson, with whom Dorothy Eisner had studied, and Benton both taught at the Art Students League and were interested in murals and the decoration of buildings. In 1932, Rivera painted a fresco on commission by from David Rockefeller Sr. at Rockefeller Center. Things went badly when the leftist artist put Vladimir Lenin on the right side and a picture of Rockefeller's father drinking with prostitutes on the left. How provocative could you be? Rivera was fired, and the work was chiseled off. By the time

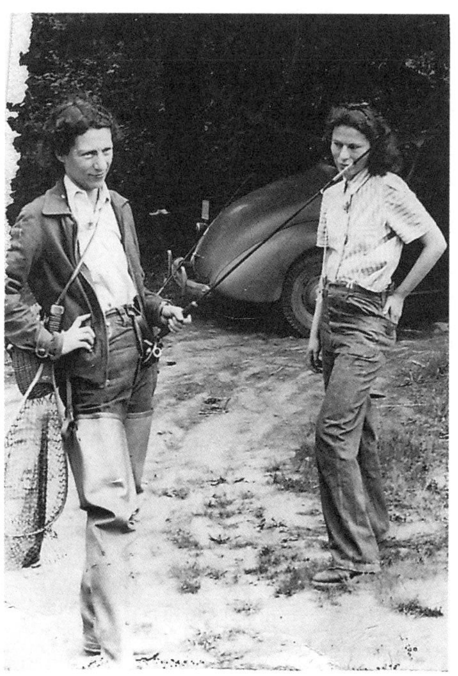

Fig. 14 Dorothy and Anne Eisner in Linville Falls, N.C., c. 1933. McDonald archive.

Anne exhibited a watercolor in the Salons of America show at Rockefeller Center in 1934, there was backlash from the Society of Independent Artists' accusations of censorship by Rockefeller Center.[9]

Anne joined Dorothy in Linville Falls, North Carolina, during the summer of 1933, intent on painting the world that Dorothy had come to know and love there. The artist Warren Wheelock—whose connection with the Eisners came through the Woodstock Art Association—had gone to Linville Falls in the 1920s and brought other artists to the area. Dorothy had spent extensive time there with welcoming local families and wrote in a 1980 exhibition catalog: "My subjects were mountain landscapes and my friends, the mountain people, civilized as Chaucer, almost untouched by modern times." Dorothy produced a body of work suffused with her fascination for this life in all its aspects—the people, the farming and fishing, and the exuberance of both music and dance.[10] Like Dorothy, Anne was excited to be in the mountains, relishing outdoor adventures. She learned to fish and hunt possum, but she did not stay long enough to immerse herself as fully in sketching and painting. (See fig. 14.)

Anne studied in Woodstock, New York, during the summer of 1935, when the Federal Art Project began. She took classes at one of the other summer schools that replaced the Art Students League, which had opened in Woodstock in 1906 but ceased to offer summer classes in 1922. The Woodstock Artists Association, founded in 1919 as the Artists' Realty Company—of which Anne's father, Will, became a trustee—drafted a constitution in 1920 with "the purpose of the Association to give free and equal expression to the 'Conservative' and 'Radical' elements [understood in painterly, not political, terms]";[11] exhibitions began in 1921. WPA support for artists and art projects in Woodstock was second only to that for New York City, enrolling some fifty artists in the PWAP. Alexander Brook (1898–1980), a summer and later permanent resident of Woodstock, was assistant director of the Whitney Studio Club, which became the Whitney Studio Gallery and later the Whitney Museum. Anne's mother, Fluff, began studying art with Brook in 1933; Will started about a decade later with Sidney Laufman (1891–1985), a painter trained at the Cleveland School of Art, the Art Institute of Chicago, and the Art Students League with Robert Henri, who also became a Woodstock resident. Fluff and Will followed their daughters' passion for art, making it their own, and their artistic practice continued throughout the rest of their lives. They bought a farm in Woodstock in the 1950s and went on to show their paintings extensively. Many artists settled in and around the village, among them Anne and Dorothy's friend George Ault (1891–1948), who painted in the American Precisionist style, influenced by Cubism and Futurism, although he remained quite realist. Woodstock was well established as an artists' colony, attracting painters, sculptors, craftspeople, and photographers, long before it became associated with the Woodstock music festival in the late 1960s. During the summer she was

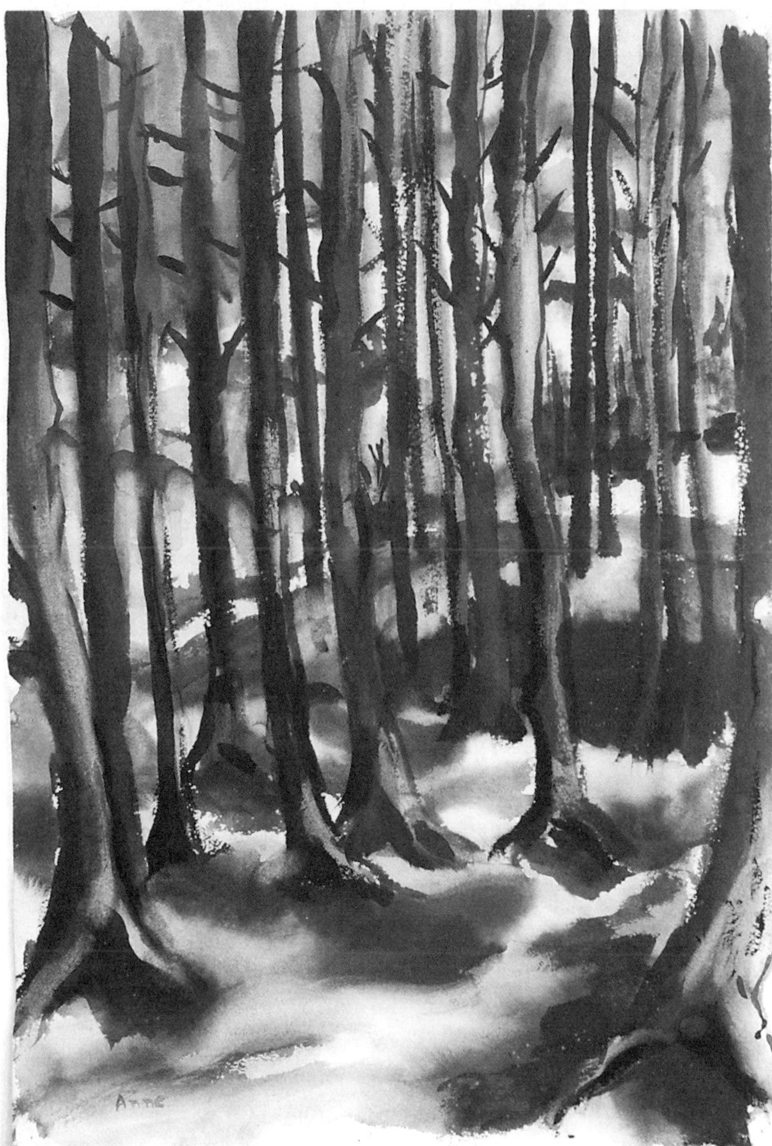

Fig. 15
Anne Eisner, *Cathedral Woods*, 22 x 15 in., watercolor on paper, c. 1939, (photographer Michael Rosengarten), McDonald collection.

there, Anne produced work for her debut solo exhibition of watercolors. In her first years of exhibiting, Anne regained a sense of self-confidence and, with high-spirited boldness, signed her paintings simply "Anne." Art reviewers loved her moxie, referring again and again to the girl "called Anne" as they singled out her work for comment in group exhibitions. A reviewer also praised Anne's watercolors shown with the Society of Independent Artists of 1934: "Particularly good may be considered the several water-colors by an artist known to her public simply as Anne."[12]

By 1943, her teacher in the medium, Holzhauer, commented about her development in the solo watercolor exhibition at the 8th Street Playhouse:

> It is always interesting to me to watch the growth of an artist from the earliest growings to mature expression. Her first attempts showed a strong grasp of the essentials in a picture, a rather quaint slant on subject matter, and arresting color. Now these qualities have become the outstanding features in her work. I know of no other woman artist who handles watercolor with such boldness and directness.[13]

Anne certainly exhibited with women artists and was conscious of herself as a woman, but it is worth noting that Holzhauer praises her in a category of women artists and does not contrast her work with that of male artists.

In one of her early watercolors, *Cathedral Woods*, painted on Monhegan Island, Anne grouped trees together to show a pattern of space (fig. 15). Her fascination with trees was to be lifelong, from distant and overarching views to closer, more existential engagement, abstracted in later watercolors and paintings (see pls. 6, 14, 15). The forest evolved throughout her work as a metaphor for life's complex problems. Little did she know that later on, both forest and life would thicken when she went to live at the edge of a tropical rain forest in Africa.

Primitive Art in New York

Anne was an avid museumgoer from her teenage years on. In 1935, the Museum of Modern Art (MOMA) opened a major exhibition titled "African Negro Art."[14] The exhibition brought together African sculptures from several countries, borrowed from European and American collections, including those of Tristan Tzara and Henri Matisse. MOMA commissioned Walker Evans to photograph the exhibit. Evans presented the objects, as the exhibition itself had, for their "formal, artistic and abstract qualities, not as ethnographic specimens, as was typical presentation of the time."[15] The purpose of the exhibition was educational: to teach the American public about African art (which had become important to Matisse, Pablo Picasso, and others). Evans was at the time an unknown photographer, who was soon to take photographs for the Resettlement Administration, under the supervision of John Carter and his successor Roy Stryker. This work produced his iconic photographs of the rural American South and some of the Northeast.[16] Evans's assistant, Peter Sekaer (1901–1950), along with writer John Cheever (1912–1982), did the printing of the photographs of the MOMA exhibition in an apartment Evans shared with artist Ben Shahn, while Evans went traveling. Curator Virginia Lee Webb commented: "Evans depicted the African sculptures using his highly stylized pictorial vocabulary, with the same concentrated yet sourceless illumination seen in the photographs of sun-soaked facades of American wood-frame houses. . . . The style of the photographs of African art is identical to the highly personalized rendering of horseless carriages, empty churches, signs, and other objects of American culture."[17]

As early as 1914, Alfred Stieglitz's gallery first exhibited "Statuary in Wood by African Savages: The Root of Modern Art." Stieglitz immediately followed that with a show that juxtaposed, as others would later, African sculpture with works by Picasso and Georges Braque, to reinforce the relationship to modern painting. The unfortunate use of the word "savage" (whose unanalyzed racism lasted through the 1950s) probably meant for Stieglitz that what appeared to be untaught or uncivilized was actually the vital source of the latest European art. He focused on a formal and aesthetic appreciation, taking the objects out of their context for a European and American public. This brought out the relationship to abstract modern art that Alfred Barr, director of MOMA, would reiterate in a 1936 exhibition, "Cubism and Abstract Art."[18]

While other New York museums had exhibited African art, they did so by providing the ethnographic context for the works. The Brooklyn Museum titled an exhibit "Primitive Negro Art" in 1921 and 1922, featuring works from the Belgian Congo (now Democratic Republic of Congo). The explanation for the MOMA displays stated a different goal clearly: "The entire collection, whatever may have been its original uses, is shown under the classification of art; as representing a creative impulse, and not for the purpose of illustrating the customs of African peoples."[19] The goal of emphasizing aesthetic qualities similar to Western art was to help the American public understand why European artists from Paul Gauguin to the Fauves, Picasso, Constantin Brancusi, Amedeo Modigliani, German Expressionists, and Surrealists had been so drawn to such objects in the early part of the twentieth century. If ethnologists were not impressed, this exhibit is still considered one of the first to show African artifacts as worthy of being shown in an art museum; later exhibits at MOMA brought the arts of the American West, Central America, and South America.[20] J. J. Sweeney, who curated the 1935 MOMA exhibition "African Negro Art," with director Barr's strong support, expressed a similar aesthetic appreciation of the "[Negro art's] essential plastic seriousness, moving dramatic qualities, eminent craftsmanship and sensibility to material, as well as . . . the relationship of material with form and expression."[21]

The exhibition was the most popular of its kind to date, with 45,000 visitors. Anne surely visited this exhibition, perhaps even multiple times. The impact of seeing African art, including bark cloths, along with statues, masks, and more that were on exhibit, may not have initially influenced Anne's work, but a decade later, African art became an active interest when she herself moved to the Belgian Congo.

Reaction to the exhibition ranged from curiosity to bewilderment, especially with the lack of context: "Everywhere amongst these curios hangs the fog of the Dark Continent. There are so many keys, as it were, to so many complicated locks. To turn them, however, is a matter of ethnology, not of art."[22] The *New York World-Telegram* marveled at the complexity of the work: "The objects have a degree of sophistication and aesthetic purity which are almost incredible considering their origin in what we are prone to consider 'Darkest Africa.' They bespeak civilization rarely surpassed in history, artistic skill carried to the highest plane, infinite passion, boundless imagination and great good humor."[23] The central paradox of equating the complexity of art that appears temporally and spatially removed (primitive and exotic) with modern art focused on the primitivist aesthetic. Appreciation rather than understanding snatched art from a Darwinian model, upon which anthropology and colonialism were based (the so-called civilized peoples might understand, in the first case, and should "civilize" those less advanced, in the second), and suggested a proto-structuralist view of balanced complexities. Harry Shapiro, curator of physical anthropology in the Department of Anthropology at the American Museum of Natural History, reacting to a later, 1946 exhibition of South Seas and Oceanic art, proposed that the legitimation of primitive art came at a moment when the "Classical traditions of Western art [had] weakened . . . as newer canons were adopted. It is not without significance that primitive art, although available to European artists since the Age of Discovery and accessible in ethnographic museums for 150 years, was discovered in Paris only at the turn of the century."[24] Such a "discovery" linked conceptions of what is oldest in culture with what was to come in modernism and countered the notion of progress in industrial society by evoking a timeless aesthetic.

Fig. 16
Anne Eisner, *Hollywood Beauty Aids*, c. 1931 (photographer unknown). McDonald collection.

Heading West

In the spring of 1937, in her mid-twenties, Anne boarded a ship headed to Oregon the long way, on the Panama Pacific Line through the Panama Canal, with stops in Havana and Hollywood. In California, she stayed with Tess Slesinger, now living in Hollywood with her husband, Frank Davis;

both of them were screenwriters. Anne enjoyed seeing Tess and getting a taste of the world of Hollywood celebrity life. In a letter, she wrote, "Salka Viertel (the lady who writes [Greta] Garbo's pictures) gave an elegant party Friday night at which I met Dorothy Parker (who was very friendly but didn't pull any wise cracks)." Salka Viertel (1889–1978) was a Jew from the

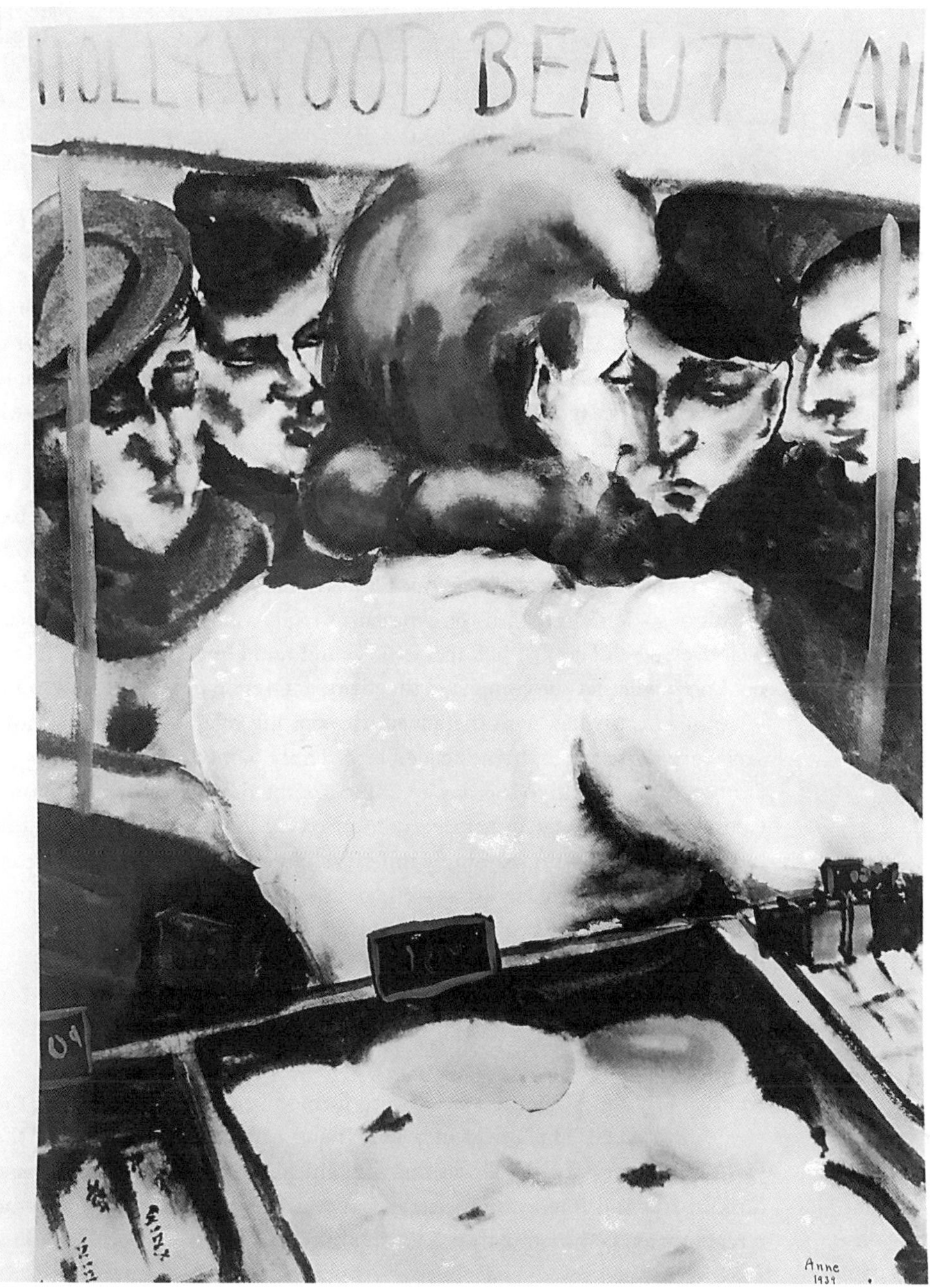

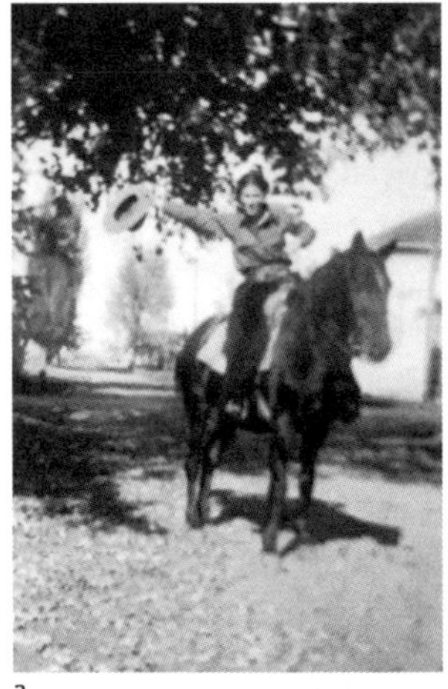

a

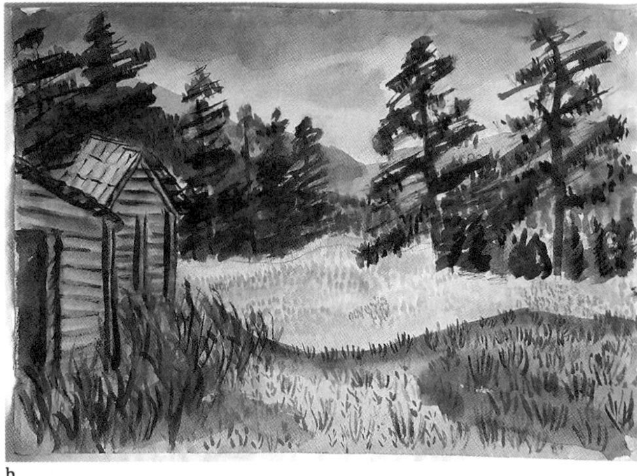

b

Fig. 17a-b
a: Anne in Wallowa County, Oregon, 1937. Photographer unknown, Houghton Library, Harvard University.
b: Anne Eisner, *Oregon Field*, 15 x 23 in., watercolor on paper. McDonald collection.

Austro-Hungarian Empire, Galicia, which is now part of western Ukraine, who arrived in Hollywood in 1928 as an actress and became a screenwriter.[25] Her salon included the Manns (Thomas and his brother), the Arnold Schoenbergs, the Igor Stravinskis, and Greta Garbo, among many others. Although it is not clear who attended the party, Anne described recovering her aplomb with the celebrities: "Instead of being a very shy movie girl sitting in a corner like a desolate landscape which was what I was afraid I was going to do and being able to describe the clothes they all wore, I had a marvelous time."[26] Anne's watercolor *Hollywood Beauty Aids* (see fig. 16) is a somewhat caustic visual comment on the women of Hollywood: the women appear well dressed and coiffed but also look "gaunt and almost menacing."[27] I do not know whether she completed this work in Oregon or back in New York.

Anne was thrilled with the adventure that life offered on the ten-thousand-acre horse ranch, homesteaded by a family named Greene, in isolated Grouse, Oregon (still to this day an unincorporated community in Wallowa County). Anne had never before experienced the exhilaration of riding out in the wilderness with seemingly unfettered freedom. She was able to concentrate on practicing her art as well, and she brought back work to exhibit in New York, choosing intimate scenes with trees on which to focus. (See fig. 17a-b.)

Politics and Art

Anne's early thinking and values were formed in the period between the two world wars. The world into which she came of age, following the stock-market crash of 1929, was one of political radicalization among New York artists and intellectuals. Anne was touched by politics through the circle of friends shared with her sister, almost all of whom were older and moving toward social and political revolution, mainly Communists and

Trotskyists, even if they were not formal members of any group. These included Sidney Hook (a philosophy professor), Elliot Cohen (the managing editor of the *Menorah Journal*, who later founded *Commentary*), Lionel and Diana Rubin Trilling (he later a cultural critic, she a writer and reviewer for the *Nation*), Max and Eliena Krylenko Eastman (he a prolific writer and political activist, she a Russian immigrant who painted, danced, and translated), Dwight MacDonald (a writer and editor), Eleanor Clark (a writer), and Herbert Solow (a journalist and political activist). Dorothy's great friend Tess Slesinger married Herbert Solow in 1928 in the Ethical Culture Society hall on Central Park West but divorced him in 1932, after which Tess wrote her satirical novel *The Unpossessed* (1934) about left-wing intellectuals' quarrels and complex social histories. Solow was a brilliant and principled intellectual, a graduate of Columbia College and Columbia Journalism School, who catalyzed his colleagues and friends to understand the political stakes of the time and to move away from Stalinism as of 1933–1934. Solow introduced Dorothy to my father, John McDonald; they lived together in 1935 (against her parents' Victorian ethos) and married in 1936. John had moved to New York City in 1932 from Detroit, attracted to it "as a place of writers, in particular writers on the left or going left."[28] He remembered that his idea then of a revolutionary was that "he was free, not realizing that this inclination was leading me to ride the two horses of Marxist and anarchist."[29] He found the pull toward communism deflected, however, by the particular brand of Stalinist communism and the lack of independence granted to writers in the Communist Party.

The year 1936 was important in global politics, as well as for artists in America. The sham Moscow Trials began that year and became a test for people on the left: Leon Trotsky was "convicted" of conspiring with foreign powers against Joseph Stalin and other leaders in the Soviet Union and charged with betraying the revolution of 1917. Interest in the Soviet experiment of collectivism dropped away as the ideals of liberty and law were upended; the Spanish Civil War gave the impetus to form a coalition against fascism. Herbert and John maintained a firmly antifascist stance, despite all the jockeying of factions on the left. John summed up their concerns many years later: "The central and by far overriding issue among left intellectuals, and for me was the imminence of Hitler's taking power in Germany."[30]

John wrote that they also "continued to be active on large issues, one of which, the Moscow Trials,"[31] demonstrating to him, Herbert, and others the catastrophic failure of the Stalinist Russian experiment. When Trotsky was granted asylum in Mexico, he had become a towering political figure and literary man, with strong appeal for this group. Anne's friend Margaret De Silver (1889–1962) became a pivotal figure in his American defense. She ran a salon at her home in Brooklyn, where she hosted passionate political dialogue and some wild parties that ran late into the night; she apparently had a good bootlegger during Prohibition.[32] Herbert Solow was a moving force in the success of the American Committee for the Defense of Leon Trotsky as discussion and plans were made for the Commission of Inquiry into Charges against Leon Trotsky in the Moscow Trials. John and Dorothy were among those who went to Mexico in the spring of 1937 for the investigation, spearheaded by John Dewey. When Dorothy had moments of doubt before leaving for Mexico, Anne could hardly believe it, emoting that she would have gone in a heartbeat. In Coyoacán, John and Dorothy worked with Trotsky at the house loaned to him in exile by Frida Kahlo's parents.[33] John worked on the material organization, running errands for Trotsky and the Commission. Dorothy painted two portraits of Trotsky, one completed after daily sittings with him in his study. Upon her return to New York, she finished the other, along with a third painting of all the members of the Commission (now in the collection of the Dewey Center at the University of Illinois in Carbondale). The fervor of political discussion following the return from Mexico pitted anti-Stalinists against Stalinists, but ultimately, although the intellectuals were "arguing the world,"[34] the Trotskyists in America did not build a new political movement.[35] John went on to cofound a journal about documentary films called *Film News*, and after the war, he was hired as an editor at *Fortune Magazine*. The magazine magnate Henry Luce gathered a group of liberal and left intellectuals to join his journalistic empire and business magazine, including John, Herbert Solow, and photographer Walker Evans. Solow, whose humor as well as his severe depression were well known among his friends, quipped about their fate: "That's the way the world will end—not with a whim but a banker."[36] As John and Herbert left their radical politics behind and embarked upon the study of business, Anne and Dorothy continued to paint. But I've gotten ahead of my story.

The year 1936 also saw the inauguration of the American Artists' Congress, a response to the request by the American Communist Party and the Popular Front for American artists and intellectuals to create groups opposing fascism. The Congress's mission was to alleviate the economic strife of artists during the Depression, as well as to oppose art as propaganda and its censorship by fascism. As the national secretary Stuart Davis wrote, the Depression had created "cracks and strains in the general social fabric resulting from the economic crisis [that] inevitably reached the world of art, shaking those psychological and esthetic certainties which had once given force and direction to the work of artists."[37] The move to unite factions around a common purpose brought artists into civic action out of a theoretically apolitical stance, inherited from a European model of the artist who held himself or herself apart from society. Art critic Meyer Schapiro encouraged artists to think about community.[38] The Congress supported the WPA/FAP, protested the Olympic Games of 1936 in Berlin through a boycott of exhibitions, and defended minority rights in the United States. Although some of the original signatories of the Congress's original "Call" were not on the left, most were. The Congress maintained a distance, for example, from the John Reed clubs, which had been discontinued by the Soviet Union because of sectarian policies no longer supported by the Popular Front. Anne did not sign the original document of the Congress, and—although it is not clear—perhaps the "troubles" she expressed with it related to the Communist domination. A friend consoled her by suggesting that many thought anyone to the left of Roosevelt must be a lunatic and cheerfully recommended that she read Friedrich Engels. Anne had exhibited a watercolor that year titled *I Voted for Roosevelt* at the twentieth anniversary of the Society of Independent Artists. In it, a down-and-outer "lap[s] at a mug of coffee . . . his face lined with misery, his eyes searching sternly for some way out," as one reviewer described it.[39] (The painting can be seen at the upper left of fig. 12.) Among those who did sign the Congress's call, however, were many artists in her milieu: George Ault, Emil Holzhauer, George Picken, and Warren Wheelock, among others.

The Congress's purpose was to become a global organization focusing on social and economic issues, uniting a broad array of artists—and this was important—without aesthetic directives.[40] The final paragraph of the "Call for the American Artists' Congress" seemed to set out clear goals: "A picture of what Fascism has done to living standards, to civil liberties, to workers' organizations, to science and art, the threat against the peace and security of the world, as shown in Italy and Germany, should arouse every sincere artist to action."[41] Aaron Douglas addressed the lack of black artists compared with musicians in his talk, pointing out that at the time, not one African American artist was displayed at the Metropolitan Museum: "It is when we come to revolutionary art that we find the Negro sincerely represented, but here the portrayal is too frequently automatic, perfunctory and arbitrary. He becomes a kind of proletarian prop, a symbol, vague and abstract. Revolutionary art should be praised, however, for pointing a way and striking a vital blow at discrimination and segregation, the chief breeding ground of Fascism."[42] Anne could not know then how important such comments would be to her later, when she would paint the Africans within whose community she would come to live.

Anne agreed with the overall mission of the Congress but had to have reacted to its response to the two reports from the Dewey Commission, *The Case of Leon Trotsky* (1937) and *Not Guilty: Report of the Commission of Inquiry* (1938). Stuart Davis and photographer Paul Strand spearheaded a letter, published in the *New Masses*, which defended the Soviet purges of political opponents (Trotsky, among others) and independent intellectuals. This stance was anathema to Anne, Dorothy, John, and others who supported the defense of Trotsky. Although formed independently, these political worlds became intertwined for artists. The turning point for many came when Stalin and

Hitler signed a non-aggression pact in 1939, which shocked the American left.

In April 1940, the unified front of the Artists' Congress burst apart when the executive committee endorsed the Soviet invasion of Finland, implicitly defending Hitler's policy and assigning responsibility for the war to England and France. Dorothy and high-profile members Meyer Schapiro, Lewis Mumford, Adolph Gottlieb, and Stuart Davis (in a seeming about-face) immediately resigned. Anne and Dorothy became founding members of the Federation of Modern Painters and Sculptors, mostly made up of former members of the American Artists' Congress. The first meetings were held in Dorothy's studio. Anne signed a statement along with Milton Avery, Adolph Gottlieb, Mark Rothko, and Dorothy, among other painters, rejecting this policy endorsing the Soviet invasion of Finland. The mission statement of the newly founded Federation read as follows:

> The purpose of this corporation shall be to promote the welfare of free progressive artists working in America. It will strive to protect the artist's general and cultural interests and to facilitate the showing of his work.
>
> We recognize the dangers of growing reactionary movements in the United States and condemn every effort to curtail the freedom and the cultural and economic opportunities of artists in the name of race or nation, or in the interests of special groups in the community. We condemn artistic nationalism which negates the world tradition of art at the base of modern art movements.
>
> We affirm our faith in the democratic way of life and its principle of freedom of artistic expression and, therefore, oppose totalitarianism of thought and action, as practiced in the present day dictatorships of Germany, Russia, Italy, Spain and Japan, believing it to be the enemy of the artist, interested in him only as a craftsman who may be exploited.
>
> Our organization shall be free from patent or concealed political control. We shall admit to membership independent artists, whose work has sufficient merit, irrespective of their religious or racial status, provided only that they share with us the belief in the integrity of the artist and the opposition to the oppressive forces hereinbefore named.[43]

Anne's active political engagement came through participation in this organization, as well as other artistic associations: the Society of Independent Artists, the National Association of American Women Painters and Sculptors, and the New York Society of Women Artists. She exhibited works in the first exhibition of the Federation at the World's Fair in 1940, and in 1942, she was first corresponding secretary and then secretary. She remained an active member of the Federation throughout the rest of her life, even during long absences from the United States. Anne was also an elected member of the Board of Control, the governing body of the Art Students League, from 1940 to 1943.

Carlo Tresca and Margaret De Silver

Anne painted a portrait of Carlo Tresca (1879–1943) in 1941. Tresca was an Italian journalist and editor who had immigrated to the United States and had at various times been a socialist, a syndicalist, and an anarchist. The term "anarcho-syndicalist" seems to have been capacious enough for the revolutionary movements that he led and in which he participated. As he was a journalist, Tresca's anti-fascist political activism was well known. He had a long history of working on behalf of immigrants whom Benito Mussolini pressured to support Italian fascism. Max Eastman wrote a bit flippantly in the *New Yorker*: "Carlo Tresca is the despair of all those young men whose idea of success and glory is to get arrested and sent to jail in the cause of the working class. Tresca holds the international all-time record in this field. He has been arrested thirty-six times. He has been tried by jury seven times. . . . He has had his throat cut by a hired assassin, been bombed, been kidnapped by Facisti, been shot at four times (once by an Ohio sheriff from a distance of eight feet), been marked for death by the agents of Mussolini."[44] This could not begin to sum up the range of activities and causes championed by Tresca, in addition to his ongoing struggle against fascism and Stalinism: the celebrated 1912 textile workers' strike in Lawrence, Massachusetts; the 1913 walkout of silk workers in Paterson, New Jersey; the 1916 iron workers' strike in Minnesota; and advocacy on behalf of Nicola Sacco and Bartolomeo Vanzetti, Italian immigrant anarchists accused of murder in South Braintree, Massachusetts, who were sentenced to death in 1927 for what many believed was not the alleged crime but their political beliefs.

By the time Anne got to know Tresca, he was editor of the anti-fascist Italian-language journal *Il Martello* and the partner of her friend Margaret De

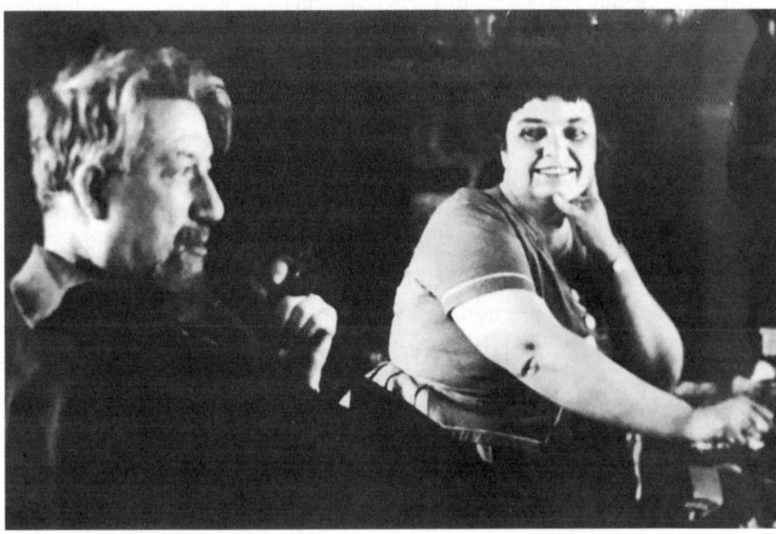

Fig. 18
Carlo Tresca and Margaret De Silver (photographer unknown). Courtesy of Susan De Silver.

Silver (see fig. 18). Margaret and Carlo complemented each other: he was outgoing and had long been a public figure; she was private, preferring to help causes and people more anonymously. If Anne found political discussions in their milieu somewhat daunting, she could paint and record the human side of Tresca's larger-than-life persona. That was what she chose to bring out in her portrait. (See pl. 4.)

Fine books have been written about Carlo Tresca, but Margaret De Silver's legacy has yet to really emerge in the histories of this politically important period.[45] She may have been somewhat shy, but she was a powerhouse in her own right. She came from a well-to-do Quaker family of "Main Line" Philadelphia. Her father, George Burnham, was a senior executive in the Baldwin Locomotive Works of Philadelphia, a successful railway business around the world. A graduate of Vassar College, Margaret married Albert De Silver (1888–1924), cofounder of the Civil Liberties Union (later the American Civil Liberties Union), on whose board she served for many years. They had three children, but Albert died suddenly and tragically in 1924, falling off a train by accident on the way to a Harvard-Yale game in New Haven, Connecticut.

Margaret met Tresca with his then-partner, Elizabeth Gurley Flynn (1890–1964), in 1924; Flynn herself was a radical leader in the labor movement. Flynn introduced Carlo to a vast network of left activists of many stripes (radical, progressive, intellectual): in addition to Eastman, John Reed, Roger Baldwin, Margaret Sanger, Emma Goldman, and Norman Thomas, among others. After they met again in 1931, Carlo moved into Margaret's house in Brooklyn Heights, where they lived as a happy unmarried couple for twelve years. Cynics saw Margaret as a source of funds for Carlo's endeavors, but Nuncio Pernicone's interviews corrected this view: Margaret, who had invested in many liberal social and political causes, helping artists and writers, among others, did help Carlo to revive his journal *Il Martello*, but they had much more than that together, personally and politically.[46] Both worked to help exiles from the Spanish Civil War fighting against Francisco Franco, for example, between 1936 and 1939.

Margaret tolerated Carlo's womanizing, a lifelong behavior that he and his friend Max Eastman (along with many other men of this period) shared. In those days, many decades before the #MeToo movement, women might squirm to avoid being pinched (literally and metaphorically), while others participated in the more radical milieu with an almost 1960s-like sense of sexual liberation; both premarital sex and open marriage were common in Anne's milieu. As Margaret and Carlo came together, he found a kind of personal and political nurturing and luxury to which he was not accustomed (both in her brownstone in Brooklyn and later in her apartment on 12th Street near the offices of *Il Martello*), and she found a soulmate with whom to share life and politics. They spent time on Martha's Vineyard and Cape Cod, enjoyed cooking, swimming, and hosting friends. Margaret's friends became Carlo's and overlapped with Anne's, Dorothy's, and John's: on the Vineyard, Nancy and Dwight MacDonald, Eastman's wife and Anne's dear friend Eliena Krylenko, Thomas Hart Benton, and others; in New York, James T. Farrell, Sidney Hook, Edmund Wilson, and John Dewey, whose Trotsky Commission Margaret had sponsored to go to Mexico. American novelist John Dos Passos, an old friend of Margaret's, commented on Carlo's analysis of politics and people as the "shrewdest" he had ever heard.[47] Through Margaret, Carlo became an integral part of this group of intellectuals, signing on to the Dewey Commission, although he himself could not go to Mexico because of his visa status. As Eleanor Clark wrote to Alan Wald, whose book *The New York Intellectuals* traces the intelligentsia's change from involvement with left politics to the right in the 1950s, Carlo was "One of the most lovable characters around . . ., a very old and good friend of Herbert [Solow's]. . . . Carlo was a real old-time Italian anarchist, very innocent by Stalin-period standards, but shrewd in some specific analysis, and brave and honest."[48] That Carlo and Herbert, despite their many differences, shared strong values in the fight against fascism and Stalinism epitomizes the relations struck up among many in this group of friends and allies, a sense of humanitarian decency and the need to rectify social injustice.

As an activist who did not herself write, Margaret may seem to have chosen to remain in obscurity, a role for women characterized by Suzanne Necker, Germaine de Staël's mother, as resembling glowworms shining so long as they remained in the shadows. But Margaret's exchange of letters with Trotsky and Herbert's reports to her during and after the Dewey Commission demonstrate not only the extent of her support but also her political understanding. Trotsky thanked her for her generosity, both for the five thousand dollars she contributed to the Commission—equivalent to about eighty-five thousand today—, her subsidy for his security later on, and for visiting him and his wife, Natalia, in Mexico (presumably prior to the Commission hearings in 1937). Margaret wrote to Trotsky after the Dewey Commission hearings: "It seems to me clear that the next war will bring *probably* everywhere but *certainly* in USA, *not* a leftist revolution, but a fascist [one]."[49]

Carlo Tresca's brutal assassination on January 11, 1943, at the intersection of 15th Street and Fifth Avenue near his office, was a shock to the entire community. Trotsky, who himself had been assassinated in 1940, had warned Carlo through Margaret in 1938 that the GPU (the Soviet secret police) was targeting him: "He should be very cautious in his movements and meetings."[50] Much sleuthing and debate ensued; some believed that Carmine Galante, presumably a hit man for mobsters associated with the Mafia hierarchy and ex-fascists, had assassinated him. Theories abounded, as Tresca had many enemies,[51] and the details of the murder remain under debate.

To mark the one-year anniversary of his death, the *New Leader*, a liberal magazine associated early on with the Socialist Party of America, published a reproduction of Anne's portrait: "Carlo Tresca. Painting by Ann[e] Eisner at the Norlyst Galleries. The last portrait of the noted anarchist leader before his assassination by a political enemy one year ago."[52] One art critic saw a likeness between this painting and the political context of Anne's Trotskyist milieu: "Murdered anti-fascist Carlo Tresca, who was a friend of the artist, is vigorously portrayed, looking more than a little like Leon Trotsky." The likeness echoed in a sense what Tresca had written to Trotsky in 1939: "You are right:—in spite of profound divergences, we do respect each other."[53]

Anne's portrait was her major contribution to these discussions, as Dorothy's portraits of Trotsky had been hers for the Dewey Commission (one of which was given to Margaret after the hearings). Anne's portrait of Tresca and Dorothy's of Trotsky given to Margaret now reside at Houghton Library, Harvard.

Art's Way

During summers before the end of World War II, Anne vacationed on Martha's Vineyard, and during the summer of 1941, she shared a house with two friends, Helen Gould, who had worked both for critic Edmund Wilson and for Max Eastman, and Aaron Siskind (1903–1991), a photographer who began as a Social Realist and later became well known for his aesthetic in dialogue with abstract painting. He went on to photograph many of Anne's paintings in documentary style, including her solo exhibition in 1944, and also to photograph her in interpretive poses on Martha's Vineyard. Siskind was working on the ways photographs could be expressive, going beyond realist description; he brought the texture of rocks, for example, into a flat plane with the human figure. Although she and Siskind did not become amorously involved, Anne clearly enjoyed playing model, and there is an unmistakable sensuousness to the photographs. (See fig. 19a-b.)

Anne had earlier served as a model for quite a few artists. In addition to photographs by Siskind and several paintings by Dorothy,[54] a painter and teacher at the Art Students League, Leon Kroll, had exhibited a "portrait of Anne,"[55] as did Emil Holzhauer, in an exhibition of "Portraits of Young People" in 1934.[56] Holzhauer also gave Anne's parents a bronze head of her that he sculpted later on.

Of course, Anne was not just a model during this period; she also won, among others, the Marcia Brady Tucker Prize from the National Association of Women Artists for *Washington Square* (pl. 1) in 1941, and the Celine Baekeland Prize for *Autumn Landscape*, a painting whose whereabouts are currently unknown, in 1944. These were also years filled with strong friendships and work. Freda Utley, a British author and political activist who moved to the United States in 1939, after her Russian husband, accused of Trotskyism, was arrested and later executed in a labor camp in 1939, wrote in a memoir that she remembered how anyone could afford to rent a place in Chilmark on Martha's Vineyard for a song. Most did without electricity or plumbing, pumping from wells or going to springs to get water. Lots of skimpy swimsuits on beaches and skinny-dipping. Utley remembered shared cooking and gatherings with Anne at the Eastmans' house on Gay Head, now Aquinnah, where Thomas Hart Benton also lived.[57] Max Eastman, who was drop-dead good-looking, had met Eliena Krylenko during his stay in the Soviet Union in the 1920s. There he observed the conflict between Trotsky and Stalin. Eliena's brother, Nikolai Vasilyevich Krylenko (1885–1938), an old Bolshevik since 1903 who rose to become the people's commissar of justice and prosecutor general of the Russian Soviet Federated Republic, had organized some of Stalin's sham trials before his own execution in 1938. Eliena married Max, and they left Russia together. Within their East Coast milieu, the Eastmans had a famously open marriage, in which they had agreed to be transparent with each other. Whether or not Anne dabbled with Max is a question I can't answer, although they remained good friends; what is sure is that Anne and Eliena were very close. Max wrote that Eliena's generosity

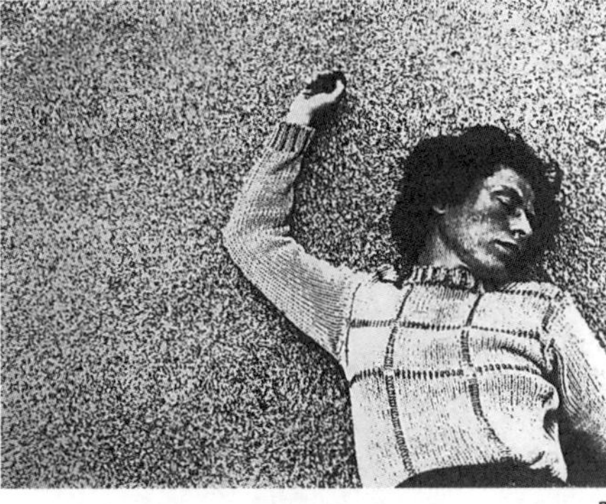

a

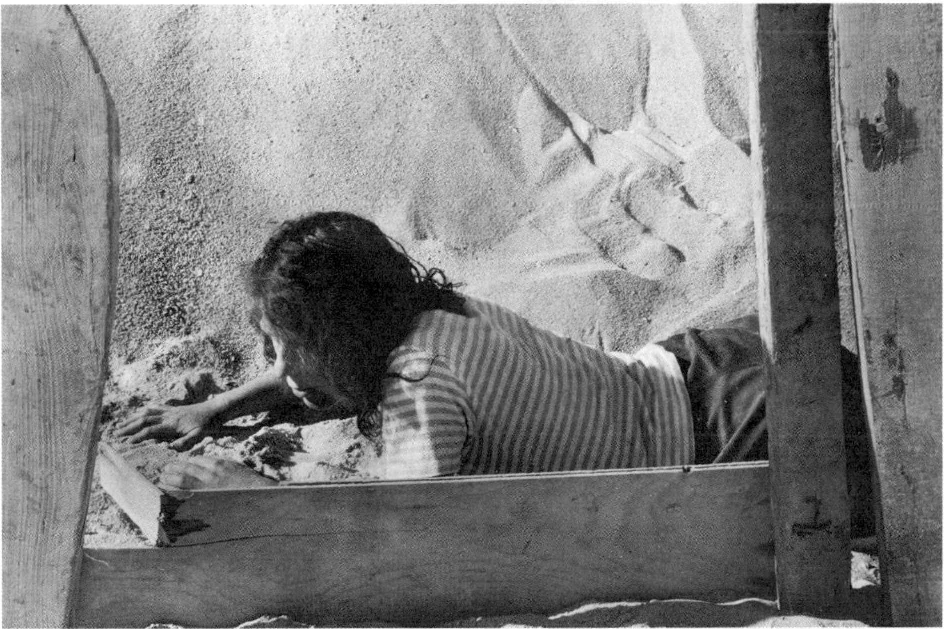

b

Fig. 19a-b
a: Anne Eisner, Martha's Vineyard, c. 1944 (photograph by Aaron Siskind). Houghton Library, Harvard University, courtesy of Aaron Siskind Foundation.
b: Anne Eisner, Martha's Vineyard, 1944 (photograph by Aaron Siskind). Harvard Art Museums, courtesy of Aaron Siskind Foundation.

toward his obsessions with other women did not come from her certainty of the solidity of their relationship. "No," he wrote, "it was not the sureness of my love, but of her own firm stance on the earth that enabled Eliena to be so generous. She had courage, and she had confidence in her own genius for living—a confidence that was magnificently well founded."[58] Anne would retain lessons from Eliena for her own marriage later on.

The years 1943 and 1944 brought exhibitions of Anne's watercolors at the Eighth Street Playhouse and her first solo exhibit at the Norlyst Gallery. The write-up for the exhibition situated her work outside all schools:

> Miss Eisner, who was born in Newark, New Jersey, in 1911, studied art in Paris for one day, and thus is essentially an American product, although not part of what is generally called "the American school." Her approach to painting is candidly emotional rather than theoretical.

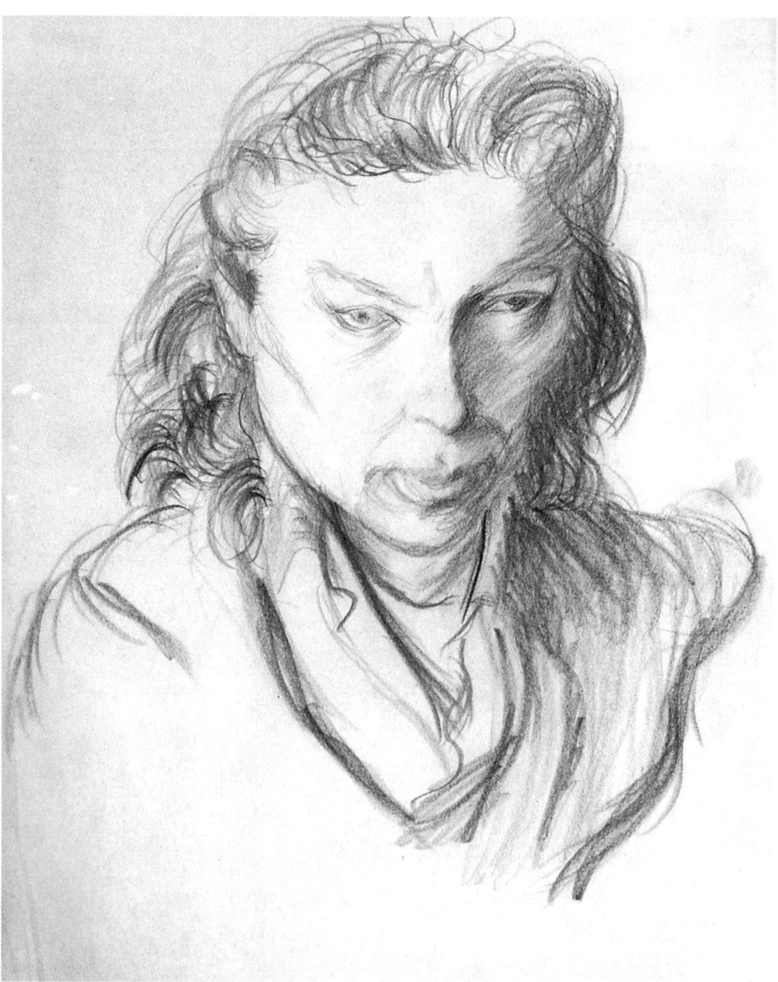

Fig. 20 Anne Eisner, *Self Portrait*, 17 x 14 in., pencil on paper (photography by Michael Rosengarten), McDonald collection.

Here was the beginning of a style effect that Anne would continue to develop. The *New York Times* characterized her style as "realism with convincing personal interpretation."[59] In this same exhibit, alongside the portrait of Tresca and landscapes of Martha's Vineyard (see Pl. 5), Anne presented two vibrantly unflattering self-portraits in pencil on paper. She had been experimenting with the idea of a series tentatively titled "The Strange Faces of One Girl." She wrote: "I've been on a self-portrait orgy. I do a self-portrait a day. I got the idea from studying . . . Rembrandt. . . . It really is hells of fun. I'm not trying to make pictures but just seeing how far I can carry them in a few hours." These exercises, meant to overcome blocking in the presence of a live model at sketch class, were both an experiment in technique and an echo of her early crisis of identity as a young woman. (See fig. 20.)

Louis Finkelstein, a friend, contemporary artist, and educator at the Philadelphia College of Art and later the Yale School of Art, where he also served as interim dean from 1962 to 1964, commented on Anne's self-portraits:

> Most apparent is the expressiveness of the gesture of drawing, the willingness to move the pencil very rapidly. And you see the act of making those lines is not only analytical, it's performance. It's almost like dancing to music, to feel the line as you execute it, while at the same time creating a three-dimensional form.[60]

Through this technique, one glimpses a sense of searching for the self in these distorted faces, looking to find a person whose identity needed constructing. They betray an inner brooding and moodiness that critics had already identified in her Vineyard landscapes.

Even within the world of the left radicals, women were accorded small acknowledgment. How many people really recall the names of strong and committed women like Elinor Rice Hayes, Suzanne La Follette, and Margaret De Silver? Mary McCarthy and Hannah Arendt were among the exceptions with whom the left intellectuals from City College (Daniel Bell, Nathan Glazer, Irving Kristol, and Irving Howe) had on occasion consulted about politics. The dialogue remained, however, almost exclusively among the men. And while Mary Gabriel's book *Ninth Street Women* foregrounds the importance of postwar women artists (Lee Krasner, Elaine de Kooning, Grace Hartigan, Joan Mitchell, and Helen Frankenthaler), with respect to the world of the painters, April Kingsley identifies a "Jewish wife syndrome" that existed among women like Krasner, wife of Jackson Pollock, who always placed the ambitions of their husbands and children above their own.[61] Anne didn't carry that particular burden: a Jew raised in a secular environment, she hadn't married or had children. Nor was this normative role for women limited to Jewish women. Magazines reinforced the cultural ideal of homemaking and beauty as the goal for all women. And her sister, Dorothy,

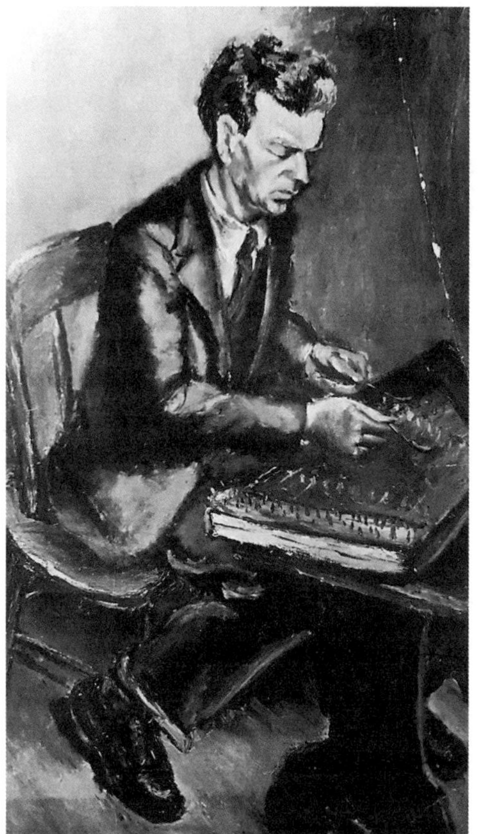

Fig. 21 Anne Eisner, *Dulcimer Player*, c. 1930s. Whereabouts unknown.

my mother, adhered quite strictly to a dual pattern in her life: a dedicated painter who never stopped working and always maintained a studio outside the home, she nevertheless subordinated her work to the constraints of being a housewife and mother. This did not diminish the importance of Dorothy's painting to herself, or her sense of being outside the mainstream as an artist, but it did dictate a life more aligned with the norms for women of the time than Anne was able to manage. Anne had had numerous lovers, a departure from the morality of the era, but the relationships always ended leaving her restless and alone. Few written traces can be found of these love affairs, but according to John McDonald, one that had particularly devastated her was with an Irishman, whom she may have met in Linville Falls. He left the country, either for Canada or to return to Ireland. A poignant photograph of her work *The Dulcimer Player*, reviewed as "outstanding,"[62] is all that remains (fig. 21).

At the age of thirty, when the United States entered the war, Anne thought of herself as unable to succeed, no matter how well she was doing professionally as an artist at the time. She sensed that the world of painters, like the world of politics, was a man's world. The way others perceived failure for a woman (and not only in her parents' milieu)—lacking babies, a husband, a "normal" life—was something she wanted to quash. By 1945, few men could have suited her, and few women could have adapted to the man she met and finally fell in love with—the seeming fulfillment of her youthful scenario.

CHAPTER TWO

Take Me Away, Baby (1945–1946)

Anne Meets Pat

Everyone has his or her own story of the summer of 1945, the liberation of Europe, and the end of World War II. Anne's started with a walk down to King's Beach, near Chilmark and what is now Lucie Vincent Beach, on the south shore of Martha's Vineyard, where she was spending the summer painting. An old friend called out, "You must meet a friend of mine. I think you will like him." With that, the friend waved to a man swimming in the very cold water, who continued swimming for another ten minutes or so before heading in toward shore. As he emerged from the water, a tall, thin silhouette appeared against the horizon, and features gradually came into focus. A beard spread itself down like a shadow flowing from his face. The stride of the naked figure splashing water was relaxed. Deep-set eyes fixed on hers and held them, with wild and gracious portents of adventure.

Anne Eisner, meet Patrick Tracy Lowell Putnam.

Pat, as he was called, invited Anne to visit his house the next day.

When she drove over, parked, and walked up to the door of a well-kept old farmhouse, a child admitted her, and she found herself in a large, comfortable room. In the center was Pat, rope around his waist, now dressed in slacks and a shirt with rolled-up sleeves, milking a goat. From a stool, he leaned out to discuss something important, judging from the intensity of his expression, with one of his guests. Who could not fall for this quirky man?

The house was packed with friends and relatives draped around the sprawling rooms. It was the wackiest scene Anne had ever seen. Children appeared to be everywhere, dashing around with urgent matters to catch his attention: *Uncle Pat! Help me with this, fix that, look at what I found!* Cats and dogs had the run of the place, as did four or five goats and various people from New York, Africa, and who knew where. An interesting lot. She felt dull not having arrived from Mars.

The scarcity of gasoline was a perfect excuse for becoming a member of the household for the night and avoiding the drive back to the house she had rented in Menemsha. Pat and Anne started talking, as they lit up cigarettes. She told him she was a painter living in Greenwich Village. She asked him what he did. He ran a hotel at the edge of a rain forest in the Belgian Congo, he said. Anne thought that the funniest gag she'd ever heard. Then the story unfolded as Pat took up the conversation again with Carlton Coon, a professor of anthropology at Harvard. Anne listened and listened. They were talking about life in the Ituri rain forest of central equatorial Africa and the Mbuti Pygmies who inhabited the region. They were the focus of Pat's anthropological interest, and a number of Pygmy families lived near his home in the Congo.

Pat ignited a passion in Anne, not only a desire for him, this charismatic figure, but also for other people and languages—for another identity. Pat asserted that he felt uncomfortable in the States, though he liked to keep in touch. Anne wasn't at all sure that life in New York as a woman and a painter was right for her anymore, but it had never occurred to her to leave for more than a few months at a time.

Falling in love with Pat was like falling in love with a story for which only the first line existed, a story strange and exciting, possibly dangerous. At the time, it felt inexplicably natural to her: walking over the island of Martha's Vineyard together, perching on fallen trees to look out to sea, talking endlessly, gathering berries. Every moment tingled. The island, too, seemed alive with excitement—children hooted from the fire truck driving up and down the road to celebrate the end of the war. Pat stood tall, and he appeared robust, a combination of lithe power and grace, so manly and so carefree. One photograph of Anne and Pat isolates a moment looking at each other. It evokes a high-voltage connection between them. Pat later said that he fell in love with her because, with her high cheekbones, her face resembled an African mask. (See photos in fig. 22a-c.)

Anne stayed on in Chilmark and lived with Pat during the fall of 1945. The two were almost never apart for more than a few minutes during the

Fig. 22a-c
a: Anne Eisner, c. 1940s (photograph possibly by Aaron Siskind). Houghton Library.
b: Patrick Putnam, 1945 (photograph by Aaron Siskind). Houghton Library, courtesy of Aaron Siskind Foundation.
c: Patrick Putnam and Anne Eisner, c. 1945 (photograph possibly by Aaron Siskind). McDonald archive.

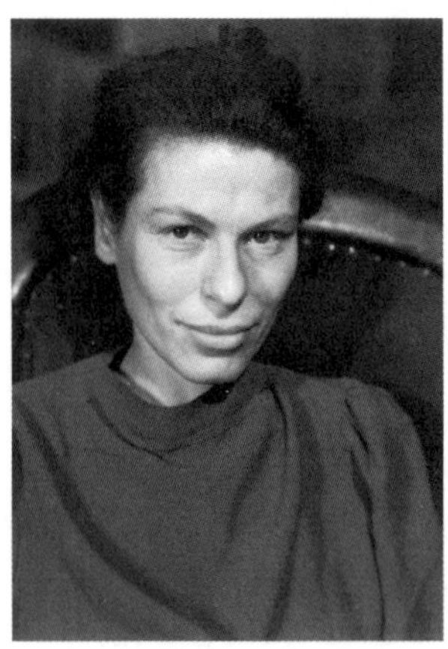
a

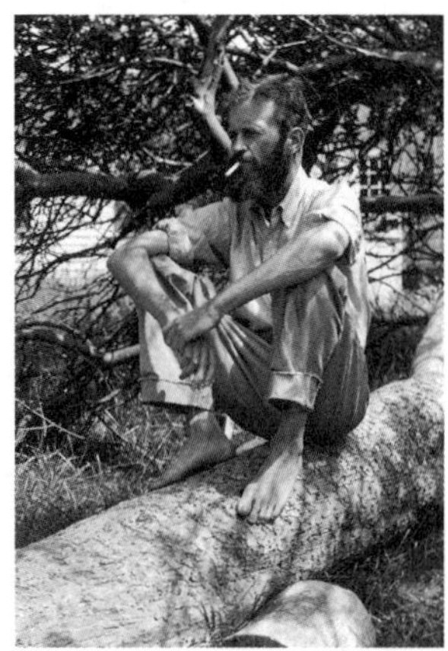
b

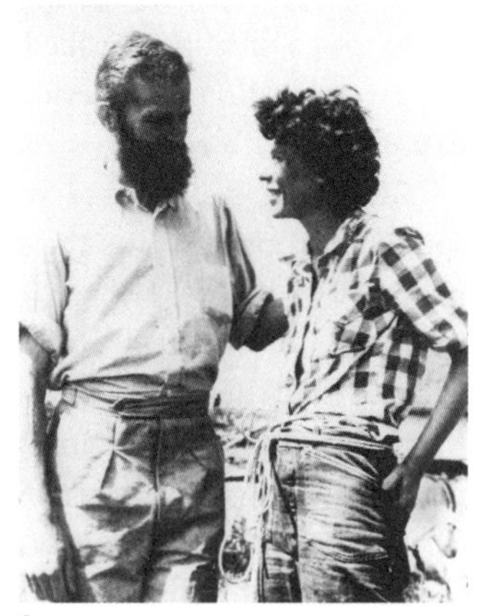
c

late summer and through the early winter in New York. The longest separation was over the Christmas holiday, which Anne spent with her family. It was a beautiful storybook romance, Anne liked to say. She adored Pat. He was as taken with her.

Pat wrote a poem to and for Anne:

To hold you in my arms is to reassure myself
That such a being is, and likes me.
Oh, Anne, it is true that I love you
And am glad you're a woman mine.
Signed: Yr. aff. ac. hsbnd, Pat [Your affectionate acting husband]

During the winter of 1945–1946, Anne produced a series of pen drawings of Pat, allowing the composition to evolve impulsively, as if saying, *Oh, I love that nose, I have to catch the person, the lips, the droops of the mustache in a certain position* (see fig. 23a-c). With a calligraphic movement reminiscent of Matisse's drawings, as Louis Finkelstein points out, Anne evokes Pat's face with a few strokes.[1] "An almost electric current drives the pencil," as Rosanna Warren notes in *Images of Congo*.[2] For now, all Anne could experience was the impetuous yearning to spend every minute possible with him. Once when they were apart, she wrote impatiently: "knowing you don't like long letters, I'll . . . just add the list of things to bring: you, you, and you, quick quick." Where the drawings suggested emotional impatience (*come on, I want to catch your essence!*), an oil portrait from 1945 gathered data in a cool fashion. In her portrait (fig. 24), Anne caught the formal side of Pat, his "Bostonian self," less in the sense of place than of lineage. Anne almost seemed to be trying to capture what it was like to come from a world alien to her and perhaps even harder to imagine than life in the Ituri Forest.

What did Anne really know about Pat? That he was descended from the Lowells of Massachusetts, among whose distinguished ancestors were James

Fig. 23a-c
a: Anne Eisner, drawing of Patrick Putnam, 24 x 19 in., ink on paper, 1945.
b: Patrick Putnam (photographer unknown). Houghton Library, Harvard University.
c: Anne Eisner, drawing of Patrick Putnam, 17 x 13 in. McDonald collection.

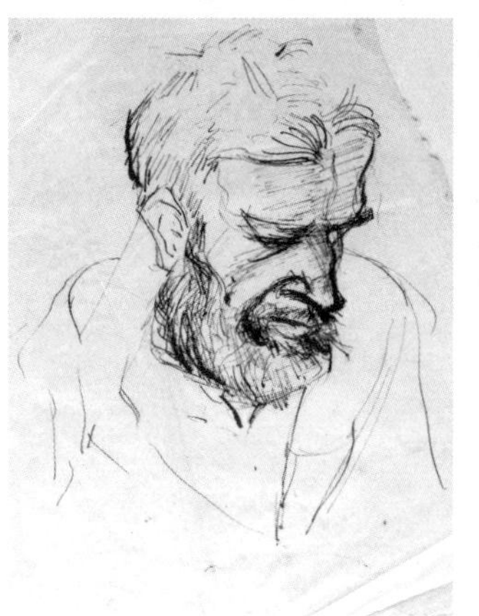
a

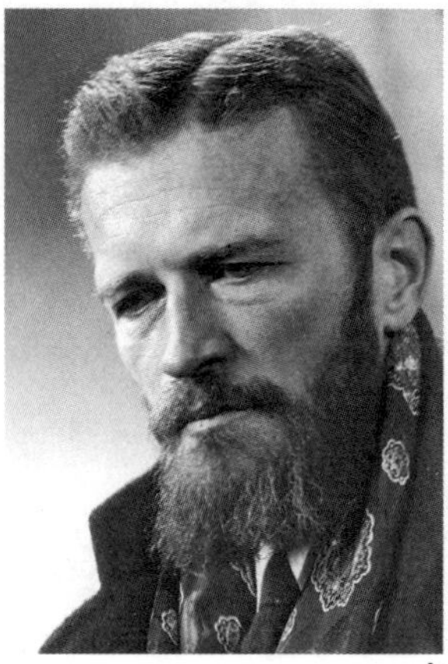
b

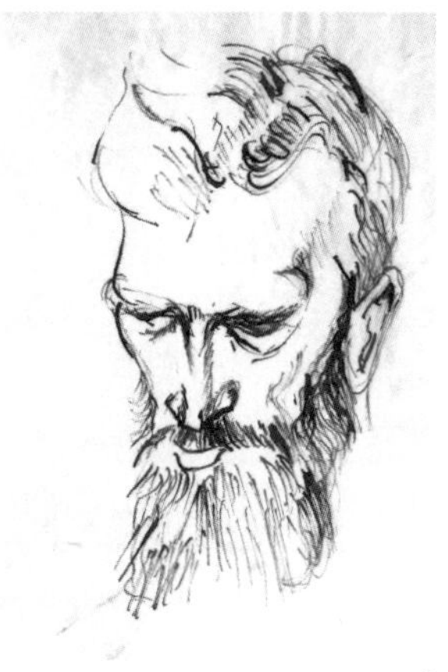
c

Russell Lowell, a diplomat and poet; A. Lawrence Lowell, a president of Harvard College; and Amy Lowell, a poet. Pat's great-grandmother, Anna Cabot Jackson, was the daughter of Patrick Tracy Jackson, whose name reflected the fusing of the old families with newer merchant and shipbuilding families. Joan Mark writes in her biography of Pat Putnam: "The eminence of the Lowells came not just from inherited wealth . . ., but from a tradition of leadership in war and in peace, in business and the arts, in education, benevolence, and public welfare. To be a Lowell was to be the New England equivalent of a European gentleman."[3] The Putnams were an old, distinguished family as well, and Pat liked to say that "all Putnams were either touched with genius or a little mad."[4] Nevertheless, there was some irony when Pat later instructed Anne to read *The Proper Bostonians* (1947) by Cleveland Amory to find out more about him; this Bostonian pedigree was but little of what she would encounter of his person.

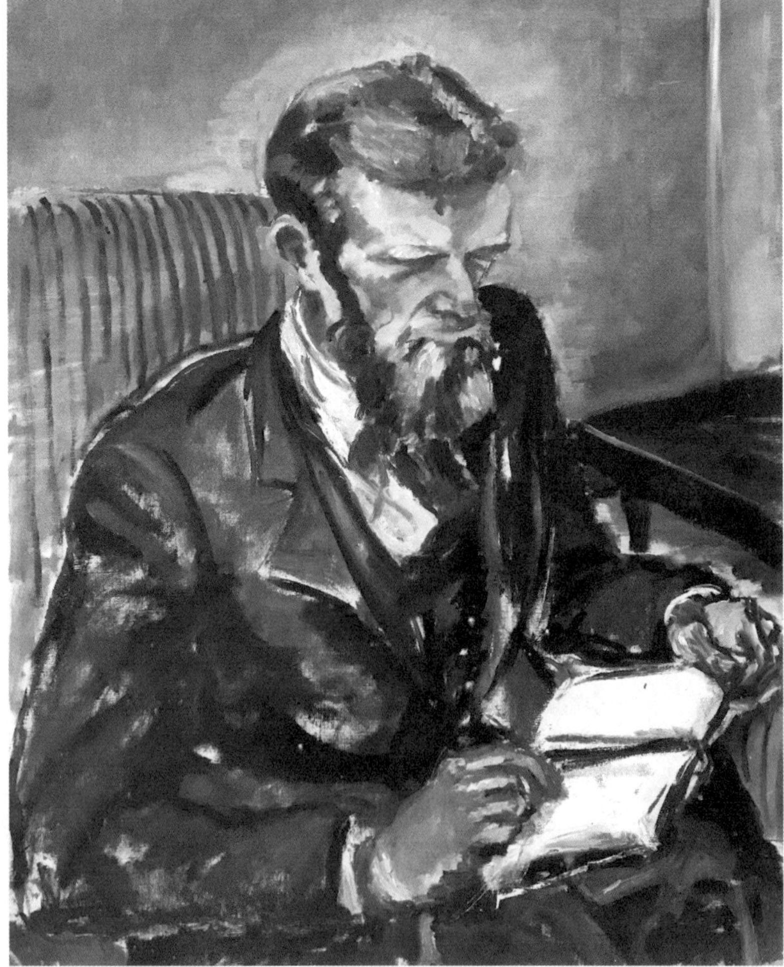

Fig. 24
Anne Eisner, Portrait of Patrick Putnam, 30 x 24 in., oil on canvas, 1945. Houghton Library, Harvard University.

Anne also knew that Pat's father, Charles Putnam, was a noted ear, nose, and throat surgeon in New York who had trained in Vienna, had himself dabbled in painting, and was a man of ambition for himself and his son. Pat's mother, Angelica Rathbone Putnam was an eccentric and strong-willed redhead. In addition to Pat, who was their biological child, Angelica and her husband adopted six children, all raised in Bedford, New York, and at Valleydale Farm on Martha's Vineyard, the large estate she populated with servants, horses, and many monkeys. Pat lived on Martha's Vineyard during summers and attended school there for several winters, before going to the Gunnery School in rural Connecticut. The Putnams believed in the effects of environment in raising children and tried to bring theirs up equally. At the same time, his father communicated to Pat, a sickly child, that he was the one who counted. Pat cared about his siblings, as is clear from his correspondence, but in his adult life, he ensured that people did what he wanted.

Pat attended Harvard College from 1920 to 1925 and, after a spotty career of resisting rules and requirements, graduated with a specialization in anthropology. After graduation, Pat traveled to New Guinea and later joined the Harvard expedition to the Belgian Congo, sent by a professor of physical anthropology, Ernest Hooton, and directed by Frederick Wulsin, a wealthy older graduate student who had traveled in China and hunted big game in Africa. During the expedition, Pat wandered off alone and was gored by an elephant; he was nursed back to health by a Pygmy woman, Abanzima, with whom he fell in love. He dreamed of bringing her home to the United States but was thwarted by his parents, who never gave in on this issue. After returning to Harvard to work on an MA, Pat ultimately decided to discontinue academic work in anthropology and took a course at the Institute of Tropical Medicine in Brussels during the fall of 1929 and early winter of 1930, becoming certified as an *agent sanitaire*, much like a Red Cross worker, in Africa. Although Pat was not ambitious about institutional life, he was curious about everything and continued to pursue the anthropological interests he had begun at Harvard. He took notes (and lost most of them in a canoe accident), measured Pygmies using techniques learned from physical anthropology, hunted buffalo and elephants, and developed an encyclopedic knowledge of his surroundings.

Pat grew up apparently unable to follow orders, endowed with a sense of abandon and invulnerability. He wanted to make the rules of his own life, while never completely letting go of the world of family and friends at home. In fact, his father and other family members had to travel to the Congo several times to care for him during his early years there. Pat translated his own sense of entitlement and leadership into a new and unpredictable context. His relationship to his own well-being and to collaborating with Belgian administrators would be complex during his life in the Congo. He began his first post as a health worker at Penge, Belgian Congo, but was fired after a year when his superiors discovered that he had bought and used marijuana—prohibited by Belgian law.

During a trek to see a dentist for persistent tooth problems, Pat found an exquisite site between Nia Nia and Mambasa, on the route from Stanleyville to Irumu along the bank of the Epulu River at the edge of the Ituri Forest (see map 1). He decided to settle on that very spot, build a hotel for European and American tourists, and make his life there. His model was the "American dude ranch": agriculturists in Argentina had saved themselves from ruination by inviting paying guests ("dudes") from the northeastern United States to visit and simulate ranch life, eventually gaining some renown and impressing Pat.[5] He applied to the Belgian colonial government for a lease to occupy thirty-six hectares (roughly eighty-nine acres) of land for agriculture and two hectares (roughly five acres) for the hotel; he received the lease for Epulu within the Territoire de Mambasa.

The scramble for Africa in the late nineteenth century carved up the continent through exploration and conquest, with borders arbitrarily cutting through villages and tribal life. King Leopold II of Belgium claimed the expanse of the so-called Congo Free State (seventy-five times the size of Belgium) in equatorial Africa and owned it personally until it came under Belgian rule in 1908 amid international protests. A system of enforced labor from the late nineteenth century to the early twentieth century inflicted atrocities upon the Congolese population in extracting natural resources (ivory, rubber, and minerals) which reduced the population by half. Adam Hochschild's book, *King Leopold's Ghost*, eloquently tracks the history of this international scandal and the beginnings of a human rights movement.[6] Pat arrived not long after the worst colonial abuses in the Congo, in 1927. By the postwar 1940s, control was maintained in designated "territories" through a network of Belgian colonial administrators and government-appointed indigenous chiefs. The territory that had been named after the town of Mambasa was renamed Territoire de l'Epulu.[7]

When Pat moved from Penge to the Epulu area, a remarkable thing happened: a family of Pygmies followed him, and others arrived later, beginning interdependent relations over decades between Bantu workers, who came to work for him and live in the village that grew up there, and the Mbuti Pygmies. The Pygmies of the Ituri Forest, including the Mbuti, Aka, Efé, and Basua peoples, are thought to have kept their culture mostly intact. As seminomadic hunter-gatherers for whom the tropical rain forest provides wild fruit, roots, and game, they exchange meat and honey from the forest for agricultural staples like plantains. The Mbuti who came to Epulu established a semipermanent village near the Bira villagers (so named for the Ki-Bira language that they speak), with whom they maintained an association sometimes described as being like a "client-patron relationship."[8]

Shortly after receiving a five-year lease for the concession of Epulu from the colonial government in 1933, Pat returned to the States to find a wife with whom to share his life and married a young woman from Massachusetts, Mary Linder (1905–1937).[9] Mary had studied to be a landscape architect, and her brother had gone with an earlier Harvard African expedition to study biology and disease. Pat returned to the Ituri Forest with his bride to create their home and the utopia he had imagined, complete with damask and fine silver from Mary's family. Mary designed the main house with the help of an American architectural firm. It included a living room called "Le Palais," rondavels (small circular huts) for the guests, and a tennis court. They named the compound Camp Putnam.

Pat's life with Mary ended abruptly when she died in December 1937 during a trip home after they had completed the construction of Camp Putnam. Pat was crushed. He nevertheless remarried four months later, returning to Epulu with his new wife, Emilie Baca. Emilie was something of a grand dame from the Southwest who had become a social worker in New York. She did not react well to life at Camp Putnam, becoming depressed from constant malaria and the isolation caused by her inability to speak the languages of the people. She ejected herself after nine months, returning to the States to live for a time with Pat's father, Dr. Putnam, before returning to New Mexico, where she obtained a divorce from Pat.

What Was Pat Thinking?

Rather than formulate a coherent political position, Pat took the stance of always being the outsider, which had permitted him ever since arriving in Africa to remain uncommitted at many levels. He wrote the following note, postdated September 1939 and marked "Just before England and France declared war on Germany":

> I do not like Hitler, or Napoleon, but I hope that Hitler will win. . . . I hope that Hitler will succeed in making the great State of United Europe which Napoleon barely failed to make. Most of the more unpleasant features of Nazi rule will disappear slowly ~~I think~~, with success and more butter, and many unpleasant features will disappear suddenly when Hitler dies. And in the end, the special of privileges of Chamberlain and his class will vanish from the British Empire, European Empire and the Adriatic Empire, [and] the Russian Empire.[10]

It is not clear why Pat postdated this note or why he kept it. The rationale for supporting Hitler, while neither fully worked out nor in any way original, presents two arguments. The first is the completion of Napoleon's failed project to unite Europe. Pat could identify in Hitler and Napoleon the notion of one leader and the project of unlimited power, a potential winning strategy in a hedge on the future. Winston Churchill deemed the comparison between Napoleon and Hitler to be unacceptable in 1940, the year the Führer visited the emperor's tomb at Les Invalides, having taken Paris in June of that year. But Pat saw Germany as but one more colonizer, extending east and west within Europe. He did not understand the corruption of power and the proportions of evil that Hitler would unleash.

The second argument provides the key to Pat's position: "I am indeed annoyed when I hear flung as reproaches against Hitlerism descriptions ~~and ideas~~ which are equally valid concerning the British Empire's attitudes toward its subject parts."[11] Humanitarianism as practiced by the British was a "disease" with which Europe had "contaminated" Africa. While granting that the English were more benevolent in their colonial despotism than others, Pat stopped short of criticizing the effects of Nazism. It was the colonial question that preoccupied him most: "My axe to grind is a desire to see the colonial system reformed. But even more inspiring to me than this desire is my personal philosophic leit-motif—*veritas*, and away with the hypocritical camouflage."[12] His assumption was that if the colonial system could be revealed for what it was—the search for power under the guise of humanitarian paternalism—then he could make his peace with it. But he had participated as an agent and beneficiary of the Belgian colonial regime, so his criticism of British power could hardly lay to rest questions about racism and Hitler's program. The Belgian Congo remained loyal to the exiled Belgian government in London after 1940, when Belgium itself was occupied by Germany.

Pat does not directly raise the question of anti-Semitism in German National Socialism. But the "Jewish question" raised in the 1930s did have a prehistory at Harvard. Pat had been a senior in college at Harvard during the tenure of his "uncle of sorts," A. Lawrence Lowell (1856–1943) as president of Harvard University between 1909 and 1933. Lowell believed in a liberal education and inaugurated the residential house system, to his credit, but when he proposed a quota system for the admission of Jews to Harvard College (and exclusion of admitted Negroes from freshman dormitories), an uproar ensued. Lowell perceived a "Jewish problem" on the campus, which became equated with an immigrant problem. (Lowell, as a member of a panel, later upheld what many—including Carlo Tresca—believed to be the wrongful conviction, due to anti-immigrant sentiment, of Italian anarchists Nicola Sacco and Bartolomeo Vanzetti, leading to their execution by electrocution.) Jews amounted to about twenty percent of the undergraduate student body, raising the presumed difficulty of assimilating for students whose backgrounds were vastly different. There followed a debate and struggle between the president and his largely liberal faculty. Lowell proposed a double standard: "The accepted theories—'that all men are born free and equal,' etc.—are not absolutely true, but true within certain limits."[13] Students had felt prejudice against Jews within the university prior to this debate. Harry Starr, class of 1921, who headed the Harvard Menorah Society, wrote: "we learned that it was *numbers* that mattered; bad or good, *too many* Jews were not liked. Rich or poor, brilliant or dull, polished or crude—*too many Jews*, the fear of a new Jerusalem at Harvard, the 'City College' fear."[14] Lowell's proposal alarmed the Jewish community, as it had considered Harvard a bastion of "liberalism, cosmopolitanism, and opportunity."[15] Lowell's proposals put this liberal tradition on the line, but the faculty and overseers defeated them, reaffirming the tradition. No student of the time could have avoided considering the issues here; where Pat stood on these discussions is not recorded.

As early as March 1936, Pat's father had alerted him to the threat of fascism, couching it in a surely ironic Ivy League rivalry: Yale was more fascist than Harvard. He presumed Pat to be as informed by radio as he himself was in the United States. By 1938, the year Pat married Emilie and spent several months in the States, his former professor of anthropology, Hooton, was publishing on delicate racial issues with the conviction of scientific objectivity, both reinforcing physical characteristics in the definition of the Jew and clearly opposing fascist ideology. Dr. Putnam, on the other hand, was still coaxing Pat in 1942 after the United States had entered World War II, expressing his hope of receiving "news of what you are doing 'for the government.'" Pat responded: "For, although you sound more patriotic than I have ever heard you, I am more of a world citizen—'mundotic'—shall we call it—than ever before, and I distrust an American or English peace only less than I distrust a Hitler peace. That is no frame of mind with which to get along in the Western Hemisphere nowadays."[16]

Hooton studied the definitions and methods for discussion of race, analyzing the ways in which broad, nonanthropological criteria, from differences in skin pigmentation to religion and language, could create confusion. He was interested in the physical criteria, looking to distinguish groups of the human race based on distinctive features, particularly "race mixtures." During Pat's years at Harvard, Hooton offered a course in physical anthropology on "Race Mixture," as well as courses titled "Races and Cultures of Europe," "Races and Cultures of Oceania," and "Races and Cultures of Africa." From his 1926 address to the American Association for the Advancement of Science, in which he defined the "Methods of Racial Analysis," to his report on the research at Harvard about race mixture, Hooton maintained a strict idea of objective analysis. He characterized his role as an institutional anthropologist as "more of the drab female type . . . which remains at home and reproduces the species while the more brilliant male roves abroad in quest of both adventure and of food to be brought back for home consumption."[17] Pat qualified as the "male" anthropologist in this framework.

However, in Hooton's studies of the Jews,[18] he brought racial analysis to one of the most controversial issues of the time. Hooton's appraisal of the Jewish question entailed distinguishing physical features that resulted from the isolation and endogamy of Jews all over the world, from North Africa to Europe to the United States. Physical distinctiveness, religious practices, and what he described as their "high average intelligence"[19] set Jews apart and made them the subject of envy. As careful as Hooton was to distinguish his own generalizations from Nazi ideology, he wrote in a 1939 article of an "involuntary eugenics" among the Jews that had brought a disproportionate number of geniuses into the world,[20] yet he had proposed "outmarriage" (exogamy) and assimilation:

> Now let us sum up the situation, not as it exists in countries where a population debased in intelligence by the dysgenic effect of a disastrous war and in desperate economic straights deliberately sets up the Jewish minority as a sort of national scape-goat to suffer for the sins of all. . . .
>
> But we cannot wait for the intellectual redemption of mankind and the revival of human intelligence, if we are to take precautions against the occurrence of such national sadism and sheer suicidal lunacy as impels the present German government to destroy that minority element which has been responsible for some of its most brilliant cultural achievements. Since we can do little with the mass of so-called civilized humanity in its present state of mental debasement, the issue must be put up to the Jews themselves, who, as a people of high intelligence and apparently endless patience, have doubtless foreseen and deliberated the several possibilities of solving their own social problems.[21]

Looking back, we could view as racist Hooton's lack of foresight about the devastation of the Holocaust, with his correlation of physical type with intelligence and the proposed plan of exogamy as a solution to the problem. Hooton's efforts in topological research on race did not correlate for him with a fascist ideology, as his acknowledgment of Hitler's "lunacy" in 1938 would suggest.[22]

By the time Anne met Pat in 1945, he had changed his attitude about Hitler and seemed tacitly to espouse Hooton's position that exogamy and assimilation were still a solution for the Jews. Sometime between 1942 and 1945, Pat made the leap from complacency about an ideology targeting Jews to falling in love with and marrying a Jew. It was not a change he could have discussed with many people in the United States, and particularly not with Anne, given her own long-standing political rejection of fascism and her position as an American Jew.

In notes written during 1945, Pat jotted down, "Sorry that Napoleon got licked" and "Sorry that the Roman Empire dwindled." The comments about Hitler had disappeared. During a talk given during the summer of 1945, Pat spoke about forced labor and opposing the "color bar" in Africa, topics on which he had taken a moral position. For him, these were the most immediate questions, although he recognized that "Tonight we are still celebrating the end of the most horrible war in history." By now, he had adjusted his thought and acknowledged the world-historical injustice to the Jews: "Anti-semitism [is] a rising thing too, although we have been fighting for these last years against its propagation by Hitler."[23] This was not so much a question of hypocrisy, I believe, as one of learning for Pat. He never pretended to have been involved in the Allied effort, citing himself (however mockingly) as a "war profiteer"[24] with respect to work he had done on rubber plantations during the war: "No great patriotic enthusiasms made me take on this job. I was bored at my place, for there were no more tourists to stop in. Washington was not sending me urgent telegrams to come back and take a special job." In fact, he admitted that he would rather have talked in the lecture about his personal experiences—being gored by an elephant, for example—but sensed the moment was not right.[25] Only this public support of the Allied triumph and mild deprecation of anti-Semitism signaled the change.

Two distinct sides to Pat's thought mark the repetition of the opposition between nature and nurture or culture. He asserts in a culturally constructed argument that all races are constituted from differences: "[I] went out there long ago with [the] feeling that natives are natives and in all these years have learned one big thing and that is that they are people differently brought up from us, to be sure, but nevertheless people."[26] While this is an argument about the universal character of people, in the second case he drew upon the context of his family when writing his will of 1946, designating the children of his [adopted] sisters, "whether adopted before or after my death," as "fully as if they were my blood."[27] Although he never doubted his being the most favored child at the center by birthright, the metaphor of adoption remained strong in Pat's sense of community.

The other side of his thought remained essentialist, as he suggests in comments about the natural tendencies of the Africans:

> I want to emphasize the fact that my own point of view is not at all that of a "mushy sentimentalist." For example, I am the first to admit that, left to himself, the Negro would fall, more or less gratefully, back into his natural way of life, with its never-ending inter-village bloodshed, and its guiding principle that the best use of man's time, aside from that necessary to produce food enough to live on, and shelter from the rain, and children to keep alive one's name, is the "dolce far niente" [carefree idleness].

This leads him to harsh statements endorsing the corporal punishment of African workers: "Again, I have no sympathy with the people who decry the punishment of flogging as abominably inhumane, for, indeed, were I a lawmaker for a Negro people, so efficacious and harmless do I consider it, that I should incorporate it into the penal code."

It was the notion of hypocrisy within the colonialist argument that most irritated Pat about the civilizing mission: "It is a great dislike of hypocrisy that drives me."[28] The humanitarian mission and ideal came up against the sense that colonized peoples needed to be coerced in order to become civilized. To decry colonial hypocrisy and yet support the flogging of "natives" carries with it the same incoherence that Pat displayed in his attitude toward Hitler. In the case of the Belgian Congo, it was to ignore the brutal history, going back to the late nineteenth century and the early twentieth century, when Leopold II exploited the État Indépendant du Congo (Free State of the Congo). In the search for labor to run the rubber plantations, terror reigned from murder, disease, starvation, and exposure, as well as a low birth rate brought on by the appalling conditions, which reduced the population by half.[29] In sum, how, then, could one declare oneself to be against forced labor and the color bar and still favor floggings?

Pat's proclaimed distaste for hypocrisy did not carry with it a need to examine the conflicts within his own attitudes and prejudices: on the one hand, believing that races are merely different, no better and no worse than one another in the African context, and on the other hand, condoning an ideology of Aryan superiority in fascist Germany and the use of physical punishment to overcome the "natural" tendencies within the black African population. He did maintain both attitudes—at least for a time.

Pat the Charismatic

In March 1946, the headline of the *Orangetown Telegram and the Pearl River Searchlight* read: "Dr. Patrick Putnam, Anthropologist, Is Woman's Club Speaker Wednesday/Thrills Large Audience with Strange Tales of Africa." The presumed doctor spoke to the Pearl River Womens Club, apparently not only thrilling but also shocking and titillating the audience with tales of illicit sexual practices among the Africans, marking out the differences as he saw them from American mores. Africans, he said, were better at compartmentalizing conjugal life from the "enjoyment of sexual excitement." Although everyone seemed to be seeking a golden age or noble savage myth, he suggested, the reality was quite different:

> Missionaries, although they would surely not advocate a return to savagery, are enemies of modern commerce and slavery, and talk too easily of the increased promiscuity under today's régime. Ethnologists and lovers of the noble savage dislike equally the savage in trouser [wearing Western clothes], and advocate a return, it seems to me utterly impossible . . . to old ways. But, at least in so far as sexual promiscuity goes, were the old days so very different from these new ones? True, punishment for partner *in flagrante delicto* may have been more terrible and swift. But Negroes have ever been good at hiding, and have always had great opportunity to hide actions which they wish to remain secret; and, more important, the types of licit extra-marital intercourse

> for married and unmarried people are so numerous as to ensure a most thorough distribution of whatever diseases may be present . . . etc. etc.

Pat here attributed the spread of disease through promiscuity to Africans and went on to discuss the lives of women: "In all the business of 'civilizing' the native, the position of their women has received very little attention. Certainly they are powerful people, the women, but they have little say in the choice of their own or of their daughters' husbands." He spoke of how very young girls were given over to polygamous marriage and how the Belgian government had tried to suppress such marriages by imposing specific taxes. But he defended the practice of child marriage, saying it "may not be so bad. The little girl may marry, as her white brother would be going to boarding school. . . . It may be 'the best thing for her' in many cases."[30]

Throughout the presentation, Pat took the male point of view toward these native women:

> Talking . . . figuratively as well as literally, they [the Africans] are less clothed than we are. At first, thousands of flabby breasts flapping in the breeze offend us; but were our women equally exposed, would they be at all less offensive? But what one sees every day becomes neutral, and so we are no longer repulsed by the ladies of the "land of breasts" . . . and cease to be unpleasantly shocking to our formerly delicate taste.[31]

Whether Anne found such comments distasteful (in identifying with women, all of whom would eventually get old) but—like so much that women were silent about—accepted it as standard male commentary is not clear. What is clear is that she did not detect anything terribly specific in what the maverick anthropologist was describing.

A Love from Different Worlds

When Anne met Pat on Martha's Vineyard in 1945, she knew nothing of his former pro-fascist views. She knew that his divorce from Emilie had just gone through, and she met Emily (Mickey) Hahn, a writer for the *New Yorker*, who was staying at the farm in Chilmark with her daughter. Pat and Emily had known each other since the 1920s, and she spent eight months with him at Penge in the early '30s; they had had an on-and-off romantic/possibly sexual relationship ever since. The end of the war brought the father of Hahn's child back from prison camp in Hong Kong, where he had been held by the Japanese, and the two were married that November.

The desire for Pat swept over Anne like a wave from behind, shutting out everything. If Anne had picked up his blithe attitude toward women, she might have questioned further, but she was herself far from the conventional gender norms and considered herself both strong and well equipped for challenging situations. She realized that to continue loving Pat meant leaving the United States to make a new life in Africa.

Anne made the decision to abandon the disciplined habits of her studio and the knowns of the City for a life without routine or predictability. She loved the outdoors, but mostly of the tame variety: Martha's Vineyard, North Carolina, Oregon. She couldn't stand insects and often reacted severely to bites, so it was hard for her New York friends to imagine her in an equatorial rain forest. Nor did she know how it would work out; she just wanted to try it.

When Anne fell in love with Pat, she also fell in love with the idea of Africa as an alternative to her present life. This passion became the reason for her to break from everything that had formed her; it allowed her a quest for another self. Anne sought sponsors who would provide advance payment for paintings to fund the trip and booked a one-way ticket to Africa. An announcement placed in *Art Digest* read as follows:

> The artist (twice winner in the National Association of Women Artists and frequent exhibitor in our national shows) plans to paint twenty canvases during her trip . . . and these are to belong to those twenty collectors who are willing to stake the lady to her fare and expenses.[32]

Among those who sponsored Anne's trip were Dorothy and John, Pat, Walker Evans, Herbert Solow, photographer Sylvia Salmi (who would become Solow's wife), and Margaret De Silver. Anne did rather well for someone who had rejected her father's world of business. By liberating herself, at least for a time, from the financial dependence and infantilization that Virginia Woolf describes of daughters who depend solely on their fathers for support, she achieved an important symbolic separation. Not only was Anne able to follow the man she had chosen, but she had given herself a job as well: to paint. Her purpose in Africa, therefore, was to be quite different from that of most of the Europeans living there at the time, who were either missionaries, colonial administrators, people in business, or their wives.

The decision to leave America was made jauntily and without regret. Anne scribbled in a note just prior to her departure:

> Goodbye to New York
> Goodbye to the Skyline
> Goodbye to the family
> Friends and Relations
> Goodbye to the City
> I love so dearly
> Goodbye, Goodbye, Goodbye.
> Off to Africa, so called land of Darkness.[33]

Part II

EPULU

CHAPTER THREE

The Voyage to Africa (1946–1950)

In the spring of 1946, Anne and Pat had said their goodbyes and boarded the ship bound for Africa, when, as Anne wrote: "During the night, Pat got desperately ill and just before the boat sailed we had to get off and rush him to the hospital where penicillin and oxygen saved his life. It wasn't till three months later that we sailed."[1] From then on, Pat's health remained fragile; Anne just didn't know to what extent. When they finally were able to leave New York on July 28, 1946, on a cargo ship called the *Freetown*, they

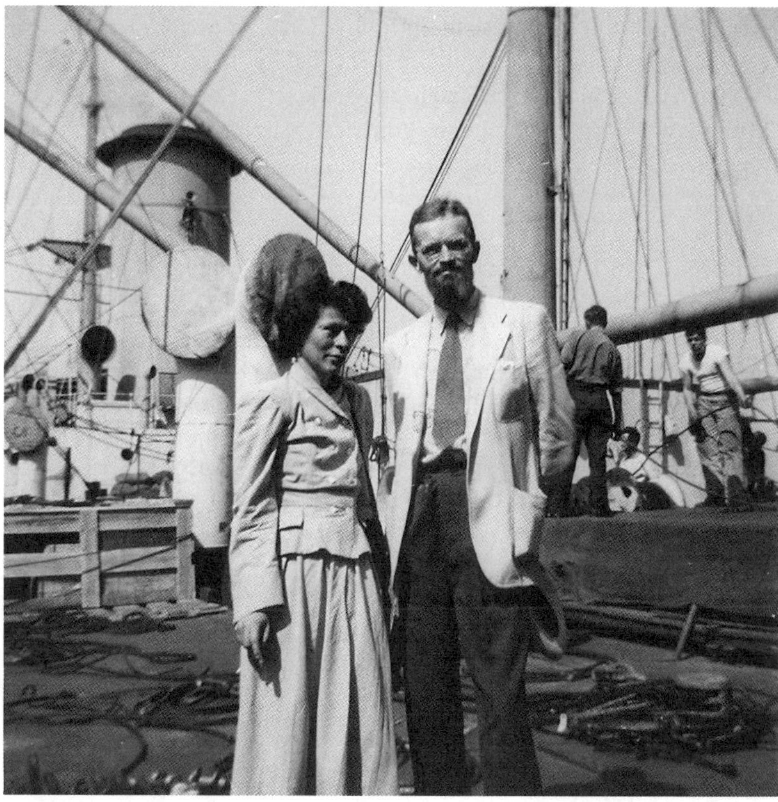

Fig. 25
Anne Eisner and Pat Putnam, departure, 1946 (photographer unknown). Houghton Library, Harvard University.

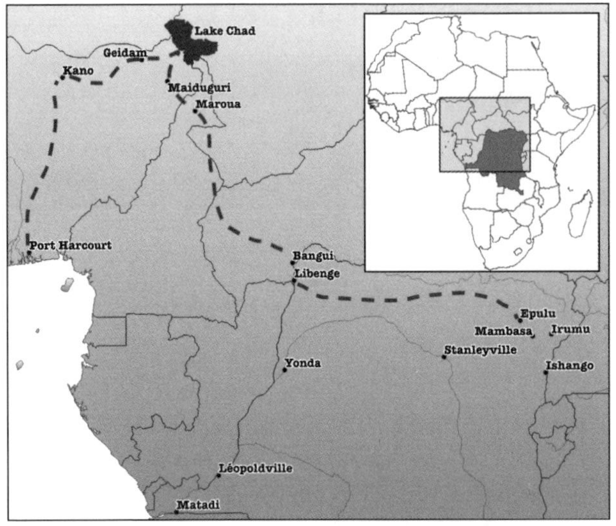

Map 1 Central Africa, showing the 1946 overland voyage (Caleb Shelburne).

sailed to Las Palmas, Canary Islands; Dakar, French West Africa; Freetown, Sierra Leone; Monrovia and Firestone Plantations, Liberia; Tsakoadi, Gold Coast; Lagos, Nigeria; Daala, French Cameroon; Victoria, British Cameroon; and finally, Port Harcourt, Nigeria (see map 1). The ports along the west coast of Africa were Anne's introduction to the continent. Pat gave Anne French lessons on board to refresh her rusty knowledge of the language in preparation for life in the Belgian Congo.

From the very first villages where their ship put in, Anne was fascinated with the shapes of the wooden carvings, masks, and stools, right down to the cooking utensils. From the 1935 exhibition at MOMA and her knowledge of modernists' interest in "primitive" art, Anne felt deep curiosity about everything she encountered. She and Pat began to buy artifacts both from individual carvers and in the markets. Pat wrote to a colleague: "[Anne] is one of the contemporary American painters known in art circles, if not outside [them], and her taste in painting and sculpture, combined with my anthropological training, makes us, we think, get stuff distinctly worth acquiring for private collectors, art museums, and those ethnographic museums which buy primitive arts as art, and not simply at bow and arrow prices."[2] They were a team: collecting depended not only on Pat's savvy about Africa and where to find objects but also on Anne's aesthetic taste. They were starting to assemble what would become two important collections (now under each of their names at the American Museum of Natural History). Anne observed the carving techniques and carefully noted down everything she observed, as she would about many of her new experiences, in a sequence of letters to her parents which would continue throughout her life in Africa.

Once they left the ship in Port Harcourt, they drove overland in the car that Anne had brought with her (see fig. 26). With its "fine patina of peeling paint, rust, dust, and patches of new paint," camping equipment piled on top of baskets, pots and pans strapped onto the front, and gasoline tins tied to the bumpers, they made their way to Kano, Nigeria, and Lake Chad; to Maroua and inland in French Cameroun; to Bangui, up the Congo and Ubangi Rivers meandering around French Equatorial Africa. Along the way, they either camped or stayed in Belgian government rest houses. At each place they stopped, Pat knew whom to contact in the colonial establishment, often the district officer and other administrators. He had undertaken several side businesses in order to make some money, and one in particular with ivory which would be shipped out in "discs" to billiard-ball manufacturers, so discussions for Pat always turned out to be operational wherever he was.

Anne arrived in Africa soon after World War II, when a change in the attitude of the colonial powers toward their colonies was emerging. Where there had previously been pride, justification now seemed necessary. During the war, Africa had been strategically as well as economically important. For example, Freetown as a deep-water port, and in due course Dakar, Port Harcourt, and overland towns like Kano had provided staging areas for the Allied campaigns in North Africa. After the Brazzaville Conference in 1944, the retiring governor-general of the Belgian Congo, having guided the colony through the war, spoke of changing the colonial policies to include reforms of an economic and social nature, with participation by indigenous people as well.

American anti-colonialism increased the pressure on imperial powers. In the Congo, the Commission pour la Protection des Indigènes (Commission for the Protection of the Indigenous) advised implementation of a plan to

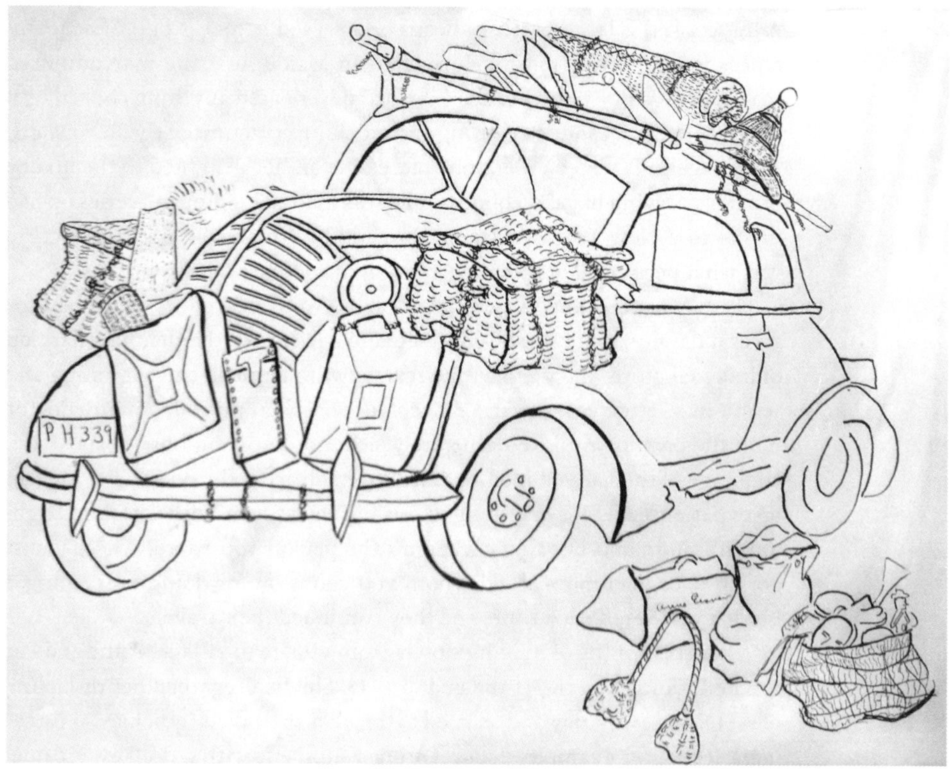

Fig. 26
Anne Eisner, drawing of car, 13 x 17 in., ink on onion skin, 1946. McDonald collection.

assimilate some Africans (known as the *évolués*, "evolved") to the status of "honorary Europeans and exempting them from racist regulations applying to Africans."[3] In 1948, a ten-year plan was adopted for economic expansion in the Congo which included internal incentives to cultivate the land agriculturally, as well as to develop education and promote health. Nevertheless, enforced labor, dating back to the nineteenth century, continued through the war and did not stop at its end. In practice, the bad ways of old had not completely been erased. The local chiefs represented the colonial administration, enforcing laws and collecting taxes.

Anne was immediately critical of the colonialist attitudes toward the Africans on the first leg of her trip: "One thing is certain that if the white people or so-called Europeans did their own work, you'd see a lot of [modern] conveniences in no time flat. It seems to me they've gone out of their way to make the jobs as tough as possible."[4] However, the "boy" who traveled with Anne and Pat and worked for them was shocked by the lack of structure in their routines. They did not eat several-course dinners or change plates with each new dish. He did not approve of them going to the market by themselves. He had been schooled in European customs, and Anne and Pat did not conform to those models. Anne wrote, "I'll never make a good colonial as I can't acquire the proper nasty voice necessary in calling for a boy. Also I don't like pink gin and eating dinner from nine o'clock on."[5] When Anne cooked a large batch of beans and served it to a group of acquaintances from a local club for Europeans in Maiduguri, one man admitted that in his twenty years in Africa, he had never eaten anything cooked by a white woman. Despite her strong and mocking criticisms of the Europeans, Anne's feelings weren't all of one piece. Part of her delighted in the luxury of a boy carrying her sketchbook—she was used to lugging groceries up five flights to a New York apartment. In addition, the colonial infrastructure was what permitted her to make this trip through several countries.

On a few occasions, Pat suddenly fell ill and was confined to bed for several days. In one case, he contracted malaria, then the flu and a flare-up of infected gums and teeth. Anne reacted with panic in the beginning and wrote in a letter years later: "Have you ever been miles from any doctor with the person you love desperately sick, not knowing how to speak the language of the natives and not a white person around, and you having had no experience. . . . It's one thing to see it in the movies with Charles Laughton. It's quite another thing when it's the person you adore, who has just gotten over pneumonia, and whom you count on for doing everything."[6] But Pat recovered each time, and they continued their travels.

After six months of moving slowly from village to village, Anne and Pat reached Kano, Nigeria, at the end of 1946. She had regained her discipline of sketching every day and learned to do what she called "quickies"—catching a scene, for example, documenting a moment with a donkey, a camel bringing in peanuts in Kano, or men building groundnut (peanut) pyramids out of groundnut bags, a key part of the economy. (See fig. 27a-c.)

On March 8, 1947, Anne wrote a long letter to her parents from Geidam, Nigeria, in which she described camping in the area, cooking ostrich-egg omelets, sketching, visiting a northern market with livestock, meeting with women in their huts (noting their headdresses and jewelry), and camel riding. She was interested in the straw huts and men who spent the day studying and writing, the trees of the area, and a silversmith shop. She described what she had learned about the Hausa, Fulani, and Kunai peoples and the history of the slave trade in the area.

Despite Pat's illnesses, Anne was upbeat, writing that she and Pat still liked "each other as much as ever, if not more, and [were] hardly even out of the other's sight. I never knew one could be so happy," and, she added, "unrestless." She marveled: "I never knew one could . . . have so few problems."[7]

As the winter went on, Anne continued to write home about her happiness with Pat. It was the inability to predict what would happen from minute to minute that exhilarated her particularly. With Pat near and well, Anne did not feel threatened by the unknown. Caught in the excitement of constant change and discovery, Anne wondered at the closeness she felt with Pat as they continued in March toward Maroua, the capital of French Cameroon. The promise of arriving in the Congo was getting closer.

After five and a half months in northern Nigeria and nine months in transit, meandering from village to village, they arrived at Libenge, a town on the border between French Equatorial Africa and the Belgian Congo, only a few days' drive to Camp Putnam. Curiously, for all Pat's knowledge and years of experience in Africa, he had neglected to check the expiration date of his passport—and the passport had expired. It was almost as if he didn't want to reach Camp Putnam. The authorities at the border of the Belgian Congo were lenient enough not to send them back to the French territories. Still, Anne and Pat were going to have to wait in Libenge for the Belgian government to renew his documents. They settled into a rest house and became temporary members of the local European Club. Anne read in French, studied Swahili, sketched, and painted watercolors. In all, it took four months for the passport to arrive and for them to be cleared to enter the Belgian Congo.

As time passed in Libenge, Anne reversed her state of mind of only a few weeks before, becoming restless and glum. At first, she developed "the itch," the colloquial name for scabies. Scabies is a skin disease caused by a mite, *Sarcoptes scabiei*, which can be transferred from person to person and produces an extremely itchy rash. Anne noted that Albert Schweitzer's book *On the Edge of the Primeval Forest* suggested a cure by bathing, rubbing the body with ointment flowers, sulfur (*sulfur depuratum*), crude palm oil, oil from sardine tins, and soft soap (the equivalent then of an insecticidal cream now); the key was getting rid of the mites. Anne also came down with malaria, for which quinine was recommended. But nothing was going to cure the problem that Anne discovered with Pat, because it was in Libenge that the bubble burst.

Anne had said and thought that she could handle anything, but she projected more of the derring-do attitude than she ever really had. Her inability to follow conventions carried a heavy price in anxiety. She believed she was prepared to leave New York with someone to whom she entrusted her passion, her life, and her future—something she had never felt for or done with anyone before. She did not know about a part of Pat's past. He had not told her.

Two events jarred Anne into the present. For the first time in their year-and-a-half life together, Pat announced that he was the husband of several African wives, who were waiting for him in Wamba (a town to the east, where Pat had awaited assignment early on from the Belgian government) and at Epulu. Then, for the first time since they had left New York, Pat left Anne alone to travel for a couple of days. The declaration and departure were to set a precedent for what "aloneness" would mean for Anne: finding herself cut off from Pat's affection as she was left by herself to cope with this news.

Anne realized that she not only was going to have to deal with her feelings of betrayal but would also soon encounter the people at Epulu, the large community named for the river that runs through it, whom she understood even less than she expected. When Pat had married Mary Linder, his first wife, he had been careful to warn her through an intermediary about his polygamous life in Africa; he had continued to visit his wives when he was away from Epulu, with Mary's consent.[8] With Anne, no such warning preceded the decision to live together or their departure from the United States. Anne knew that Pat had lived with African women in the past, but she was unaware of any current wives. Pat's strategy of luring Anne to the Congo without telling her suggests a desperation which he never admitted. That he needed a woman from a relatively similar background who spoke English—as a reminder of his American self to balance the African side—seems clear. He had fallen in love with Anne, he said, because her face had the bone structure of an African, and he seemed to need her in his own way more than she needed him. Did Pat so fear that Anne would lose interest in

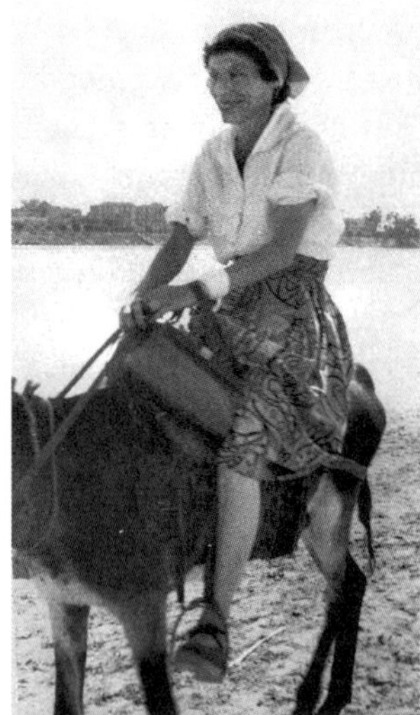
a

Fig. 27a-c
a: Anne on a donkey in Kano, Nigeria? c. 1947.
b: Anne Eisner, *Kano*, 14 x 16 in., ink on onion skin, 1946. McDonald collection.
c: Anne Eisner, *Kano Pyramids*, 15 x 22 in., watercolor on paper, 1947. McDonald collection.

coming to Africa with him if he explained his polygamous situation that he hadn't prepared her for the life he wanted? One in which she would share everything, including the relationship to him with other wives. Perhaps Pat's plan was to wait until after Anne had become entirely dependent on him during their travels to tell her about the other wives, understanding that it would take her some time to process what she had learned about his

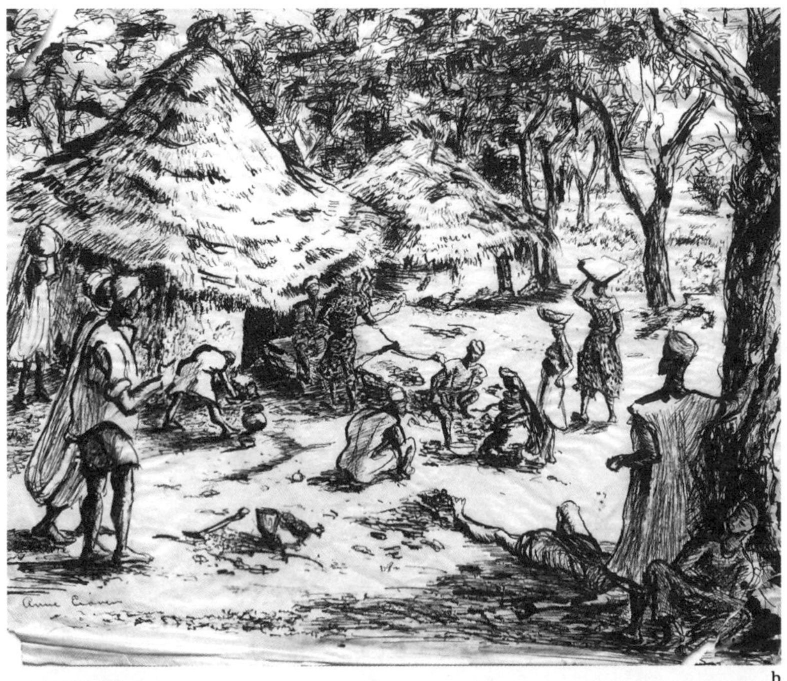

b

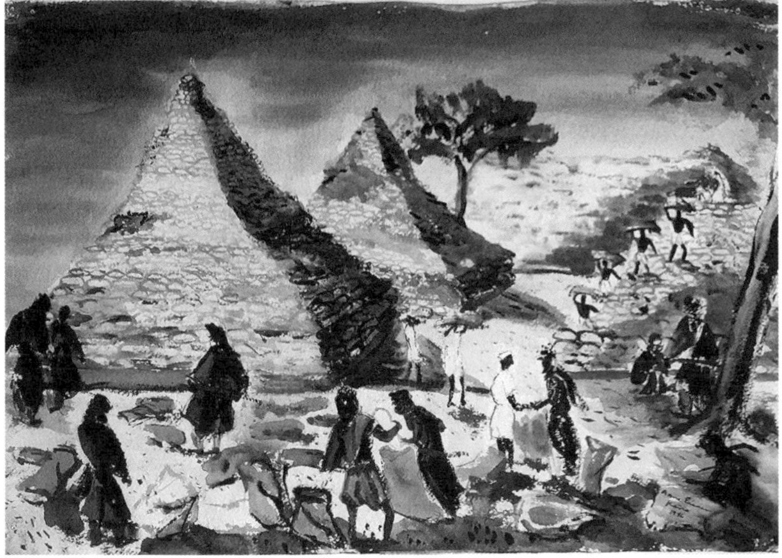

c

(and now her) situation and that then she would adapt to his ways.

Anne and Pat had just spent an entire year and a half together, from living together in the United States to their trip across Africa, during which they were virtually never separated. It was far from clear how things would go once they arrived at Epulu. Anne was only beginning to gauge the extent of what Pat meant by living in two cultures. She became depressed, not knowing how to react (see fig. 28). She was unable to write home even to her mother or sister, whose support she had always counted on, about this humiliating news. Stunned and struggling to get her bearings, she continued to write mechanically what she had written with such enthusiasm a few short weeks earlier: how Pat was the most wonderful traveling companion, how much she loved him, and so on.

Privately, she wrote:

> What happened to Anne in her African wonderland? She certainly drank out of the wrong bottle. It wasn't that she felt tall or that she felt small she just felt lousy and grim. Everything was wrong, everything felt wrong. All food tasted bad . . . and her skin itched and itched and itched and she scratched and scratched. But that only made it worse. Nor was that all it seemed, as though everything she did could only displease. Nothing she did was right. Nor could she work.
>
> She couldn't speak to anyone, as everyone around her spoke strange languages. The "blancs," as they were called, spoke something called French, and the "noirs" spoke an even odder gibberish. They seemed to act as though they understood each other within each group. Only nobody could understand her. Even if they spoke English, they didn't seem to be able to understand hers. She felt very lonesome.... Poor Anne: Where, oh where, is your African wonderland?[9]

When Pat arrived back from his first journey away from Anne, visiting one of his African wives and working on a business venture, he brought back a baby monkey as a gift. Pat had always had chimps and monkeys as their friends had cats and dogs in their lives. It was a way of showing his affection and giving her back something in exchange for the monogamy he had just taken away. He attempted to make her feel better. Anne took some cheer in the companionship of the monkey and even the guinea pigs that Pat threw in for good measure. What the future held was still unknown.

As they left Libenge, Anne wrote that the trip had been "like a Kafka novel. We're always on the way, but we never get there." This feeling wouldn't end soon.

Home, (Bitter)sweet Home

By the time they did finally arrive at Camp Putnam, and although Anne could not yet think about her future, she had recovered her aplomb and could again feel enthusiasm for the beauty of the place. Pat loved spectacular entrances, and he made a great show of their arrival. After stopping to see an animal hunter named Jean de Medina about fifteen miles from Epulu, they arrived at night under a full moon. As they approached the turnoff from the road, the message rang out: "Putnami's here! Putnami's here!" Pat honked his horn all the way down the road, as people started running alongside, yelling and shouting. He stopped the car at the entrance. Anne wrote: "In between huge trees with only the moonlight and a couple of small blizzard lamps, you could see an archway of red flowers through which you got a sweep of white huge bell flowers, and a slight glimpse of a tan mud house with a little thatch showing, the whole view composing like

Fig. 28
Anne Eisner in a Geidam headdress, 1947 (photographer unknown). Houghton Library, Harvard University.

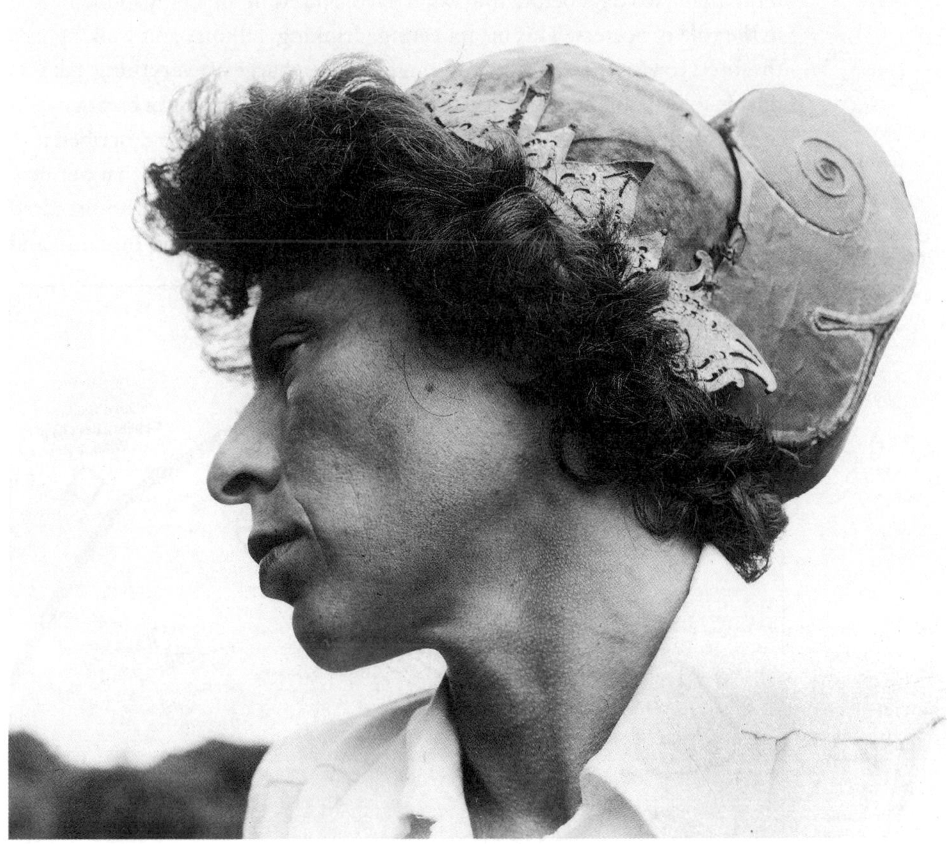

nobody's business."[10] (See map 2) She sat in the car, taking in the nocturnal view of high trees, feeling shy about meeting the people who had clustered around to greet Pat. When she was introduced, the handshaking stretched into a lengthy performance before they went inside. The central room was austere and elegant, a large room with a fire in the center and three enormous logs burning on top of a stone structure, and two open doorways with windows. Other than the mud structure, there was no furniture. In the morning, Anne saw the view from the grand living room called Le Palais overlooking the Epulu River, stretching across to the trees of the rain forest (see fig. 29). Her bedroom had the same view. The forest was far less scary than she had imagined, and not in the least claustrophobic: the trees formed a high canopy overhead.

After an absence of two years, Pat immediately reclaimed Camp Putnam and the hotel from the men who had worked there previously and with whom he had left it. Anne and Pat paid hotel rates for a month because it had been a source of income for the men while Pat was gone. Pat then devised a system so that they could share in the responsibility of the hotel, but he could benefit from the revenue to pay for repairs and himself receive income. It didn't take more than two days before tourists arrived, and Anne suddenly found herself in the role of hostess. This meant eating, drinking, talking, and walking into the forest to visit the Pygmies. Although he took charge of everything, Pat was unable to walk in the forest because he experienced shortness of breath.

Life at Epulu was "magic" for about three weeks, as Anne described it in letters home. Then it turned into a crisis, as she had to accept that her new home included Mada Gobaneka (1915–?), Pat's African wife who predated Anne by many years. Pat assumed his place as head of Camp Putnam, and

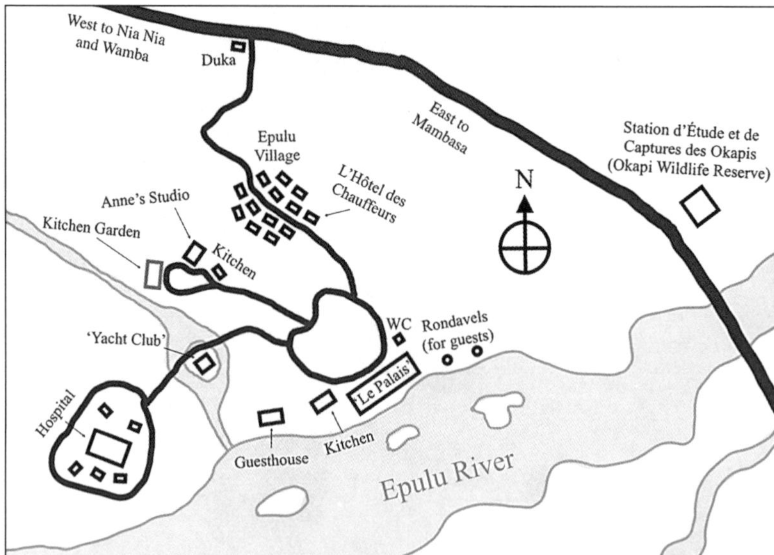

Map 2
Map of Epulu as it was in 1952 (Schuyler Jones original map, revised by Caleb Shelburne).

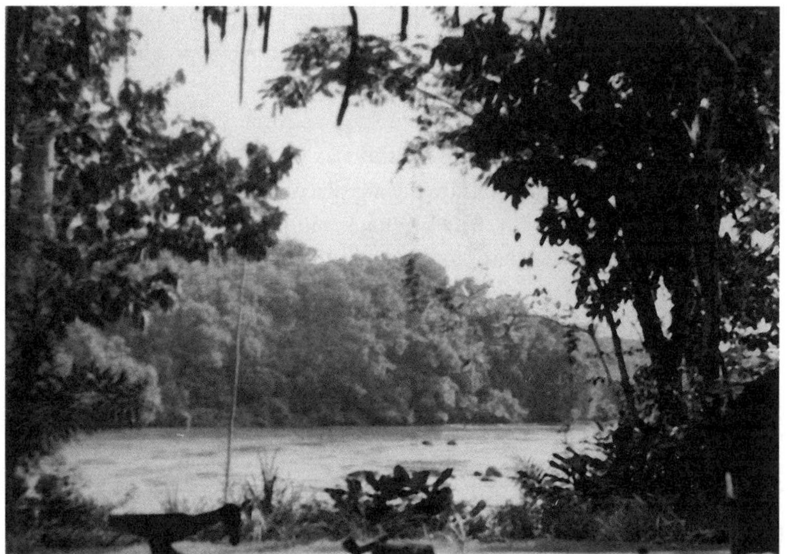

Fig. 29
View of Epulu River from Le Palais, 1952 (photograph by Schuyler Jones). Houghton Library, Harvard University.

he seemed to find it quite natural to be with Mada as well as Anne. Anne found herself in the position of the other woman. It was a shock, no longer abstract or imagined but lived concretely, minute by minute. As Anne might have expected, Mada didn't like her. Anne didn't have any status at Camp Putnam, and yet she had far too much of another kind as a white woman, whereas Mada considered herself to be an integral part of the establishment. She had seniority, and Pat seems to have respected this. Anne didn't like her any more than she liked Anne, and Anne was tormented by jealousy and her separation from Pat. She had lived and breathed her relationship with Pat, in passion. With none of her other lovers had she constructed a romantic dream. The Pat she fell in love with was a character they both wanted to believe in: the tall, handsome frontiersman in Africa. That he couldn't sustain this role dismayed them both. Pat had not only reclaimed his rights as landholder and hotelkeeper, but he also retook his position as *seigneur* (like a feudal lord with rights). Anne rarely saw him after their arrival.

Anne could not conceal her emotions. She told him that this wasn't what she had expected. This wasn't what she wanted. They no longer seemed to have the same view of their relationship. She felt that she had been drawn out there on false pretenses. She began to doubt his seriousness, whereas for her, their relationship was everything. She had stated and shown her passion in no uncertain terms: she had left behind her family, her friends, her life, to follow him. He thought he had given her his love, too, although they seem never to have discussed the issue of polygamy until their extended stay in Libenge. Pat called it being "African," but Anne didn't see how misrepresentation and selfishness could be simply defined as cross-cultural. Pat said he wouldn't think of "poking" a white woman with his "beloved wife" only five hundred or six hundred feet away. Anne spat back that if one was going to be abstract about making love, whether it was with a white or a black woman, a "poke" was a "poke."

Blue thoughts became more depressing, as Anne wandered around her no- man's-land, not knowing where she was or where she was going, not liking where she was but not knowing anyplace she'd rather be. She was unable to speak to anybody in their language, but in any case, she would have had no one in whom she could confide (and she did not write home about it). Grievance after grievance, hurt after hurt, piled up. She tried to understand and organize her feelings, like stringing a necklace of beads one by one, but instead they became jumbled and overwhelming. No rains washed the feelings away. Nothing seemed strong enough to push away what she was feeling. She needed to erupt like a volcano, and the explosions between Pat and Anne became like molten lava.

What was Pat doing to and for Anne? What did he expect her to do? Join the wives' group—of tourists or his other wives—upon arrival? Become his "efficient" "Advisor on Conjugal Problems and Grand Chief Dictatrix of Pygmies," as he titled her? He had given Emily Hahn a similar name years before.[11] That wasn't Anne's style. She didn't want to observe the erotic relationships of others from a distance; she wanted to be in the relationship, the only woman in it. Anne noticed that none of the men and women ever sat together in the village as couples except Pat and Mada. She could only assume that they did so to flaunt their relationship in front of everybody and make a point to her.

But unlike his former wife Emilie, who had only been able to endure Camp Putnam for a few months, Anne had different survival skills. Her impulsiveness disguised a defensiveness that allowed her to find her way. As Anne was writing home about the possibility of deadly leopards in the area, the most immediate threat came from Mada's jealousy. Once, early on after Anne's arrival, Mada made a plan to kill Anne, and she came over to visit her carrying a knife. Sensing something amiss, Anne "nicely" offered Mada a beer and went on to gossip with her on the porch. Mada, succumbing to Anne's "charm," abandoned her plan. Left on their own, Anne and "Mrs. P.," as Anne called her, might have worked something out.

Yet there was never any compromise on Pat's part, from the smallest to the largest matter. What changed between the two of them upon their arrival at Camp Putnam was their sense of being equals. They both were strong-willed and, up to that point, had been engaged in their own lives. Anne viewed her dependence on Pat during the trip to Epulu as merely contextual. Once there, she saw the renegade Bostonian gentleman transform into an absolute ruler, benevolent to everyone but her. She was meant to assume a subservient and accepting role, but Anne wasn't a person to take things easily or silently, and in that, Pat had perhaps misjudged her. Anne might have appeared weak to others through years of trying to groom a feminine image (her mother always told her to let men win at the games she played too well), but she recognized the desire to control in those around her, and she didn't plan on yielding to the pattern. "I can manage quite well on my own in Africa," she wrote.[12] Anne had defended herself with humor and defiance against the authority of her father, and she assumed this would work as well with Pat.

In Anne's initial resistance to Pat's inflexible regime, however, she questioned his authority in a crucial way. She could not know that Pat had always ruled his wives unchallenged at Epulu, and in her boldness, she introduced a new element to the scene. Although she was still in love with Pat, her sense of trust was severely damaged. Anne was noisy in all the senses of the term *kelele* (she would become known as Madami Ya Kelele): boisterous and strong-willed, repeatedly letting Pat know that she didn't like him sleeping with other women. Oddly enough, Pat appeared less able to cope with the situation than either Mada or Anne. Pat began to reject Anne for her noncompliance. His solution? Avoid the problem. Leave.

For a while, Pat only disappeared for a few days at a time and then returned, having gone only as far as Stanleyville (several hours by car), where he would look for new business opportunities. In the beginning, Anne didn't mind his absences. She went into the forest with the Mbuti Pygmies and got back into the swing of work: "I sketched all morning with my litho pencils. Everyone moves so damned much and there's no sense in my painting until I know them better."[13] She wanted to capture the feeling of life in the forest; she needed to be part Pieter Breughel to catch the animation, part Vincent van Gogh for the color, and a touch of Sandro Botticelli for detail. During Pat's short absences, Anne felt free in a way that she couldn't when he was there.

Anthropologists had taken an interest in the Pygmies because they were considered to be a group whose origins dated back to the beginning of humankind. They were considered less evolved and thus worthy of anthropological study as remnants of early human biology and culture. Anne, cutting through the Darwinian presuppositions to explain or justify the colonialist "mission" of bringing the "primitives" closer to the "civilized" cultures of Europe, echoed Michel de Montaigne's saying: "They may be one of the most primitive people, but I would call them about the most civilized as far as manners, curiosity and the art of living [go]."[14] Pat praised Anne's ability to stay out in Pygmy camps, even as he stayed away. For all his years in Africa and his accumulated knowledge about Pygmy life, Pat had rarely spent time living in their camps. The more time Anne spent with the Epulu (Mbuti) Pygmies, as they were called, the more other groups began to invite her to visit them. Anne became quickly aware of the importance of gift exchanges, in which she gave salt and cigarettes and received meat from the Pygmies. She guessed early on that the invitations had to do with this exchange and the relationships between the different groups at Epulu.[15]

During this period, she gained a sense of what it meant to live collectively, and her painting *Pygmy Camp* reflected the sense of communal life (see pl. 7).

However, as time went on, the relief from not having to fight with Pat and her excitement at spending long stretches of time in camp with the Pygmies turned to agitation and anger. At Pat's suggestion, Anne went to visit him briefly in Stanleyville, and for all his ostensible indifference, he waited nervously, fearing that she might not come. In one worried note about Anne's life in Pygmy camp, Pat wrote that he shouldn't be "such a benevolent dictator" and signed off: "Much love even though you don't believe it. Under present circumstances, absence seems to make the heart grow fonder."[16] And so it was: within three months of Anne's arrival at Epulu, Pat took off on a trip that lasted six months, to Léopoldville, much farther away; he wasn't going to come back anytime soon. Anne pleaded: "Please, please come back to the Epulu, Pat, it's where you belong, not in a grim hotel room in Léopoldville."[17] Pat had done the same thing to his family as a teenager, and not infrequently to his previous white wives as well—off he'd go, without a word. When he decided to settle in Africa, his mother wrote a similar plea for him to come home. But Pat did not calculate the effects of his actions on others. He told his family stories about his own disappearances with an *Oh, that's just my way* attitude, the charm of "Pat the unpredictable." Of course, Anne knew now that he had also left his African wives for long periods of time. His current behavior was in character, even if Anne hadn't seen it before. But what good could this knowledge do her now?

Pat left Anne at Epulu with Mada and everybody else. If he could not face the situation he had created, Anne had to, or else leave. The problems were greater than just this *ménage à trois*: Pat had had to reclaim his authority at Epulu at a time when there were more people there than he could afford to employ, and his income was more meager than it had been in earlier years. In the 1930s, when Pat and Mary created the compound, there were anywhere from twenty to forty workmen, boys who worked at the hotel, and medical aides in the dispensary (and all their families); it is not clear how many were still working there after Pat's return with Anne. But from the road, he instructed her in how to run the operation, specifically ordering her to fire people one at a time.

Today we might say that Pat was gaslighting Anne in his explanation for why he needed to stay away from Epulu:

> But as for Epulu . . . I can't face it, I can't face it, I can't face it. For, except for those wonderful first three weeks or so, our time together at the Epulu has been, shall we say, not very pleasant—or shall we say, Hell.
>
> I really am busy here, and I hope profitably so in a financial way. But I know that in spite of business, seeing you would have lured me away, or getting back to the Epulu, would have lured me away. But visions of seeing you at

> Epulu—visions of seeing the Epulu with a strange Anne there—are enough to make me feel that [this] business in Leopoldville is absolutely essential. I think that must account for my long stay here. What do you think?
> I wish that some solution of this problem could be reached. But I wonder what solution. What do you think?[18]

By spring, Anne was fed up with Pat's theory about the difference between "poking" with white women and "poking" with black women, and she was damn well ready to pack up and leave. She thought of going to Rwanda, where she knew a few people. She wasn't ready to concede failure: the end of her passion for Pat and for Africa. She wasn't going to return to New York; the first moments back might have been comforting and fine, but then what? Go to Martha's Vineyard? Rebuild the life she had decided to leave? Anne was determined to live out this "African wonderland" with or without Pat. She even thought about staying for a while in a Pygmy camp while trying to figure out what to do. At the time, she thought that if Pat didn't want her at Epulu, he didn't want her as part of his life.

However, threatened by the reality that Anne might leave for good, Pat sent telegrams and wrote daily letters to her, some very chatty, to keep communication going. He had tested her to the breaking point and began a process of mending and courtship. Pat needed Anne, although he wasn't willing to admit it. But why? To run the hotel? As a connection to his American life? To care for him if his health deteriorated? Each of these needs played a part, I believe, in what to Anne was perplexing behavior.

On her side, the sense of happiness that she had felt during the cross-country trip had transformed into a push to survive emotionally and find a life she wanted. She decided to act first to set down roots and become part of the broader community of Epulu, even though she couldn't express herself well in any of the local languages yet. She knew what it was like to be alone, without a partner, and she was not afraid. After one year of exceptional dependence on Pat during their travels, to be treated as a personality in her own right, not just as his appendage, was almost a heady sensation during those months at Epulu without him.

Anne couldn't help but wonder how Pat's former American wives had dealt with his polygamy. What about Pat's first wife, Mary Linder, who had brought her damask and New England silver and a life to go with these fineries? How had she dealt with this? Mary's memory was inscribed in the buildings and design of Camp Putnam. These remained for Pat signs of a lost, if imagined, idyll. Part of Pat's charisma for those close to him was the ability to project an ideal that no one, including himself, could live with or live up to. From a distance, he seemed indifferent or cruel. Lore among the "colons" had it that Mary died of grief and jealousy. And Emilie only lasted nine months at Camp Putnam.

Anne wondered, too, how Mada felt about the white wives. Her lot was far more difficult than any of theirs, and not only because they came in sequence. Mada was used to being one of several black wives, and perhaps they all kept one another company. She was now about thirty-two and had come into Pat's life at the age of fifteen, when Pat already had two other wives (one being his first love, Abanzima).[19] When Pat had lectured to the Pearl River Womens Club defending child brides, he was defending his own experience, although he didn't acknowledge it openly. But what did Mada do in 1945 when Pat went back to the States? He didn't take her with him. She, like the others, must have felt abandoned, even if she could always go back to her own family. Emily Hahn, who lived with Pat for several months in the 1930s, wrote in her novel *With Naked Foot* (1934) about the fate of African women who became involved with white men, how they were often used up and discarded. She argued that in some ways, the cruelest men were not those who abused their wives verbally or even physically (although there are limits to this argument) but those like Pat who, despite their compassion and conceptual egalitarianism, abandoned their black wives to return to their own families, mostly in Europe, leaving the women too old to attract another partner. In most cases, the presence of a white wife in the colonialist context ensured a strict boundary between Europeans and Africans. Mada must have had a difficult time, just as Mary and Emily did. But Anne had not yet committed herself institutionally to Pat; although they had lived together for more than a year, they were not yet married.

The fight that raged between Pat, in Léopoldville, and Anne, holding down Camp Putnam, went on for a couple of months and then abated. Anne wrote in April: "I miss the Pat I met, but am glad the hateful one is gone."[20] He addressed her as "my darling dictatrix." Then, in May, after nearly six months away from Epulu, he wrote asking Anne to marry him. He seemed almost to have been waiting for her to calm down. Whatever each of them had been doing, and perhaps the epistolary fight was a kind of negotiation, he made his terms clear: "I think it would be a fine idea if you came down here and we got married in Leopoldville, on the clear understanding that conditions at the Epulu would remain unchanged. Now don't let off a ream of comment, but just say 'yes,' or else say nothing."[21] Pat had proposed to Emily Hahn a month after Mary's death in similar terms: "I could write reams, but I won't. I ask you to send me a telegraphic answer, either 'No,' or 'NO THANKS' or 'YES AWAITING DETAILS.'"[22]

Hahn had said no; Anne said yes.

Marriage

Pat admitted to being attracted to Anne because she resembled his first African wife, Abanzima: "She was honest, direct, and without any pretenses."[23] Pat projected onto Anne both the more animal, sexual creature he had found in her on Martha's Vineyard and an idealization of her as an artist. He called her the Madonna of the Pygmies. In February, when Anne and Pat were engaged in bitter arguments about life at Camp Putnam, Pat—letting on nothing—wrote to his father: "[Anne] has turned into a pigmy. . . . Her painting is wonderful."[24]

While still outwardly confident, Pat was vying for his own psychic as well as physical survival at Epulu. He acknowledged that Anne was important in his life: "Curious thing is that I have never dreamed of Mary since I met you." And more directly: "You do figure in my thoughts. I'm afraid, no matter how sore you may feel, that you and I are psychologically married."[25]

Pat summed things up in a letter announcing his marriage to a friend: "I got my divorce from Emilie and met a young woman of 35 years, a painter-artist spoiled by her industrialist father. . . . Having tried Epulu for quite a long time, Anne Eisner (that is her name) joined me and decided to marry me in Leopoldville, where I had come to make my fortune in urena lobate" (a fiber plant, Congo jute, first grown for commercial purposes in the 1920s to make cord, sacks, and carpets).[26] Pat's description is heavily economic: Anne has means, and he is seeking his fortune. They will be married. To a colleague, he wrote "Anne Eisner . . . finds big doses of Africa and of me fairly pleasant in the long-run, so she decided to marry me."[27] In the late spring, Anne and Pat made a kind of contract. Pat with Anne, Anne with Mada. He said nothing would change at Epulu. Anne figured she could manage it. She gathered her wits, took a deep breath, and walked over to Mada's house. Anne told Mada that she was going to marry Pat; she hoped they could change from being enemies to being friends. Anne and Mada then struck a deal: Pat would spend one week with Mada and then the next with Anne. Each had her own house. Anne communicated that they should try not to fight anymore and to respect each other's life. They sealed their wives' contract with a bottle of whiskey and took a stroll around the village together. Mada planned to stay at Epulu while Pat and Anne were in Léopoldville. It turned out to be a long time, nine months in all, what with problems getting the marriage license and the overland trip back. Anne never saw Mada express anger toward Pat, or even toward her, despite the failed coup against Anne. Yet Mada let it be known in a letter to Anne from Agaranga Nunziotika, the head man at Camp Putnam, how "sad" she was and that she was threatening to leave if Pat didn't get back soon.[28] In the end, Anne and Mada became used to each other and developed almost a sympathy one for the other.

The time that Anne and Pat spent together in Léopoldville before their marriage in late July 1948 and during the cross-country trip back to Epulu was much like their first year of traveling together. The event of Anne and Pat's marriage was consecrated by a researcher, Alfred Emerson, who named termites from Epulu after each of them: *Microtermes putnami* and *Odontotermes annae*. Throughout the trip back to Epulu, they got on well together, traveling through the Kasai, Sankuru, and Kwango areas of the Congo, again collecting art, musical instruments, baskets, and more, as Enid Schildkrout discusses in *Images of Congo*.[29] Anne by then had requested a copy of the 1935 catalog from MOMA with Walker Evans's photographs and was studying the scant amount of scholarship about African art and crafts to learn as much as she could. As they bought artifacts, they sent off cases of masks to Epulu and several museums: the Peabody Museum of Archaeology and Ethnology at Harvard, the Brooklyn Museum, the American Museum of Natural History (AMNH), and the Musée du Congo Belge in Tervuren, Belgium (now the Royal Museum for Central Africa). Notably, Anne was trying to situate the art and ethnographic objects she was seeing, including trying to identify the artists to better honor their work. Schildkrout points out that Anne marked the name and village (Antoine Nsito of Mwela village, N. Kwango) of the maker of a mask that came to the AMNH. Anne and Pat were thinking about the art market in the States as well. When they returned to Epulu, they found that much of the art they had bought on their first trip across Africa was gone. This only spurred them to rebuild and continue collecting. Schildkrout estimates that in the end, they collected somewhere around one thousand artifacts, of which five hundred eventually went to the AMNH (about which more later).

Once they returned to Camp Putnam, however, the honeymoon was over. Pat criticized everything Anne did: she wasn't fixing his trousers, couldn't start the car with its weak battery, and so on. He stonewalled her with anger. He didn't like to be fakey polite, he crabbed, and explained that his reasons for ignoring her at public gatherings were linguistic; he did not want to break the decorum of conducting social life in French. Anne did more than crab back. She yelled and told him those arguments weren't good enough. What was going on? Pat appeared, on the one hand, quite impatient with her dependency. On the other, he did not welcome the discovery that Anne had connected with the Pygmies and become an integral part of Epulu independently of him. With Pat, it was no-win.

Epulu was *Pat's* terrain, and having brought her into it and delegated managing the hotel to her, he didn't want to make room for her as an equal. He behaved like a feudal landlord who wanted relations to be only on his terms. His name for the central living room, "Le Palais," or palace, reflected how much of colonial life was about preserving a sense of the *ancien régime*. It replicated a sense of white entitlement, however affectionately or ironically it was meant. Anne mostly registered the hurt. Unable to write to anyone about all this in the early years, and having no one to talk to, she coded little stories to herself, fictive and real, changing this or that name or detail to avoid the confessional mode:

> A European man whose family had stayed in Europe when he came to Africa lived with an African woman and had a child with her. This was common practice before World War II wherever the colonialist had arrived. When the man's sons came for a visit from Europe, he showed them around his plantation with great pride and introduced them to his African wife and child without any explanation. It never occurred to him that this discovery might upset his sons. Quite dense for an intelligent man. I knew what the sons must have felt.[30]

Daily life was not simple in this multicultural community of Bantus and Mbuti Pygmies, brought together around Pat's compound Camp Putnam—particularly for Anne as the "new wife on the block." No one tried to explain it to the outside world in those days. Not Pat in anything official for Western consumption, not even Emily Hahn in the book she wrote based on Pat's life, *Congo Solo* (1933), in which, along with name changes, Pat's black wives are free-floating characters never described as related to him. So many stories to make the white man stand alone when he was so dependent on black women's love. Mada was not the only African wife of Pat's at Camp Putnam. There had been and were to be other wives, up to five at a time.

Anne accepted the situation. For her, the contract was emotional, to keep the feelings of jealousy shut out. She did better at it once she and Pat were married officially, because at least then she had a secure position at Camp Putnam. Once she and Mada had made their pact, they were able to conduct their lives—at least for a while—on terms that the two of them had chosen.

Visit to New York

In the United States, 1950 was a turbulent year: the Korean War began; with tension from the Cold War between the Soviet Union and the United States, President Harry S. Truman made the controversial decision to intensify research on a hydrogen bomb; "McCarthyism" began with Senator Joseph McCarthy's crusade to investigate government officials and citizens in the United States believed to be Communists (most famously, among other artists, folksinger Pete Seeger, actors Orson Welles and Charlie Chaplin). Many of the old friends who had been on the anti-Stalinist left in the 1930s were by now moving to the right and anti-communist.

That year, Anne returned to New York for the first time in four years and felt the jolt of switching cultures, measuring which home was home and who she was. When she had originally left New York to be with Pat, she loved her work painting all day, but in Africa, she exchanged that life of concentration for one full of people and action. Now she brought back paintings of the Pygmies, stories of Camp Putnam, and objects from various parts of Africa—all traces of her life in the Ituri.

What had changed for her? She was no longer just a painter. She was also Mrs. Patrick Tracy Lowell Putnam, whose address was Epulu, Belgian Congo. Was she still the artist who signed paintings "Anne"? The same woman who loved to giggle with "Sister" about the smallest thing and who had to struggle for independence from her parents? When she followed her sister, Dorothy, to become an artist, she thought they were to be the Eisner girls for a lifetime; they had chosen art as their world, their language. But after two years in Africa, far from her former community, could she ever be an Eisner girl again?"

Anne arrived in New York in April 1950, without Pat. Her parents met her at the airport. There was her mother, elegant in a navy-blue suit with a blue and white silk scarf, her father looking very "Uptown." She was elated for a moment, but then felt the claustrophobia of being back with them. On the ride in from Idlewild Airport, the view of the New York skyline brought back ambivalent feelings, the ease of familiarity tinged with an almost simultaneous sense of emptiness. How would she present her life in the Congo to them?

Anne's parents lived in a penthouse apartment at 180 West 58th Street in Alwyn Court, a tall building covered with complex terra-cotta decorations inspired by the French Renaissance. It epitomized the high culture of early-twentieth-century New York and their bourgeois world (a positive term for these second-generation Viennese). At the apartment, Anne performed a snatch of Epulu life for them, narrating events and describing people, talking loudly and gesticulating. She reenacted what the Pygmies did when they returned from a hunt, dancing and singing the story of the catch, her raspy voice simulating the metal thongs of the *lukembi* (a musical instrument that is plucked), then the drums.

Anne passed out presents, among them a set of ivory chessmen from Pat to her father as "wife's payment." Will Eisner responded intuitively to this manly bonding, and Anne brokered the exchange between these two men in her life as both the object and the agent. At first, Will and Fluff hadn't been too sure about the tall, extraordinarily seductive man who made his home in the Ituri Forest, but they soon came under Pat's spell. By 1950, they had not just resigned themselves to Anne's choice of a man, but they were very proud of his work at Epulu and excited by her accounts of life there.

The next day, Anne headed out past Carnegie Hall and the Steinway showroom on 57th Street, across the street to Bonwit Teller, and down to her old haunts in the Village, including Klein's, the bargain store, where you could dress for next to nothing. That period of her life felt a world away.

The focus of her trip was a party for the sponsors who had pre-bought paintings to fund her original journey to Africa in 1946. The paintings she brought back were from her trip across Africa and her life at Epulu. The sponsors were a varied group, among them the attaché of the Belgian Information Agency, Jan Albert Goris, along with her old crowd of family and friends—among them, her sister Dorothy, Dorothy's husband John, and Margaret De Silver. The party was a smashing success—lots of booze and talk and dancing. Most people seemed pleased with the paintings they received, and Anne felt relieved. It was the end of her first era of painting in Africa.

When Anne had left New York to live with Pat in 1946, the term "abstraction" designated decorative networks, linear or in cubes.[31] Despite the popularity of abstraction in the art world, at Epulu, Anne had criticized the concept based on the lack of emotion:

> As I sketch and look at the banana tree it has the most beautiful abstract shapes. One leaf is swinging into another. But it has more than just the dead endism of abstraction. It's got life, sap, bananas to eat, the leaves make fine umbrellas in the rain. The pygmies even make their houses out of their leaves. There's nothing sterile about it. . . . Just as they play a part in our lives whether we like it or not. But I've got feelings and moods and am a fairly warm-blooded creature. That to me is . . . important and interesting.[32]

From 1947 to 1950, while Anne was in Africa, the art world in New York had changed dramatically. The two main movements that burst onto the scene after 1947 within Abstract Expressionism were gesture painting and color-field painters. Adolph Gottlieb and Jackson Pollock had moved toward myths in their experimentation with abstraction; Mark Rothko and Barrett Newman had looked to universals. Henri Matisse, Milton Avery, and others had related color to affect. Looking beyond figuration, the color-field painters transformed color into their content. Emotion had become the dominant ingredient, rather than play with form. Anne shared with all of them the concern with depth and surface on the canvas. Like Rothko, she had already undoubtedly been marked before she left for Africa by the important Pierre Bonnard retrospective in 1946. But 1950 in New York was a watershed year for Abstract Expressionism. Rothko, Gottlieb, and Newman exhibited in January, and Hans Hofmann, Franz Kline, Pollock, and Willem de Kooning showed later in the same year.[33] New York had become the center of the art world.

For a while, it felt good to see the old faces. All the faces had aged except Pat's father, who appeared "as crickety as ever," Anne wrote. Dr. Putnam and Anne had had strained relations before she left for Africa. He was perhaps as suspicious of Anne as the Eisners were initially of Pat. It is hard to imagine that Dr. Putnam had doubts about Anne as an artist, given that his own interest in art and artists had also led him to study at the Art Students League and should have provided a connection. She was, in any case, Pat's third white wife

(Emilie having become a responsibility for Dr. Putnam when she returned from Africa) and no shrinking violet. Dr. Putnam might have worried that Anne only added to the peculiarity of Pat's African world rather than giving it balance, although she was no more unusual than most people in Pat's life. As for Dr. Putnam himself, he was just as much a mix of conservatism and liberalism as were Anne's parents, perhaps even more so. Whatever his reasons, Dr. Putnam did not like Anne, although it was unclear why.[34]

Unlike in their first meetings in 1945, however, Dr. Putnam seemed more outgoing to Anne during this trip. The return of ownership of the Valleydale Farm from Pat, who had inherited it from his mother, and Anne (as a gesture of goodwill), who could inherit it from Pat under Belgian law, to Dr. Putnam and his second wife Margo (whom he married in 1946 after Angelica's death in 1940), as they had requested, seemed to have relieved the tension. They viewed a film together in which the Pygmies, Pat, and Anne all appeared. Dr. Putnam magpied through the whole film, and when Pat came on-screen winking savvily at the camera, his father waved and called, "Hello, Pat!" As for Anne, who appeared in the film as much as Pat did, Dr. Putnam asked her at the end why she hadn't been in it. He couldn't see her.

Anne had been quite indifferent to her own mother's sadness when she left home at age twenty and then again at her more definitive departure from New York in 1946. Anne thought she needed to cut her mother off. Fluff kept her feelings to herself but had herself become a painter after her children were gone. With time, Anne came to see how important her mother was to her and how much her mother believed in her and in her work. Fluff was convinced that Anne would have something important to say through her art, and for all the years Anne was in Africa, she acted on her daughter's behalf, submitting Anne's drawings and paintings to juries, to the annual exhibitions of the Federation of Modern Painters and Sculptors (one of Anne's Vineyard paintings even went on tour to Rochester, St. Paul, San Francisco, Houston, and Kansas City) and to the American Association of Women Artists. The drive to get Anne's work into circulation seemed to activate Fluff on her own behalf as well. It was as though Anne's traveling and her life at Epulu had reawakened an audacious spirit in her mother. If it hadn't been for Fluff, none of Anne's work would have been shown during the years she was in Africa.

After three months back, however, Anne no longer felt relevant in New York. She had pounded the pavement looking for a gallery without success. Gallery owners seemed enthusiastic but did not offer to represent her as an artist. When she showed her paintings to Goris from the Belgian Information Center, he liked her work, but his idea of a compliment was to say that they looked as though they had been painted by a man. Her former teacher, John McPherson, gave her good criticism. It wasn't like the old days, showing her work at the annual Washington Square spring exhibition and wherever a jury accepted her work.

Anne found the cost of living in New York very high: a sandwich and a cup of coffee cost fifty cents! To make some extra money, she sold several artifacts that she and Pat had collected and, sensing interest in her life at Epulu, launched a novice public-speaking career to Woodstock papers and radio stations. She adapted her desire to speak about the joy and pleasure of life at Epulu to an audience of the Woodstock Historical Society that wanted only facts; on one Kingston program, she did describe women's lives. Anne started work on an autobiography about her life in Africa with her friend Helen Gould, who had been secretary to Edmund Wilson and Max Eastman. She also finished about twenty drawings, including some in ink from Kano and Libenge, with which she was very pleased. She intended them to accompany the writing about her life. That manuscript, despite energy and work on the part of both women, was never published.

Anne was reluctant to tell her family and friends about the difficulties with Pat. She stayed silent about the other wives and how lonely she could feel in Africa, even when surrounded by people. All she would admit was that marriage could be difficult. Anne sensed that even the people closest to her, her mother and sister, sometimes grew exasperated because she was unable to take up her life where she had left off. The art world, her friends, the city—they all seemed to be saying, *How about a little interest in us?* After all, New Yorkers always thought that almost nothing could possibly happen anywhere else.

Anne no longer felt herself to be part of the New York art world. Her own path had swerved away from this life and—as with everything else in her life—would again in her own way: back to Epulu and the work she was doing there. In Africa, 1950 marked the beginning of an era that would change everything and everybody in the colonial world.

CHAPTER FOUR

Back at the Epulu Ranch (1950–1951)

After Anne left Epulu for New York in early April 1950, Pat waited impatiently for the mail. Without news from her, he imagined a plane crash. Anne wrote often and passionately ("Darling," "Pat my love," "Pat my darling"), but the letters took time to make their way from New York to Camp Putnam. Pat was so used to people moving in and out of the forest with messages, the pleasure of both communicating and maintaining a distance through his endless little scribbled pieces of paper, that he must have felt very cut off. Anne cabled that everything was fine upon her arrival in New York. He wrote a letter that he "felt awfully sick and tired all the time" before receiving the cable, but "fine and full of pep, bossiness and business" after that. He wondered if it was cause and effect or just *"post hoc sed non propter hoc,"*—after all but not because of, one of his favorite sayings. Demanding more than a telegram, he appealed to Anne as "a poor, overworked dutiful married woman" and taunted, "I should certainly get news of how many Yardley men fell your way." Promising sexual bliss with soap and cologne, the Yardley ad stopped short of what Pat had in mind:

> Don't forget that I am more than half African. As the Irish politician said in a speech to get the Harlem vote, "My skin may be white, but my heart is black." An African custom is that any wife worth having, when she goes home to Mama, makes a few connections with personable gentlemen, and all the husband insists upon when she gets back to him (whom she loves best, after all) is that she tell him all about them; and if she has had any syphilis she might have got from them treated before she comes home.

There was more than African custom at stake here—and more than their relationship. Pat went on "encouraging" Anne:

> If she comes home pregnant that's fine, and I mean it for me, too. However, I'm a little afraid that both of us, by the same damned disease, have had a baby-making apparatus spoiled.[1]

Pat had been unable to have children with any of his wives, although he had been hoping that Anne would get pregnant. It isn't clear what disease Pat thought he might have contracted that would have led to infertility or whether he might have transmitted something to her. Anne's early wild days were behind her (I don't know that she ever contracted any venereal disease, for example), and she responded that she hadn't met anyone while away.

In any case, Anne already struggled to balance the complexities of married life, the demands of the hotel, and her painting, and she was not at all sure that she could handle having a child under the circumstances. Even less could she entertain the taunting request for her to become pregnant through a New York fling. Pat had a way of mocking his own eccentricities, playing up his outrageous antics, which only fueled the rumors circulating about. It was often hard to tell whether he had always been odd, a maverick inside and outside all institutions and conventions, or if he masked his feeling of losing control with self-mockery. It was easy to let go of one's customs in the Ituri Forest, and both Pat and Anne were marginal even to the European colonialists, missionaries, and administrators. How did the others perceive them? Pat, amused, commented on advice given in Beni to a journalist:

> "It's not worth a visit [to Camp Putnam], and Putnam is crazy." The last part of that remark is, to me, quite flattering, but it seems, to my mind, that that very insulting first phrase is in direct contradiction to the second one: for, if you were an explorer-journalist wouldn't you go out of your way to meet all the reputedly crazy white men scattered throughout the bush of the country that you were journalizing-exploring? For my part, were I one, I would certainly do so.[2]

Anne was by now used to Pat's flamboyant sense of being a maverick.

Anne kept in touch with what was happening at Epulu more practically in newsy letters from Agaranga Nunziotika. Agaranga had followed Pat to Epulu from Penge, had taught himself to read and write (later espousing Protestantism), and had become the headman or chief of staff at Camp Putnam. He taught Anne KiNgwana, the lingua franca from the eighteenth century on, when she arrived and worked closely with her as she took on managerial responsibilities for Camp Putnam. He wrote to her whenever she was away, sharing news of Pat and the others at Camp Putnam, now requesting that she return with clothing for one of the workers.[3]

Anne's Return to the Forest

Anne left New York in the summer of 1950 after a busy three-month visit and returned to Epulu through London and Paris, wearing herself out until she had "museum eyes" at the Louvre. Pat had written in a letter asking

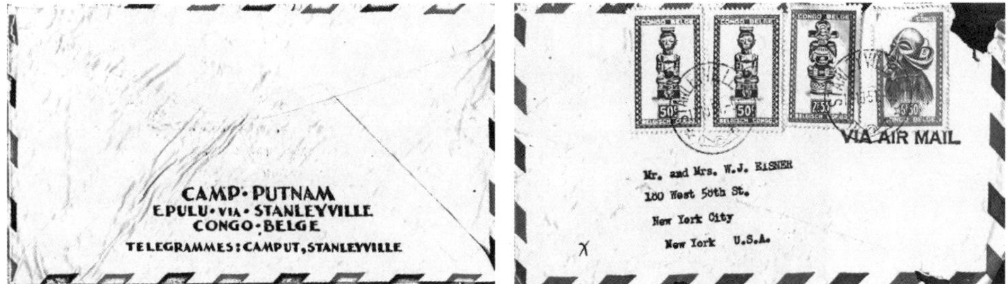

Fig. 30
Camp Putnam stationery. Houghton Library, Harvard University.

why she was coming back so soon: "Do you think I'll welcome you like the prodigal daughter when you get here?"—before adding, with his typical ambivalence, "I do love you, and in spite of hating you."[4] Anne returned to a life that was again fragmented: living with Pat and living without Pat, tending to the hotel and the routine chores of life, alternating between Epulu and Pygmy camps as a retreat to paint, a happy expatriation from expatriate life at Epulu. She became addicted to the discipline of sketching and painting as the one thing that had always given her a sense of who she was.

Over the years, in addition to sketching and painting, Anne had also developed a need to write, relying on correspondence as the link between two worlds: the one of family and friends in New York and the other life at Epulu. At times when almost no mail got through, she felt as though her letters launched words into space, perhaps never to return. Yet the very act of writing confirmed that she was still Anne Eisner; the weekly letter home provided a format for framing her experiences into a story or chronicle. (Fig. 30 shows a sample of Camp Putnam stationery.) Anne also began to take notes on life at Epulu and would transcribe a number of Pygmy legends as time went on.

Writing accompanied loneliness, shadowed the present, giving it shape and sense. By contrast, painting, for all its stabilizing discipline, could be daunting, in much the same way Epulu was: demanding exploration, adaptation, change. Before leaving New York, Anne had written confidently: "the start of a journey or of a canvas seems to have that same marvelous quality that anything can happen. The possibilities are unlimited. I don't know just when the limitations set in on a journey. I trust not quite as soon as on canvas. But it's true that you bring yourself along in both so that the limitations are yours."[5]

When Anne had first arrived in the forest, she found she needed to adjust the vision of it she had gleaned from reading books about Africa and seeing movies. She expected wild jungle, dense foliage, tangled underbrush, contrasts of dark and light, like an Henri Rousseau painting. She quickly discovered that the forest isn't like: huge trees stand far apart; vines hang down and twist about in between them; small, detailed designs of the flora,

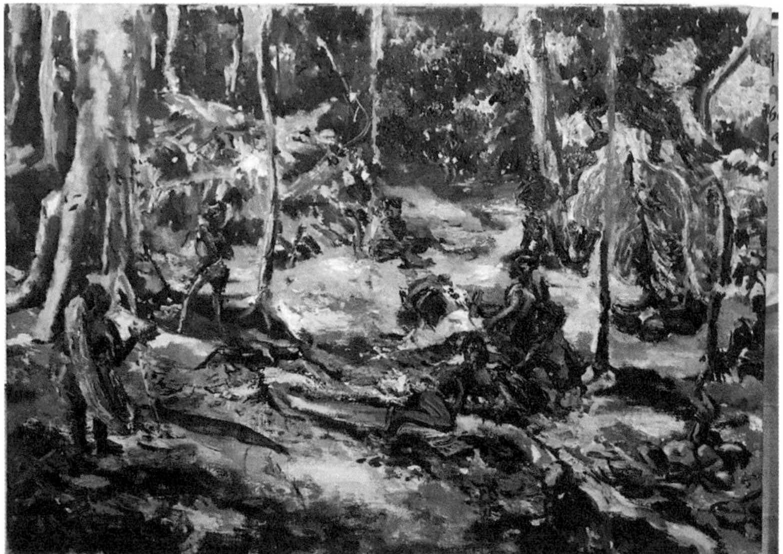

Fig. 31
Anne Eisner,
Ituri Forest with Figures I,
20 x 28 in., oil on canvas, 1948.
McDonald collection.

with large mongongo leaves and low-lying ferns crisscross without obvious patterns (see fig. 31).

Anne had spent several years before her trip to New York fine-tuning her vision to make sense of the forest landscape and the people who populated it. In 1947, three years earlier when she had first arrived, she found it difficult to accustom her eye to the way the forest light creates a dreamlike pale yellow with cerulean glaze. She missed the dark blue-green of American forests and wanted some red. Her drawings of Africans had begun to catch some characteristic gestures and postures of the tall villagers and smaller Pygmies. She still felt the challenge of getting the delicate nuances, the tilt of a back, or the angle of a face. Each person was so different. By now, life in the forest was familiar, and she enjoyed living with them in their temporary hunting camps; her sense of what and how she wanted to paint was more assured. (See pl. 8.)

As Anne prepared to go into the forest, Pat wanted to know how many "minutes tipoyable and how many minutes not tipoyable" the journey would be, referring to the *tipoy*, a carrier chair shouldered by several men. It was as though he was trying to determine how far away the camp would be made and whether he might even be able to make the trip himself. Everyone said that Pat had been a terrific walker, better than any white man they had ever seen. Now, though, with his failing health, he would have had to be carried through the forest in a *tipoy* if he were to visit. (See fig. 32.)

During the early winter of 1950, Pat had been in bed most of the time, downed by one of the many illnesses that afflicted him. Emphysema was the most evident and obviously debilitating (they referred to it as his "puffing disease"). Despite his decreasing ability to move, Pat had re-opened the medical dispensary—often referred to as the hospital--supported by the

Belgian government. As an *agent sanitaire*, Pat received people from all over the area—giving shots and treating whatever people presented: venereal diseases, leprosy, and yaws (a skin infection related to syphilis but not contracted through sexual contact). It was like running a hospital that had only an emergency room.

Setting Up Pygmy Camp

It was the dry season and a comfortable time to go into the forest. Anne gathered up pens, pencils, and old paints, as well as shirts, a sleeping bag, itch medicine, a food basket, camp beds, a table and chairs, lamps, cigarettes, a novel, and she and the Pygmies were off. She knew this path well and checked the changes in terrain: a termite hill, a fallen tree. The woods were full of birds, and although their songs could be heard all around, they perched so high up in the trees that one rarely saw them. The heavy foliage filtered the sunlight, but here and there, a ray glanced off the mongongo leaves, shining them up like patent leather. One of the Pygmies stopped, cut a thick liana, held his head under it, and drank the liquid. The curious, pungent odor of rotting figs permeated the forest.

Women carrying baskets on their backs, holding their ever-present

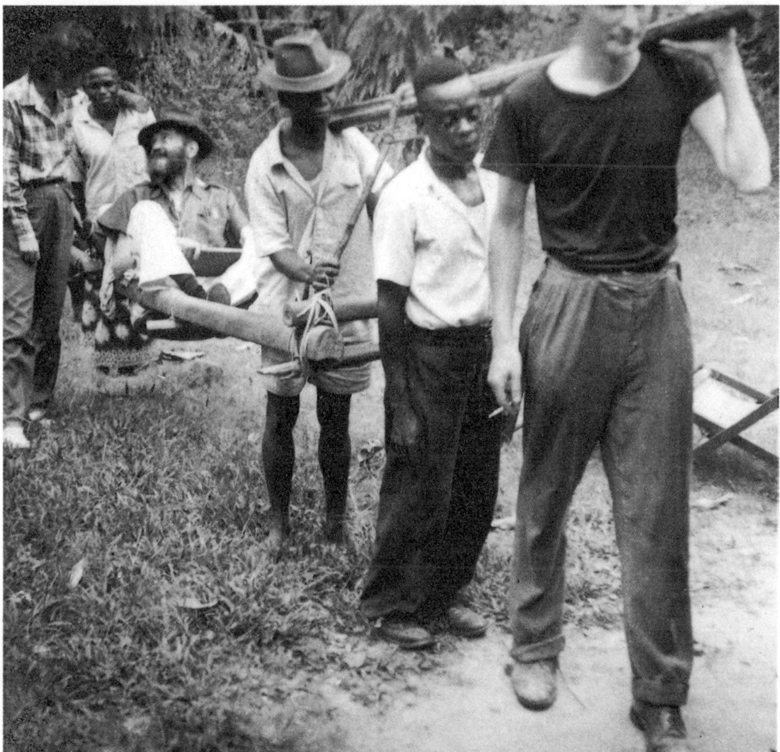

Fig. 32
Anne, Pat (in *tipoy*), workmen and Schuyler Jones at Camp Putnam (photograph by Keith Lawson). Houghton Library, Harvard University.

Fig. 33a-c
a: Anne Eisner, *Pygmies Walking*, 11½ x 13½ in., ink drawing on onion skin, c. 1951.
b: Anne Eisner, *Pygmies in Forest*, 17 x 13 in., ink on paper, c. 1951, McDonald collection.
c: Pygmy hut of mongongo leaves, c. 1952 (photographer unknown), Houghton Library, Harvard University.

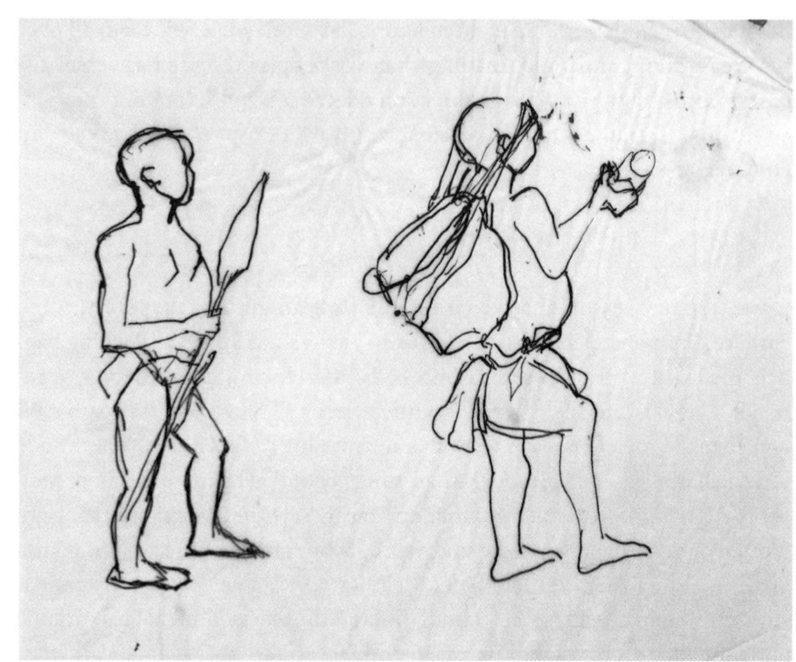

a

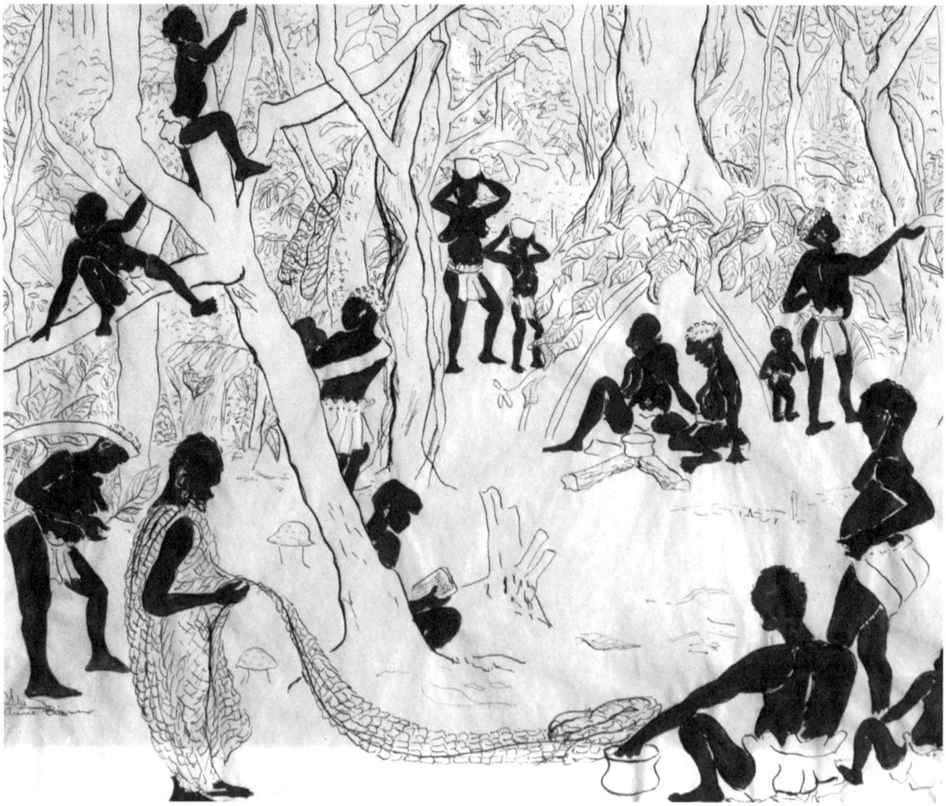

b

embers to make a fire, and men with spears (they were net hunters but made spears for defense) caught up and passed Anne. They were strong and purposeful. The first time she visited a Pygmy camp in 1947, she had been treated as some fragile lady explorer, riding high on a *tipoy* decorated with flowers and whatnot. Now she walked as they did and admired their agility; like solo ballet dancers, they executed intricate maneuvers to avoid trees, roots, and vines. She found that Pygmies would often squeeze under a fallen tree rather than climb over it, which she could not do. She'd had to convince them that she was not fragile, but she had also learned from experience and observing them not to look up and admire the view, as she was bound to stumble on a vine or get stung by ants.

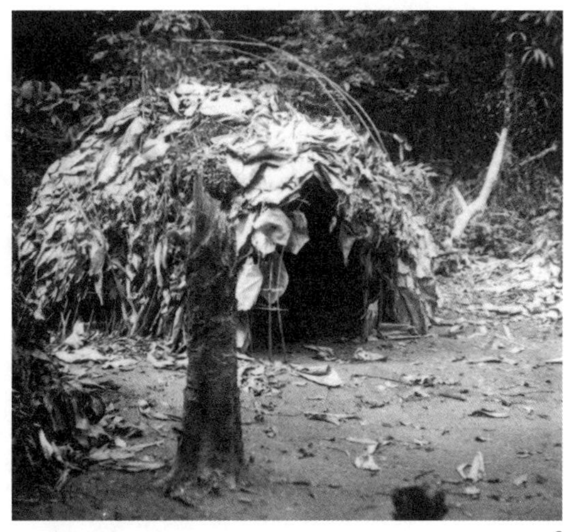

c

Each new camp had to be constructed within the forest near streams for water and firewood for cooking. This time, as always, when they reached the chosen campsite, each man cleared an area while the women started cutting sticks and gathering mongongo leaves to build houses (see fig. 33a-c). Pygmy camps were arranged in a circle around an open clearing. Families built their own structures, with a man, wife or wives (although unlike the villagers, few pygmies are polygamous), and children in each one. Anne found that seventeen huts constituted a large camp. Families stayed close together, and women tried to build their homes as close to those of their friends as possible. When the men finished their work, they sat down. Most of them stayed near the large fire started in the center of the clearing, where they talked to one another and watched their wives. The women were expert in building, placing sticks in the ground and bending them until they met over their heads. To complete the frame, they wove horizontal strips and then notched the stem of each mongongo leaf. Covering the frame with the leaves was a quick operation, and in front of each hut the embers kept the fire going. The men repaired their nets in preparation for the hunt. Anne's painting *Pygmy Camp* (see pl. 7) evokes all of the activities of a camp within the circle of families: tending to nets (for hunting), tapping of bark (a constant activity to make bark cloth), and preparing food.

Anne contracted malaria almost immediately, so Pat sent quinine, with strict instructions about the dosage and a gruff but caring message (she had learned to read between the lines) that she was to come back to Epulu "pronto" if it got worse. The Pygmies rocketed back and forth through the forest with communications and supplies, and they soon brought another note from Pat: "My dearest Anne, there may be other people with other names, but so far as Annes go, you are my dearest."

Pat had never been out with Anne in a Pygmy camp since she had arrived at Epulu in 1947, and he didn't come out this time. She settled in, painting life in the camp and the forest, once so exotic and strange to her and now so familiar. She went into a working binge: drawing, painting, eating, sleeping, drawing, painting, eating, sleeping. The routine of work provided emotional ballast to the stress of life at Camp Putnam. Just stretching a canvas had helped to calm her.

At the camp, people were always together in a physical way that took some getting used to. At first, she felt uncomfortable with people around, staring at her sketchbook or canvas. Whenever she went off by herself to sketch or paint, someone always wanted to keep her company. She learned that there was no such thing as privacy. On their side, during Anne's first stay in a camp in 1947, the Pygmies had been as jittery with her as she was with them. They had made a new camp to hunt for animals, and they thought she was there to spy on the meat catch. Anne had been mystified by their secretiveness, since they had always been very open at Epulu. It didn't take long before she learned to paint even amid the bustle of the camp, and she grew to understand their concerns and love the sense of being part of a community. Although the experience until then on both sides had been a complete anomaly—Anne was the first white woman to spend extended time in a Pygmy camp, and Pat had not done so—the Pygmies now accepted her joining camp life to paint and be part of the community. Everybody was relaxed. (See fig. 34.)

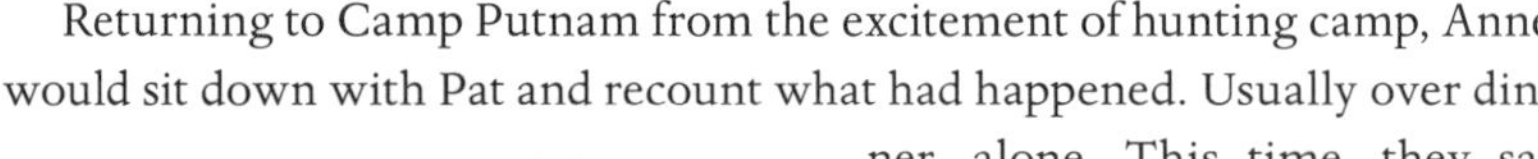

Returning to Camp Putnam from the excitement of hunting camp, Anne would sit down with Pat and recount what had happened. Usually over dinner, alone. This time, they sat under the umbrella tree, with the moon's light filtering through the high trees. He listened carefully, leaning his slim torso back in a chair, before lighting a cigarette and commenting in detail on Anne's notes and methods of observation. This had become their ritual. Anne could go where Pat used to go, do what he used to do; she had become his eyes and ears.

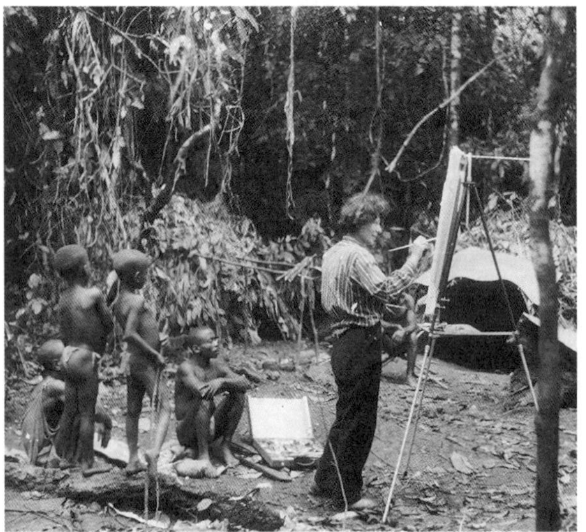

Fig. 34 Anne Eisner painting in the forest, 1957 (photograph by Colin Turnbull). Houghton Library, Harvard University.

Thanks to his anthropology training at Harvard and his long years in the area, Pat had come to know more about Pygmies than anyone save perhaps the Austrian missionary Paul Schebesta (1887–1967), who had written extensively about them. Through their conversations, Anne had learned from Pat's techniques how to record what she saw, ask questions, and observe differences. For the moment, she was his best pupil; he gained confidence that she would report information he found significant about the life of the Pygmies. Early on, Anne's observations from camp only became meaningful for her once they were transmitted to Pat.

But that relationship was changing. A need to write down what she was learning had taken hold, not unlike the need she felt to write letters as a way of chronicling her experiences at Epulu. The transition from sketching as a form of note-taking to writing ethnographic notes was to be more challenging. Not only was she dyslexic, but unlike drawing or painting, where her hand moved steadily with habit developed from years of practice, words often escaped her—even orally. When she spoke, they were too loud. When she wrote, she often misspelled. In French, her *débit* was as quick as a Pygmy running, but the sounds, so beautiful when she listened to others, were like the crackling knees of a stiff hippo rushing to her mud bath. She had resumed learning French from Pat on the ship over in 1946 and then continued in the field, as it were. Agaranga was coaching her in KiNgwana, a form of Swahili and the local traders' language. She had been a quick study as soon as she arrived at Epulu, of necessity, and had become fluent in KiNgwana—though Pat said she spoke like a Third Avenue fish peddler. With effort and practice, and despite Pat's jibes, Anne became proficient. She no longer got coffee when she asked for a lamp. She understood now and could communicate in the lingua franca. She took notes in English and later transcribed Mbuti legends from KiNgwana.

One of the Mothers

Pat left this note for Anne on Valentine's Day, 1951:

> TO THAT WOMAN, MY WIFE
> To dear, cantankerous Anne,
> Who's my sweetest Valentine;
> For though she surely can,
> And does, too often, whine;
> Yet when she loves her man,
> He feels the whole world's fine.
> PTLP [Patrick Tracy Lowell Putnam][6]

Anne had decided to decorate the long dining-room table for an elegant evening meal. As she was talking with several people in the room and arranging the flowers that would form the centerpiece on the white damask tablecloth, a man arrived. "Bwana sends you a message," he said, handing her a note: "Anne, A three-day-old orphan. Get milk bottles ready, P.T.L.P." She called for Abazinga, the man in charge of the small "zoo" at Camp Putnam. They had chimps, monkeys, mongooses, vipers, hyraxes (a small animal similar to a marmot but actually more closely related to elephants and manatees), and more, but their collection was most known for holding the rarest of the rare: the okapi, an animal related to the giraffe, living only in the deepest parts of the Ulele and Ituri.[7] Discovered in the early 1900s, okapis are quite remarkable in appearance, with red-brown velour-like fur, legs decorated with white stripes, and huge black eyes that peer shyly around. It was a sight Anne never tired of, this animal with its long, narrow tongue quietly curling around the leaves that were hung up daily between palm trees for food. Abazinga and Anne gathered the bottles that were used to feed the animals. All the nipples had large openings from extensive use by the okapi. Abazinga and Anne both assumed they were to receive a new animal, though probably not an okapi, since the messenger would have hooted about its arrival and announced a celebration—so prized were they.

Then a well-dressed BaNgwana—member of an *arabisé* or Islamic tribe[8]—who introduced himself as Ayulu Kapapela arrived with a delegation of Pygmies speaking KiBira (a Bantu language of the villagers to whom the Pygmies are attached). He announced in KiNgwana, "Bwana said I should come to you and said you should get milk ready for this baby whose mother died." With that, he turned to an older woman, a Pygmy who carried a faded blue sling strapped across her. She timidly opened it, and there, wrapped in bark cloth, was a baby, a beautiful little boy. He took Anne's breath away. She still hadn't registered that the baby was for her.

The visitors, none of whom knew Anne, were terrified; it was clear that unlike the Pygmies at Epulu, they weren't used to being near white people. Kapapela was the *bakpara*, or master, of the baby's father,[9] who had brought the baby from the village of Koki. He was from the Bira tribe, which had the closest ties to the people of Epulu among the various Pygmy communities in the region. He and Anne talked while waiting for the bottles to boil. Two days earlier, the baby's mother, Belekonde, had not had any apparent trouble giving birth, but she had died an hour or so later without warning. The baby's maternal grandmother had

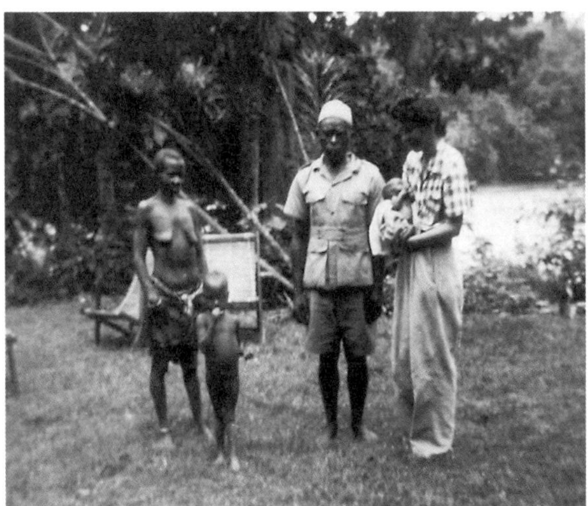

Fig. 35 Awanza Mufalume, her grandson Toko, Kapapela, Anne, and the infant William J. Kokoyou at Camp Putnam, 1951 (photographer unknown). Anne Eisner Putnam papers, Houghton Library, Harvard University.

assisted at the birth and then kept the baby alive for two days by pouring infusions of banana water into his mouth from a folded leaf.

Kapapela was a relative of Hamadi Koki, the chief of the Babombi, a chiefdom created by the Belgian government. It was Hamadi who suggested that they walk the twenty-two kilometers to bring the baby to Putnami. Kapapela had to carry an authorization with him, the *feuille de route*: "The person named Kapapela is authorized to take from Koki to the Infirmary at the Epulu a little baby to Mr. Putnam who will have it brought up by the Mothers. Signed, Hamadi Koki, le 14/2/51. *Le chef des Babombi.*"[10]

Kapapela explained that the woman who held the baby was the baby's paternal grandmother, Awanza. Anne couldn't tell how old she was, though she guessed her to be in her early forties. A young man of about nineteen (who is not in the photograph in fig. 35), was too afraid to look at Anne and turned out to be the father, Apekanu Mufalume. This was not his first child. He and Belekonde had had twins three years before, though only one, a boy named Toko, survived. Toko stood there wearing only his string of beads and huddled close to his grandmother.

Anne knew that it was customary to adopt orphaned children of relatives. She also knew that Camp Putnam had historically functioned like a surrogate family. The children called the adults mother or father, whether or not they were their biological parents. The villagers and the Pygmies had followed Pat to Epulu years before and maintained a relationship. And Pat had early on named two of the rondavels, the adobe-like huts, Umba ya Mama ("House of Mother") and Umba ya Papa ("House of Father"). But this was the first time anyone had brought a baby to them. To be "brought up by the Mothers," the *feuille de route* said. Anne wondered if she was a mother, one of "the Mothers." The answer was yes.

Anne was excited and worried. The baby was to be given to the mothers, and Pat had sent Kapapela to Anne. It was like discovering that you were pregnant as you are delivering the child, certainly not the opportune moment to reflect on what's happening.

The bottles were ready, but Anne had no idea how to prepare milk for an infant. Despite her inexperience, she didn't let on to the assembled Pygmies, as the women would have known what to do (as Awanza had). She told them to bring the pot for milk and to follow, whereupon they all descended on Pat at the dispensary.

At the time, a number of epidemics were raging: pneumonia and paratyphoid were the worst. At the dispensary, they gave penicillin injections constantly. Anne helped out as much as she could, and she did admire the work that Pat was doing for the people who came from miles around. But he was no more in the know about infants than Anne and suggested a look at their encyclopedia. As avid readers, they had an array of books, from Henry Morton Stanley's *How I Found Livingstone* (1872) and *Through the Dark Continent*

(1878), to Joseph Conrad's *Heart of Darkness* (1899 serial, 1902 book), to an eclectic array featuring James Joyce, Giovanni Boccaccio, and a Sears Roebuck catalog. Nothing on babies. And by now, the poor infant was crying from hunger. Besides, this really wasn't a situation for bookish solutions. Then Anne remembered that there were measurement tables on the cans of evaporated milk. She calculated the measures in grams and liters, and *voilà*, she made the baby his very first bottle. The Pygmies had never seen such an event, since they nursed their babies for a very long time. They thought it all quite astonishing. The baby took to the bottle immediately.

After the second feeding, they left. Anne felt at a loss. The infant was so tiny, seemed so breakable. Until then, she had been so busy fixing bottles she hadn't had time to think about her relationship to this baby. There he was: she was one of the mothers, the one left to take care of him. It didn't take long to learn that every four hours for an infant meant at least every four hours. Period. Since Awanza didn't know how to fix bottles, nor was she prepared to feed him every four hours, Anne knew that she was the one responsible. She wasn't sure who would be willing or able to help out. But she was going to adapt to this, as she had adapted to everything else at Camp Putnam.

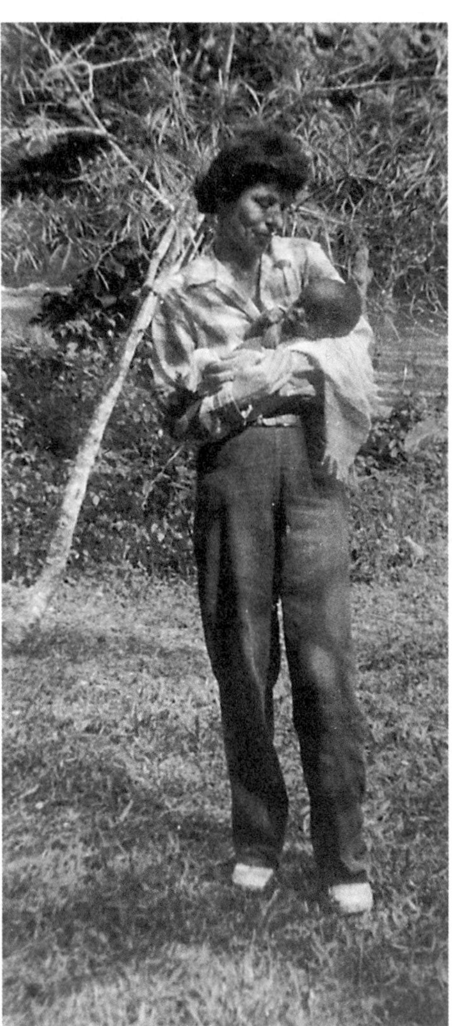

a

Fig. 36a-b
a: Anne and W.J. Kokoyou. **b**: W.J. Both at Camp Putnam, 1951. Anne Eisner Putnam papers, Houghton Library, Harvard University.

Whereas an expectant European mother has plenty of time to get diapers and all kinds of things ready, Anne was in the same situation as a Pygmy mother, except that she decided to make diapers. She gathered the simple curtains she had put up in one of the rooms to cut into diaper squares. She found a paper carton to make a crib and used a pillow for a mattress. She draped an old sheet that she had cut up over it and cushioned the sides with towels and blankets. When Pat came up from the dispensary, everything was under control, and they went out on the veranda. There were the dinner decorations for Valentine's Day. Here was their baby. They discussed what to name him. They agreed that he probably should be called Abe Lincoln because he had been born on Lincoln's birthday but decided to name him after Anne's father instead: William J. Anne's father later wrote a formal letter accepting that his name be carried on by an African Pygmy; it was a great honor, he wrote, which he humbly accepted. How he really felt wasn't clear.

Pat then asked who would be coming to give the baby his Pygmy name, and Awanza answered that his name was Kokoyou, "the one who is alone." His BaBira name (given by Kapapela's tribe, with whom his parents were associated) was Kangangiloke. Now he also had a Western patronym after his adoptive mother's father, so this was bonding according to the rules of three cultures (Pygmy, Babira, and Western), and he was no longer alone (fig. 36a-b).

Anne loved young William from the moment she held him, and he became the best-dressed Pygmy in the Ituri Forest. After the first week, the cook, André, would bring visitors right into Anne's bedroom and open William's cupboard with a sweeping gesture, saying, "This is the baby's wealth." Anne felt embarrassed at the ostentation. Each cloth she made for him was more than any local child ever had; if a Pygmy child had one cloth, he was considered very wealthy. No sooner had William J. Kokoyou accumulated the fantastic number of nineteen diapers and six sheets than his wealth began to dwindle, because Anne began distributing them to all the infants in the village. Anne's reasons were complex. She had never felt like she made the cut as a white woman in Africa, because she felt it was unjust to eat something special and not share it. She felt a lot of liberal guilt at her own privilege, and now that privilege was passed on to her adopted son. William J. Kokoyou was going to be singled out from all the others. The differences between his life and the lives of the other babies were rather stark. Anne and Pat both worried that those differences because of growing up with them might prevent him from ever returning to the Pygmy community.

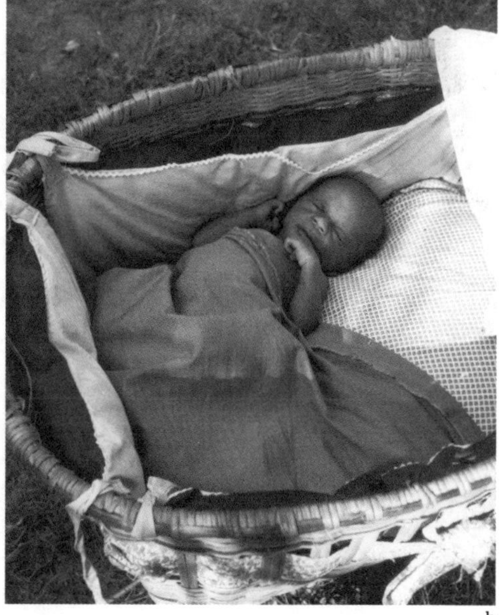

b

On their side, the people of Epulu were asking philosophical questions about the consequences of Anne and Pat becoming parents of a pygmy child, the classic debate between nature and nurture. Would he remain small and still look like a Pygmy if he was brought up by them? Pat was more than six feet tall, with a flaming red beard. Black children adopted by whites were also considered white. The problem was how could he be Anne and Pat's child and remain a Pygmy? Part of the solution lay with the extended family, and part would come about by the force of events.

Grandma's departure after three days posed new and serious problems for Anne. Who would help her take care of little William, and how would Anne keep Grandma connected to him? Anne's time was occupied with running the hotel and being a painter, and she had not questioned whether to accept William J. as her child. None of these issues was well thought out, and like so much of what happened at Epulu, one adjusted as fast as events occurred.

Most of the village women were busy working at their banana and peanut plantations, and they seemed to think it beneath their dignity to take care of a Pygmy baby. Anne becoming one of the mothers of a Pygmy was crossing a line that villagers did not cross. Pygmy women married both villagers and white men, but Pygmy men could not marry villager women.[11] Pygmies could dress in European textiles and come into the village to use implements of the villagers. Village women and men could also wear European textiles and cloths, but they never cross-dressed with the Pygmies; there is no evidence of any villager wearing a bark cloth (Anne put one on over her clothes on some festive occasions). Nevertheless, one of the village women, Katemana, offered to help for a time. She learned how to fix bottles.

Anne had always admired the relationship between parent and child among the Pygmies and thought them wonderful parents. Soon Pat and Anne, too, were watching each coo and gesture with the same enthralled rapture that parents experience for any first child. Everyone made a great fuss over W. J. Kokoyou. Anne thought about the lore that African babies didn't cry. They didn't cry as much as Western children did, as far as she could tell, because they were constantly being held by somebody. At the first whimper, the mother would give the child her breast. Anne seemed to have to pick William up every minute, too. When his father, Apekanu, arrived back with Kapapela, they brought gifts, eggs, and a chicken, and his uncle Masimongo cut a liana and sprinkled its juice (and there was plenty of it) over W.J. to make him strong.

Anne's mother wrote that she was delighted at the news of W.J.'s arrival, but she encouraged Anne rather insistently to get help to care for him. She was concerned that Anne would never be able to leave and come back to visit in New York. It did not occur to her that the child might come back with Anne. In her fantasies, Anne had imagined that she could bring him with her in the future if she were to return to New York. She chided her parents: wouldn't they like to see their grandchild? Anne thought wishfully that everyone would be excited, intrigued, and involved. Her mother thought otherwise, perhaps remembering what had happened to Ota Benga, the

Pygmy who was put on display in anthropological exhibits at the St. Louis World's Fair in 1904 and the Bronx Zoo in 1906: "I think little W.J. is better off in Africa. Here he would just be a little curiosity and freak—your tales will interest everybody."[12] She sensed that he was only partially in Anne's charge and should stay in his own familiar environment. The risk that he would be made into a spectacle was unacceptable. What Fluff couldn't see was how close William J. Kokoyou and Anne were becoming. She did ask Anne to do sketches of him, and Anne knew that meant that she was trying to understand.

In April, Anne turned forty. On the day, Pat sent a boy carrying a soft new cushion with her name printed in safety pins—the equivalent of pearls in the region. Next came boy after boy with bunches of flowers, wishing her a happy birthday.

More New Arrivals

Toward the end of that month, a charismatic young Englishman, a student of philosophy in India for two years, came motorcycling by on the recommendation of a friend as he was making his way across Africa back to England. His name was Colin Macmillan Turnbull. He arrived with a young American music teacher, Newton Beal. Everybody liked Colin immediately. Like Pat, he was tall and seemed to be able to fix anything. Colin was also fascinated with the forest and the Pygmies, in much the same way Pat had been when he first came to Africa as a young man. He was articulate and clearly talented in practical matters as well as intellectual ones. Pat and Colin got along immediately; Pat had knowledge, Colin had energy. Colin fixed the car and soon was helping Pat build a dam away from the center of Camp Putnam, down on an island, among other projects. Colin was interested in everything Pat knew and did. The more Anne and Pat grew to know Colin, the more they liked him. By the time he prepared to leave in early June, after about three months at Epulu, he was already talking about coming back to visit and to study the Pygmies. The men who worked at Camp Putnam, Pat, and Anne all hoped he would be able to do so.

Building the dam, with a longer plan to construct another camp on the island, seemed like just one more of Pat's many projects. Once Colin left, however, Pat remained on the island, his passion for the dam becoming a way of life. He liked "vacationing" two hundred yards away, "hidden in the great equatorial jungle," living surrounded by his snakes and all the other creatures he kept. He could not walk at all anymore; just going from the bedroom to the parlor in the Palais now seemed too difficult for him. That was one of the main reasons he liked his camp, where he had arranged his room like a steamer cabin, the worktable within arm's reach of the bed. It was also becoming evident that Pat wanted to isolate himself, at least from white people. He no longer liked even to come up to the hotel, saying he always stayed up too late and was sick in bed for days afterward. He confessed that it made him feel less like an invalid when he could control the comings and goings of visitors. Only a few "chosen spirits" were allowed to see him.

Pat still worked from morning till night, still seeing patients and overseeing a baby okapi, as well as other animals, with Abazinga. Sometimes Pat wanted Anne to come sit and watch him. It wasn't easy to think of him as an invalid, because he was still more active than most people. But Anne and Pat were now, in fact, separated and only saw each other during the day down on the island. Anne missed him, she but could see he planned to spend the rest of his life there. She thought that if he were back in the States, he would be in bed or in a wheelchair all the time—he was better off this way.

Anne was now running the hotel alone. The visitors kept coming: members of the Explorers Club arrived to do an article for *True* magazine about Pat, Anne, and the camp. An odd visitor , Morris Tenenbaum, from Hackensack, New Jersey, rode in on a bike. Then twenty Belgian Boy Scouts arrived. And there were many more.

Behind the scenes, things were, however, falling into disarray. Getting palm oil (one of the staples) for the hotel was difficult, and the boys had threatened to go on strike. Relations between the villagers and the Pygmies had been strained since January. Cooperation was poor. The Pygmies had been bringing less and less meat to the market to exchange for agricultural products, because someone was taking it—though it wasn't clear who had done it. There was even talk of the Pygmies themselves splitting up. For a couple of weeks, Anne received no meat at all. Then a hunting camp disbanded after a number of people became sick, three of whom died. Anne sent messages encouraging them to bring the ill to the dispensary, but there was new resistance (Anne didn't explain why) to Pat's medicine.

Pat spoke of discipline and keeping things in order. He taunted Anne about finally understanding how her father must have felt running his waxed-paper company in New Jersey. Anne responded sharply that she never wanted to be a boss, but under the circumstances, she had to manage. They had been having difficulty staying afloat financially, and she was now responsible for their hotel as a moneymaking operation. The Institut pour la Recherche Scientifique en Afrique Centrale (IRSAC, the Institute for Scientific Research in Central Africa), a Belgian research institution with several stations throughout the Congo and in the Ruanda-Urundi Protectorate, was a welcome connection, but it owed Pat and Anne a couple of hundred dollars for okapi milk. Anne was in such debt at the store where she got provisions that they had already capped her credit, so she had to pay cash. Her anxiety about finances brought on sleepless nights. Life had become too expensive. Anne managed to downsize the staff, but there were always unexpected expenses. As Pat withdrew, Anne's responsibilities and problems increased.

In July, a premature baby was brought in. The mother was extremely sick, and when her breast milk stopped flowing, Anne started the baby on a bottle (they were all experts by this time!). The infant's survival was uncertain throughout his first weeks at Camp Putnam, and his mother died in early August, but he ultimately recovered. Anne found herself with another bottle baby. This time, the question of choice didn't even arise. She took him as her second child. Katchelewa Bangama was his name, and he was tiny, only two pounds at birth. Over the weeks, he gained strength, and Anne was hopeful. He received a few hand-me-downs from W.J. Kokoyou, including a basket. Unlike W.J., Katchelewa had many relatives at Camp Putnam. His father was an important person in the next village, and it was easy for Anne to keep them involved in looking after him.

Nevertheless, Anne worried about her ability to care for the young babies, especially with Pat's health worsening. She knew that William Kokoyou would have to go back to his family when he was old enough.[13] In the long run, she believed that William would be happiest with his family. Keeping them involved, though something of a struggle, was her long-term strategy, and it worked. Grandma Awanza came and stayed, helping to take excellent care of William. André's wife also helped supervise him. And William Kokoyou was with Anne every day as well. Like the other baby, he was being taken care of by the mothers. With Anne, he ate soup, cereal, flour, milk, and butter. With his grandmother, he got bananas or papaya, smashed cooked plantains, pounded manioc leaves, and rice. His diet was only one sign of how he lived between cultures.

CHAPTER FIVE

Grim Days (1952)

When did it start exactly? Anne couldn't remember, really. Pat's illness worsened, but not just physically. He seemed to be losing his mind. Only a few of Anne's notes from early part of 1952 remain:

> Is Pat on the verge of madness? What am I to do? What is happening? What is going to happen? Is anything going to happen in the next few hours? Or is it just going to be a beautiful sunny day with Pat . . . unwilling to see me? Is he going to call for me and spend two hours insulting me, lecturing me or what? . . . What the hell is happening to Pat? What's happening to him, what's happening to him? what's happening to him?
> Where oh where is there help? Will we both go mad? What caused this hate on his part? What made him turn on me? Is it just his sickness? Do I have such tremendous lackings? Are people to be trained like horses or worked like marionettes on wires? Not even allowed to use their own wording? . . . I did not get married at thirty-six to be trained to be god knows what. I got married to be a wife to a man I was very much in love with. A man who had greatness, possibilities of being one of the world's really great men. A man of charm, personality and brilliance, a good talker. Original.

When in his illness Pat started losing control of his faculties, he turned against Anne in 1952; it evoked all the feelings of rejection that she had experienced on arrival at Epulu. But things were also radically different now. Anne had set down roots in the community with the children and their families, and she was deeply invested in extended family life. She could speak KiNgwana fluently and French reasonably well.

Although Anne later tore up letters that she wrote to family and friends in New York, she needed to memorialize the situation. She wrote little stories, in either the first or third person, often only thinly disguising their autobiographical basis, crossing out names. One was clearly about how Pat had begun to destroy Camp Putnam: a man throws down a Coleman lamp, smashing the glass chimney into shards on the cement floor, where barefoot men and the narrator look on, shocked. The incident happened when Pat [name scratched out] called the hotel boys together demanding to know why a new lamp didn't work.

> Faithful, one-eyed Ibrahemu had said "Well, it may be the palm oil in the kerosene." "What do you mean palm oil in the kerosene?" "Oh they sent the [~~palm~~] wrong drum to the store instead of the kerosene one." "Well if you saw it had palm oil in it why did you pour it into the lamp?" "I didn't think that the palm oil would do it any harm." At that X [~~Pat~~] threw the lamp on the floor with all his force. There went the only [pump] lamp that worked.

The narrative continued:

> The blacks and whites in the room held their breaths. "Bah," said the tall thin blue-eyed bearded man from his chair "that's the last God damned lamp that's coming into this place. Your reign [to the narrator] is over." "Of all the disorganized, badly run places, this is it. From now on I'm taking over. It doesn't matter if I'm sick. You've wrecked this place."

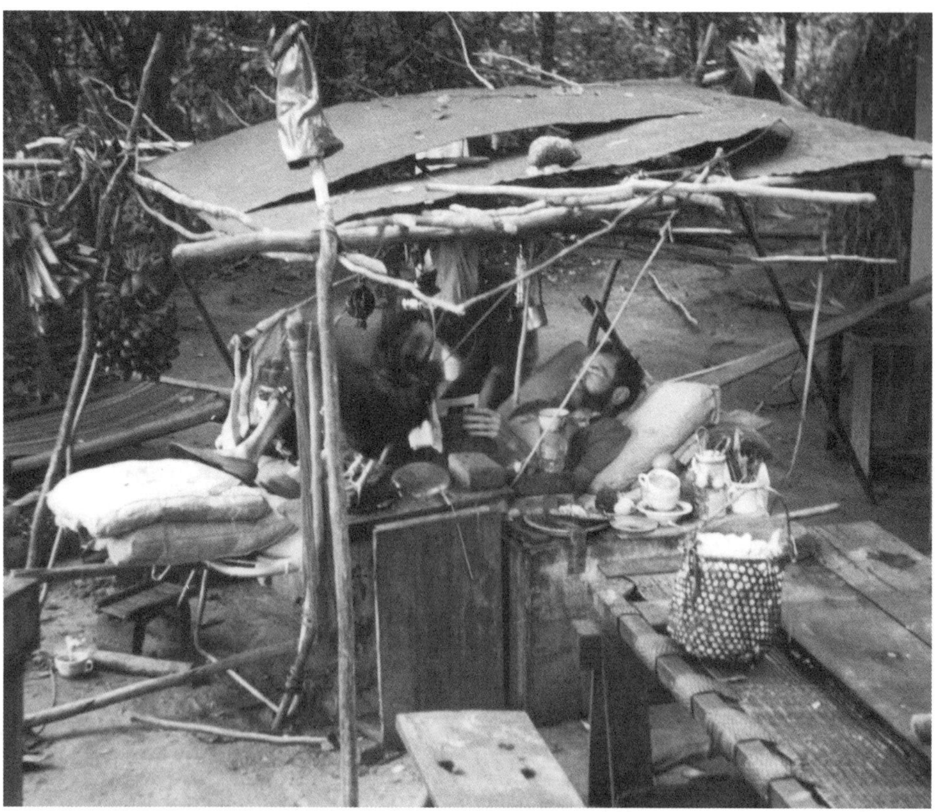

Fig. 37 Patrick Putnam, 1952 (photograph by Schuyler Jones). Houghton Library, Harvard University.

Anne retorted in her scribbles, giving herself away as author: "I was stunned, I was mad. Nobody had a right to speak to me the way he had, sick or not sick. One doesn't throw lamps."

Then, written in a different, finer pencil: "I didn't realize at the time that that was merely a mild preview of what was in store for us--nor had I really heard what he said or paid attention."[1]

As Pat's health deteriorated, he rejected Anne. The more he needed her, the more she wanted to take care of him, and the more he seemed to resent her. Indeed, Pat's ambivalence about those he loved was there long before Anne came onto the scene. Marcel Proust wrote that one is really only an accomplice to the psychic structures of another—it was this involuntary structure that Anne found difficult to resist. As Pat became sicker and Anne became more committed to running Camp Putnam, she searched for causes. Why he did he resent her presence so? What was this mental illness? She found no answer, only more worries about their situation.

Pat stayed on the island where he had built a hut and a new dispensary (see fig. 37). Up at Camp Putnam, life bustled. But Anne had little money to run it, and she hadn't received subsidies promised by the government. When she could view the hotel as a movie set, as she had when she first arrived, she knew it was a relatively good moment. When she could no longer maintain a distance, distinguishing what seemed like a screenplay from her anguish, she felt defeated. During that period, she took a lot of tranquilizers—"jitter pills," as she called them—to keep calm.

The year started like a roller coaster and continued that way through January and February. March gave some relief: Pat recovered a bit, and a young man fresh out of high school named Schuyler "Skye" Jones from Wichita, Kansas, happened by and stayed for three months. He himself had little money and was traveling around Africa with his camera. Tall, with a great shock of brown hair, and full of positive energy, he took immediately to helping Anne and Pat with anything that needed repair or building.

Skye was fascinated by life at Epulu and took many photographs (see fig. 38a-d): the beautiful and rare okapi, the collection of African objects, and interiors of the Palais, among many other aspects of life at Camp Putnam. Skye would go on to extensive travels in Africa, Asia, and the Middle East, and he later studied ethnology at the University of Edinburgh (MA) and Oxford (PhD). He was the director of the ethnographic museum at Oxford University, the Pitt Rivers Museum, from 1985 to 1997. But even at this time, as a very young man, Skye took extensive notes about Pat and Anne, his own visits to Pygmy camps, and the organization of Epulu.

The one outstanding event that both Skye and Anne wrote up in their notes was Pat's operation on a woman whose stillborn child had died in utero sometime before. The woman's husband was being treated for gonorrhea and had been a patient for a few weeks at the Camp Putnam dispensary, when he suggested that she be brought to Pat. The scene was grisly: the dead baby's hand and part of its arm were hanging out of the woman's cervix; they were discolored and starting to rot. Anne, Pat, and Skye knew that the doctor in Mambasa was away, and Irumu was too far to go under the circumstances. It was not clear how Pat could extract the baby's body from the mother. Pat was not a surgeon like his father, and he had never even delivered a baby, let alone a stillborn baby. Yet he took on the challenge for humanitarian reasons and also to prove he could do it. Alternately smoking his Astrid cigarettes and coughing from emphysema, he thought through

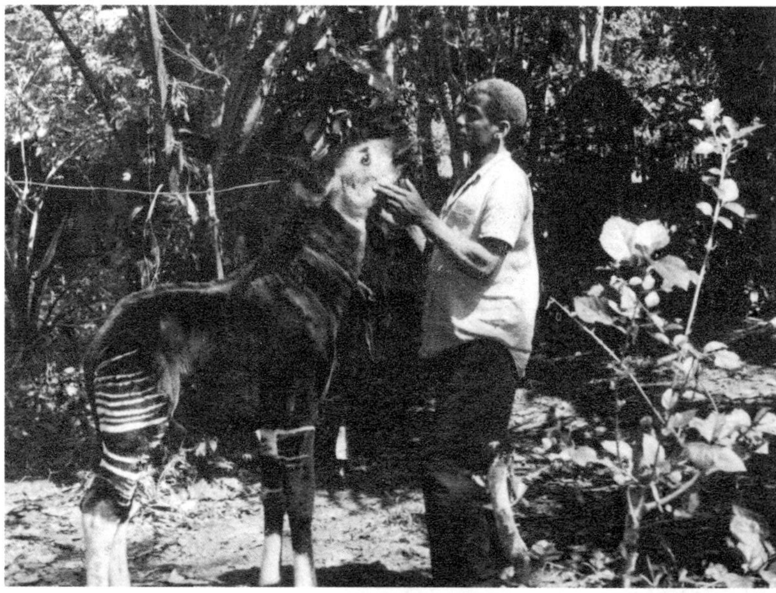

a

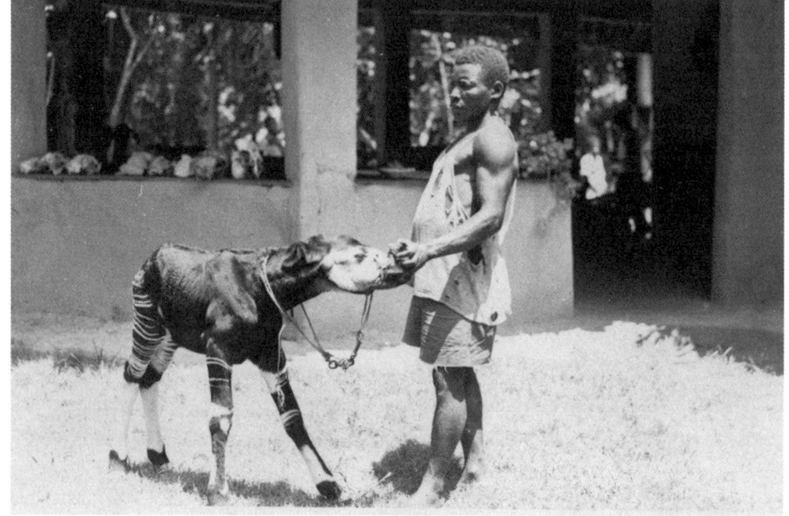

b

Fig. 38a-d
a-b: Unknown with okapi and Abazinga feeding baby okapi, c. 1952 (photographer unknown). Houghton Library, Harvard University.
c: Schuyler Jones and Keith Lawson with okapi, at Camp Putnam, 1952 (photographer unknown). Houghton Library, Harvard University.
d: Mbuti bark cloth and bird-shaped headrest, probably made for Anne, 1952 (photograph by Schuyler Jones). Houghton Library, Harvard University.

each step of the gruesome but necessary operation. With Skye and Anne assisting, they worked without any proper instruments (though the ones they had were boiled to be sterilized) in the dim light. The stench of decay was overpowering, according to their respective notes. After many hours, the operation was a success, and the woman lived. Much was made of this feat at the time, because it proved to them all that Pat still had his wits and powers about him and that his Western medicine could save lives.

Once the emergency was over, Anne later learned more about the circumstances that had led up to the disaster. The woman had been in labor for three days when the baby stopped moving. As her contractions grew excruciatingly painful, she became afraid and confessed to her family that she had been having an affair at the time she became pregnant. They decided with the elders that the only way to save the baby was to have her make a public confession in her husband's village. She was taken there, all the while in labor, to name her lover. But to no avail: she still had not delivered the baby. It was then that they decided to bring her the five kilometers from the village to Pat. She came by *tipoy*, then by truck.

Anne didn't think much at the time about the discrepancy between this woman's situation and Pat's encouragement when she was away in New York for her to be very African by having affairs and even becoming pregnant. She also did not know that when Pat's first and most beloved wife in Penge, Abanzima, consorted with a local man, Pat beat her, made her carry her bed through the village, and chained her to a tree during the daytime for a week. Emily Hahn had witnessed this very distressing behavior and had been unable to do anything but leave.[2] What Anne could see was that in the case of this woman, the penalty of confession—by delaying medical help—could have been fatal to both her and the child. Thankfully, the mother's life was saved.

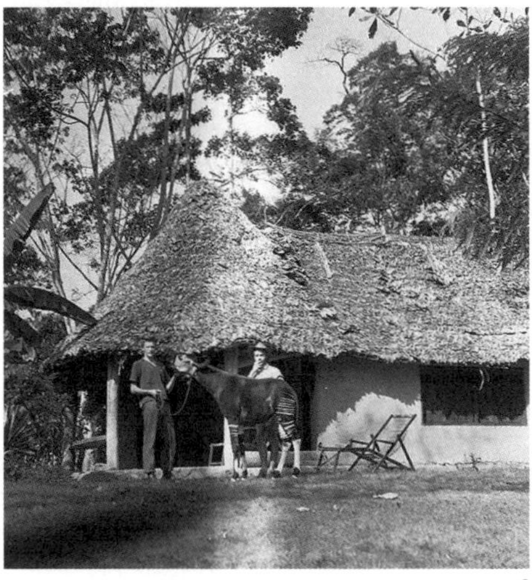
c

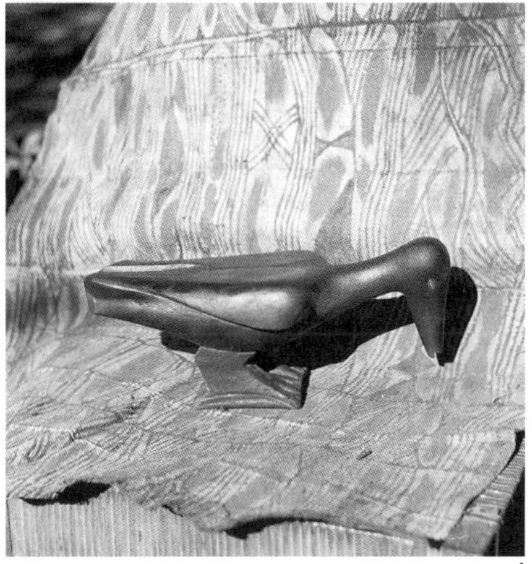
d

Throughout all of this, Camp Putnam was still abuzz with visitors, including the prince and princess of Liechtenstein. She wore blue jeans, diamond brooches, and pearls, and he forgot his briefcase money and passport, so he had to come back and stay longer. As gifts to Anne, he left an elegant outdoor Abercrombie and Fitch shower bucket, books, and a baby's hot-water bottle. A clarinet player arrived with missionary musicians, accompanied by a former Miss Montana, a man in the merchant marines, and an Australian who kept calling Anne "Sweet." It was an odd assortment of people, to say the least.

When Pat felt a little better in March, he moved back to the Palais to be with Anne, bringing along a number of his creatures, a couple of snakes, a hyrax, and a baby monkey, which played by leaping in and out of the mosquito netting on her bed, rolling around and getting caught. William Kokoyou, almost one and a half years old, now had six teeth, wore some fine beads of red and green, and was eating with gusto (see fig. 39). Grandma took care of him all day long, and he slept with Anne and Pat at night. At seven kilos, he had a huge stomach, large black eyes, a big bald head, and a sweet, sweet smile. Anne was convinced he was beginning to say her name, but it was mixed up with his other noises.

Anne's father, Will, hearing of Pat's illness—though not the full extent—from her letters, had called Pat's father in the hope of getting support to encourage them to return to the States. Dr. Putnam said he thought that they were happier and better off in the Congo. While it was clear Pat could have gotten better care in the States, he had chosen the life at Epulu, and Dr. Putnam may have understood this and, perhaps more than Anne, knew what was wrong with Pat.

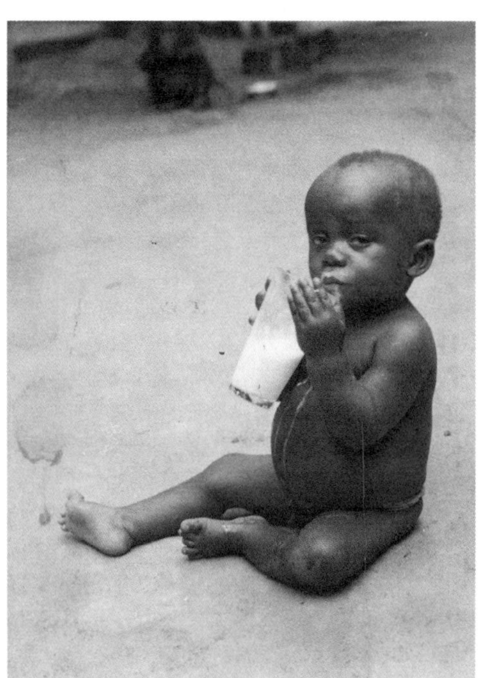

Fig. 39 W.J. Kokoyou, 1952 (photograph by Schuyler Jones). Anne Eisner Putnam papers, Houghton Library, Harvard University.

Anne's mother sent letters of encouragement and wrote of a beautiful Cézanne show that was on in New York. She wrote lovingly, suggesting, for instance, that Anne do a sketch a day to keep her mental balance. But this might not be enough; Fluff insisted that a return to New York for a while would help Anne recover her strength and tranquility. When she wasn't around her mother, Anne found it easier to accept such suggestions. The ups and downs of Pat's health left her feeling that everything was being drained out of her. She took her mother's first suggestion, deciding to do some abstractions from paintings and drawings that she had previously done "from nature." (See pl. 8 and

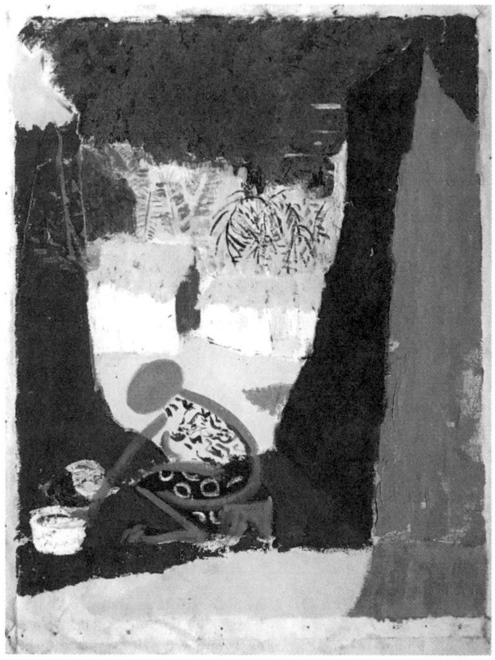

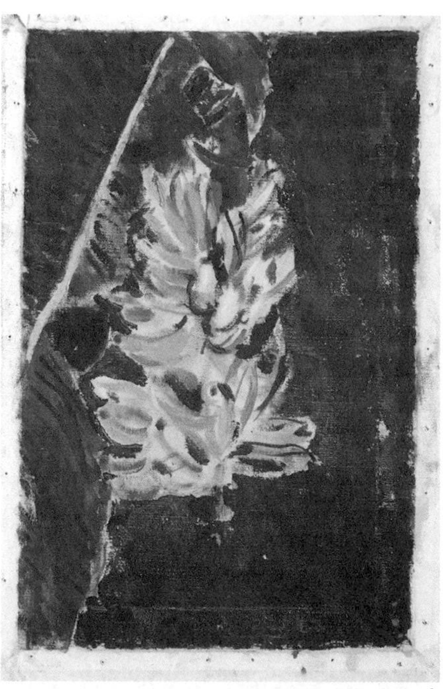

a b

Fig. 40a-b
a: *Woman Cooking*, 24 x 20 in., oil on canvas, c. 1953 (photograph by Michael Rosengarten), McDonald collection.
b: *Bunch of Bananas*, 24 x 16 in., oil on canvas, c. 1953 (photograph by Michael Rosengarten), McDonald collection.

fig. 40a-b.) It was a first step toward taking control. She did not realize how much this practice was going to help her survive the next few years.

At this point, in addition to caring for the children and dealing with the hotel, Anne was still able to keep working when she went to spend time with the Pygmies. As she pondered abstraction, she had come to think that the composition of a canvas needed to include the particularities of context. The question of whether one was an Abstract or Surrealist painter seemed remote in the Ituri. In 1949, she had mused:

> I am surrounded by wonderful masks and statuettes most primitive in character but I find that I don't think I can work like that, much as I love them. Maybe subconsciously my work will be under their influence but it feels as though to try and to be directly under their influence is a little bit like a woman trying to be sixteen when she is really forty. How can I dream up masks of leopard skin, copper and beads. They are not part of my life, though they are a very definite part of the lives of the people who made them. I have seen rugs made that seemed as abstract as hell but the maker of them will tell you that this is a knife and this is a person but they have done it as a natural and not because it is *à la mode* on 57th Street, or because they saw the last Picasso painting. I think one should evolve as a painter even as one does or at least should as a human being being able to absorb ideas, take what one wants from [them] . . . and carry on from there but not . . . get too hyped on any one theory that makes one inflexible, [or] . . . to be so flexible one is nothing.[3]

Now, still connected with the New York art world even at a distance, Anne was revising her own sense of what it meant to do abstract work which could include the forest and the buildings of Camp Putnam; these subjects commanded her interest, and she would follow her own sense of abstraction. That meant to see and interpret.

Dialogues with Mbuti Bark-Cloth Paintings

Anne decorated a white wall in the living room of the Palais with a beautiful Mbuti bark cloth, not one of her own paintings. (See fig. 41.) She hung a Kota reliquary figure in the middle of it and placed pieces of African furniture and masks sparsely around, as a tribute to at least two African traditions: the Mbuti artistry of bark cloth and African mask making in the primitivist modernist art tradition of Picasso, Matisse, and others. We do not know who painted the bark cloth, though it was possibly Akinadema, an artist Anne had identified as one of the prominent women painters of bark cloth.[4]

Anne's interest in figuration, abstraction, and creativity in relation to the context around her was her way of thinking aesthetically about living

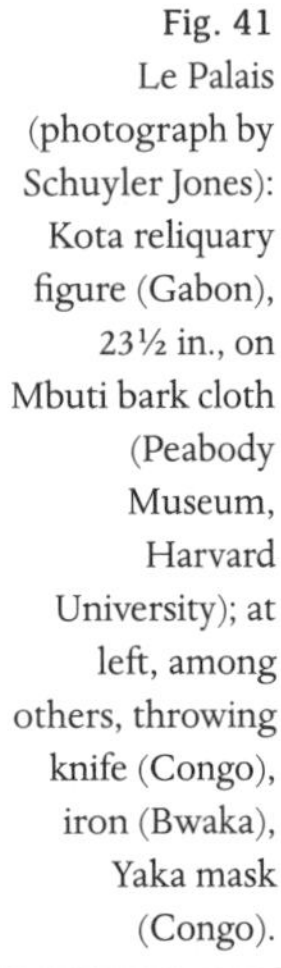

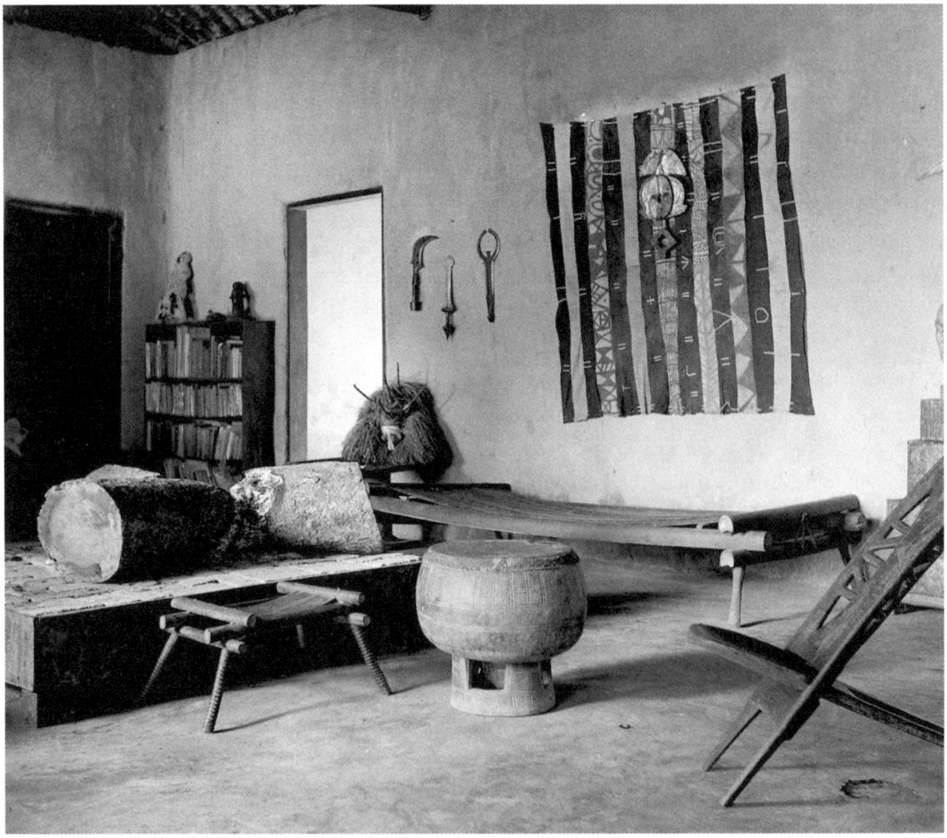

Fig. 41 Le Palais (photograph by Schuyler Jones): Kota reliquary figure (Gabon), 23½ in., on Mbuti bark cloth (Peabody Museum, Harvard University); at left, among others, throwing knife (Congo), iron (Bwaka), Yaka mask (Congo).

between cultures. Her interest in the bark cloths set the stage for changes in her own work. During times as difficult as these, her commitment to her artistic practice showed that it was still a source of self-understanding and joy. Anne was fascinated with bark cloths from the moment she began spending time among the Pygmies in 1947. (See fig. 42.) The men beat the bark from six different kinds of trees in the Ituri Forest into a soft fibrous textile (the tapping sound can be heard when approaching a Pygmy camp). Bark cloths are loincloths of differing sizes (the twenty-two Anne collected and later donated to the American Museum of Natural History range from 46 x 43 centimeters to 144 x 128 centimeters) worn by the Pygmies. Once the textile is made by the men, the women take over and begin to paint geometrical motifs with pigments from roots.[5]

When prompted, the artists would show how the abstract designs on bark cloths referred to the world they inhabited in the forest: for example, vines were shown with twisted and knotted cord figures.[6] This understanding was an important influence on her iconic painting *Pygmy Camp* (pl. 7); in it, the forest surrounds a Pygmy camp where making bark cloth is given equal space to sorting and repairing hunting nets.

In *Images of Congo*, both Enid Schildkrout and Suzanne Blier address the mutual influence between Anne's Western-trained artwork and the Mbuti women's bark-cloth designs. Anne noted in a letter that the Pygmies went to "a lot of trouble to decorate their bark cloth because they knew I'd like it."[7] Although we cannot know the extent to which Anne's art in Pygmy camps influenced the women artists' painting of bark cloths, Schildkrout and Blier make a convincing argument that Anne and the Mbuti women dialogued through their work.

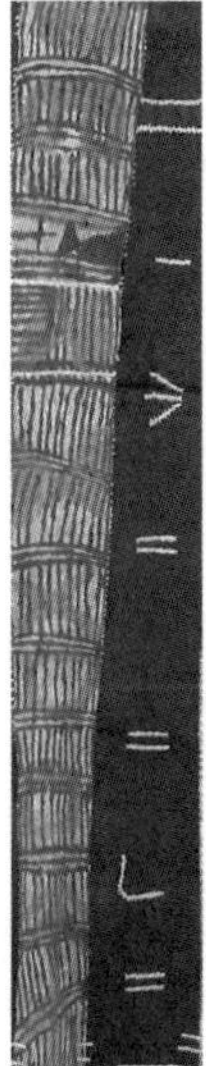

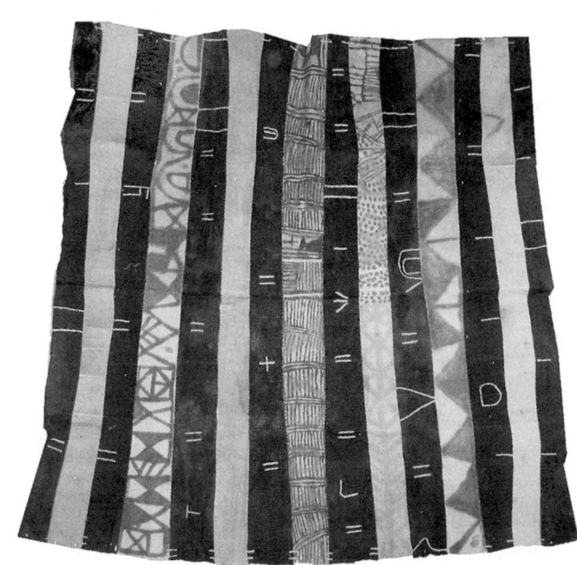

Fig. 42
Bark cloth and center detail of bark cloth, formerly owned by Anne Eisner (see fig. 41), now at Peabody Museum, Harvard University.

The rectilinear fibrous vine bark cloth—*lengbe* or *pongo* in KiBira, *murumba* in KiNgwana—are like a "canvas," as Blier points out, on which the women artists of the Ituri Forest painted. She shows that despite remarkably different backgrounds, these artists and Anne had shared interests in womanhood and the confluence of culture and environment. They could use a kind of artistic agency to address one another despite significant differences: from a mostly anonymous artistic tradition of making works for use in everyday life to the work of an artist trained in the Western tradition of painting.

Mapping places and patterns on bark cloth was significant to Mbuti women, similar to Anne's expressions of the link between culture and place. One of the places Anne began to fuse what she had seen during her last visit to the New York art world, especially color-field painting, and the strong bark-cloth paintings of the women was in a sequence of paintings that involved color and the partition of space—inside the forest and out, indoors and outdoors. (See pls. 9, 10, 11.)

April 1952 was not to be the cruelest month at Epulu. There were numerous visitors: a French photographer, Pierre Verger (1902–1996), and a deep-sea diver also interested in rain forests, Otis Barton (1899–1992), were filming the Pygmies. And when the chief of the Belgian Tourist Bureau came from Léopoldville with his assistant from Stanleyville, as he had done before, Anne sensed that while Belgian officialdom was received everywhere with a great deal of protocol, at Camp Putnam, they would be greeted with the everyday confusion of her life. For their visit, Pat purposely let a chimp loose to create havoc. It did. When things calmed down, the Pygmies demonstrated their dancing and various other activities.

Thinking about Family Life

In April, Anne inherited her third orphan, a Pygmy boy named Ndeku. His mother died at the dispensary just after he was born. At the time, Anne had finished weaning young William from the bottle and was preparing to wean Katchelewa. William showed spirit, scooting around on his rump, and little Katchelewa exuded charm with his quiet gurgles. This time, the father and one of his aunts offered to help take care of Ndeku, for which Anne was grateful. Still, even with this help, she was now raising three babies together with their families.

Life in the families of these babies was no simpler than life back in the States. Anne learned that William J.'s father, who lived in Koki, had gone off with a woman from Epulu, Basalinda, a great personality and one of Anne's favorite women. She was very vocal and always had a lot to say about almost anything that happened in the camp. Years earlier, Basalinda had been married to Andonata, a local Pygmy, in the common practice of a sister exchange (a woman of his clan must marry a woman in his wife's clan). Andonata had been one of the first Pygmies Anne got to know at Epulu. He had an unforgettable way of bounding into view, wearing a wide red bark cloth and carrying his bow and arrow. Anne marveled at how his eyes expressed such animation and curiosity, even before she learned to speak with him. Basalinda had a number of children by Andonata, although people suspected that her child Teliabo Kenge (around age thirteen in 1952) had a biological father who was Bantu. Kenge would later become the iconic Pygmy in Colin Turnbull's influential anthropological study of the community, *The Forest People* (1961).

When Anne first arrived, Basalinda had a small baby named Aberi, whom she showered with careful and loving care. Although she and Andonata seemed to get along well, on at least one occasion, she had gotten angry during a hunting trip, torn down the house she had just made, and stalked out of the woods back to the village, carrying her basket, her log (with the embers for her fire), and Aberi. This was her way of giving Andonata hell, and Anne remembered his resigned, almost beaten expression. Andonata would have been left homeless for the night had he not had another wife. He did, but this was unusual for a Pygmy. At first, Anne wasn't too sympathetic to his plight (because she also had a husband with another wife) and identified much more with Basalinda. Anne had trouble believing in his evident distress, because he could simply turn to his other wife. Still, she saw that he was devoted to Basalinda.

One day, Basalinda came to Anne in a rage, accusing another Pygmy, Nzuki, of tearing off her clothes in a plantain field. Nzuki was in his early thirties, and although he had had infantile paralysis when he was very young, he still got around with amazing speed and agility, even net hunting. Anne thought Nzuki looked like an intellectual, with expressions radiating great beauty at certain moments, especially when he was telling a story. This incident, which today would be called sexual assault, was taken seriously in the community, and Pat convoked a jury to rule on the matter. They found Nzuki in the wrong. Anne was thus puzzled when Basalinda went on to have an affair with Nzuki later, but what really interested her from this convoluted tale (given Pat's multiple wives) was Andonata's feelings after his discovery of Basalinda's adultery. Anne had never seen someone change as much as he did. From that time on, he seemed to be broken, hardly ever coming to visit Camp Putnam or caring about what happened. Still, his other wife stayed with him. Some of the Pygmies were convinced that Nzuki had put a *bolozi* (the feared spell of the evil eye) on Andonata, and there were hard feelings between Nzuki and the Andonata family, most people siding with Andonata. When Andonata fell ill with pneumonia, Anne rushed him down to the "hospital" (the way they referred to the dispensary) to give him penicillin, which saved his life. Basalinda, however, did not want to take care of him. It took effort on the part of the Pygmies, Pat, and Anne to persuade her that it was her duty.

As soon as Andonata recovered, Basalinda went on a trip to the village of Koki, taking Aberi with her. When she failed to return, Anne learned by chance that she was now living with W.J. Kokoyou's father, Apekanu Mufalume. Basalinda was much older than Apekanu. Basalinda and Andonata both went against expectations in their community. Was there any lesson for Anne here, other than that people could hurt each other in many ways? She felt herself sympathetic to both Basalinda and Andonata, and she also wanted to keep William Kokoyou's father involved with his care.

The situation with William's grandmother, Awanza, was quite another story. After several months at Camp Putnam tending to William, she became restless and wanted to go home. Anne wrote to Kapapela that she needed someone to help take care of William if Grandma left. Kapapela himself came, saying that he could find no one. If Grandma wanted to leave, he was perfectly willing to let W.J. go to one of the Epulu Pygmies to be brought up. That did it. Grandma had been very jealous of W.J.'s love for Anne. When she heard Kapapela's suggestion, she made her decision: young William was her baby, she loved him, and she was going to stay. That, of course, was what Anne wanted. She knew more than ever that there was a chance that she would return soon to the States, and then what? The next time Awanza came back after a visit to her village, quite a few Pygmies came with her, and she was unusually cheerful. As Pygmies usually have relatives around, Anne didn't realize for some time that one of the unfamiliar faces was Awanza's *grand amour*. Anne was surprised that Awanza, a grandmother, could also be a femme fatale—an older woman involved with a younger man was not a norm back in the States—but Anne realized that Awanza was happy now with both William and her lover nearby.

What to Do?

In July 1952, Anne's old friend Herbert Solow came to Camp Putnam. He was conducting research on a story for *Fortune* magazine about business in the Belgian Congo.[8] Though no doubt useful to his project, his stop at Epulu was primarily to visit Anne. Anne felt terribly happy to see him. He was associated with those closest to her family and friends in the States. She told him about Pat's physical and mental problems. Things were getting dramatically worse on both counts, even though there were days and times when he almost seemed fine. Anne kept trying to remind Herbert of the redeeming qualities of life at Camp Putnam, but she didn't convince him—or herself, for that matter.

Herbert looked with fresh eyes on Pat's state, and he saw the situation in stark terms: the Belgian government could ship Pat back to the United States if he got any worse, since residence in the Congo was conditional on posting bond for passage home in case of sickness, committing a crime, or becoming a public charge. Anne didn't think the colonial administration would do anything like that, because Pat knew all the right people and would convince them that he needed to stay; besides, people who knew about Pat's condition popped in whenever they passed by to make sure she was all right. Moreover, Anne didn't believe that Pat could survive the long voyage home. For his part, Herbert wondered how they could stand *not* making the trip. He told Anne that even if Pat refused to go, she should return to New York with him, leaving what he viewed as the "veritable heart of darkness" of Camp Putnam.

Anne was loath to give up her nostalgic or idealized vision of Camp Putnam and Pat (despite all the difficulties). She told Herbert it was impossible for her to return to the States without Pat. He was her man. No matter how hard he was on her, she couldn't leave him permanently when he was in such trouble (just as she had argued with Basalinda when Andonata was ill and needed to be taken care of). As Herbert left, he could see that people liked Anne and that she knew her way around. At least for the moment, he predicted that she could handle the situation.

By the end of the summer, there were many rumors traveling around about Pat and the state of things at the hotel. Visitors began to dwindle in number, no doubt frightened off by the more dramatic of these stories.

Anne's conversations with Herbert, as well as her realization that the hotel was beginning to fail, led her to reevaluate her relationship with everything, including William (see fig. 43). She decided it was best to separate herself from him slowly; a sudden break would be too traumatic for them both. Following through on her plan to give him back to his grandma, she

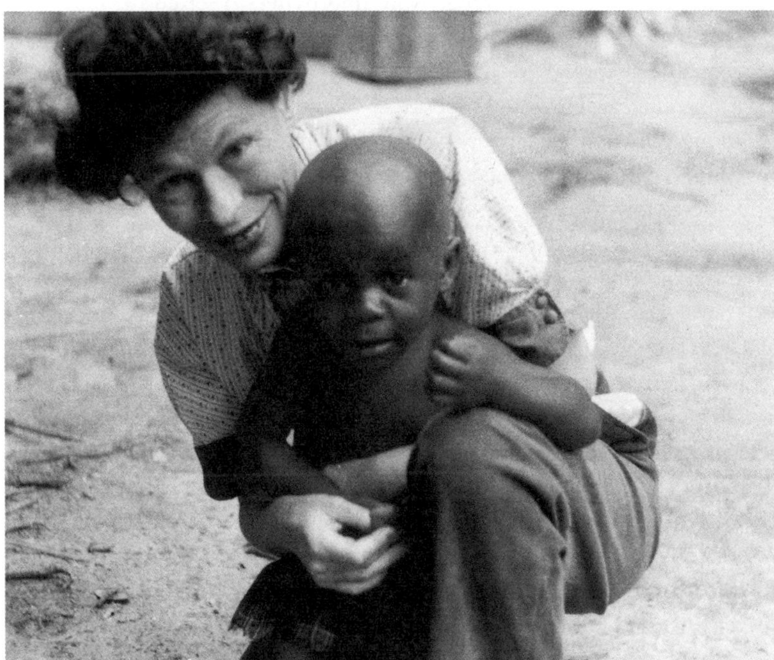

Fig. 43
Anne with W.J. Kokoyou, c. 1952–1953 (photographer unknown). Houghton Library, Harvard University.

arranged for him to sleep with Awanza for a week. Anne missed him terribly—his little noises and laughs, the games they played in the morning when he woke up. She would visit the village during the day to play with him, and every afternoon they had a little party at the five o'clock feeding. Even though she wanted him to be in his own culture, she was still surprised to see him asleep in his bed of banana leaves on the floor. It wasn't so much the difference in custom but that his return to Pygmy life was a sign of her loss. Their separation left a dull ache. She longed for his little hands around her neck. She wanted to hold and protect him. But in the long run, she knew now that she couldn't do that with Pat so sick.

Pat disagreed with Anne about W.J. Kokoyou's future, and during this period, they frequently argued about him. Although Anne had complied with just about everything Pat wanted, on this she stood firm; she insisted that she would first involve his family and ultimately let them take over. Pat had wanted children. Anne wondered whether it was syphilis that had prevented him from having children with any of his wives. Was this the disease that was now destroying his mind? She figured she was never going to know the answer to that. In any case, Anne knew Pat was unable to make decisions about a child at this point. She had made up her mind in William's best interest.

Anne was thankful that what she thought were the grimmest days were over for the moment. She could only hope that they would never return. She had broken down and written the news to her family about how destructive Pat had become in the early winter, then quickly telegrammed before they received the letter, saying things were improving, to soften the blow. Her parents wrote of their love and worry, which made her weep. Words were inadequate to express how much what they said meant. Anne badly needed their unconditional love and support.

Young William was starting to get around, but with quite a bit of difficulty for his age. Anne thought his trouble might be due to a wicked burn he had gotten crawling too near the coals of a fire while Grandma was asleep. But then, after he returned from the village one day, he suddenly couldn't walk or even stand. Anne worried that he had turned his ankle. Pat thought a nerve was paralyzed. Pat's *infirmier* recognized the symptoms and announced that W.J. Kokoyou was paralyzed in one leg. Anne wanted to rush him to see a Dr. Legrand in Irumu, but Pat felt there was nothing that he could do. The effort would be wasted. For now, he said, their only option was to massage the leg.

However, Anne was not going to be dissuaded when it came to the well-being of her adopted child. She was determined to do all she could, and that meant getting a doctor's diagnosis. Bright and early the next day, Anne collected W.J., Awanza, and Awanza's lover, Marabo, and went to the road to hitch a lift. A swanky car came by and stopped, and by a stroke of luck the driver turned out to be a doctor from Costermansville. He gave William an examination then and there and confirmed the diagnosis: infantile paralysis, or poliomyelitis. The Pygmies were relieved that no one had to go to Irumu or the hospital, and they held a dance. W.J. himself seemed unfazed and was happily crawling around, though he didn't try to get up or down much. For Anne, though, the news was heartbreaking. As she watched him struggle to do things he could do the week before, she thought about how much a Pygmy needed his legs to live in the forest.

The polio epidemics of the 1940s and 1950s are thought to have paralyzed or killed more than five hundred thousand people in the world every year. It was the very year W.J. Kokoyou contracted polio that Jonas Salk tested the vaccine (when sixty thousand cases were reported in the United States), though it would not be available until 1955.[9] Pat's nonchalance about W.J.'s polio might have come from his own diagnosis of it in France, for which his father had prescribed only hot baths and massages in 1932.[10]

Nor was W.J. the only one of Anne's adopted children to cause drama in this period. Much as she did with W.J. and Awanza, Anne encouraged Katchelewa's relatives, especially his uncle Kopo, to take care of him. After a weeklong fishing trip with his nephew, Kopo returned to Camp Putnam at the appointed time to ask permission to take Katchelewa out again. Pat, however, announced that Katchelewa looked as if he hadn't been taken care of well, and thus the baby should stay at Camp Putnam under his supervision, at least for a few days to recover. Kopo's wife raised hell at this proposal, which only enraged Pat—the notion that they didn't want Katchelewa to stay with him! Ultimately, they convened a jury to adjudicate the dispute, which by then had escalated to a communal affair. Pat was still confined to his bed, but he raised it on boxes so he could still be higher than everyone else. Fifteen people came to hear the case, packing themselves like sardines into Pat's small hut on the island. Anne's dog Mademoiselle had recently had puppies, who scampered between everyone's legs, occasionally letting out angry yips when they were stepped on. The decision ultimately came in favor of Pat. Katchelewa, who was shy and wanted little more than to stay with his aunt and uncle, had to stay with him for four days. Abazinga took on most of the responsibility, but even with his attention, the poor baby was unhappy and cried for most of the time.

In mid-November, the chief, Kapapela, who had first brought William Kokoyou to Anne, declared that Marabo, a Bira Pygmy and Grandma's lover, should come back to Koki. It seemed unacceptable to Anne that Marabo could not have a say in his own whereabouts, but she was in no position to challenge Kapapela. Until recently, she hadn't even realized that by staying at Epulu, Awanza was being deprived of her lover. Then Kapapela and Anne had a misunderstanding about Toko, William's older brother. Toko had been a problem child, and Anne thought that he needed more attention, which would be most likely if Grandma took care of him. Kapapela mistook Anne's concern for an attempt to steal his wealth, that is, his Pygmies.

When Anne asked him why he didn't leave the child with Grandma for three months as she had suggested, he replied, "Are you trying to buy him?"

"No," said Anne. "I don't buy people. I'd like to see him happy."[11]

It was confusing to Anne to be caught in the complex system between villagers and Pygmies, where the alliance of the old system based on reciprocal need had been transformed by colonialism. Whether it was from the vestiges of history of a slave economy or the brutality of the colonial regime, the villagers now seemed to see the Pygmies as their servants, at their disposal without choice or agency. The Pygmies, it seems, did not think that way. They did not recognize authority from the villagers, even though they interacted economically; and even though they adopted their languages (and, for some, KiNgwana), they did not embrace the cultural mores of the villagers.

One night, after a fight with Pat, Anne stalked out of Pat's house, heading toward her own. In the dark, she accidentally stepped on what she thought was a stick, which flew up and hit her in the ankle. It turned out to be a medium-sized viper. Anne screamed bloody murder and rushed back inside Pat's house. Since no one could find the antidote, Pat made an incision, and he and the boys sucked the blood out. After a week in bed, relieved from the day-to-day management of Camp Putnam, she left her house, only to discover that in the meantime, the dispensary had collapsed and all the patients were gone. At the same time, news had spread that the Belgian government was sending new medicine that was like magic for leprosy, and lepers were starting to arrive.

When she had first arrived at Epulu with Pat, Anne had been shocked to discover that Singa (Basalinda's brother), Pat's favorite and by far the most important Pygmy to him early on, had contracted leprosy. Singa was most known in the community as a skilled ritual doctor, but he was also a born comedian—as great as Charlie Chaplin, Anne thought. At the time, she was torn between admiration for Singa and fear of his leprosy. No matter how many times she was assured that leprosy was the hardest disease in the world to catch, she was still afraid to have Singa near her or to let him touch anything. She also wondered whether she needed to separate him from the hotel guests. Singa resented the idea of being excluded, because he thrived on entertaining tourists. The first time Anne asked him to remain in the background, he retaliated by sending all the men and most of the women off hunting. Anne thought things over, tried to understand more about the disease, and decided to ask him to sing and dance with the people who remained. He was pleased, and she felt better.

After the experience with Singa, Anne knew that with the large number of lepers coming, it was important to build a separate leper colony near Epulu for both villagers and Pygmies. She understood a lot more now about the disease and what was necessary to ensure everyone's well-being. They would make it as nice as possible, so that the patients would enjoy staying there and take pride in it, despite their separation from the rest of the community. And at least for the moment, Pat seemed delighted at Anne's idea to have a village built for them—as he used harsh methods of dealing with their grievances. Anne had ten houses built by the workmen to accommodate the people with leprosy, and despite still recovering from her viper bite, she oversaw the work not far from Camp Putnam.

I interviewed the great leprologist, Dr. Michel Lechat (1927–2014), who served as the primary source for Graham Greene's novel *A Burnt-Out Case* (1960). Greene had visited Lechat in Yonda, his leprosarium in what was then the Equateur Province of the Belgian Congo. Yonda was the prototype for the modern care of leprosy patients, where there was no segregation of the thousand patients who lived there and whom Lechat and others treated. They came and went, had families, and went to school. Lechat recognized that leprosy was not very contagious: no more than ten percent would have been infectious out of roughly one hundred thousand patients in the Congo.[12] Although Anne's philosophy about the leprosarium that she was building was similar to Dr. Lechat's, she probably did not know about his work. Perhaps she had heard that when Albert Schweitzer won the Nobel Peace Prize in 1952, he used his prize money to build a leprosy colony near his hospital in Lambaréné, now part of Gabon. For his part, Lechat told me that while he had never met Pat, he had heard about him and knew of Epulu.

Late in the summer of 1952, Monroe Stearns, who was editor at Prentice Hall, a distinguished trade and educational publishing house in New York, wrote a letter to Anne. Stearns was also an art historian, and he had seen one of her paintings of Monhegan Island hanging at a friend's house, read some of her letters shown to him by her family, in which she described life at Camp Putnam, and wanted to hear more about her story: "I should be very interested in having you write a book for Prentice Hall, Inc. about your experiences in the Congo. . . . It seems to me that this would make a most interesting volume which would be likely to have a considerable sale in this country. If it could be illustrated with drawings or paintings by you and also perhaps with photographs, it would be a most handsome book."[13]

Stearns admired both Anne's painting and her writing and believed that her unique experiences could attract a broad readership in the United States. Anne replied somewhat defensively: "Some people would say that my painting had bad spelling and grammar. In writing there is no doubt that my spelling and grammar are fantastically 'incorrect.'" Pat often said that Anne should compile her letters and send them to a publisher. With his typically outrageous sense of humor, he suggested that she should leave all the mistakes. Anne recalled later Pat saying, "'Anne, your weekly letters are gems. . . . But part of the fun is that ineffable misspelling and absence of grammar. Be sure . . . if you have them retyped that no corrections be made.'"[14] Anne didn't agree.

She had already attempted to write her story, in the short-lived collaboration with her friend Helen Gould during her trip to New York in 1950. After the failure of that experiment, she thought that working with a professional writer would be a better strategy. Since she was still in Africa, the family could provide the writer with her weekly letters, and she could send supplementary material to fill in any gaps. She wanted to include some of the sketches she had already done, although she wasn't too keen on adding photographs—worried most probably about stereotypical images of Pygmies and Africans that had been distributed for decades.[15] In the end, with the help of her family, she would choose a high-profile writer, Allan Keller—a columnist for the *New York World-Telegram and Sun* and faculty member at the Graduate School of Journalism at Columbia University—to ghostwrite her memoir.

Anne felt a surge of energy as she thought about the prospect of a book. Something to look forward to, another way to make sense of the confusion of this life, as her correspondence home had done. She set about gathering the copies of her letters, diligently copied with carbon paper (memorializing for herself what was happening in real time), and typed out the parts about the Pygmies that seemed to be of most interest to her.

Dementia?

Anne could not bring herself to write home about the events that followed until long after they happened. During the fall, Pat's psychic state suddenly took a turn for the worse. Pat wrote to Anne:

> I do not think you realize yet that there is room in these here woods for only one pair of pants and only one kiku ngufu, and those are my pants and my head.
>
> No doubt my verbal messages are ingeniously devisive [*sic*] perhaps intentionally to keep matters boiling between us in a way amusing for the public. . . .
>
> Your [affectionate] husband, PTLP[16]

To Anne, Pat seemed hardly human anymore. She understood now that she was way out of her depth.

Anne thought she had proved to herself that she disliked running things. What she really did not like was when things went out of control. She had no desire to be a big shot. More introspectively, she knew that she didn't like being privileged when she couldn't share. That was the big difference between her and Pat: he liked direct power, to be the boss, to live as an African in African terms and yet enjoy the privilege of a white man in Africa. The struggle between his different sides had given way to a grasp for absolute power in the despair of his illness, but the two sides had battled each other for most of his life. Power over blacks was gained and wielded easily by the colonial whites in Africa, and the colonial structures themselves were very hierarchical. In a way, how could he not repeat the colonial patterns for white men in Africa? It was a dilemma he couldn't himself solve, and he wasn't alone in that. But as an American, Pat lived with ambivalence and paradox and his own agency in the world he had created. He said he hated absolute leaders like chiefs and emirs (despite his early interest in Hitler and Napoleon); he would have nothing to do with them. Yet he loved making everything run according to his rules, and this grew more pronounced with his declining mental state.

Anne had to face it: the situation had turned into a horrific nightmare. Pat had a throne built from which to look down on people. He ordered the boys to construct a maze for both Pygmies and villagers to demonstrate how they would literally stoop to his will.[17] On one occasion, people had to wend their way through the maze carrying red-hot coals.[18] Herbert was right: Epulu had become the heart of darkness. Pat had been furious when visitors called him the "King of the Pygmies," but now he was acting the part. Almost as disturbing as his physical diminishment and mental derangement was his continuing power over all of them—Anne, the boys, the Pygmies. They all somehow complied with whatever he asked. The day Pat had Anne's chair raised so that it was almost on a level with his, she wanted to resist her role as accomplice but didn't know how to dissociate herself from him. She tried to understand what he was doing and why.

Call it what you will—madness, dementia, or megalomania—Pat's behavior was destroying his long-standing and extraordinary relationship with everyone in the Epulu community. Destroying in a short time what it had taken many years to establish. Did any of them realize how far he had overstepped the boundaries he had aspired to for treating everyone equally? Yes and no, because Pat always lived at the edge of conventions and norms anyway. Here he was transgressing the very terms of a life that he himself had established.

Mostly, Pat did not appear in public and kept to himself. The boys gave him constant updates on what was going on in the village. They also reported to Anne on Pat's condition and let her know about his particularly damning comment about her: "She's not a woman anymore, she's a man." That Jean de Medina (the man who ran the nearby government animal station) thought so, too, reinforced the stereotype of a white woman's restricted role in the Congo.

Anne's dilemma was that she had to do what Pat could no longer do. At times, she had even come to enjoy solving problems, but to her, defining which jobs were "feminine" and which were "masculine" made little sense. Anne simply knew that she had to act.

Every day, she debated with herself about whether to stay and take it or call it quits and leave. She would talk to herself: *All right, Pat is very sick and in his sickness does not want me to run things. All right, I'll let things go and go to*

New York for a few months and take a much-needed vacation and whatever happens happens. She hadn't been sure where to set her red line. She was fortunate that the people at Epulu were remarkably loyal, and surprisingly few had left. In any case, she herself had planned to go back to New York for a visit in the spring. Shortly after Pat made people go through the maze, she abruptly decided to make plans to leave in December. She needed to get away for a while.

Anne informed Pat that she was going to New York and would come back with the energy to withstand whatever awaited them. She thought about how she would return with a tape recorder to get Pat to record his knowledge, as it might give them a project together. She would write her book about the good days at Epulu, about the magical world that she still hoped to salvage for all of them. That world had only existed with all of them together. And it seemed to be gone.

Before her departure, Pat dictated two letters, the first to his medical superior, Dr. Legrand:

> Since "Hope springs eternal in the human breast" I hope you will be able to have my contract suspended for "raison de santé" rather than terminated for "raison de santé." . . .
>
> I think that my convalescence if by some miracle it should occur at all, will be accelerated by [Anne's] absence. I put her in the same category as alcohol and nicotine things I should hate to be without. She is kind [to] disappear and I wish alcohol and nicotine would do the same. Anne is kind enough to write this for me so it is English.

The other letter was to Dr. Louis Van den Berghe, the director of IRSAC, the research institute for Central Africa, which had long collaborated with Camp Putnam:

> I lost out, Anne and I went on squabbling about the reorganization. She often directed toward me hysterical attacks which shocked my proper New England tastes, and I sometimes got blue in the face and exploded, at great expense to my slight remainder of energy. Of course there were minor irritations too.
>
> Of course, too, some people would say "Post hoc sed non propter hoc" [after all but not because of] anyway I found myself flat on my back with a blood pressure of about zero. . . . I am putting the hotel and animal business "en veilleuse" [on hold]. Anyone less optimistic than myself would say I was putting them out for good.[19]

CHAPTER SIX

Life Is Difficult (1953)

Contemplating the future on the plane ride back to Epulu from New York in March 1953, Anne reread letters that had been received from Pat. The first one was to Pat's aunt Elsie, Miss Elizabeth Putnam, his father's sister, who had been a supporter and dear friend of Anne's, dated December 1952. From the hospital in Irumu, Pat had written that—philosophical discussions aside—he was contemplating bringing "his life to an end," now that his body was almost completely useless. He had wanted to express his love to his aunt and requested that she notify others:

> I don't know at all what may give me the little shove needed to actually make me do it, rather than merely think about doing it, for hours at night
> You know how I have loved to argue in all my days gone by. But now I am too tired to argue whether or not it is cowardly, "wrong," or cruel to others to do this deed. Certainly I remain as selfish and as stubbornly impervious to good advice of well-wishers as I have always been.
> The physical cause of these suicidal feelings, which I have never had before except for a few months after Mary died, may be simply lack of oxygen in the brain cells, as in all the other cells of my now nearly useless body.

Anne knew that he was tormented, but she didn't think it was over yet. She had written him often from New York; he had written her back only twice, once to prepare her for a "memorandum of sad news, and sad decisions, and certain recriminations against" Anne, with copies to his father, his father's wife, Margo, his aunt Elsie, and Anne:

> Here below I try to make clear the most weighty of what I believe to be my reasons for not wanting [Anne] to rejoin me, at least at the present moment.
> 1. We continue to love each other very much. Why we do, I cannot guess, but I know it to be a fact.
> 2. I have always been, psychically, abnormally aberrant from the arbitrary norm. I have had many characteristics making me unpleasing to other people,

as well as other ones, which make me pleasing to other people. My present stage of chronic somatic disease tended strongly to arrest all manifestations of the pleasing side of my character, and to accentuate the manifestations of the unpleasing side of my character.

3. Anne, in her own different direction, is psychically, abnormally aberrant from the norm. For about a year, the sum total of my actions toward her have been so distressing to her, that they have irritated her to the point of acting in ways very distressing to me.

4. As a result, our contact with each other during this last year has been unusually very unpleasant.

5. An aggravating factor of this I believe to be caused by the fact that for about two years, my ever-increasing short-windedness has made it impossible for me to dare to indulge in sexual intercourse with her, in spite of the desire to do so being still strong in me and the potency of my sexual organ only slightly, if at all, impaired. So, among the important things we enjoyed doing together, this one, at least, no longer is feasible.

6. Although this period in Irumu Hospital of mental and physical rest, with nothing irritating to me, has to some extent attenuated my mental derangement, I fear that being with Anne at the Epulu, which was in the first years on the whole so pleasant to both of us, would now result in even more mutual unpleasantness than what we suffered during our last year there together. . . . Now, as to the possibility of it ever again becoming wise for her sake as well as for mine, for us to rejoin each other at the Epulu: if my somatic illness should become perceptibly diminished I think it would be a risk for us to rejoin each other at the Epulu.[1]

But Anne couldn't stay away. Pat had been in the hospital in Irumu since December, and neither Agaranga, the head man at Camp Putnam, nor the others had been paid. Sale, another villager who worked at Camp Putnam, had written to Anne as soon as Pat went to the hospital, explaining that she had to get back—and soon: "Mr. Putnam is not here with us at the Epulu; he has gone to the hospital in Irumu. Now we find ourselves 'orphans' in the real sense of the word."[2] In his feelings of abandonment, Sale expressed the sense of family that existed between Bantu, whites, and Pygmies—not your usual colonial separations. Anne wondered how her babies were doing.

Pat needed Anne, even though he didn't want her back yet. The workers needed her. She was not sure how much the Pygmies needed anyone outside-but themselves, but Anne needed them and Epulu.

So there she was—back after three months in New York, having landed in Irumu. To her surprise, their young friend Skye Jones came to meet her at the airport. She learned that he had been in Irumu for two weeks since mid-March and described the return after his last visit, a year before. In Northern Rhodesia, he had run into Frank Livingstone, who tried to visit Pat in the late fall of 1952 (Livingstone was a recent Harvard graduate who would later go on to become a distinguished professor of physical anthropology at the University of Michigan). Pat wouldn't see Livingstone. So Skye decided to go see for himself. He had found Epulu deserted, everything overgrown, and Pat's hut "crumbling," though his sign still stood: "Epulu Yacht Club Members Only." This club (or what Pat had earlier called Camp Stanleyville) was only half a joke, since for the past year, Pat had only received people by appointment—including Anne.

Skye had taken right off for Irumu to find Pat, and Pat had greeted him like a long-lost friend; they talked and talked. Pat had left the hospital three weeks before and moved out, against medical orders, to a government rest house with the help of a lovely young nurse. He couldn't be kept down. At one point during his stay in the hospital, Pat had convinced a visitor that he was well enough to be driven to the airport. Once there, he had walked over to a twin-engine passenger plane parked on the tarmac, climbed up into the plane as though he owned it, and told the startled pilot to give him oxygen. He sat in the pilot's seat pulling oxygen in through a mask for a few minutes. Then, abruptly, he climbed out and ordered the visitor to take him back to the hospital. That day, Pat walked more than he had in almost three years.

Skye informed Anne that Pat seemed in better health. Skye had been sleeping on the floor near Pat, helping with all kinds of chores. Despite the evident physical and mental changes, Pat seemed to Skye "well enough to cause trouble" and in pretty good humor.

But when Anne walked into the rest house, Pat's mood darkened from what had been described. Skye left them alone together.

"Why have you come back when I asked you to stay away longer?"

"I want to be with you."

"I don't need you."

"Yes, you do."

"I am doing just fine. Leave me alone."

Anne thought he put up a good front, not wanting anyone to see his pain, and his best defense against pity seemed to be gruff rejection. For Anne, walking into his den felt like ripping off a bandage from an as-yet-unhealed wound. Nevertheless, she talked about New York, his family, hers, and gave him the blanket she had brought back for him; he softened and smiled, put it around himself, and asked a few questions. They talked about Camp Putnam. Long silences. Anne noticed that his body was much thinner than before she had left. When Skye returned, nothing Anne could do or say was right. Pat would ask a question, and if she hesitated for a second to answer, he would shout, "Get on with it, God damn it." When she spoke too softly, he forbade her to speak for the rest of the evening. She continued to speak, though. It was one thing to think about how much he had been through, another to cope with the mind shifts.

Skye reasoned that—whatever its source—Pat's illness accounted for how difficult he had become. Perhaps Pat's particularly strong reactions to Anne were because she challenged him in a way nobody else did and reminded him of his incapacities. Skye thought this was understandable, given Pat's condition. Anne couldn't see it that way. She had already started her own campaign to figure out what was wrong with Pat physically. She wrote to his relative, Dr. George Sturgis, who responded that during the incubation or "prodromal" period of serum hepatitis, changes in the liver might set off the kind of psychic disturbance Pat had gone through. If so, there shouldn't be any recurrences. Anne hoped he was right, though she was not optimistic.

Upon her return, Anne found Epulu in a sad state. Supplies were almost gone, except for meat brought in by the Pygmies and beans and lettuce from the garden that Agaranga had watered while Anne was away. She managed to get some peanut oil. But there were no eggs (a disease had gotten the chickens), and for the moment, there was no way to get coffee or canned goods, since the Mambasa traders were away.

Anne noted changes that appeared to be in the offing, and none appeared too welcome. Jean de Medina—whom Pat had gotten to know during the war when he was working on a rubber plantation at Banalia—had plans to develop an animal station across the road. De Medina's mother was a Mubua from up the road at Akati, and his father was Portuguese. The family had been ennobled by Leopold II. He had been educated in Portugal, and because his father had recognized him, he was considered white despite his dark skin. He undoubtedly had been a great hunter at one time, and now he intended to capture okapi, which had once been the main attraction of the Camp Putnam zoo. De Medina spoke as if the station were only to be temporary; he would be moving out by the end of June. However, Anne believed that he was placating Pat, who could no longer manage animals (or people, for that matter). Anne thought de Medina was there to stay.

Anne invited him over to dinner to smooth things over. L. Kempinaire, the administrator for Epulu Territory, came by and joined in. The territorial division gave tight control to the colonial government. Kempinaire's policemen had recently raided the village, checking who had permission to be there and who didn't; they took seven people away. Kempinaire had matters to discuss with Pat and Anne as well—namely, that Pat was five years in arrears on rent. Kempinaire stressed that the government had been very kind; almost anyone else would have evicted them, because land values had gone up. He suggested that Pat write and ask if they could get some kind of stay or exemption, given new laws for large hotels. Pat wondered if it made any sense to fix Camp Putnam up if he only had a short time left to live. Anne said that whatever happened, she would like to run it for a while. If she didn't want to live there by herself after a time, the boys could continue running it, as they had done earlier. Anne liked to think that it was for Pat that she was offering to continue. It was, partially. But it was also for her; she could not imagine letting go of Epulu. She hoped that Pat, seeing how much she cared, would feel reassured and become more positive. The two of them had a rather tender moment exchanging thoughts. Pat understood her gesture: "I want you and the boys to continue to run the hotel when I'm gone and to take in the people who come for lunch and drinks. The rest of the time, I want you to paint and write." Welcome words on an otherwise rough sea!

Anne set to planting the seeds she had brought back from the States. She wanted to try to grow okra and other vegetables to cut down on the expenses for food, adding in a few zinnias with a touch of scarlet.

However, Anne knew that Pat wouldn't write a letter to the government as Kempinaire advised. He tended to concentrate on only one thing at a time, and he had once again become occupied with the medical dispensary. The deadline of May 10 set by the government for payment of back rent meant nothing to him. Not even the threat of being deported from the Belgian Congo could get him to hurry. Anne thought that she had enough to pay half of the back rent from the advance she had received for her book while in New York.

The local storekeepers keep dropping in to visit, reminding them of their debts.

Catching Up

Hearing women singing in the village, Anne went up to watch them dance. She sat in front of Agaranga's house by the fire, and Abazinga (the man who took care of Camp Putnam's animals) came and joined them. They talked about different things, and in due course, the conversation turned to the children. Anne was concerned about William J. Kokoyou's infantile paralysis. Abazinga said that Mrs. André (the wife of Anne's cook, André) had taken good care of him while Anne was away (and Grandma helped, too, apparently). Abazinga scarified W.J. weekly and combined the stem of a dandelion-like flower with goat manure to put in his wound. Mrs. André administered the pit treatment. She showed Anne the five holes she had dug. While W.J. was in the pit, she said, she kept washing him with hot water, and he ate and drank and played in the dirt. This went on for a month. At first, she said, he cried. But he soon got used to it, and everyone stopped by and played with him, so that he thought it was a game. This wouldn't have been Anne's first choice for treatment. W.J. was, in fact, now starting to walk with a stick and could go about ten to fifteen steps before sitting down. He could crawl anywhere, and he had taught himself to climb trees. He was clever and observant, learning to read the forest, and could point out the smallest ant or bud.

Anne also learned that Andonata (who had a complex relationship with his wife, Basalinda, mother of Kenge), who before she left for the States had been strong and healthy, had contracted TB and become a shadow of himself. Anne realized that she had to make time for him no matter how busy she was, or it would be too late. The boys moved him into the peanut storeroom and transferred baskets filled with peanuts over to another room. Pat put him on a diet of rice, plantains, and oil, and Anne saw to it that he got soup, sugar, and tea daily.

Andonata's son Kenge at first wanted to take his father back to die in the Pygmy village. But his Bantu patron, Ibrahemu, and Pat wanted to let him die in peace where he was. Andonata was lying on a bed, dressed in a khaki nightgown provided by the government, instead of on the floor by the fire, as was his custom. Anne called for his family and then went home. When she came back later that evening, she was surprised to see Andonata busy chewing away on a *ndizi* plantain, still conscious of everyone.

The next morning, however, Anne woke up to wailing; Andonata had died during the night. He would have to be buried at the Epulu cemetery on the other side of the small stream called the Nepuse, in the forest not far from the hotel, because de Medina had built his okapi camp on the burial ground. Nothing felt good about this displacement. Andonata's brother arrived on the scene, waving his hands and arms, demanding that Andonata be taken across to another area of Epulu. Kenge stood in the doorway and said, "Absolutely not." This was his father's earth, and this was where he was going to be buried. Anne backed Kenge, who convinced his uncle that since Andonata had lived there for at least fifteen years, this was where he belonged.

Reorganization?

In May, Pat gave Anne permission to clean and fix up the hotel to try to get it running again. He had been in such a rare good humor that he even said she could repair a mud wall that had fallen down from a year's neglect. Anne went right to it, accepted reservations for a group of tourists, and started on an inventory and repairs.

De Medina arrived with a bucket full of ice and a bottle of cold champagne for Pat. His assistant brought out a bottle of whiskey for the rest of them. The boys got glasses and poured drinks while Anne took the champagne to Pat. He was examining a patient, so she returned later with de Medina and his assistant. Once inside Pat's room, Anne realized that a bottle of formalin, a formaldehyde solution used as an antiseptic, had broken. It reeked. Her eyes smarted as she entered the room; it caught the throat. Pat would hear nothing of moving to another room. He scribbled a note for de Medina to come in. They made space for everyone, sat around scrunched like sardines, eyes watering, and drank the champagne, then went back to work. An example of how nothing seemed odd anymore.

The next day was market day and payday, always a tough double whammy for Anne. Everybody chattered while she calculated amounts in Astrid cigarettes and palm oil, recognized units of value in the area. There was almost nowhere to spend money except at the *duka* shop (whose owner was called, as all shopkeepers were, Dukandar) at the corner turnoff to Camp Putnam. For that reason, most of the pay was in the form of goods. By the end of payday, Anne's head would often be aching. She tried to run everything Pygmy-style, by consensus, without exercising arbitrary authority. But there were times when she felt she had to arbitrate.

This was one of those days. There was a shortage of plantains. André the cook came to tell Anne that the women of the village were starting to buy up all the plantains before the drumroll sounded to signal the official opening of the market. Anne knew that this meant the Pygmy women, who had free time, had come and bought up the plantains before the workmen were paid and had a chance to get theirs. She saw several Pygmy women dashing off with batches of plantains, including the wife of one of the workmen, Émile. Anne asked Sindanu, her gardener, to retrieve the batch. In what seemed like only seconds, he reappeared with his face bleeding and said he intended to quit working at the market forever. Anne sent him over to the dispensary to be treated and tried to figure out what had happened. Émile's wife, it seems, had gone into a frenzy at the thought of having her plantains confiscated and had really given it to Sindanu. He was a strong Pygmy, but she had knocked out one of his teeth. Émile and Anne looked for her, but she was nowhere to be found; Anne was as upset as Émile.

In the middle of this confusion, an American missionary from Wamba arrived. She asked permission to spend a couple of days at the camp and save the boys' souls. Anne wasn't cordial; it seemed like the last straw. The missionary said she wouldn't be any trouble, that she was going to stay at Agaranga's house. Anne said she was welcome and to please have lunch with them, but at that moment, they couldn't spare anyone, particularly Agaranga. The missionary said that was all right, not to worry about her, she could quite understand that Anne needed Agaranga. But Anne could feel Agaranga's anger boiling up at her. She knew it was an important moment in his life, and he wanted to be a good host. Anne would have been glad to do anything to help any other time, but she was trying to cope with the market and finish up preparations for guests. Agaranga pushed back, asking if she couldn't spare a different workman. That was it. Anne blew her top. Lunch with the missionary hadn't been ready until two p.m. None of the leaks that one of the workmen, Kopa Kopa, was supposed to have patched had been patched—they were still all wide open—and there were forty kilos of sugar to attend to with very few dry spaces anywhere. Anne was so tired and frustrated that she dumped her spleen on Kopa Kopa—she also thought he deserved it. Because of the leaks he hadn't repaired, he'd have to keep the sugar in a safe place in his house and be responsible for it. It was a mean trick; he loved sugar, and for him to have it around without being able to eat it would require exceptional self-discipline. But Kopa Kopa got his revenge. Anytime they needed sugar later on, it became one hell of a struggle to get even a single grain from him. If Anne was not around and anyone asked him for sugar, he said, "Oh, no, Madam said I was responsible." He even refused when Pat asked for some.

When, in Camp Putnam style, a jury was called to decide the dispute about the plantains between Sindanu, Anne, and Émile's wife, the wife was said to have bought her plantains right *after* the drumroll. Anne didn't believe that was the way it happened, and much to her amazement, the jury charged her a greater fine. That burned Anne up. Ever since she had been home, people had been complaining that the market had fallen to pieces and the BaBira hadn't been bringing in enough plantains. Anne had to get the market going again.

Then several people—who seemed to feel badly about the outcome—came to Anne. She apparently hadn't understood the verdict; Émile's wife was really supposed to pay fifty francs, and Anne was to pay twenty-five. Anne retorted that as far as figures went in KiNgwana, she had by then been offered plenty of opportunity to learn how to count and had understood perfectly well. It had been years since she had misunderstood the price of a debt she owed.

Anne swore that she wouldn't have anything further to do with the market—not because she shouldn't have sent Sindanu off to get the plantains but because she literally couldn't afford to be involved. In retrospect, what none of them could measure at the time was how Anne's growing sense of responsibility, passed to her from Pat, was changing the relationships among all the people in Epulu. Their complaints to Anne about the disarray of the market had led her to feel that it was her duty to help set things right. Her intervention in the plantain drama revealed Anne's arbitrary rule for the market—like the beginning of an event at an American county fair—which was to start at a precise moment. Anne's actions had no basis within any one of the traditions of peoples at Epulu, even though it seemed like a good idea at the time. The Pygmies and the villagers had their relationships, based on exchange in a hierarchy, but no history of mediation existed, outside of Pat's authority, among all the different groups soldered together at Epulu. They were like an unwieldy large family that was not simply genetic, racial, or contractual, and they had had to invent and negotiate their traditions as a group.

The violence that had resulted on that market day came as much from the imposition of rules as it did from their infringement. Without realizing it, Anne had begun to behave like the "colons" that she had always criticized. In that sense, her fault was indeed the greater one, not because she enforced the rule but because she created it. Pat had run things with an iron fist when he was in charge, as everybody had expected him to; he tried to teach Anne to do the same. However, Anne attempted to run things differently—according to her own sense of fairness. She didn't like the idea of being boss and wanted to decide problems by consensus, Pygmy-style, yet her own sense of authority was not clear to her. What Anne wasn't able to see in that moment was that the others could not possibly be expected to understand what she herself could not communicate. She needed to learn to negotiate to keep some order and sometimes found that she had to use her privilege of power, colonialist-style. This created a disturbance. She knew that everyone respected her and wanted life to be harmonious. Anne certainly wanted that, too. The question was, with goodwill on all sides, how could things just fall apart as they had in this instance? Anne didn't have time to reflect on that question at the moment. But she was coming to realize concretely how—within their little world—questions of authority and economics threatened them all.

The days were pretty hectic by now. There were lunches with the IRSAC people, the Pygmies singing and giving demonstrations. Most of the meals and entertainment had gone without a hitch, and life seemed to have a goal: the reorganization of the hotel. Anne felt good about having met the deadline and about Camp Putnam humming with activity.

Two men arrived in the first half of May from IRSAC, the Belgian research institution with several stations throughout the Congo and in the Ruanda-Urundi Protectorate. Frank Lambrecht had come to do entomological research, looking at the bloodsucking insects (particularly the *Aedes* mosquitoes) that might transmit "jungle yellow fever" in monkeys of the *Cercocebus-Colobus* group. They were found between Epulu and the Andudu region, about sixty miles away. Marcel Chardome was with him to study chimp parasites in the Andudu. He was interested in the banana groves where the mosquito larvae suggested a sequence in transmitting yellow fever from monkeys to humans. They were also searching for monkeys, dead and alive, and had found the malaria parasite in some of the dead monkeys. Pat managed a brief visit with them. Lambrecht also wanted to collect various insects such as the tsetse in the trees at different levels in the forest. Anne helped organize two groups of Pygmy men to go out with him—one for the insects, the other for trapping animals.[3]

Pat's old friend James Chapin, the celebrated ornithologist who had co-led the Congo expedition with Herbert Lang from 1909 to 1915, arrived on his way out to spend two years at IRSAC. Pat had never had any sense of time, and even less so since he had become sick. He said he would see Chapin in fifteen minutes, but minutes stretched into hours before Pat finally agreed to receive him. Chapin was shocked more at the personality change, which was breaking everyone's heart, than even his physical appearance.

Perspectives on Life at Epulu

A letter came from Anne and Pat's young friend Colin Turnbull, who was heading to visit accompanied by his cousin Francis Chapman from Toronto. His first visit on a motorcycle in 1951 had been such a happy time for them all. Looking forward to his return, he expressed his utopian vision of Epulu: "I think you have the most wonderful place and lead the most nearly perfect existence I have ever come across." If only he understood what it was really like . . .

The article in *True: The Man's Magazine* about Camp Putnam, and mostly about Pat, arrived. *True* was a men's adventure magazine; in the same issue, there was another article on "How to Lasso a Shark." Inaccuracies in the article ranged from getting Pat's name wrong—it was not Patrick *Russell* Lowell Putnam but Patrick *Tracy* Lowell Putnam, and Pat cared about getting it right—to their adoption of a baby Pygmy *girl*. The biographical write-up focused on Pat's transformation from a "rich young bachelor" to a dedicated health worker giving his life to save the lives of Africans under almost impossible conditions in the Ituri Forest. It recounted the history of Pat's arrival in Africa and his work on the rubber plantations during World War II for the Congo—which had remained loyal to the free government of Belgium in London—without mention of the atrocities sustained on these plantations around the turn of the century. Few people in the Congo could forget that history. But that is not what people in North America wanted to read about in the 1950s. They wanted adventure—wild animal hunts and the growth of a frontier. The article only granted a few scant sentences acknowledging Anne as an artist but moved quickly to how they were married in New York (wrong) and how Anne ran the hotel to free Pat's time for his medical work (really?). Did it bother her that this was the story of a hero and his helpful, if talented, little wife? Yes, it did—all of it—but she didn't say anything.

Pat didn't even want to see the article. He had given up reading: first the medical journals went, then the magazines (the *New Yorker*, *Time*, and the *New Statesman*), finally even the detective stories he used to read, signing each as he finished it, "PTLP has read."

Skye was preparing to leave with Frank Lambrecht. He wanted to say goodbye to Pat and went down to Camp Stanleyville unannounced. Mada, Pat's African wife, was sitting in the room with Pat when Skye walked in. Pat barked at him to get out. Skye turned around and walked back to camp; the next morning, on June 20, he left Epulu, never to see Pat again.

With hindsight, Anne could see that Camp Putnam was not and never would be a viable business. If they had had the capital to invest in accommodations approximating Western standards, they might have been able to make a go of it. But neither Pat nor Anne had wanted those things; they resisted the kinds of improvements that might have made it a financial success.

The three rondavels were pleasant, if sparse, with whitewashed walls, but they could only accommodate about six people, maximum. They still had no refrigeration and limited supplies of rice, coffee, and other staples. Anne loved Epulu as it was—a kind of romantic dream—and didn't want anybody there who didn't feel the same. But the dream had turned into a nightmare several times over, and it was about to happen again.

The Grim Days Return: Opioids

In early July, Pat kept a setting hen in his room, and it didn't take long for chicken lice to invade. For two days, the boys and Anne disinfected everything, from sheets to towels to mats, a process that included putting furniture and bedding out in the sun, scratching themselves every minute. It was as though the mind took over from the body—an itch here, then there, then everywhere. Pat replaced the hen with a hyrax and her young one, neither of which seemed to have any bugs. This was about par for the course; as Pat declined mentally, so did his sense of hygiene. Pat's ups and downs continued, becoming more aggravated throughout the month. Anne looked for signs of another breakdown. If only there had been something she could have done to help him. The worst part of it was accepting that he could never get well.

By the middle of July, Pat was enacting elaborate sickbed scenes; he'd holler for hot-water bags as though he were about to pass out. With closed eyes, he'd shout, "Who's there?" Pat had always been dramatic—no, he had always been extraordinarily charismatic. It was not hard to understand why the Pygmies and the boys had followed him out to this isolated spot on the Epulu River. After all, Anne had done so, too. She remembered how taken she had been with his magnetic blue eyes when she met him. But now he looked like a sick person, with his long hands and spindly arms. Oh, the histrionics! He ordered someone to act as clerk and take down every word as though it were a courtroom. If he thought Anne was not paying enough attention during his scene, he got rotten angry (but then again, when didn't he get angry these days?). She tried to remain unfazed. But on one of these occasions, Anne blew up at him, a luxury she could ill afford; no matter how mad she got, it was an error to answer back. Yet to remain a dummy was almost unbearable, and sometimes her emotions just *took off like a pack of wild horses stampeding.* She felt guilty for *blowing like a geyser* (and to cool down, she often poured a bucket of cold water over her own head). Like everyone at Epulu, she still thought of Pat as the leader there.

Pat worsened as the summer wore on, not only refusing to see Anne but sabotaging functional parts of Epulu—holding up the mail, for example. He was no longer interested in anything that was going on. He didn't read the mail but instead would just toss it aside, and in due course, it would get lost. Writing letters and receiving mail were among the few activities that had sustained Anne throughout her time there. Tauntingly, Pat offered to give back the typewriter that he had confiscated from her—but for outlandish fees. "Damn Skye for letting Pat know that I liked the typewriter," she noted in a *cahier.* She took to longhand.

Pat was so severely under the effects of morphine some days that he spoke like a person asleep. As his breathing became more difficult, he increased the dosage, and then to sleep, he took double doses of sleeping pills. Anne had come to the point where she thought it would be better if Pat simply died. She wished that he could just float off on an overdose rather than linger as he was, with the potential for another spell of madness. She felt guilty about this wish. But in constant dread of his condition worsening and with no hope that he could recover, she could not think otherwise. Yet there was no way that she could do anything; she couldn't order an overdose of morphine. Even if Pat had been close to her in those days, it wasn't her decision; it would have had to be his choice. Given his state, he could last for a few days, another month, or a year.

When visitors came through, Anne felt better. But when it came time for them to leave, she felt like crying out (whether she liked them or not): *Take me along! Don't leave me like this!* She restrained herself, however. How long she could go on, she didn't know. Spencer Chapman, a visitor from the Royal Geographical Society, sensed her despair when he stayed at the hotel for a few days. How right he was. She was very sorry to see him leave, needing the company of people who seemed connected to a life outside.

A bacteriologist from the Pasteur Institute in Paris turned up with another man from Yangambi to take blood tests of the Pygmies for research on infantile paralysis. And a Swiss doctor named Boris Adé, who had been through in April 1952, came out; he was being transferred from Wamba to Mambasa. He looked tough, with very black hair and a protruding jaw, and at first Anne didn't like him much. He had been sent on a special mission as *médecin de la colonie* in Mambasa to scout out a hospital location and study medical practices in the region. In his work, he had been treating white and black individuals, and in his spare time, he was taking physical measurements of Pygmies for his research on Pygmy dwarfism.

As time went on, Anne discovered that Adé and she had a lot in common—not only their connection to the Pygmies but also a keen interest in painting and African art. It initially seemed strange to dislike one of the few people who was interested in all of the same subjects as she was. But she grew to like him. He was sensitive and thoughtful, giving encouragement about the transcription she had undertaken of Pygmy legends into English, and especially in trying to get her back to painting. Adé's sense of culture and purpose helped set Anne on a path toward finding herself again, as she realized how lost she was feeling there without Pat's companionship. Adé often came out on weekends to help. He would examine Pat and then look at any of the other patients in need of treatment—people Pat could no longer treat or old people in the village too weak to come to the dispensary. While he was there, he worked on impressions of Pygmy teeth and took various other measurements for his research.

When the *agent sanitaire* from Mambasa, a Mr. Francine, came out to examine people, Pat insisted that this take place in his room—a room in which no one but Pat was normally allowed to work. Francine refused and moved examinations to the carpenter's shop. It was the first time anyone, young or old, had countered Pat's will. Anne hoped that Pat would realize how loyal everyone had been and how strange his own behavior had become. More likely, any resistance probably just reminded him of how very much of an invalid he was.

Camp Putnam Closed (Again)

By the time Pat finally brought the typewriter back to Anne, he had confiscated almost everything else, prohibiting visitors from having lamps, sheets, or even water. Anne realized that she could no longer run Camp Putnam, although she didn't like to admit it. The reorganization and revival had been short-lived. Pat had managed to destroy all the mattresses, sheets, blankets, towels, mosquito nets, cushions, and so on. Anne could not have received guests even if she had wanted to, except for close friends.

She wanted to get out, but she didn't think she would have been happy anyplace in the world knowing that she had walked off. The boys had all made it very clear that if Anne quit, they would, too. She was determined to try to stay it out. All she could do for Pat was see that the boys took care of him and that he got his wish to finish out his days at Epulu. Some of them had left already. Nobody could blame them. Anne also knew that those who remained had transferred their trust to her.

She felt much stronger than the year before, when Pat had experienced his first breakdown; she felt ready to face the situation. She also realized in early September that as far as she was concerned, her Pat had died more than a year ago, and this person had very little in common with him. Part of the tragedy was that at some level, he also realized it. Whether he actually continued to live for a year or more, Anne was in mourning.

Epulu Études

As was always the case when the Pygmies would return from away camps, Epulu suddenly came alive again with shouts of joy. They would string a vine from two trees and make a swing. A person would swing once, and then, as the swing returned, another Pygmy would run and somersault into the swing as the first one jumped off. It was as beautiful and exciting as any trapeze spectacle—the Flying Wallendas of the Ituri! The young and the old could do it alike—women, men, and children—and Anne could easily "waste" hours watching this game.

Anne took to doing what had always made her feel best: daily sketching. It was a good discipline and gave structure to daily life. She started off each day with a new subject, but if she happened to pass by any of the women fixing each other's hair, she had to sit down and sketch them right away. She called it the "beauty salon" (she would later do a number of paintings and watercolors from memory from the resulting sketches, and it was her favorite subject (see fig. 44).

At first, Anne had known the men much better than the women—both the village men and the Pygmies—and she had convinced herself she wasn't very interested in the women's domestic lives. In an early letter, she asserted:

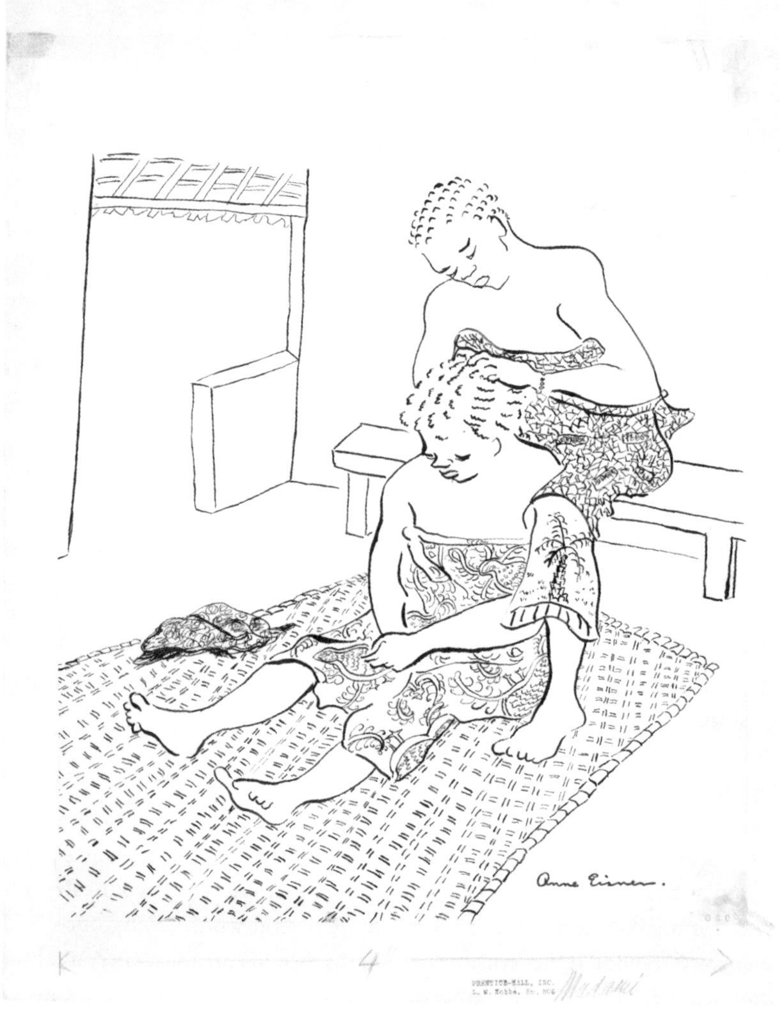

Fig. 44 Anne Eisner, *Beauty Salon*, 13 x 16 in., ink on paper, c. 1953. Later published in Anne Eisner Putnam, with Allan Keller, *Madami: My Eight Years of Adventure with the Congo Pigmies* (New York: Prentice-Hall, 1954), 157. McDonald collection.

> I think that Pygmies lead a right and most beautiful life, but I should hate to be one of their women. They work like hell all day long and their work is the hard work: building the houses, cutting the wood, getting the water, cooking the meals besides hunting all day. If I mention the women less, it's because I hardly got to know them. They spend their time in the background, working or sitting in front of their huts, and seldom, if ever, sit at the main fire with the men. They speak less KiNgwana and their constant chatter is KiBira.[4]....

But since Anne had become one of the mothers, what she most loved to draw were the women, the village women and Pygmies who took such lovely care of each other. Braiding little plaits for hours on end, together, was such a sweet activity. Anne talked less and took fewer notes about the women, but she sketched them more. She had been drawn to the women around the time William J. Kokoyou and the other babies were born. As her life and theirs intertwined, she expressed an increasing sense of community in her art. They were soon to become some of her most important subjects (see fig. 45a-b).

During the worst moments of the previous year, Anne had decided to do work directly from life at Epulu and then create abstracts from the sketches and paintings. It was a way for her way to think about issues concerning artists at home who had been part of the American Scene movement. *Should* they change their aesthetic sense? *Could* they transform their style of painting? The Abstract Expressionists were having a heyday in New York. In the forest, Anne didn't have other painters with whom to mull over these changes, or galleries to check out, and she had to make her own path. Until now.

Fig. 45a-b
a: Anne Eisner, drawing, 11 x 6 in., ink on paper, c. 1952–1953.
b: Anne Eisner, *Woman with Mortar and Pestle*, 12 x 12½ in., ink on paper. Both McDonald collection. Both later published in Anne Eisner Putnam, with Allan Keller, *Madami: My Eight Years of Adventure with the Congo Pigmies* (New York: Prentice-Hall, 1954), 256, 123.

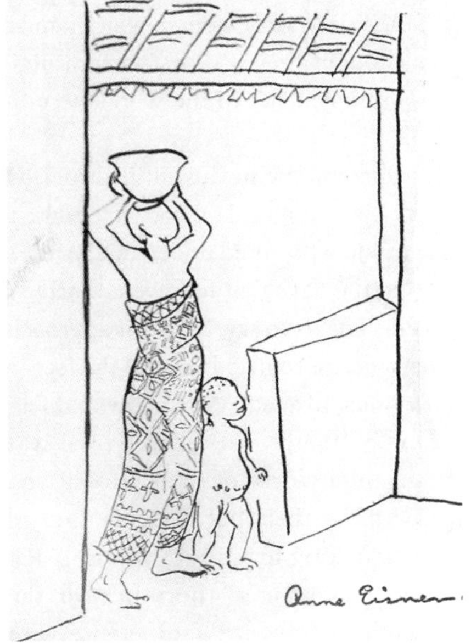

a

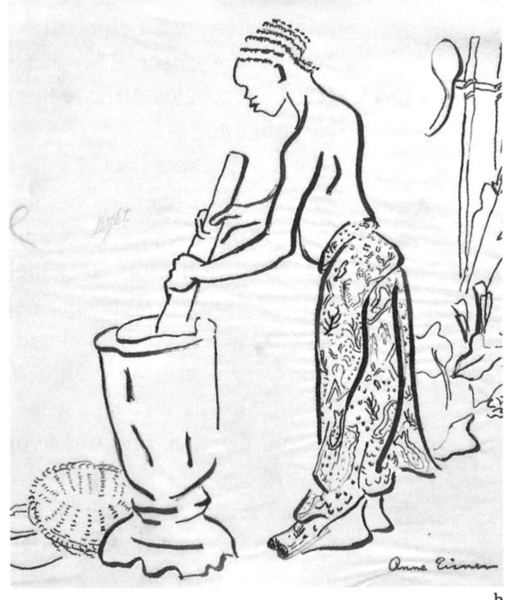

b

A Belgian Artist Arrives

On September 18, Adé drove out to Camp Putnam with a Belgian painter, Marthe Guillain, whom he had met on the crossing from Antwerp to Madadi. Marthe seemed strange to Anne at first. Tiny in size and wiry, she was "of a certain age," as the Europeans say—but what a powerhouse. She traveled all over with no fear, alone. True, almost everybody in Africa was hospitable at the time, and there seemed to be virtually no danger. Still, she was particularly independent. The Belgian government had awarded her a grant to come out to the Congo. In the 1920s, Marthe had worked as a Fauve and exhibited alongside contemporaries Fernand Léger, Chaim Soutine, Suzanne Valadon, Paul Signac, and others. Having moved through most of the avant-garde movements, from Fauvism to Cubism, she was involved with Expressionism by the 1950s. Totally dedicated as an artist, she took time to paint wherever she was and immediately transformed what she saw through form. Hers was the best art Anne had seen by a *blanc* in Africa, and the work she did at Epulu turned out to be some of her best.

Anne had seen an influx of Belgian artists, most of them also on grants, but they stayed only long enough to learn that the roads were bumpy and muddy or dusty and to get the idea that the black people lived in mud houses. They seemed to prefer spending their time in the big cities. Anne approved of scholarships but thought that these artists needed to spend more time trying to understand the context in which they found themselves. She felt the same way about some of the anthropologists who passed through and became instant "experts."

Marthe settled herself in, connecting with Anne and the people at Epulu immediately. What especially struck Anne was Marthe's outspoken manner and her enjoyment of provocation. She thought they had that in common. Marthe reminded Anne of her father—a scrapper out in the world, accomplishing things.

Adé suggested that Marthe keep Anne company in this difficult period and encourage her painting. She did both. Marthe stayed on and gave Anne a unique kind of support; she was there, a friend who could understand Anne's life. Marthe offered Anne a lifeline during the days that followed. Marthe's feelings about Pat were not as Anne's were. That is to say, Marthe's approach toward Pat was not logjammed between a desire to help him and the fear—and resentment—of his unpredictable moods. Instead, Marthe revered Pat, having already met him when she came by Epulu in 1950 when she was visiting her son, who was living in Yangambi (north of the Congo River, west of Stanleyville). She had spoken with Pat then, but it seems she had missed seeing Anne, whom she had been looking forward to meeting. Pat had described Marthe to Anne as "an old lady painter" (born in 1890, she was sixty), an "expressionist" (and he wondered about the difference with regard to "impressionist"). Now back at Epulu, Marthe visited Pat every day for tea, fascinated by his history in the Congo. Marthe, too, was a fascinating person; she had met her husband (Médard Maertens) on the front lines in World War I—she as a nurse, he as a wounded volunteer. At the beginning of World War II, after Hitler invaded Belgium, she had been imprisoned as a resister. Now, bringing her own experience to bear in this new, difficult context, Marthe confirmed Pat's desire to keep Anne away and could warn her when Pat was going out of bounds. Perhaps most important, Anne felt that Marthe cared for her from the moment they met, and she needed that badly.

Adé, Marthe, and Anne attended a wedding together at Dar es Salaam, a little place not far from Camp Putnam named after the great port on the east coast. It was a rare happy moment. September was traditionally the month of the marriage ceremonies, because at that moment of the year, food is readily available, with lots of fruits, nuts, and mushrooms to be had. Marthe planned to paint a triptych from the dances at the wedding. Anne took advantage of Adé's visit to use his typewriter and write up her notes about the wedding. These were BaNgwana Pygmies, different in their customs from the Mbuti Pygmies at Epulu because each group adopts the customs of its Bantu patrons. They spoke Arabic and kept up Islamic traditions; the bride wore a headscarf entirely covering her face. Anne couldn't help but think that with all the rigors and difficulties of life in this equatorial forest, Pygmies had been successful in maintaining the feelings that knit a family together; they married for love, and they wanted someone with whom to deal with daily problems they encountered in life.

During a trip with Marthe to Mambasa, Anne found out about a scandal that was brewing around Adé's research. Adé had been called out to Camp Putnam too late to save a woman; despite his working all night, she had died. Since no family member stepped forth or claimed the body, Adé had preserved the cadaver in formaldehyde, intending to send it back to Belgium for research; seven such bodies had been sent back without objection, and this was in his view a unique opportunity for science. He wrote to various anthropologists and officials in Belgium who reacted positively, but without warning, his medical superior in the Congo ordered him to bury the Pygmy and reassigned him to a forsaken outpost where research was virtually impossible. This professional slap in the face took him off guard and triggered an international scandal. The Swiss press called it a loss for science.

Adé had been studying the anatomical differences between racial dwarfism and dwarfism of a pathological character. This was close to Carlton Coon's work,[5] situating studies in physical anthropology along the Darwinian evolutionary line. There was a similar attitude between this kind of research, based on Darwinian theory, and the paternalism of most colonialists. If evolution is based on physical and social adaptation, and races predate species—as Coon theorized—then not only could one chart where different races were situated over the long term, but it also would somehow become the job of those who considered themselves more evolved to enlighten those considered to be less far along. In this sense, approaches such as Coon's attempted to use science to justify the best and the worst of colonialism in equating civilization with progress. The term *évolués,* referring to a certain class of educated blacks in the Congo, translated this attitude blatantly.

Anne's concern had to do with the sense that Adé was a good person, deeply interested in those around him. He understood the kind of complex pressures of life at Epulu, coping with Pat and the complications of Epulu. In the midst of the scandal, Anne wrote on his behalf, but the reactions to her letters brought her up short; they communicated a perspective that her view from Epulu didn't offer. She was in touch with the attaché of the Belgian Information Agency in New York, Jan Albert Goris (Joannes Alphonsius Albertus Goris), who had moved to New York during the Nazi occupation of Belgium in 1942 and lived the rest of his life there. Goris wrote back with great care and administrative acumen, explaining to Anne why she had not seen anything in the Belgian press about Adé. She still had much to learn about the scars left from the ugly history of the rubber plantations from the beginning of the century. Goris told her that in the not-too-distant past, there had been a problem concerning canned food. When American canned goods arrived on the shelves in Elisabethville with labels featuring the head of an American black man, a riot broke out; the image was interpreted as testimony to the canning and selling of blacks who had died at the hands of Belgians. The Belgian government wanted to avoid this kind of misunderstanding with the Adé affair. Why had Adé not taken an internal administrative route through IRSAC? Goris's attitude from a distance was that there should have been a middle road, allowing for the continuation of research while following regulations intended to maintain public order. It was startling for Anne to realize how little one sometimes understood of the context in which one found oneself.

Meanwhile, the problem was whether Sindanu and his wife were going to keep the dead woman's baby girl or whether she should go back to the as-yet-uninterested father. Anne thought, *We can deal with that; we have by now lots of experience with babies.*

Part of the excitement of life at Epulu had always been that one never knew what would happen from moment to moment: people dropping in, problems to solve, and so on. Anne thought she had learned to respond quickly, recalibrating her mental reflexes to adapt. But she could not really prepare for the way in which Pat's volatile ups and downs affected all of them.

As the fall of 1953 progressed, Anne's journal notes and letters became more fragmented. One moment, a visit to Pat would find him in better form. To Anne, he could still look quite magnificent, in his chair with red cushions behind his head and various eccentric still lifes in the room: flowers, dead birds, and rats smoking over the fire, assorted books, soap, and a chamber pot, and so on, lying around. While the artistic tradition of still lifes—with which Anne was very well acquainted, as she had practiced the genre often—gives a sense that death is close at hand, seeing Pat in a tranquil pose was for Anne reassuring for the moment. (See fig. 46.)

Another moment could follow swiftly, as when Marthe returned from a visit enraged. Pat had presented her with her bill for the week, charging an outrageous sum for a quarter of a cup of coffee, a piece of wood, and so on, and then had the cheek to ask to borrow one thousand francs from her. Or, for example, the day Anne got word that someone had sent plantains by mistake to Pat, who took all of them. With organization so completely out of control, the workmen would go hungry, and not for the first time.

Pat's most peculiar spectacle came the day he organized a safari parade through the village—his first time out in a very long time. At his best, Pat could be majestic and dramatic, showing off his kingdom and his Pygmies; his greatest accomplishment may have been that he was the first white man to win over the confidence of the Pygmies in the days when they were afraid of white men. This day's extravaganza put everyone in high spirits, because Pat hadn't been out since his breakdown almost a year and half ago. Helena led off, wearing a blue cloth. She was the young girl and sickly orphan staying in Pat's room, where he tended to her and she to him. Helena pulled Katalina the chimp in tow. Next in line was Abazinga, who walked with Katchelewa. Then came Pat, feebly officiating from his *tipoy* decked with

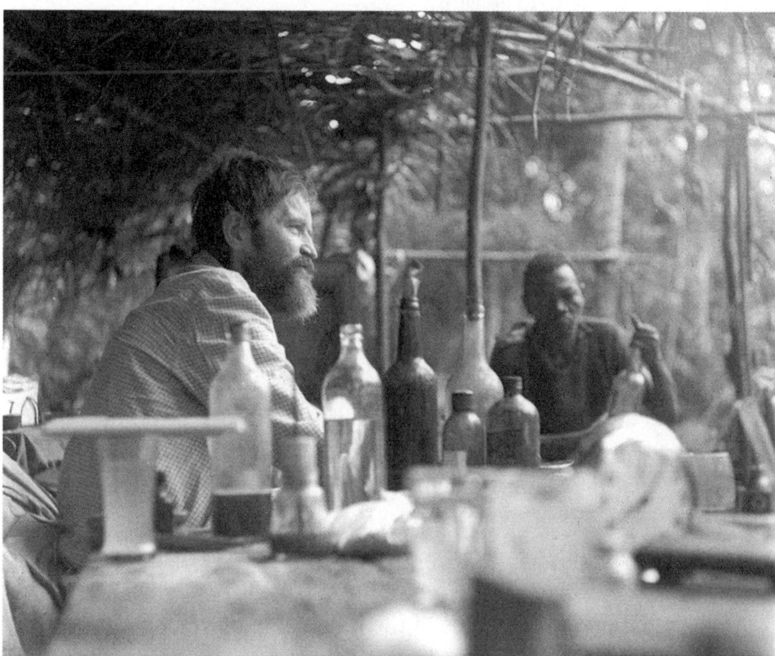

Fig. 46
Patrick Putnam in 1953 (photograph by Schuyler Jones). Schuyler Jones collection.

a canopy of palms. He sported a faded blue bush shirt and pink corduroy pants. Looking far too thin, he wore his shabby brown felt hat with a faded yellow bath towel that reached over his ears and across his shoulders. He held a mirror in one hand and a small bottle filled with what Anne guessed to be whiskey in the other. At the end of the procession, Alili was pulling a wheelbarrow full of objects. In it, of all things, was the trophy typewriter! Agaranga said that later Pat picked up coffeepots and cups and all kinds of things he found along the way in the village. He ended up at Sale' and André's veranda, where he stayed from eleven in the morning until seven in the evening. For a person who hadn't left his room except for a trip to the hospital in Irumu, this was quite something. It was difficult to make out what he was saying: *I'm Putnam. I hear you have beautiful flowers. May I have some? Is this your concession? Do you pay the taxes? Did you design and build the house? Isn't it dangerous to close off a road that doesn't belong to you? Have you heard a rumor that I've been sick? It's not true. I've been on a long trip for many years.*

Marthe brought up the rear of the procession (she recorded the adventure in her own notes). Anne watched from the sidelines, more than worried.

When Marthe left to go see her son, she got a handsome send-off, as her presence had been much appreciated at Epulu.

Reign of Terror

On October 17, Anne lost the thread of events. Only certain moments still stood out. She wrote to keep calm:

> As I was going to the bathroom, he got in a rage, grabbed my hands. His hands are as strong as a chimp, and he hit me in the face. He then threw a lamp at me.
> After I left, he hit Kopa Kopa with a large piece of wood.
> Issaca with wood and with arrows.
> Sunday morning.
> André Pichi with wood and he threw everything including medicine.
> Monday he had a knife fight with Abazinga and threw dishes which he broke on him and threw knives. He grabbed Kopa Kopa by the throat.[6]

Anne beat it for Mambasa on October 19 to request that Adé and Kempinaire come to help deal with Pat. They drove out and made it clear: they'd have to send him away if the violence continued. Among the three of them, they discussed declaring Pat unsound; none of them wanted to. The visit had an effect. Pat calmed down.

For Anne, the only relevant question had become: what would she do next?

As she'd done so many times in the past, Anne moved out to a Pygmy camp. But for the first time ever, she asked the Pygmies to leave their village and make a camp with her. The only requirement was that it not be too far away, so that if she were needed back in Camp Putnam, she could walk back quickly.

The leaves felt good underfoot. They were full of moisture. The path was overgrown, muddy, and slick; it was the rainy season. The Pygmies discovered that they, too, were sick of being in the village and were glad to be back in the forest. The tiny river called Mai Abazinga was so full that the rock Anne usually crossed on was underwater, so she waded across the stream. The Pygmies insisted on carrying her piggyback at the second ford, with much hilarious laughter. Water in the larger Lelo River was high. Faizi (a great hunter and storyteller) told her that long, long ago—before his time—a Pygmy had fallen into the deep pool there and had been taken by the water spirits. Not a reassuring thought as she balanced on a giant log, but she felt secure with steadying hands helping her to cross.

Once they arrived at the site where the camp would be built, everyone sprang into action. The house that the workmen began to construct for Anne was huge, the largest one she had ever had. For the first time, she was not embarrassed by its size—or its "ostentatiousness," as she would have said on other trips. She was delighted with her home for the next month or so. They built her a veranda, and inside they made shelves for paints, washstands, and books. They also set up a shelter for Anne's canvas shower bucket from Abercrombie and Fitch. It was, she felt, pure luxury.

The children were there, too, and it was fun to have them around as young members of the camp. Little W.J. Kokoyou was thrilled. He had been living as a village Pygmy, and this was the first camp he was old enough to visit. Everything excited him; he kept calling Anne to point out a stick, a bug, a house, an arrow, an *indizi* plantain, a leaf. The children swam or went fishing and caught baby crabs and baby fish. They were a noisy bunch. With peeled sticks and twine made out of lianas, they tied a piece of wood on as a weight, and from then on, it seemed to be nothing but screams and laughter.

By evening, all the huts were completed. There were eight in the circle next to Anne's house, all Epulu Mbuti Pygmies. Then there were the Matiabu Pygmies, with three houses where Grandma and young William J. Kokoyou lived. In a third circle was another group called the Cefu Pygmies. It was much like Anne's first experience of Pygmy camp in 1947, when she was so thrilled by everything that happened. It had all seemed new and marvelous back then. This time, she was content with the sense of belonging and respite; she felt part of the community. Life in the forest was still about the most wonderful way of life she knew. She could think of no place she would rather have been, lulled by the calm sound of the Lelo River nearby. "Pygmies are fun, good, and not only a dream, but real, real, real. They have all that's important in life: love, life, family, nature, dancing, and singing."[7]

Anne sat and listened to the chatter in KiNgwana and KiBira. It seemed like the first real vacation she had had for a long time—like reveling in the first sunny days of spring after a long, hard winter or the warmth of the sun on a beach, relaxing the muscles. Why hadn't she come long ago? For a while, she didn't read, write, or think. She just ate and slept. She didn't even take notes for the first few days, either. Most of the Pygmies went hunting by day; a few stayed back. Little by little, Anne started to draw, and then a rhythm set in, from seven in the morning until five in the afternoon. Her problems seemed to disappear into a sylvan idyll.

While Anne was at camp, the women conducted their inauguration ceremony for the young women coming to maturity: the *elima*. The women were singing full force when the men decided to call out their *essumba* animal for men only. Anne had asked in the village whether the *essumba* was a bird or an animal, and Mada, Pat's BaNdaka wife, had responded, "We women don't know about those things. Only the men do." When Anne asked how the men knew, Mada said, "They are told when they go through their circumcision school." Unlike the women, who sang a cappella, the men were accompanied by drums—and the competition was on between them. Anne had never heard such marvelous music in all her years.

Journal Entries

Having read the recently published memoirs of James Boswell, *Boswell in Holland*, which included daily memos written to himself, Anne began her own journal entry thus:

> I'm a chatter box. Since Pat is so sick, and I have no one to talk to, or maybe it's because I've just finished *Boswell in Holland* this minute. Not that I can compete with Boswell in any way except gloom.
> Courage, everybody says I have courage. How little they know. To live here does not take courage. It would take it to move out. I know one can be just as miserable and lonesome in New York. It can be worse. I . . . know I'd walk out of a bad situation and into a nothingness. I have to find myself again, and I'm afraid that until I find Anne the Painter I can't find myself.[8]

Anne did really have the feeling that she and they were better off at Epulu than in New York. Even in her private handwritten notes to herself, however, she still insisted on building Pat up and reproaching herself. It was a way of recognizing differences between them, coping with guilt, and setting limits on what she could do:

> But Pygmy experts there are few if any except Pat. Pat has never written. He's too sick to write. To say I can carry on the work of Pat is nonsense. His knowledge and desire of knowledge is endless. Mine has definite limits. His energy

> is relentless. Mine gives out quickly. His is a disciplined mind though he in his way is as undisciplined as I am.

Anne recognized that Pat wanted to stand alone: "His desire for knowledge is for himself." She, on the other hand, wanted to be connected through language: "I can't bear not sharing anything I know with everybody. I like publicity. He thinks he's god, so he doesn't need it."

She had longed to do serious work on the Pygmies; Pat's knowledge plus hers would have made a wonderful combination. But it was too late for that:

> Pat, Pat, Pat, why did the gods, fate, whatever one wants to call it let you get this damned sickness, and then crazy. Sick was bad enough. Crazy, mean without heart is too cruel. Too tough on you, the boys and me.

Looking at her own handwriting, she saw how shaky it was, almost like her grandfather's when he was very old. She noted:

> Tomorrow is your birthday. You used to like birthdays and so did I. There's no sense going into it all and remembering past ones. It hurts too much. You'll be 49 and I feel 100. *Basi* ["enough!" or "finished!" in a mix of KiNgwana and French].[9]

Progressively over the two last two years, Anne had begun to assume the role of boss. What else could she do? These responsibilities were now thrust upon her, and she accepted them.

She had also been thinking that she would have to mention Pat's illness in her book. Too many journalists passing through had written to and about Pat; too many people had seen him in bed. Not to mention that it was a major part of her existence. She suggested to Allan Keller, the ghostwriter whom Monroe Stearns had contracted to write with her, that they might deal with the lighter aspects (no tragedies, please, she suffers in silence) and how wonderful the boys and neighbors had been.

In early November 1953, Anne received a letter from Keller, to whom she had been sending her notes (typed or handwritten). He had requested anecdotes of "excitement" and "terror," and now he came back with this:

> Let's put it this way. You've been down there damn near eight years and nothing has happened to you except the viper bite. Things have happened around you, to natives near you etc. etc. but you haven't been chased up a tree by a buffalo nor even chewed a teensy-weensy bit by a leopard.

Anne felt herself begin to boil. Allan and she had been corresponding since her return from New York in March 1953, and they had been collaborating on her book project since that January, yet he seemed to sense little of her experience. He had been reading the weekly letters that she sent to her parents chronicling life at Epulu, heavily expurgated, of course. Now her words poured out in a rage, not so much against Allan or Pat as against the self-imposed silence that she had tried to maintain as some kind of (misguided?) protection of her family and friends. She was the one in need of protection, not them; whom was she kidding? Protection was in words, not silence. Anne could see that now. She sat down and wrote and wrote, piercing the silence; it felt good. As in 1952, during the grim days, she did not send her letters; her emotions still burned too dangerously hot. She waited to cool down and wrote several more drafts of letters she contemplated sending. Allan's apparently benign comment revealed the distance between his perception of Anne's life and her own experience. It got her angrier than she had allowed herself to be in a long time, and it was an important moment. Not only because she could for the first time write with some abandon, but because by piecing together the versions, she articulated a history of the difficulties at Epulu in a way she never had before. Anne poured out at length about her early period in Africa, about Pat's illnesses. Allan lacked the context in which to situate what he was looking for in order to edit the manuscript, and Anne wasn't withholding certain feelings anymore:

> I read your sentence, "you've been there eight years and nothing has happened to you." I have died a million times. I've had to forget what sensitivity is. I've had to act and think and feel as though this is a book I'm reading, not [something] really happening to me. I've had to send the boys back to take care of [Pat] after he's tried to kill them. I've discovered who are the brave, who are the cowards, and I know damned well I'm one of the cowards. If I go back to that room and don't desert it's only because I know if I leave everyone will.[10]

For all that Anne did say, she still wasn't able to tell Allan directly about Mada or the other wives; she couldn't bring myself to use the term "African wife." She couldn't admit to polygamy. With all that had been written about Camp Putnam—by Pat, by Emily Hahn, and by the other writers who had come and spilled ink afterward—no one had ever talked directly about Pat's wives, the black wives. Was she going to have to explain how she fit in? No. Anne wanted to take the "high road" about Pat and retain what she thought of as self-respect.

This letter was nevertheless an admission of what she wanted to deny: not only was life at Epulu no longer perfect, but it never had been the utopia Anne had hoped it would be. She wanted Allan to respond but remained ambivalent. Part of her wanted the adventure and romance of Epulu to live on. Part of her wanted to kill the bad side, making of it a redemptive tale. And part of her wanted to tell both through *her story*.

"Come Immediately I Am Awake!"

Anne was out at the camp sketching when Agaranga and Émile arrived on a late November afternoon with a note from Pat (see fig. 47):

> 22-11-53 Well, Anne!!! Good god!!! I woke up an hour ago. Come immediately I am awake!!!!! I woke up about $^3/_4$ of an hour ago—to be as precise as I like to be. Come in at once, rain or shine. There are five thousand (to be imprecise like Anne) things that I want to tell you while they're still fresh in my mind. I've told Ibrahemu to make a nice light supper for two. PTLP.

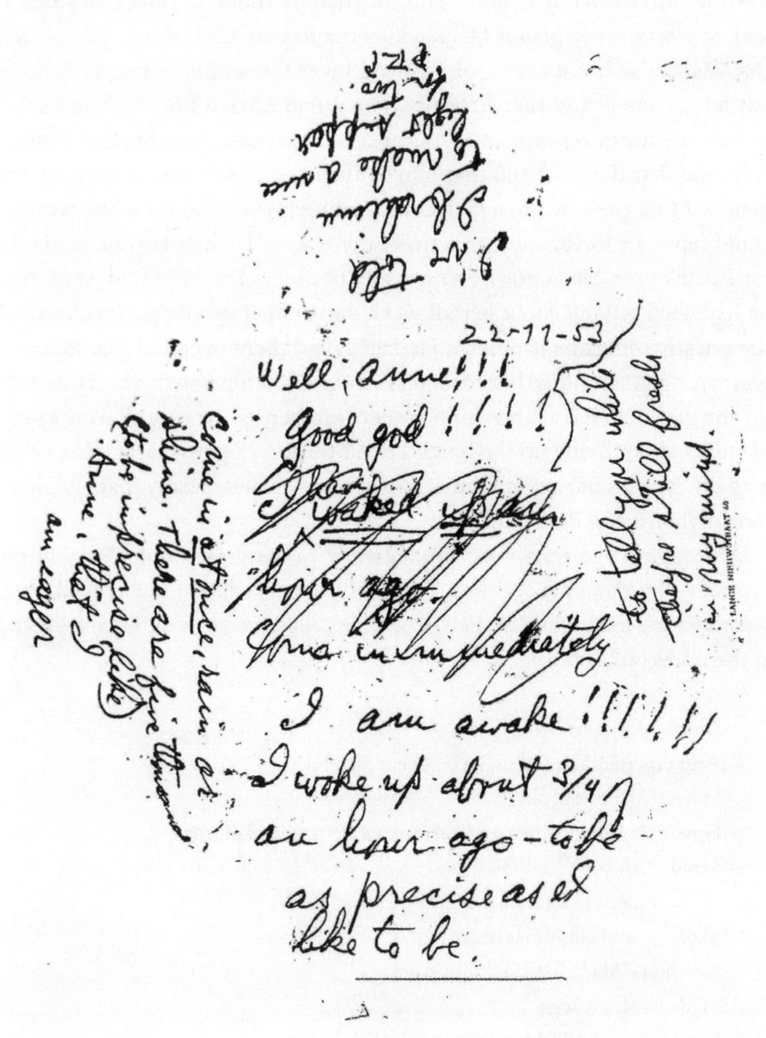
22-11-53
Well, Anne!!!
Good god!!!!
Come in immediately
I am awake!!!!!
I woke up about 3/4
an hour ago—to be
as precise as I
like to be.
Come in at once, rain or
shine. There are five thousand
(to be imprecise like
Anne) that I
am eager
to tell you while
they're still fresh
in my mind.
I've told Ibrahemu
to make a nice
light supper
for two
PTLP

Fig. 47 Note from Patrick Putnam to Anne Eisner, 1953. Anne Eisner Putnam papers, Houghton Library, Harvard University.

Like Rip Van Winkle, he had awoken from a six-month nightmare. Glad as Anne was that he was better, she put her paints away reluctantly. She knew that she was leaving a world in the forest that was good for her and to her, in order to enter into an unpredictable scenario directed by Pat. On the way home, Émile and Abazinga gave her the news that de Medina, manager of the Station d'Étude et de Capture of okapis and elephants for the Ituri Forest, was indeed cutting a road in the forest that was to go very far. She shut it out as soon as they told her, because she didn't want to hear any more bad news.

When Anne arrived at Camp Putnam, she was rather surprised to see that Mada had returned. Anne thought that Mada had been gone for quite a while, uttered a curse, but then immediately thought, *Now, that's ridiculous.* She was really glad if Mada had come to take care of Pat, but she felt that Mada also had a talent for showing up at the wrong moment. Perhaps Pat felt in some way that African women had nursed him back to health before (a pattern repeated on a number of occasions since his first Pygmy wife had first done so) and that maybe they could do it again. Perhaps Pat believed that these women had some healing power that no white woman could have. Unfortunately, this time, there wasn't much anyone could do for Pat. Neither Mada nor Anne nor any of them. The boys told Anne that he had been talking about her all week; he seemed to have just realized all the ghastly things he had done. He had called them over and told them he was wrong. Anne noted her reaction in her Lelo camp notebook: "Does that do any good? Will it change him? Is there any sense in trying all over again? He talks about fixing up the hotel. I don't think I've got what it takes to do it again. Besides our reputation is so bad now and deservedly that I couldn't face anybody. Nor do I want to."[11]

Although Anne responded immediately to his urgent note, Pat—in his typical style—kept her waiting. She went home, washed and changed, then went visiting for a while in the village. He called for her at dusk. She looked at the notes on his table:

—*Divers*
—Paul disassemble silly snake box near *fauteuil*
—Have snake box brought in
—Have Sale bring copper and galvanized netting and all corn
—Scold Mada . . .
—Mada pound corn on table and siève [*sic*] flour . . .
—Mada go and get francs [from Anne]
—Sale make Mada bank account page . . .
—Mada wash my legs
—Enema for me ? Taildressing . . .
—Mambasa order[12]

Anne and Pat ate dinner that evening in the moonlight under the umbrella tree. She stayed until about ten. Pat was even interested in hearing a little bit about the *elima*. Anne recounted to him what happened, and he commented how very special it was being allowed to see it, that she had to be careful with the information. It was like a nostalgic moment out of the past—when in the early days together, Anne would come back full of what was happening out in the forest, and he, not so able to get around, would gloss every detail, filling in background and explaining what this or that meant.

Afterward, Anne noted:

> He wants to talk about what happens to one under the influence of morphine and laudanum. . . . He thinks his crazy period is over. God knows I hope so. To see him slightly sensitive hurts because one remembers one's love for him which he has killed. One is broken to bits again, and to survive one has to remember that one must tell lies. Not be taken in or your everything will go the next time he's sick; . . . you don't know how temporary all this is. One has to lie, so difficult for me, about pump lamps—that seems like a small thing, but lamps are precious and one of his phobias is to take all my lamps. One has to learn that one can't tell all. It's hard after so many years of being honest. But one knows what it's like to see everything taken from coffee, flour, light. Only the clothes I wear and the blanket I use left to me. Pots, pans, knives, forks all taken. Presents that were given on trips being worn by lepers or people with the itch. Everything one loved destroyed.[13]

Anne puzzled over what he told her, trying out yet more hypotheses about his illness. He attributed his breakdown entirely to morphine and laudanum (an extract of budding opium poppies cultivated especially in the British Indies, which Pat said was dissolved in diluted alcohol). Anne wasn't convinced. His breakdown came the year before he took morphine. She knew he had been taking it but had no idea how large the doses were (only he had access to the drugs at the dispensary). There seemed to be two schools of thought generally about the benefits and dangers of taking morphine: one that if it helped him, he was so sick that he should simply take it; the other that he should not under any circumstance, because morphine was addictive. Only the Irumu doctor took the latter position. There was no doubt about the onset of his dementia in 1952. Did the morphine push him over the edge? He hadn't taken anything for more than a month, and he was not deranged at the moment, it was true. But knowledge from his experience seemed very unreliable. Anne didn't know. She just didn't know.

The next morning, Anne and Pat had breakfast together. Around ten, they decided she would take the typewriter to her house—a real truce—and their peaceful moment at Camp Putnam together ended well.

Then, without notice, Pat moved his bed out to the roadway and began flagging down cars. Before anyone realized it, he had gone to Mambasa. He had apparently just learned that de Medina intended to build a village of brick across the road, with a hospital, houses, stores, probably even a movie theater. Pat left to protest. It wasn't clear which was more upsetting, de Medina's plans or Pat's departure.[14] In his condition, his move didn't make any sense. He was far too ill.

De Medina came by and expressed surprise that Pat was gone. Anne invited him in for a beer. He couldn't understand why they were angry with him; everybody wanted a big hotel there—the river flooded with electric lights and two or three ice boxes. Why, they'd have hundreds of people! Anne told him that they didn't want hotels across the river. He invited her to his place, but she wanted to return to the forest. Back to the forest, which was still full of excitement. The *elima* and the *essumba* were going full force.

Farewell to Pat

Although Anne shuttled back and forth from the Lelo camp to Epulu, and to Mambasa once in December, she mostly remained out in the forest.

As she was finishing up some of her field notes, a messenger arrived: "I have bad news for you. Bwana [Pat] is very sick and they've sent a truck to get you. The chauffeur has a note for you." Anne gathered her comb and brush, asked a Pygmy, Angoli, to pack up her things, and left Lelo camp. She wondered whether she would be too late, though she knew in her heart that it already was. Anne met Abazinga carrying a large spear; he acted as though he just happened to be strolling down the path. Agaranga appeared a few minutes later, and he said, "Close your heart, Madami. He is dead." She replied, "I thought so, Agaranga."

Agaranga had heard the news from the chauffeur but had not told any of the others; they knew only that Pat was very sick and that Anne had been sent for. Anne thanked him, and they walked on in silence, with their own thoughts, for a few minutes until they got to the crossroads. The facial expressions of the men standing by the truck told Anne they all knew.

Someone handed Anne a letter. She walked into her house, opened it, and lost her head a bit when she saw it written. She tried to pack her suitcase but couldn't think of anything she needed. Everyone knew that the practice of wailing to mourn, as was their custom, would make Anne hysterical and that she couldn't carry on if that happened. She said, "The letter says Bwana is desperately sick. I think he is dead." She then asked each old-timer if he wanted to go to Mambasa with her. Nikiabo loved Pat very much and said he would; Pat had worked on him for years, trying to cure his yaws. Abazinga and Ibrahemu said they wanted to stay and see that nothing was stolen; they knew that the day of departure or death was when thieves came out.

The short trip to Mambasa in the store owner Rozos's truck seemed to last forever. Anne thought about the many miles she and Pat had driven to Epulu, about all their trips and hopes. She hadn't expected it to end like this. Pat had always said he wanted to die at Epulu, and he had died in Mambasa, a place he had never liked. When the truck pulled up to Rozos's store, he came out to greet Anne, offering a welcome glass of whiskey. The boys hung around outside. Rozos recounted being with Pat until twelve o'clock the night before, and he gave her a last letter from Pat to her, dated December 9; it was now the 12th:

> Anne, Don't come in. It's really unnecessary. When I get strong enough to be able to do some real good at the Epulu I'll be back and will get out of this expensive hotel into a cheap place, because we're pretty broke. . . .
> When you were here, the after-effects of the laudanum were in real fact pretty strong.
> Now I need to recuperate from six months of undernourishment and a vitaminless diet.
> And there's really nothing you can do here—you're much more needed at the Epulu. I'll get you some pillows back. . . .
> You have *carte blanche* to use André and all the men to reroof, rebogolong, and shine up.
> P.S. I sleep all night and almost all day. Appetite for normal food coming back only very slowly.
> Jacques and Alili [the two boys taking care of him in Mambasa] have it very easy now, we turn in between 8 & 11, and one gets waked about 2 a.m. because they will forget to tuck the blanket properly under the mattress.
> I wake up anywhere between dawn & 8 o'clock. Shocking. Disgraceful! Positively UNMANLY!!! PTLP

Anne found a letter from Pat to Rozos two days before his death contesting his bill and asking for more credit at Rozos's store, inquiring of him if anyone had "personally known a morphine addict or a drinker of a tincture of opium [laudanum]."[15] Rozos's response isn't recorded, but he refused Pat the credit. There was a telegram that Pat had written to his dear aunt Elsie shortly before his death: "Just emerging from six months laudanum stop both terrible stop please request father to telegraph seven hundred and telegraph me notification. Putnam. Mambasa Hotel." In the last days, the *agent sanitaire* in Mambasa treated him for a light case of malaria and some kind of infection in his arm. The night of December 12, Rozos, who had stayed during the evening before he died, had also written Anne a note saying that he thought that her company would give Pat pleasure. Pat died at four that morning.

When Anne finally asked Alili and Jacques about the details of Pat's death, Jacques recounted word for word the history of each breath Pat took, what he said, how he told Jacques to take the watch, take his pulse, write it down, how many deep breaths he took. He'd been trained by Pat to record such data in detail, and his account offered a kind of clinical accuracy. Pat had died peacefully, not choking as he had always feared.

A government official whom Anne had never seen before arrived and announced that the burial was to be that afternoon. He informed her that he had locked the door to the hotel room because Pat's boys stole all his money and his watch. Anne didn't believe it, but there was nothing she could do to straighten out the problem at the moment. Those boys had been through hell taking care of Pat. Anne knew that even if it were true, neither she nor Pat would have locked the room.

Anne had looked at Pat's body, which she thought resembled a Byzantine painting, but she knew she could not assist in dressing the body, so Mr. Francine, the *agent sanitaire,* took care of it while Anne went to her hotel room. A mailbag of bills arrived from the Mambasa post office, along with a *New Yorker* and a long letter from Marthe. The coffin, made of the kind of trees surrounding their Epulu house, arrived. Anne felt it was all wrong for Pat to be buried in Mambasa, but a law required that a person be buried in the place where he died. Too upset to pressure anyone about burying him at Epulu, Anne discovered that people seemed relieved; they were afraid of his *satani* (an ancestral or evil spirit)—even Agaranga, who was now Protestant.

Anne wanted to be with those who knew and loved Pat. A crowd of black people had gathered, some of whom she recognized. But the *blancs* in their uniforms were all new faces. Rozos, the Woodhamses (the medical missionary and dentist from the United States who had been there since 1918 and had treated Pat), and the Francines were among the few people she knew. There was a large wreath of flowers with a sign, "Epulu Territory." She had no flowers. Pat and Anne loved flowers—not wreaths—so Anne went looking for some and found some red *Myosotis* (forget-me-nots). She brought them to put next to his coffin, along with a lemon flower full of latex that gummed up her hands. She then had to shake many hands, with hers all sticky. She thought, *Pat didn't go to Mary's funeral, why do I have to go through this?* They began a procession with the coffin and the territorial wreath, leaving her flowers behind. She wanted to rush back and get them, to scream, *These are more important than those!* But she walked quietly behind the coffin, which was draped in a flag. The cemetery was a horrid place, all fresh earth with nasty weeds in the background, near the prison. In his bad French, Dr. Woodhams read something from the Bible having little to do with Pat or any part of the Bible that Pat liked. When Woodhams had finished, Anne started away; she didn't want to watch them put him in the earth, but she was called back. She threw dirt into Pat's grave. Then the whites threw a shovelful, after which the Africans did the same.

Anne telegraphed New York: "Pat died Saturday morning December 12. It is better so."

Grieving Together Alone

The boys came back to the hotel with Anne to see if she was all right. When everybody finally left, she went to bed, stunned. Hadn't she been prepared for this for a very long time? Why was it such a shock? *Perhaps we are never as prepared as we think we are for the loss of a loved one.*

Early in the morning, Rozos sent his truck. The boys packed Pat's things, and they made their way back to Epulu. Anne was never left alone; she noticed someone always hanging around the kitchen. She said something like *It's all right, I can be alone.* "No, Madami," they said, "When some relation dies, it is our custom, as you know, not to let them alone, and it does you good to be near someone and talk if you want to." They were right. Just then, the children came, and that was good.

Anne gathered her courage to go to the Palais. Sitting in the "beer" chair and looking at the river, she felt more peaceful. When the people of the village came by to pay their respects, they were requested not to wail. Agaranga stayed nearby, but when the lepers came, they did wail. In the evening, Ibrahemu and Émile came by, and they talked about their customs to keep Anne's mind occupied. They stayed until somebody else came to sleep in the next room. When the Epulu Pygmies heard that Pat had died, they broke up camp right away and returned to the village. They had been hunting desperately to be able to have a dinner and mourn, as was their way. There had been a full moon all that week, and the drums were pulsing throughout the Ituri Forest.

Anne called everyone, the men and women, and she read Pat's letter to them. She said they had to let the dispensary and the animal station go, but she asked them whether they wanted to continue the hotel or close it up, too. She told them they were very broke and had many debts. André Pichi said: "Bwana may have left you poor in francs Madame, but he left you his wealth in Pygmies." Someone else said, "We were hungry when we came here with Bwana. We cut down the forest and planted food, and now there are lots of plantains. We don't mind being poor for a while." Then the people of Epulu—the chiefs and villagers for miles around—presented Anne with the forest, saying that Pat had left it in her hands. Anne responded that she was a woman and knew that Africans didn't like a woman as boss. She didn't know how to tell them then that it didn't seem to her that she could ever feel, as Pat had, that the forest could belong to her. Her way was simply not proprietary. All said that they wanted her to continue in order to sweep away the bad memories of Pat's sickness and try to bring back the wonderful memories they had of him.

The boys said they would be willing to work for nothing, and soon the white people would come back. Anne replied, "Well, if that is so, then we have to get to work right away." Anne said she would like to have a bundle of mongongo leaves for a New Year's present so that they could begin rebuilding roofs. They all agreed that this was a good idea. Anne stated, "Now I get twenty-five dollars a week. We cannot go into debt anymore." Out of this twenty-five dollars, half was theirs to be divided, and the other half would go toward paying debts. They knew that Anne had been carrying the financial burden and constantly worrying. They knew all. They knew her family helped out.

They all began to fix and clean up the hotel, to repair the damages that neglect and Pat's sickness had wrought, each mourning in his or her own way. Émile said that he thought the white man's way of carrying on was a good one; Anne reciprocated.

The spirit of this diverse and inclusive community and its magnificent setting were, to Anne, a work of living art. There was no canvas as beautiful that she could paint in an empty room in New York. But she was no fool. She knew that with Pat gone, everything had changed. She made a pact with the boys and the Pygmies: they were going to rebuild Epulu. She didn't have any illusions that she could keep this up for years. Besides, the boys were getting old, and in a year or two, they would be ready to retire. This was, she thought, the only way they knew to grieve for their loss together and make peace with themselves for the rest of their lives.

PLATES

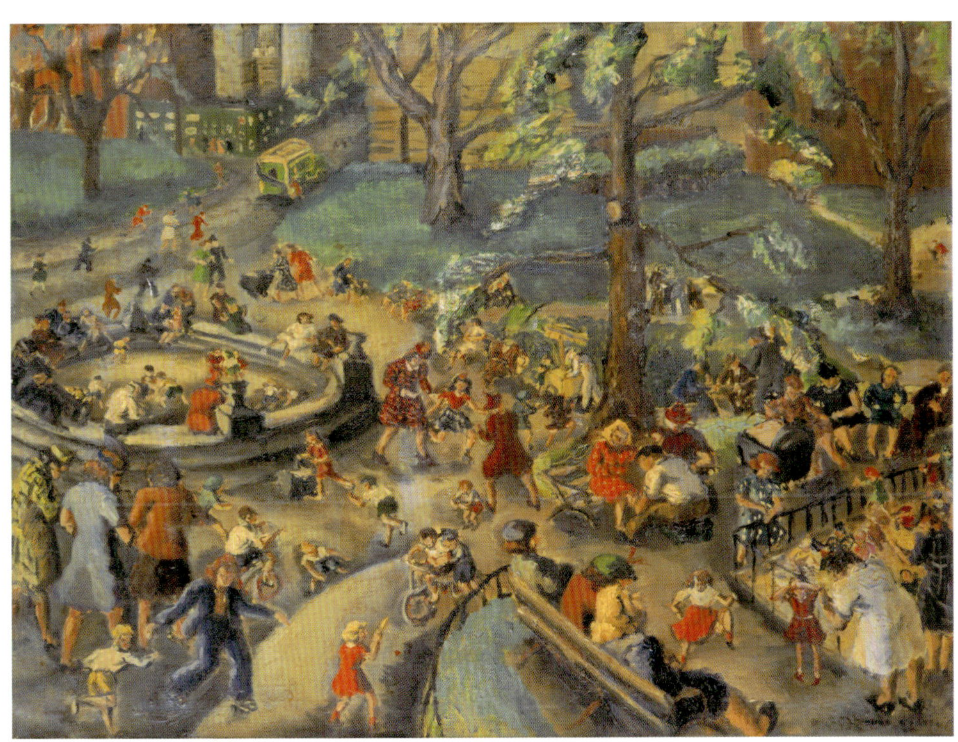

1. Anne Eisner, *Washington Square*, 30 x 40 in., oil on canvas, 1935 (photograph by John Hill). McDonald collection.

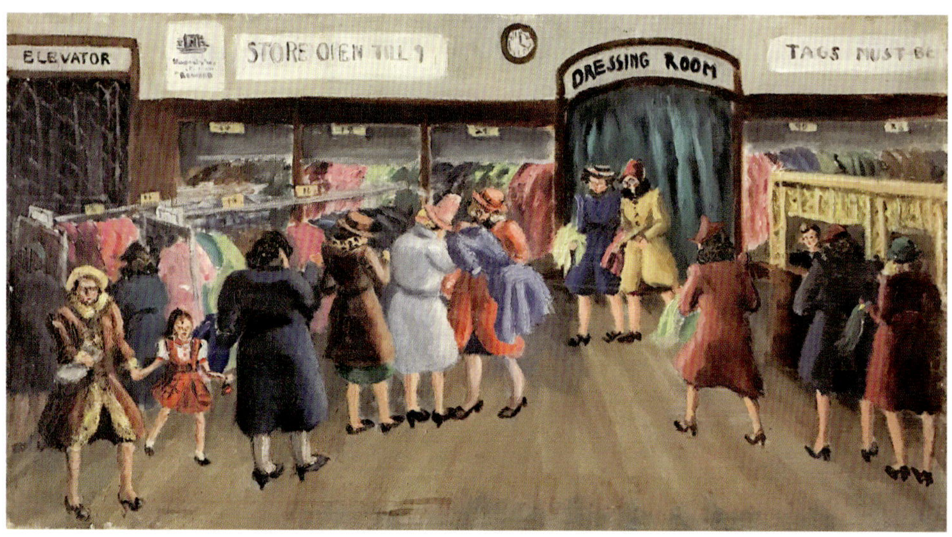

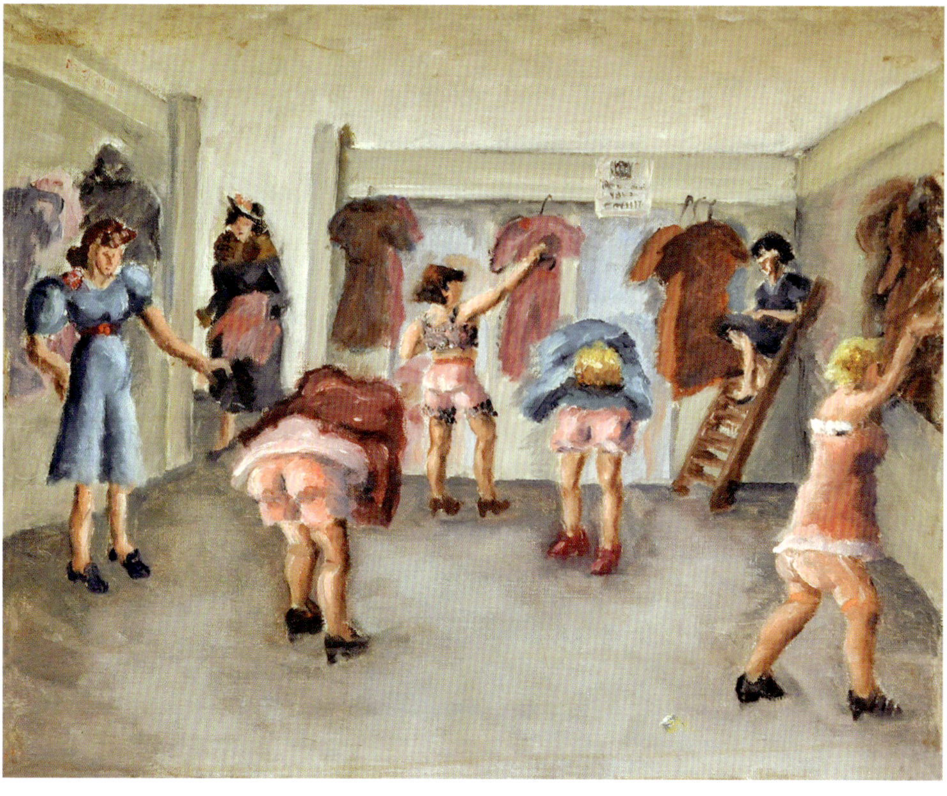

2a / 2b. Anne Eisner, *Klein's Outer Sanctum*, 16 x 30½ in., oil on canvas; *Klein's Inner Sanctum*, 161 / 4 x 20½ in., oil on canvas, c. 1934–1938 (photographs by Michael Rosengarten). New-York Historical Society and Museum.

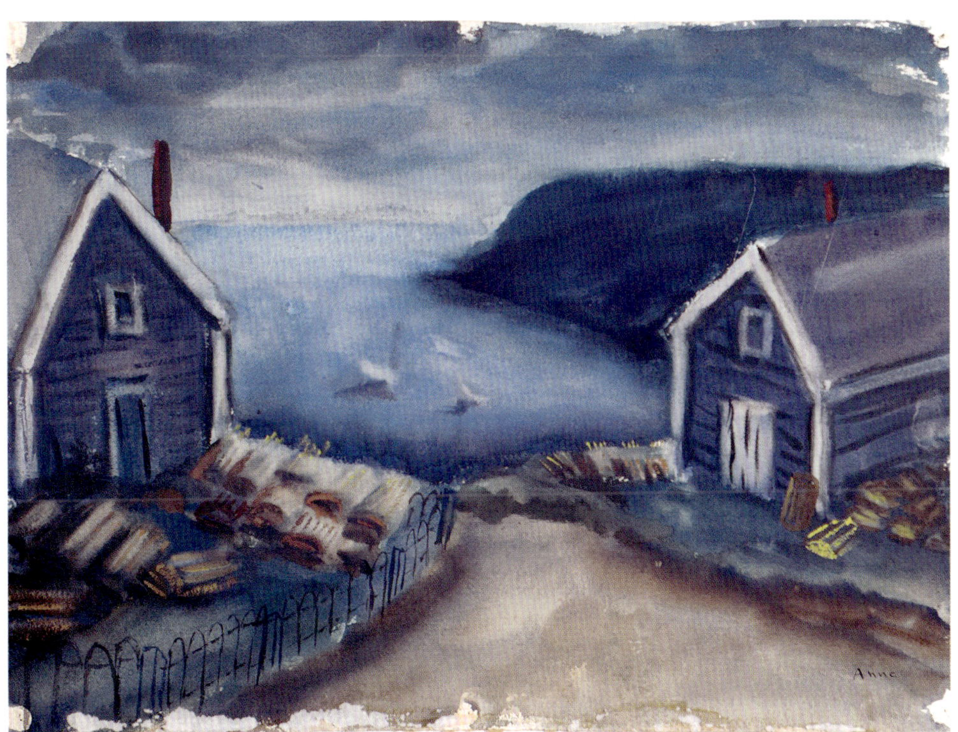

3. Anne Eisner, *Monhegan Landscape*, 15 x 22 in., watercolor on paper, c. 1939 (photograph by Michael Rosengarten). McDonald collection.

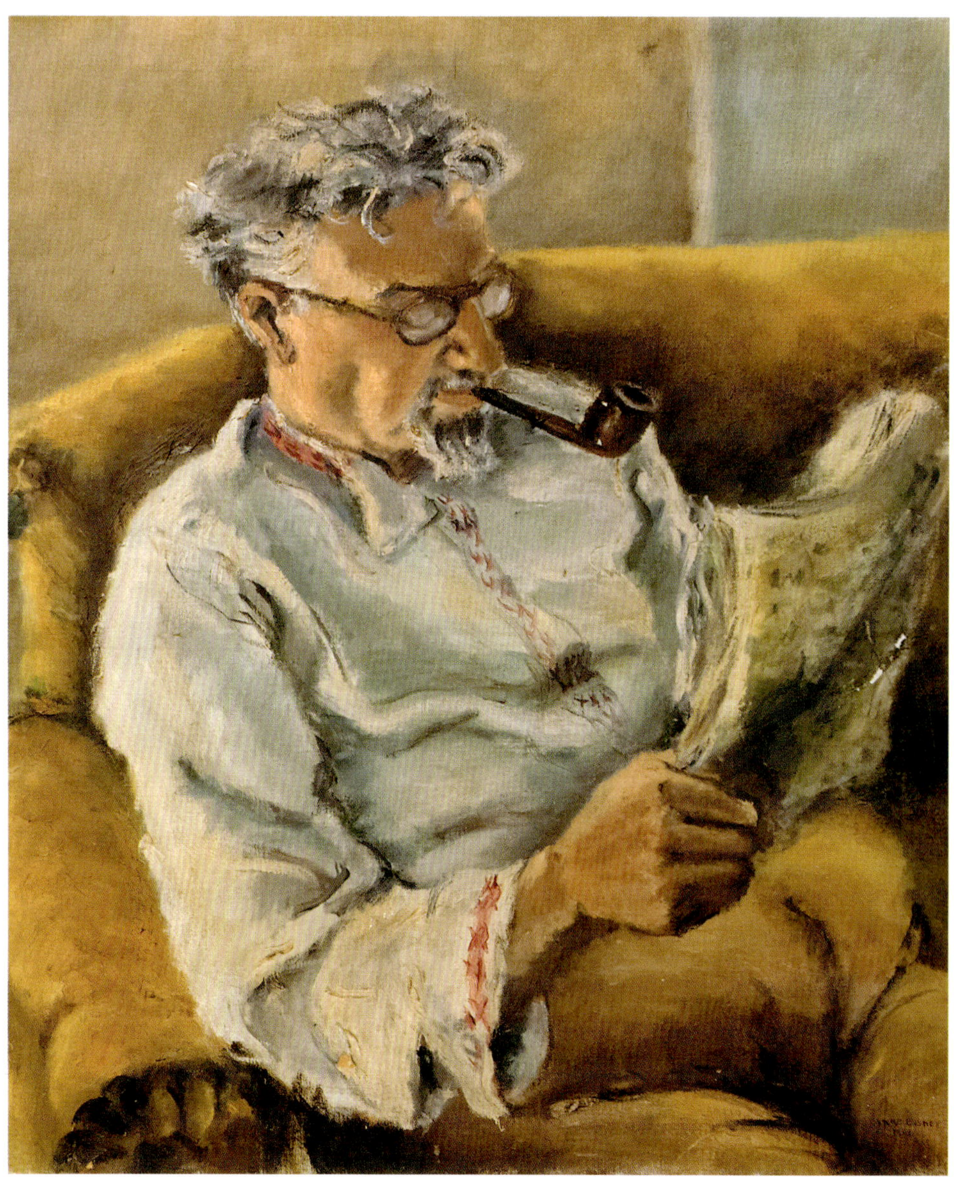

4. Anne Eisner, *Carlo Tresca*, 31 x 26 in., oil on canvas, c. 1941 (photograph by Michael Rosengarten). Houghton Library, Harvard University.

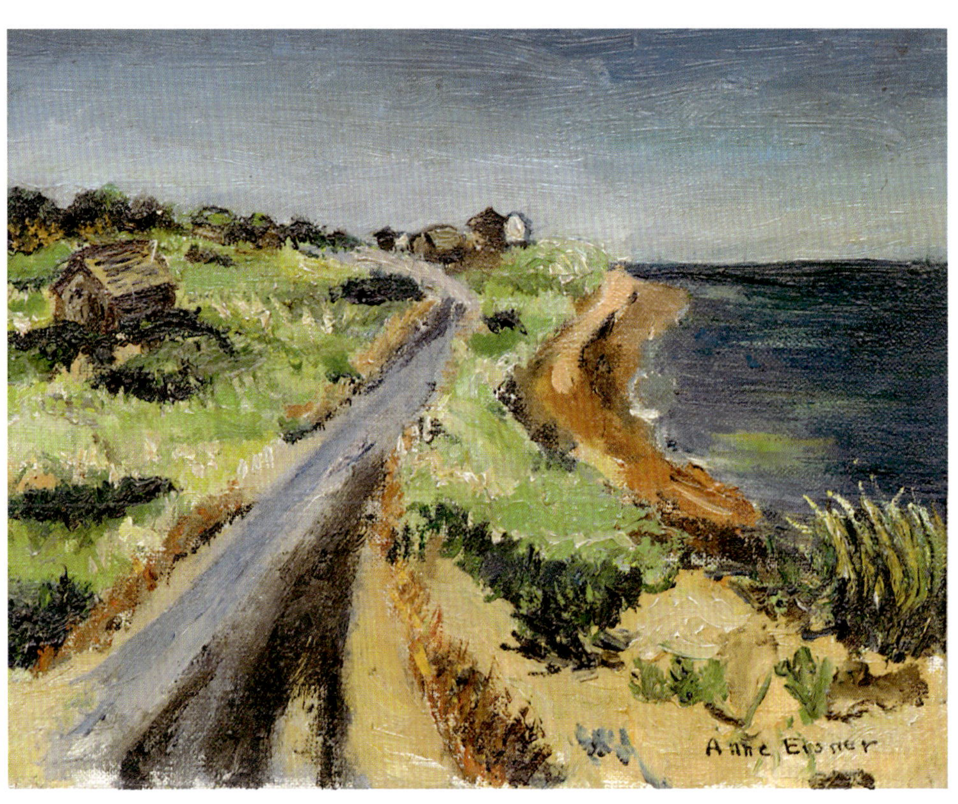

5. Anne Eisner, *Martha's Vineyard I*, 8 x 11 in., oil on canvas, c. 1944 (photograph by Michael Rosengarten). McDonald collection.

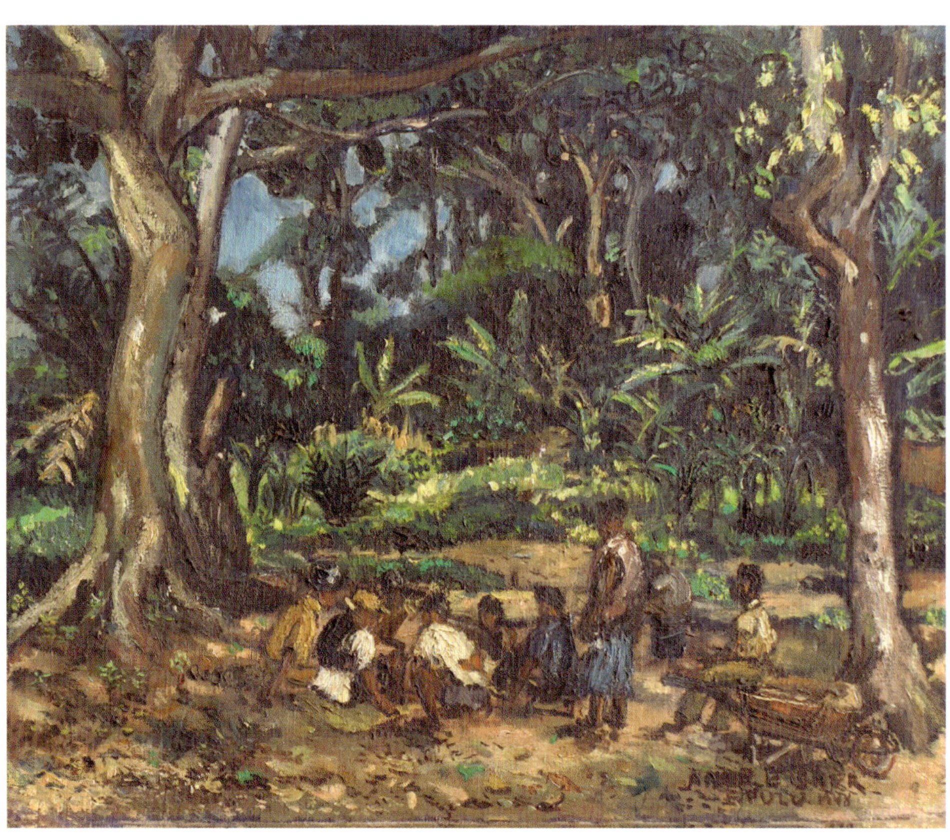

6. Anne Eisner, *Forest and Figures*, 20 x 24 in., oil on canvas, 1948 (photograph by Michael Rosengarten). McDonald collection.

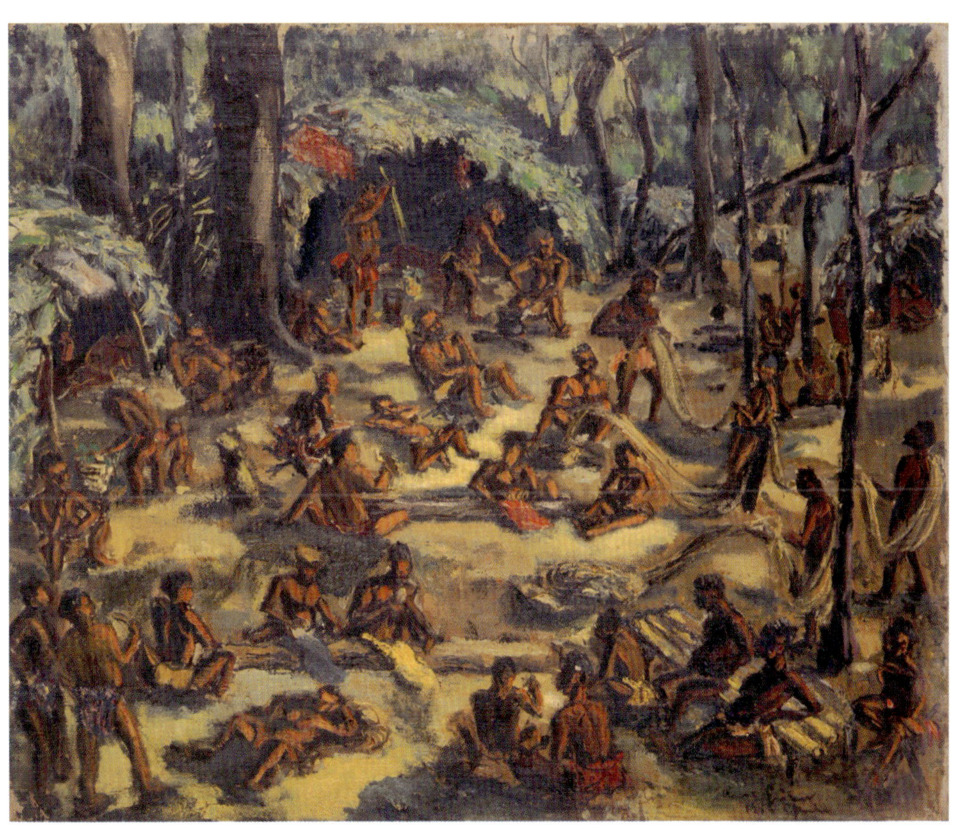

7. Anne Eisner, *Pygmy Camp*, 25 x 30 in., oil on canvas, 1948 (photograph by John Hill). McDonald collection.

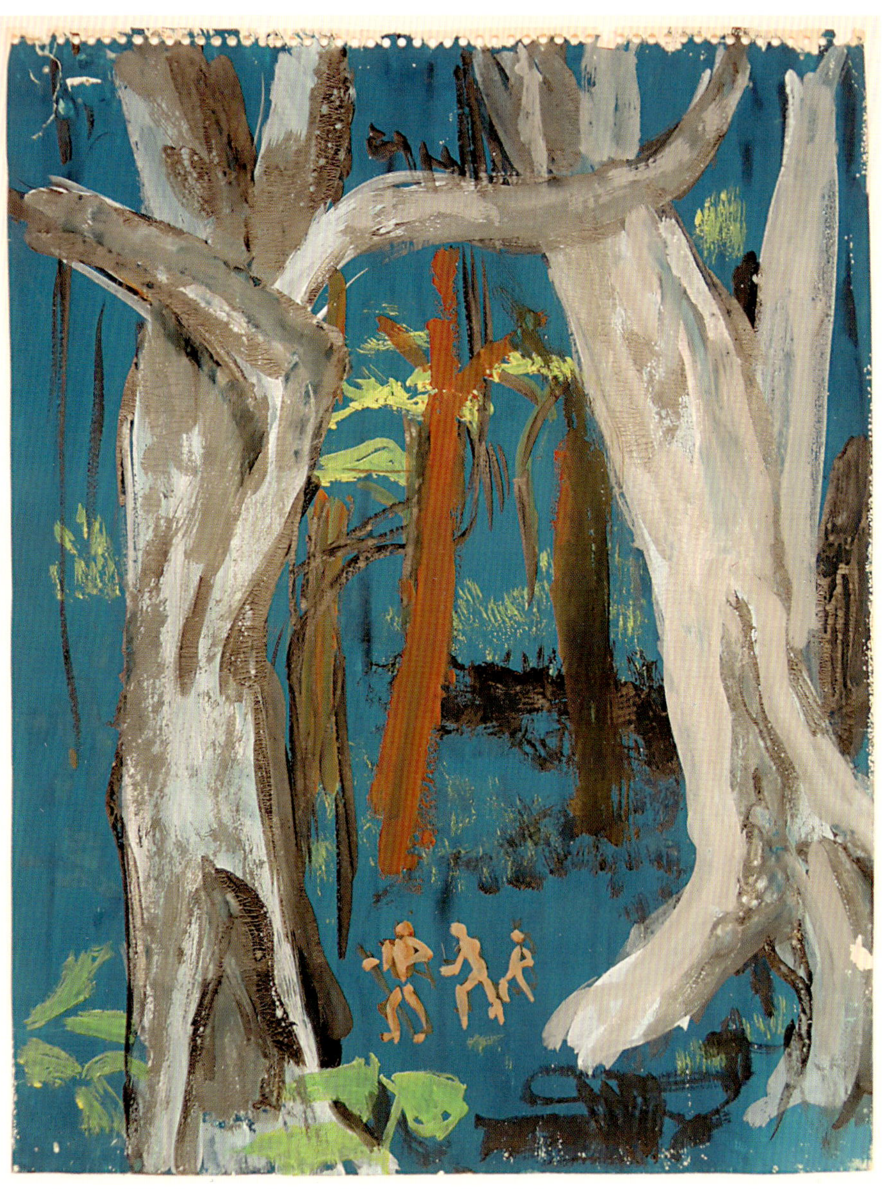

8. Anne Eisner, *Pygmies in Forest I*, 14 x 11 in., gouache on paper, 1951/1952? Musée du Quai Branly, Paris.

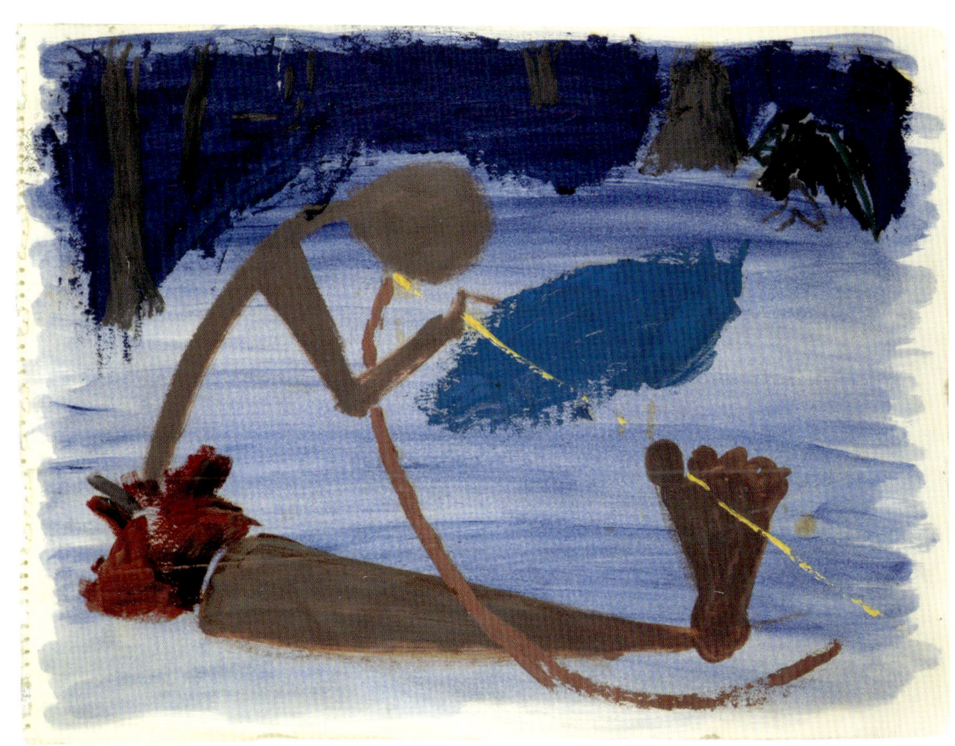

9. Anne Eisner, *Musical Bow I*, 18 x 23 in., gouache on paper, 1956 (photograph by John Hill).
Musée du Quai Branly, Paris.

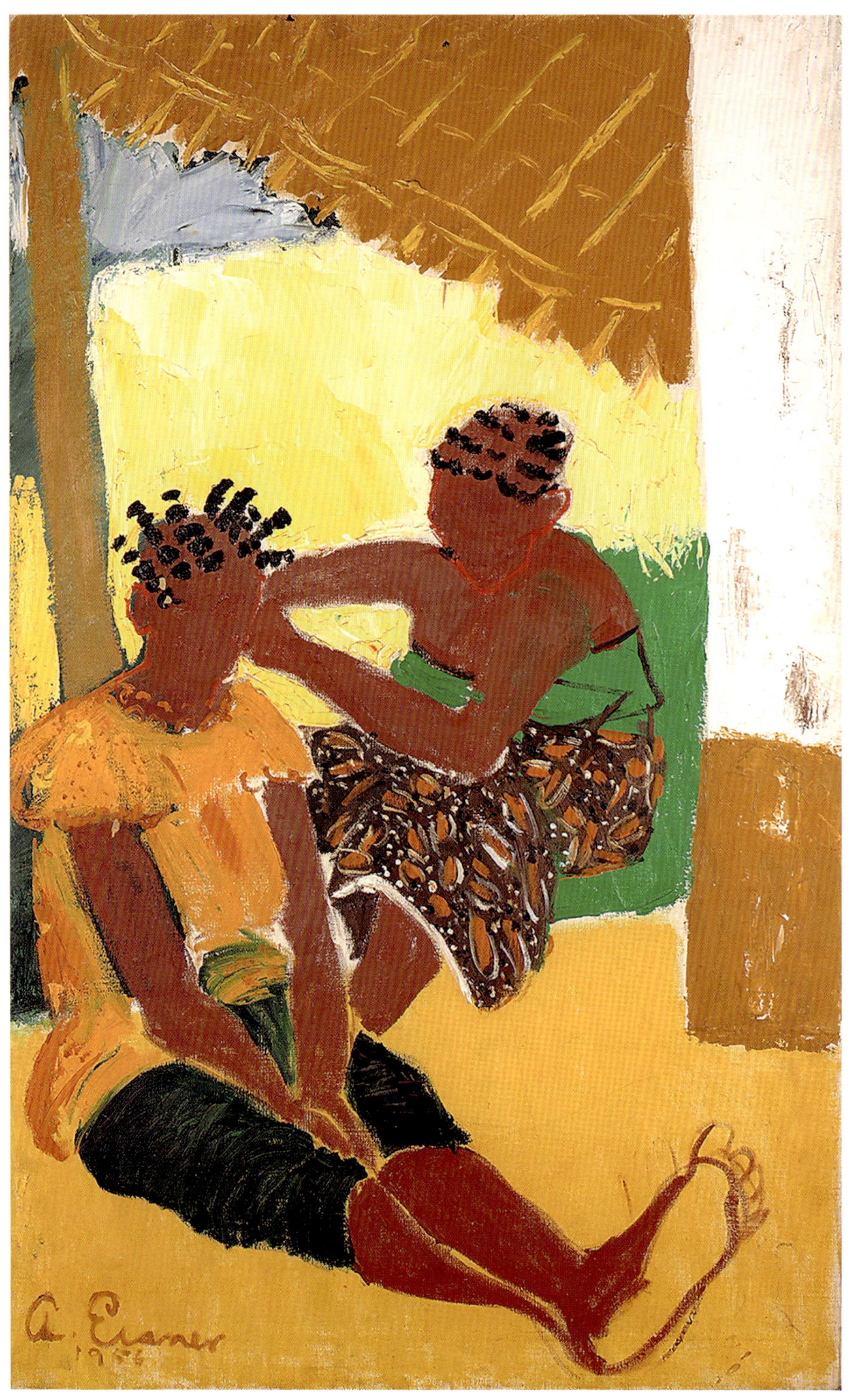

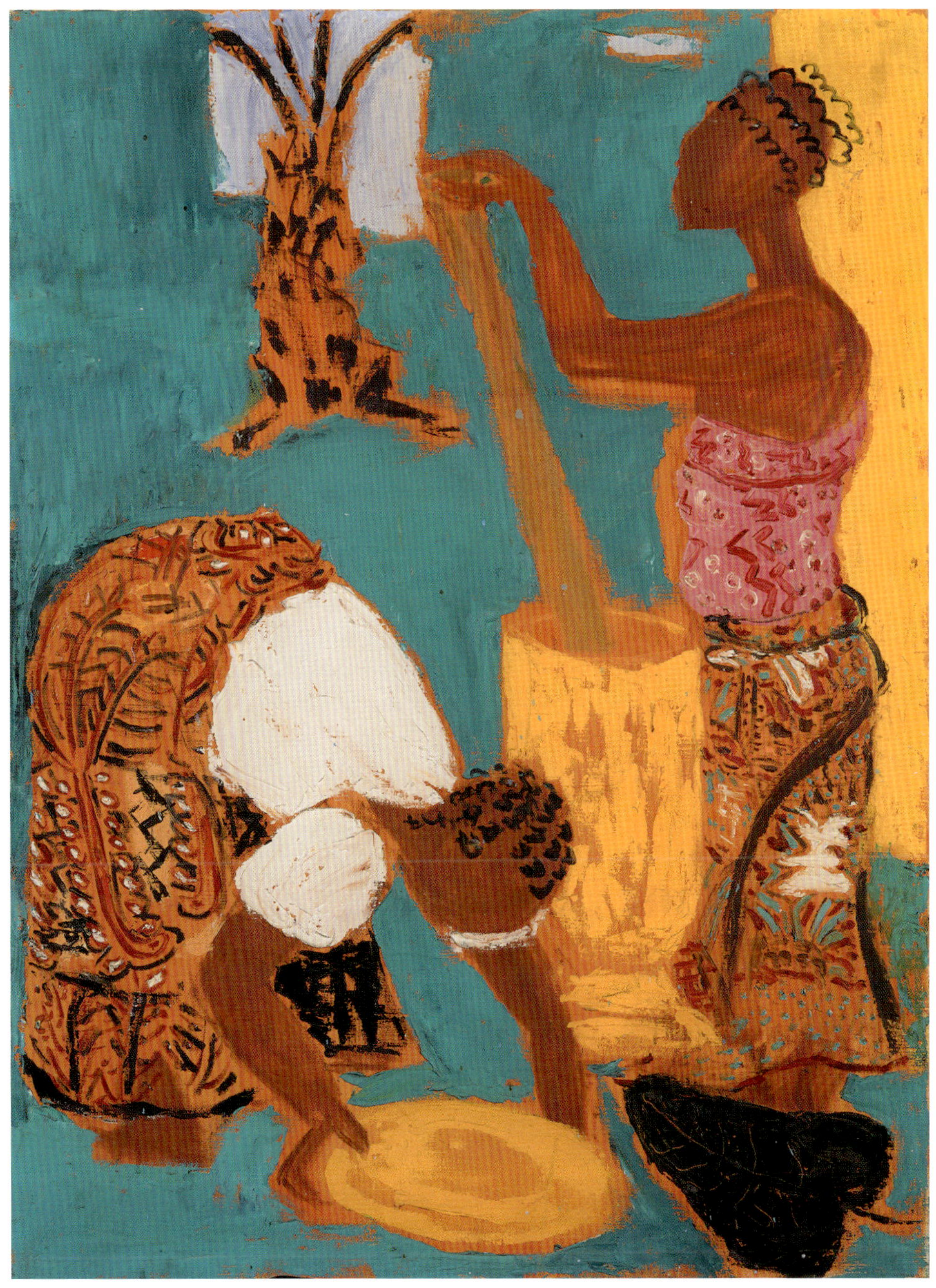

10. Anne Eisner, *Beauty Salon III*, 403/4 x 253/4 in., oil on canvas, 1956 (photograph by Whatcom Museum). Whatcom Museum, Bellingham, Wash.

11. Anne Eisner, *Two Women Working*, 40 x 30 in., oil on canvas, 1956 (photograph by John Hill). McDonald collection.

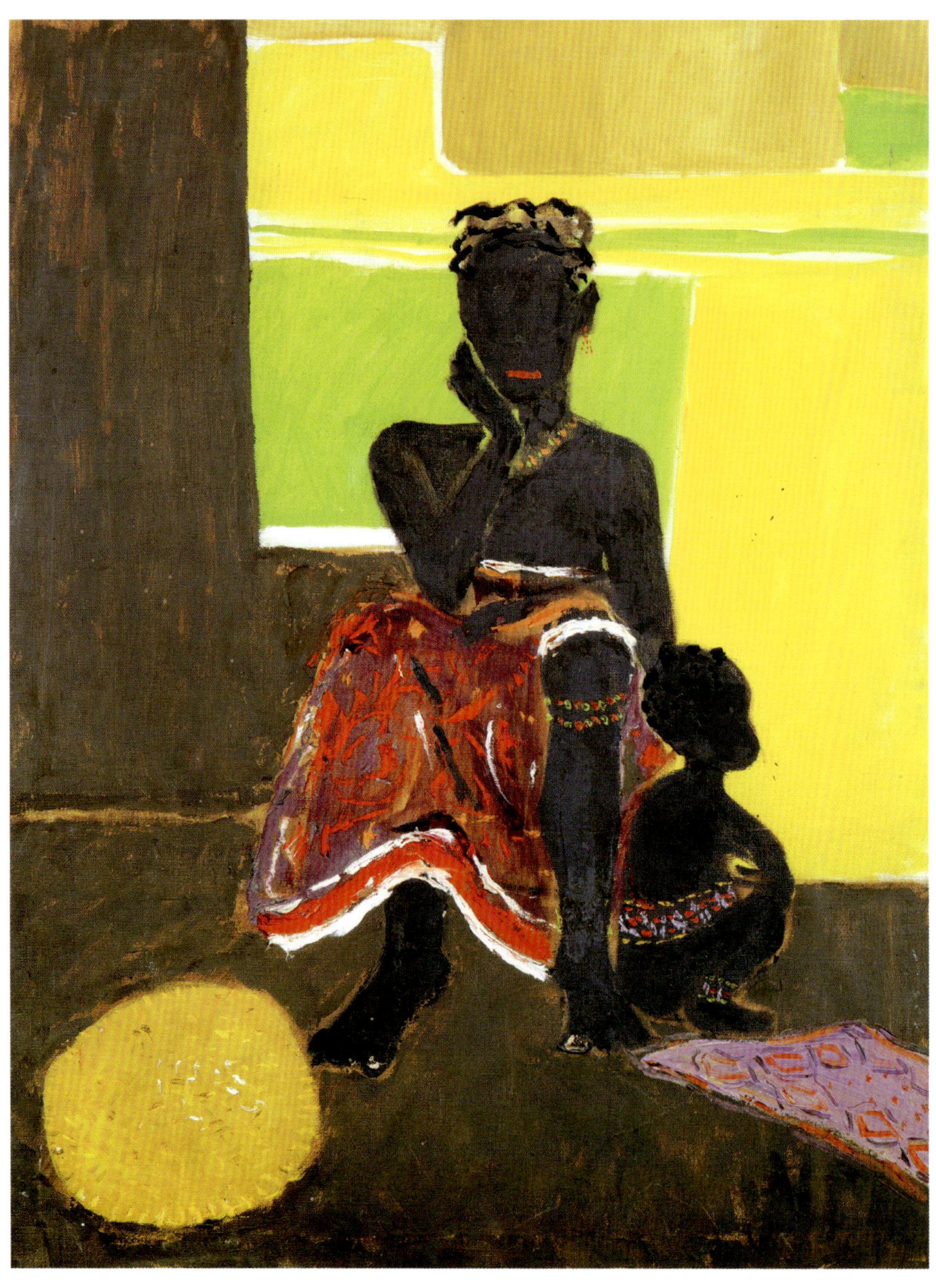

12. Anne Eisner, *Mother with Child II*, 41½ x 31½ in., oil on canvas, 1957 (photograph by John Hill). Musée du Quai Branly, Paris.

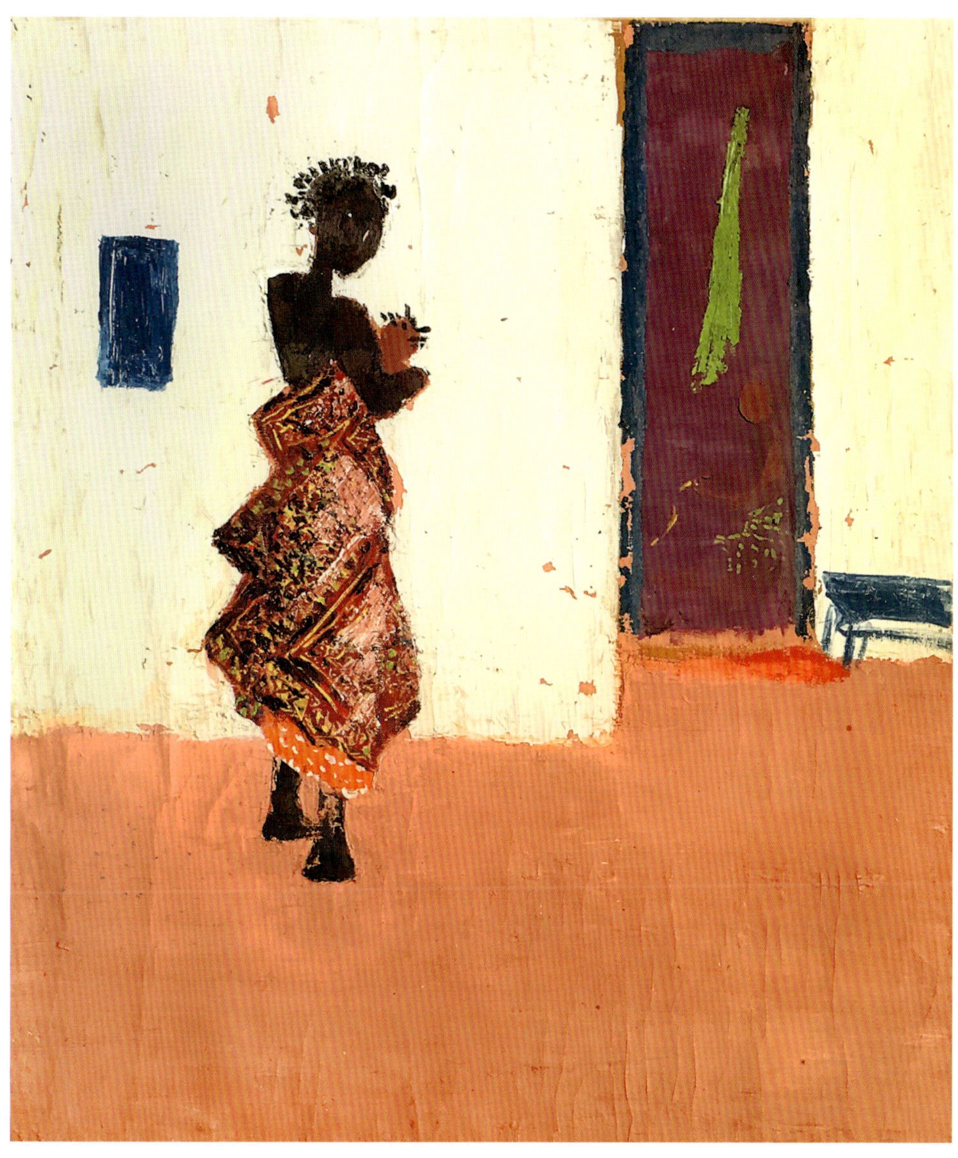

13. Anne Eisner, *Mother with Child IV*, 36 x 30 in., oil on canvas, 1956 (photograph by Michael Rosengarten). McDonald collection.

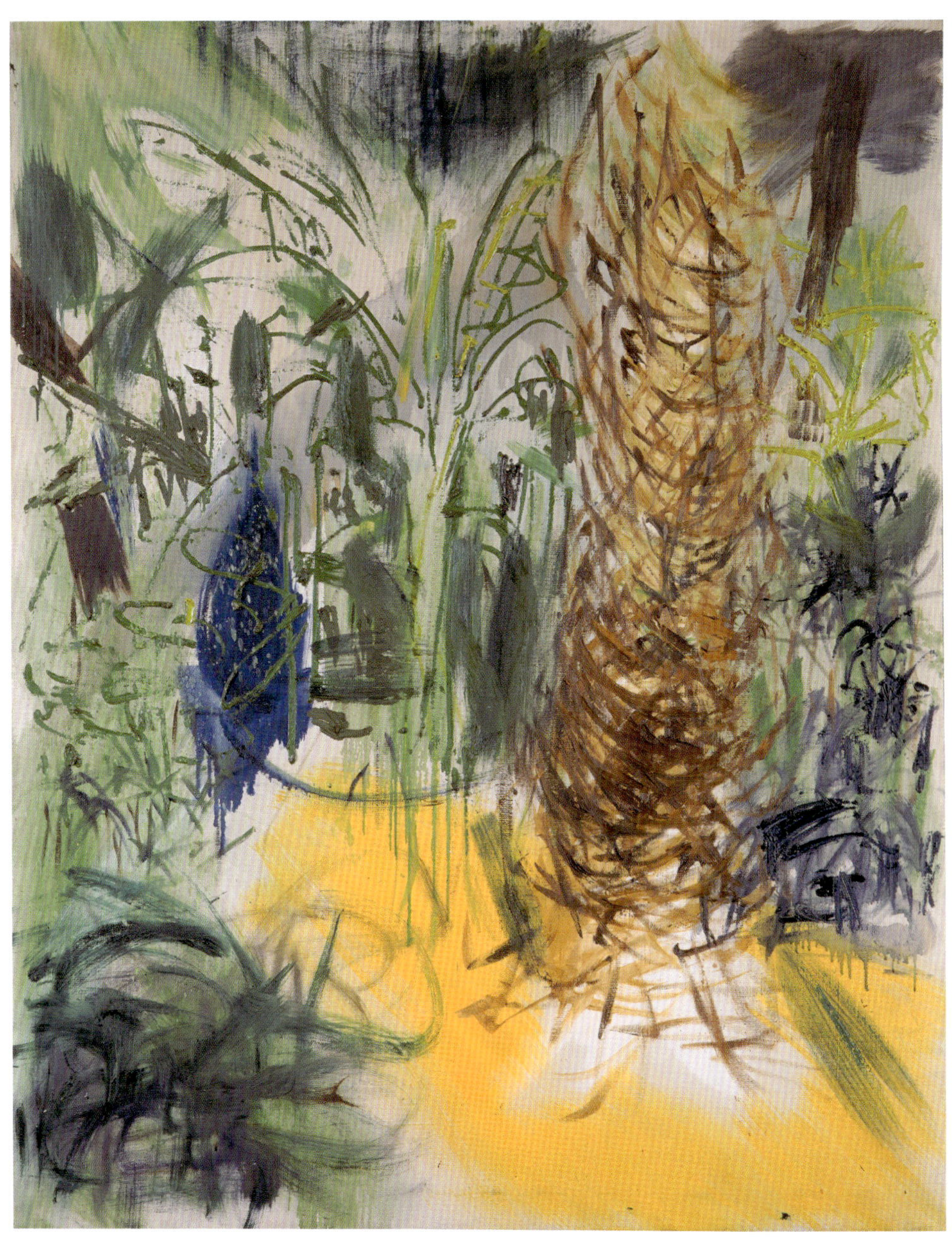

14. Anne Eisner, *Entrance to Camp Putnam*, 50 x 40 in., c. 1960 (photograph by John Hill). Musée du Quai Branly, Paris.

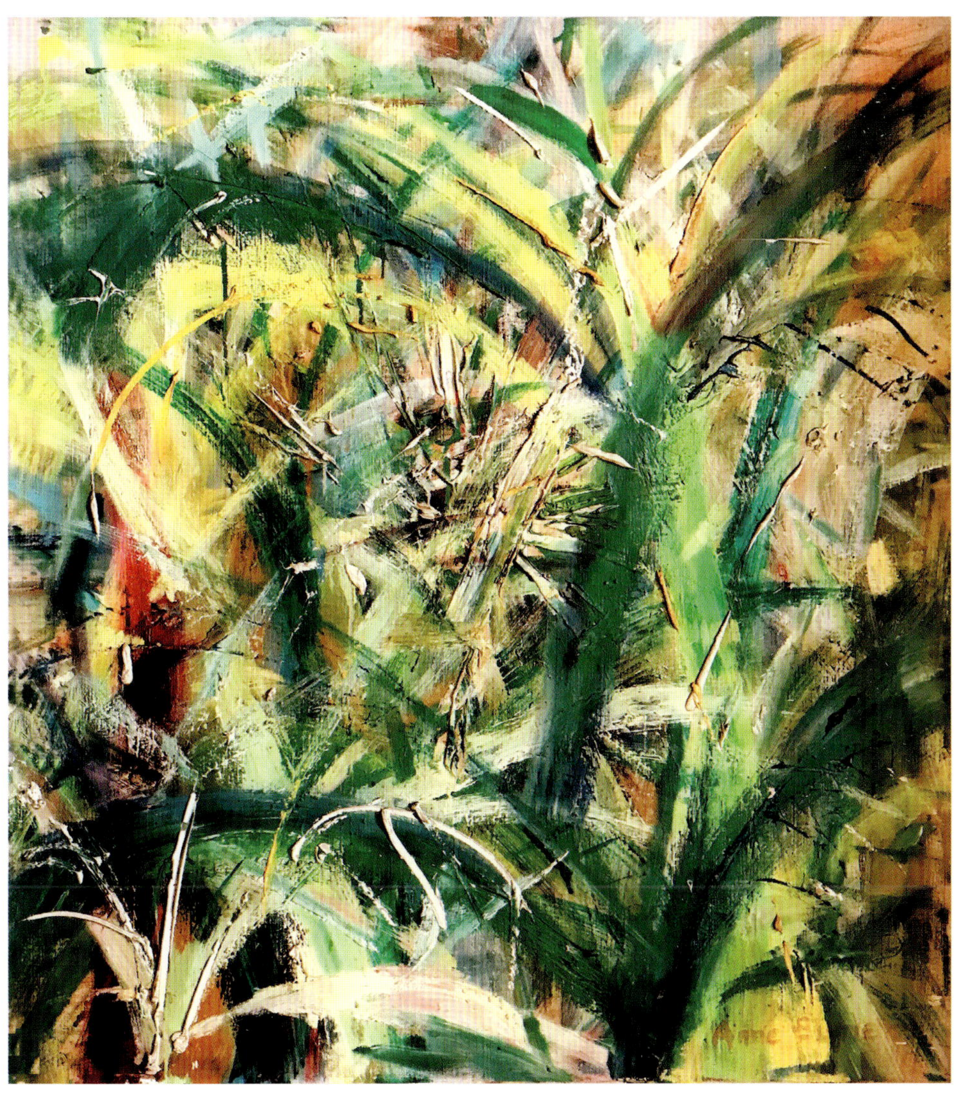

15. Anne Eisner, *Ituri Forest II/Plantation*, 39 x 36 in., oil on canvas, c. 1960 (photograph by Michael Rosengarten). McDonald collection.

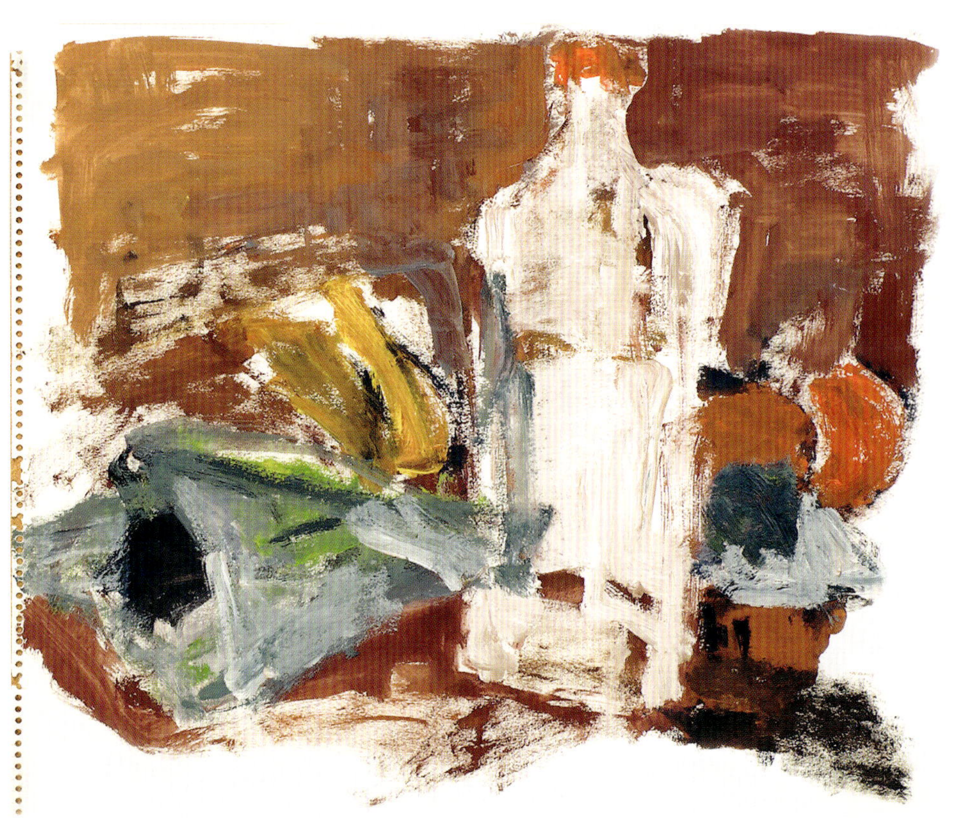

16. Anne Eisner, *Still Life with a Bottle*, 14 x 17 in., oil on paper, c. 1954 (photograph by Michael Rosengarten). McDonald collection.

Part III

EPULU AND NEW YORK

CHAPTER SEVEN

Sisyphus's Sister (1954)

Marthe spent Christmas with Anne at Epulu. They had a special dinner and overdid it on delicious termites; Marthe got indigestion. The boys decorated the hotel with flowers everywhere. Anne prepared presents for the New Year's party—trifles from Mambasa and some of her old clothes. Market day went on as usual (see fig. 48), and later the Pygmies brought their promised presents of mongongo leaves.

In late December, Anne went down to Stanleyville to deal with Pat's papers and pay the back rent. Marthe went along.

Anne wanted to stay at Epulu and make things work. She wanted to take care of the people who had taken such care of her and Pat. Some of them had been with him for twenty-four years, and others—the younger ones—had been there ever since Anne had arrived. She had no idea how long she would or could stay.

Fig. 48
Village women on market day (Anne and Agaranga in front of house), c. 1953. Anne Eisner Putnam papers, Houghton Library, Harvard University.

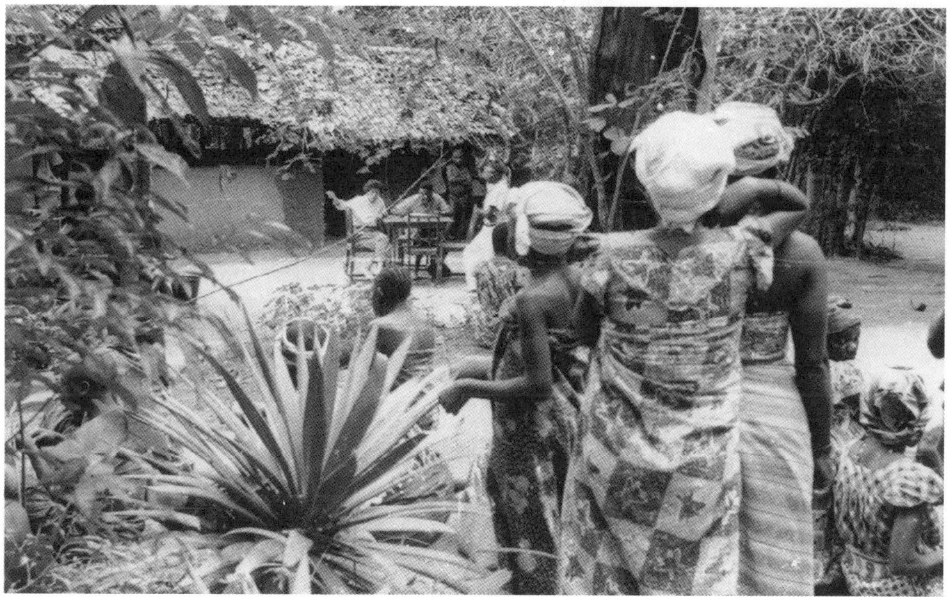

Anne knew that Africa was changing. Unrest spanning from the Congo up to North Africa was beginning, and she sensed that the political situation was about to erupt in a few years. Rumors about the violence were circulating through to their remote part of the continent. While Anne did not think that she was personally threatened, one could see how long-standing tensions created by colonialist rule, as well as changes in the area (both continued westernization and economic changes), could ignite a powder keg.

But I am getting ahead of Anne's story here. When she arrived in Stanleyville that December, she filled out administrative forms at the Service des Titres Fonciers de la Province Orientale (the land office). The clerks were reassuring; they informed Anne that she had only to pay for the two hectares (the ones on which the hotel was located). She paid the whole amount with the help of money sent by Pat's aunt after his death, hoping for a one- or two-year renewal of the lease at Epulu.

Anne paid a visit to the governor. He reiterated doubts expressed earlier in December about letting her continue at Epulu. The permanent okapi station run by de Medina had become too valuable. Would he push her out? It didn't make any sense; Camp Putnam had been an important research and cultural center and should continue to be one. "With friends like this, who needs enemies?"—or so the adage goes. No joke. She picked up some paint and a couple of pairs of sneakers and was so anxious to get out of Stanleyville and back to Epulu that she splurged on a ride partway there with the Vici Congo, the state-run company for the railroad. When she arrived home, her reception touched the hearts of even the hard-boiled transporters who drove her the final leg of the trip. People came pouring onto the road to greet Anne.

Still, she was shaken by the governor's words, unsure of how to proceed.

Just after Pat's death, de Medina had told Anne that if she intended to stay on, she would need to deal with a man named Mr. David, who was planning to build a large hotel next door. Pat had originally acquired a lease on about thirty-six hectares (about eighty-nine acres) and two hectares (roughly five acres) for the hotel. He had thought that this land stretched from Nia Nia to Mambasa but only recently had discovered that one kilometer had not been included after he had signed the papers in Brussels back in 1933. Anne suspected that David had been helped by de Medina to acquire land without telling anyone at Epulu. De Medina introduced her to David shortly after Pat's death, during an evening when he projected films of elephants with the radio blaring—a kind of Coney Island effect—and Anne seethed about the future. On the way back to the Palais that evening, she had blown up, shouting about how she resented David moving in without warning. David was taken aback that a woman would dress him down and worried that everyone would laugh. Anne didn't care if they laughed at her; her distress had arisen from the idea of Epulu now being destroyed by what she thought of as the crassest form of culture. David signed the papers for the land; Anne wrote to the governor.

David wrote to Anne, attempting to explain his position: the project of a modern guesthouse was much needed, he said—a "fact" confirmed by the International Commission on Tourism. It would not compete with her "primitive" establishment. He had not defamed the memory of her husband by taking up a much smaller space than they had. And he couldn't understand why the black population from Epulu had been surprised that he had not let them in on these plans.

With all that had happened, Anne wondered if she, too, was becoming paranoid. Why had she lashed out at someone like this, who, after all, might not have been so ill meaning? Maybe David just happened along at the wrong time for her and for Epulu. Her jitters were perhaps an overreaction.

Would that it had been so. The next mailbag brought bad news from the Titres Fonciers: Anne's request for a lease had been refused, and she was to be evicted from Epulu. The letter said that the two leases—one for agricultural land, the other for the hotel—had run out on December 17, 1949!

Pat had never answered any of the correspondence, and the last eviction notice was dated April 1953. Anne had learned of this fact in early September and discovered that the bank had apparently bounced all checks written by Pat. Moreover, when she sent money, the government returned her check. Under Belgian colonial law, Anne was subject to the authority of her husband. In order to have acted independently and made rent payments, she learned retrospectively, she would have had to declare Pat unfit—a decision she had refused to make at the time. Now she was alone, and she had one month to get out. If she didn't, she would be forced out. All of this was communicated to her in a letter signed by Pat's dear friend, the governor himself.

Anne knew that she couldn't possibly gather up her whole life (her art and particularly the collection of artifacts that she and Pat had collected) under duress in the time allotted. Still, she began to pack—not only her clothes and whatnot (such as they were) but also Pat's papers, her drawings and paintings, and their entire collection. It was an impossible task; there was neither a box nor a shred of string to be had in the forest; they would have to make their own boxes, weigh everything, and note it for customs, which took money and time.

Meanwhile, Anne continued to search for a way to retain the lease. She looked to the powers of the world and wrote to Léo Pétillon (who served as governor-general of the Belgian Congo from 1952 to 1958), over the head of the governor of the Oriental Province. Upon Pat's death, he had sent a cable of condolence, citing the importance of Pat's work. Anne also wrote to the American consul in Léopoldville; everything was in order, she assured him, and they just wanted to reconstruct the compound and the hotel. She wrote to Goris in New York at the Belgian Information Center, to Herbert Solow, to Allan Keller, to everybody she could think to ask for help.

Anne suspected that de Medina was probably looking to expand and take over Epulu as well. The boys informed Anne of his new campaign to turn all the villagers and Pygmies against her, trying to incite them to riot. He told them that she was being evicted because she had "pickled a Pygmy" (an allusion to Adé's ill-fated attempt to conduct research). Anne called everyone together to discuss what had happened. Most knew and understood already; Pat had conducted classes for the *infirmiers* and children and anybody else who would listen, explaining that when he dissected antelope, for example, it was to learn and perhaps save other antelope and okapis. Pat had always explained why he did what he did until his breakdown.

De Medina had become Anne's villain, and he played his part well. While she was away briefly in Mambasa, he came over and taunted the boys: "Hasn't Madami gotten the bad news yet?" André said that had de Medina been a black man, he would have hit him. De Medina had ordered him to bring him the imported beer Anne had in stock for guests visiting the hotel, then refused to pay for it. The power play had little effect; when de Medina sent someone to pick up the beer the next day, the boys discovered there "wasn't anymore." Passive resistance—just Anne's speed.

Part of Anne was prepared for de Medina's next move; the other part was scared—scared of him, scared of her own volcanic feelings. When she learned that he was leaving on a trip the day before she was to be evicted, she sent over a bottle of champagne to him with a little taunting note to say that he should celebrate her defeat in style. De Medina stormed over to Epulu, called all of the men and Pygmies around, and threatened to hit her with the bottle of champagne. One of the boys grabbed it from him, as Anne walked off laughing sarcastically, which made de Medina all the angrier. He said that he didn't understand why all her people didn't leave her—that she was a bad woman and to remember why the governor was kicking her out.

Anne thought: *If they do evict me, I shall make it the end of my book.*

The same day, however, a cable arrived from Vice Governor Hendrik Cornelis and Goris, who said that they were reviewing the case. Then, a week before the deadline, word came that Anne wasn't going to be thrown out after all. All of a sudden, the local *blancs*, who been avoiding her, became friendly again.

The villagers and Pygmies were less surprised by the good news than Anne was. Bwana had been more important than the governor, and the forest had belonged to him, they asserted. Everybody knew that, they said. So the government offices couldn't put their Madami out. Maybe they couldn't, Anne thought, but they had sure tried. She was awarded a new contract for five years, more than she had requested.

Anne was reading *Kon-Tiki*. Here was a man very afraid of water who set out to sail from South America to Polynesia in a balsa raft to prove a point, no less. They had said he couldn't make it in the raft, but he did. *If he could finish his adventure,* Anne thought, *I can finish mine.* She reopened Camp Putnam to tourists with announcements in the *Courrier d'Afrique*, through Thomas Cook & Son, African Car Hire, Overseas Touring Company, and L'Office du Tourisme du Congo Belge. She was as ready as she was ever going to be.

Agriculturally, 1954 was a difficult year and the longest dry season in all the years Anne had been there. It was the first time there had been a bad crop of plantains—due to a worm that had invaded the plants—and the food shortage was serious. Even if it had been a good year, there would not have been enough food to go around, because now, with the okapi station across the way, there were two hundred or more people in the area. In the village, people grumbled about hunger, fights broke out, and the price of plantains went up from five francs a bunch to forty or fifty. Anne was very concerned. Food had to be imported, but the storekeepers from Mambasa were not always able to fill the orders. After months of trying, Anne obtained some sacks of rice, which everybody loved, and beans, which everybody hated, plus a large quantity of dried manioc that was to tide them over during the worst of the situation. The hotel was filling up again, and Anne needed food. When more than half of the Epulu Pygmies went off toward a WaLesi village about eighteen kilometers down the road to Nia Nia, she saw nothing of them for two weeks and received no meat (see map 2). They were hunting, hoping to exchange their catch with the WaLesi for plantains, rice, or anything they could. The WaLesi chased them off, and they arrived back looking so thin that she was shocked. Anne herself went into Mambasa to get what food she could. Although she could hardly afford such gestures, she felt that it was her responsibility.

An athletic young Greek, Marinos, replaced de Medina, who had gone off on holiday to be presented to the king in Belgium (now Baudouin, grandson of Leopold II and son of Leopold III, who had abdicated in 1931), or so it was said. Marinos, Kempinaire, and Anne agreed to move the market from Epulu to near the road by the entrance to Camp Putnam so that it would accessible for everyone in the area. Soon, however, Marinos faced a mysterious problem: the okapis were being poisoned, and he had lost five in a month. Although Marinos himself didn't believe in magic, he understood the kind of cultural and social power he could wield with it, and so he decided to call in a ritual doctor to put a spell on whoever was responsible. Punishment was to be paralysis or blindness in one eye. The poisoning stopped immediately.

Anne had come to believe in the power of magic.

Marinos and de Medina had been good friends at one time, and Marinos was looking after everything at the okapi station, including de Medina's family. But now de Medina was double-dealing his friend Marinos for fear of being replaced. Marinos poured out his heart one evening to Anne over a series of scotches. His distress at de Medina's betrayal confirmed her own reading of de Medina: a rough character. But Marinos startled Anne when he said of de Medina (whose mother was black): "Je ne savais pas qu'il avait la mentalité d'un noir" ("I didn't know he had a black person's mentality"). The attitudes that cohabited within people were so complex, Anne realized, as to take one's breath away. Marinos, after all, lived with a black woman, Charlotte, who called Marinos "mon blanc." De Medina ended up returning to the animal station early and casting out Charlotte and Marinos, who was still technically in charge; then he quickly called in another ritual doctor against Marinos with another spell, using Marinos's own method against him. Marinos moved out of the animal station and nearer to Epulu. Perhaps he didn't know how to wield the power of magic in such conflictual circumstances; perhaps he was a poor diplomat. Or perhaps the complexities of living between a white world and a black world were causing things to start to unravel.

Marthe Returns

Anne never did feel good on her birthday when she was alone, and so she usually immersed herself in some project. She was reading when she heard a truck struggling down the road in the mud, and she sent someone out with lanterns. To her surprise, in walked Marthe, who was delighted to be back.

Anne was both glad and not glad to have Marthe with her again. She was fond of Marthe. But Marthe was also very intense and difficult (not that Anne herself wasn't!), and Anne always felt exhausted after an hour or two of heated discussion. It was fine once they both were painting, and Marthe was still the best company Anne had.

Marthe was very generous with her creative energies. She painted two panels of unbleached muslin to make a curtain for one of Anne's closets. Then she painted a bedspread, using color to highlight the rhythm of shapes in such a fine painterly way that Anne felt they deserved to be exhibited rather than put in her room. Both painters agreed that Marthe's work seemed too avant-garde for the *blancs* living in Africa, especially after the letdown Marthe had felt at the somewhat disappointing reception of an exhibition of hers earlier that year. In December this year, however, Marthe's paintings, including the *Triptych* she painted of the wedding that she and Anne had attended in 1953, would be recognized as strongly avant-garde and individualistic in their relation to the Congo.[1] Anne admired Marthe's discipline and dedication; she thought her a talented and fine painter.

There was more. Marthe's warmth ("you must get back to painting, it will do wonders, you'll see"; "*allons*, don't get discouraged"; "I will come and stay with you to keep you company") and her involvement in everything that happened at Epulu showed how much she cared. Nothing more important than this companionship could have happened for Anne during the dark moments of Pat's illness, his violence, and his continuing rejection of her in the fall. Marthe was Anne's friend—her faithful friend.

The relationship was nevertheless complicated. Anne had offered Marthe

the house next to hers if she decided to stay for long periods of time. They had named it Umba ya Matisse. Anne had always had a sense of her mother's friends' loving relationships with other women but had herself been too focused on men in her life—and, most important, was still grieving the loss of Pat. Anne struggled to respond to what she felt about this woman who could, by age, have been her mother.

So many questions remained in Anne's life that uncertainties about Marthe were submerged in the challenges of living minute to minute at Epulu. Marthe's comprehension and her care often short-circuited Anne's tendency to deflect rather than deal head-on with a problem. She knew from Marthe's looks and from the touch of her hand that she would have liked a more intimate relationship. But Anne couldn't begin any new relationship, with a man, let alone a woman. She had to rebuild slowly and look out for herself once more.

A letter from Skye arrived from in Paris, where he had met up with Anne's parents, and he sent photographs of them all together. She showed the snapshots to the boys, who thought her parents looked *mafuta mingi* ("quite fat"). They were astonished to see Skye in a suit and tie: "You said he was poor and had no money. Look at him wearing a *cravate* and a new suit without a single patch." What surprised Anne in this letter wasn't Skye's sartorial effect but his offer to come back to Epulu while Anne was to be away in the States, and to stay perhaps indefinitely. He expressed his love for Pat and the place. He had written a good part of his manuscript, *Under the African Sun*, about Epulu. Anne shared his attachment to the romantic side of Epulu: the charm, the ideal, what it stood for. But times were changing quickly, and a new era whose effects couldn't yet be measured was just beginning.

If someone had taken over, it would in fact have been an enormous relief. Not only was Anne replacing all the material things that Pat had destroyed and trying to pay back debts, but she was also accumulating expenses of her own. Part of the problem was that she refused to establish a profit margin when she sold palm oil, cigarettes, or food during this period of relative famine. She didn't like to make anyone pay a higher price than she herself had paid. Not good business thinking. But Anne never made decisions based on business alone. In fact, she never was really in business in the first place—something that only became acutely clear once these financial crises engulfed her. She hadn't been able to make enough from the hotel and didn't have sufficient backing from her father to support the people at Epulu.

Nevertheless, the reconstruction of Epulu had done the boys and her a world of good. The roofing of the hotel was almost finished, a pavilion begun during Pat's illness was freshly mudded, and all the buildings had received a mud touch-up. Restoration felt good.

In May, Marthe readied herself to leave, although she couldn't stand the idea of saying goodbye. Anne was going to miss her, too.

Colin and Francis Arrive

At the end of May, Colin Turnbull arrived at Epulu. He had wanted to return ever since his visit in 1951. In 1952, he had written suggesting that he and Pat work together on a biography of Pat. But by the time he was able to formulate a project, Pat was no longer in a state where he could respond. In the short time they had been acquainted, Pat the American and Colin the Scots-Englishman had been drawn to each other. Was it a communion between English and American blue-blood men that Anne could have no part in? Whatever it was and despite the age difference (Pat had been forty-seven and Colin in his mid-twenties), the similarity between the two was striking: both white, tall, charismatic, one educated at Harvard and the other first at Westminster School and later at Oxford, and both fascinated by African culture.

Colin's enchantment with Pat and Epulu spilled over in his letter, and he expressed great warmth toward Anne as well, reiterating his determination to find a project to get him back out to stay at Camp Putnam. He had convinced his Canadian cousin and budding filmmaker Francis Chapman to accompany him on the trip, and together they had gathered equipment for filming and recording music. They had left North America in October 1953 and were unaware of Pat's death when they arrived at Epulu.

Colin and Francis had come down from Morocco through the Sahara Desert, taking the least comfortable way through the Tanezrouft—known as the Desert of the Terrible Thirst—bordering Algeria, Niger, and Mali, in order to get to the Gold Coast (later Ghana). They had continued their journey toward Epulu through Nigeria and the Cameroons, finally making it in May 1954. Shouts and greetings from Pygmies and villagers welcomed Colin back, to which Anne added her own greetings.

She threw a large party with the villagers, who killed two goats to welcome them, and they collectively downed a case of beer. Every time someone arrived who had last been there when Pat was alive, Anne celebrated to dispel feeling the sadness at his absence. When Colin had first visited in 1951, Anne was building life at Epulu, Pat was still reasonably well, and William J. Kokoyou had just been born. The party focused them all on the present.

Francis began to plan his film, and Colin started taking notes on Pygmy customs. In the midst of the excitement, a comment that Anne's sister, Dorothy, had made many years before in an entirely different context came back to her: "Now that you love him, I hope you like him." The boys and Anne had been crazy about Colin and looking forward to his visit for months. Wouldn't it be awful if he had changed, she thought, or if they had? She didn't foresee any serious problem. The first days were marvelous.

Colin wanted to record music of the Pygmies; he was an accomplished musician himself, having played keyboard instruments, particularly the organ. It was the kind of event Anne liked to organize. She invited all the musicians from up and down the road for a recording session and even went into the deep forest, somewhat off their usual trails. People came from miles around. Colin and Francis buried a generator in an aardvark's hole, running a cable back to the camp in order to record. The moon lit up the forest. Each person played his instrument, with three songs from each tribe, the BaBira, the BaNdaka, the Mabuda, and the BaNgwana. Colin and Francis recorded.

A very smart-looking couple dropped in at the guesthouse while the music was under way. Despite being told by government officials in Stanleyville that Camp Putnam was closed, they had flown their small plane to Mambasa and come over. He was Lowell Thomas Jr. (1923–2016), son of the legendary radio announcer and an adventurer (much later to become an Alaska state senator). His wife, Mary Taylor Pryor ("Tay," 1927–2014), was a writer. They looked just the way one imagined a young couple who stepped off a single-engine plane in the forest should: young, energetic, and handsome. On their fifty-thousand-mile trip flying as pilot and copilot from Europe to Africa—and later to the Middle East—they had come for a week to make films.

Anne accompanied them to a Pygmy camp for filming, staging a scene of the Thomases' arrival with the Pygmies emerging out of the forest. The Pygmies were playing their own game, too; always there when the sun was gone, they vanished instantly when the sun was out. The Thomases nevertheless managed to get the footage they needed and slept in the camp overnight. The next day, after more niff-naffing around in and out of the sun, the Pygmies just couldn't wait to get away to harvest honey in the trees; it was the season.

Tay Thomas seemed surprised by the open and easy relationship Anne had with all the people of Epulu, picking up on her talents and her self-deprecation: "[Anne Putnam] spoke [KiNgwana] in her usual boisterous tone, explaining to us that her husband had always insisted that she was the only person in the world who spoke Swahili with a New York City accent." She also remarked on Anne's difference from Europeans. Offbeat compared both to people back home and to the "colons" who tried to replicate Belgian life in the Congo, Anne caught Tay's attention. Tay remarked: "Anne Putnam's attitude toward her Negroes and her Pygmies differed so greatly from that of most of the white people of the Congo that some among them were convinced that she had 'gone native.'"[2]

Over the years, there were contemporaries of Pat's who certainly thought he had gone "native," or "primitive," reasoning that he had remained too close to the blacks and the Pygmies for too long and had become more and more like them. This might have been explained by an atavistic resurgence of his primitive nature. If Anne—who hadn't been there as long—had "gone native" by the same logic, it must have been the innate wildness of her primitive *female* nature reappearing. Anne's view was more practical; like the women in their ever-changing camp settings, she had had to adapt, and she did. All the people of Epulu had to live together and respect each other's differences. Anne changed, they changed, they all changed—however modestly—in order to be able to live together. Was this something to criticize or laud? Was it better to maintain one's traditions rigidly? Was this one great difference between a (European) colon—whose tradition was longer, more established, more important to the identity of the individual—and an American like Pat for whom assimilation (in the first half of the twentieth century) was still a basic value? Wasn't there some middle ground—somewhere between maintaining tribal differences and assimilating? Anne thought so.

Sometimes she wondered whose account of herself to adopt, the one about whom others wrote or the one she had been developing in her own letters. Moving through life was like a trek through the forest. The way seemed impenetrable at first, but the more you learned, the more you could make out a path—a matter of opening perspectives. Anne remarked that the Pygmies were never blocked because they knew how to forge alternative routes in the forest.

Maybe there isn't just one version or one voice for any of us.

Colin and Anne visited all the workmen's plantations to see how serious the food shortage really was. They talked about her financial situation. Rozos announced he could not give credit in his store in Mambasa any longer. All of his white customers owed him money, and if he supported anybody else, he would be unable to get credit himself. While it made sense, it put Anne on the spot.

Francis's presence was definitely a comfort to Anne. She was very much the old lady of the party (she preferred calling him and Colin "the boys" rather than *les enfants*). He was not only good company but, like Colin, he also had a knack for fixing things, so for the first time in years, almost everything was in working order again.

However, Colin and Anne quite soon began to tangle. Although the reasons often came down to minor nitpicking, Anne got Colin's dander up, and Colin made Anne hopping mad. After each spat, they would patch things up and go on with their respective projects, repairing the damage on a day-to-day basis. Colin was the new kid on the block who had one strong and compelling bond in common with Anne: Epulu. From the moment Colin arrived, it became quite clear that their needs and points of view about the place differed radically. Anne needed all her energy for making decisions about the future—her future and that of Epulu as a whole—whereas Colin needed his energy for his music and the copious ethnographic notes he had begun to take on Pygmy life.

If Anne had harbored a glimmer of hope that she might keep Epulu going, it was probably nourished by a fantasy formulated prior to Colin's arrival: that because he so resembled Pat, he might want to help her run the place in some kind of partnership. Colin, however, was not interested in partnership. Young and driven in his own charismatic way, he zeroed in on his passion for ethnography. He was going to construct his version of Epulu.

The beginning of July marked the onset of the circumcision camp of the young Pygmy boys. This was a long-awaited event, and people started dancing three or four days ahead of time in anticipation of it. When the Pygmies had learned from Anne that Colin was planning a trip back to Epulu, they had put off the circumcision ceremony until he'd arrived. In theory, no whites and no children who hadn't yet been circumcised were allowed. But Anne remembered that back in the "class" of 1950, a small seven-year-old BaNdaka had snuck into the camp out of curiosity. It had created a dilemma. Let him stay? Send him back? It was easier to apply the rules to a child than to a *blanc*. But the Pygmies broke the rules for Colin; the ceremony got started, and Francis filmed. They called Colin Monsieur Mulefu, the "long or tall" one, and Francis was Monsieur Mudongo, the "short" one.

Colin had moved in on their world and Anne's—the people she considered family, her community, her almost-exclusive source of support and love—as he became increasingly interested in the Pygmies. Colin knew that they were like a family (a note written in 1951 had wished the "Epulu family" a happy Christmas). But he didn't want to share with Anne, even as she continued to share her world with him, and she felt excluded. A rivalry was developing between them.

Colin wanted to be Pat's disciple, and he saw Anne as the wife—the widow, rather. But the welcome offered to him at Epulu in 1954, with Pat no longer there, depended on Anne's connections. Had she not held the community together for the previous two years and rebuilt much of Epulu over the last months, it certainly would have been a very different place. It would take quite an effort to blot Anne out of Epulu.

When Colin made it clear that he didn't want to share information with Anne about the circumcision camp, the arguments between them escalated. It wasn't just that Anne couldn't attend this ritual; she had never been able to do that. It was more that Colin wanted a "pure" relationship with the Pygmies, as though none of the rest of them existed—not the villagers, not Anne, not anybody except the Pygmies (and the rest of them *did*, after all, constitute a rather important part of Epulu).

How one gathered, interpreted, and shared information became a contentious issue between them. Anne was a painter, not an anthropologist. And—in Colin's view, worse still—she tended to check her notes with the villagers. She might have had her own romantic vision of the Pygmies as a people close to the origins of mankind, but who, she wondered, could claim a neutral or objective eye? Was a villager's information any more skewed than a Westerner's? Anne admitted that she often interpreted the information she received early on from Pat. From her own experience as an artist, Anne wondered if interpretation wasn't, in fact, what everyone does in selecting material, or even in transcribing it. She had been transcribing legends while in the Pygmy camps, taking down word for word in English what each of the narrators recounted in KiNgwana (see fig. 49a-b).

She had also taken extensive notes about their lives. Anne had been transferring the discipline of drawing to note-taking—she had learned that from Pat. Colin hadn't yet been trained as an anthropologist; was he more precise than she was? Perhaps. But what gave him authority over Anne other than being a tall, white, male European?

Anne could feel her voice going out of control, her gestures getting wilder. What was the matter with him? Why wouldn't he listen to her? Was he repeating the worst side of Pat, trying to push her aside at the very moment she and the workers had almost completed the reconstruction and restored the good parts of Epulu and its past? She had to regain control; she had to calm herself down. She needed to think clearly, not wishing to repeat old history—and certainly not with Colin. One time, Anne yelled to Francis to get a bucket of water and throw it over her head to calm her down, which he did. The splash of coldness doused the yelling, and the words ceased sputtering out of her mouth. Anne's anger sizzled and smoked; the fire was out, and she began slowly to cool down.

But this relief was only momentary. Anne's closest ally had turned into a competitor for the world that was her lifeline, and the tension between them became a permanent ingredient in their relationship. How many times in quick succession, Anne wondered, could one be excluded? First by Pat, then by the Belgian government, and now by Colin with this symbolic male-only ritual? Were these signs that she had no place in this world? If that was the message others were trying to send, Anne thought differently.

Anne was caught in a bind. She needed Colin's support—of that there was no doubt. At times, he was wonderfully charismatic, warm, and sensitive. He gave what he could and plenty of it (on his terms). At other times, he was stubborn and adversarial, working all around Anne like a spider outmaneuvering a fly. But Anne was no unsuspecting fly; playing victim was not her cup of tea. She was extremely independent and strong-willed and did not need someone to put her in her place.

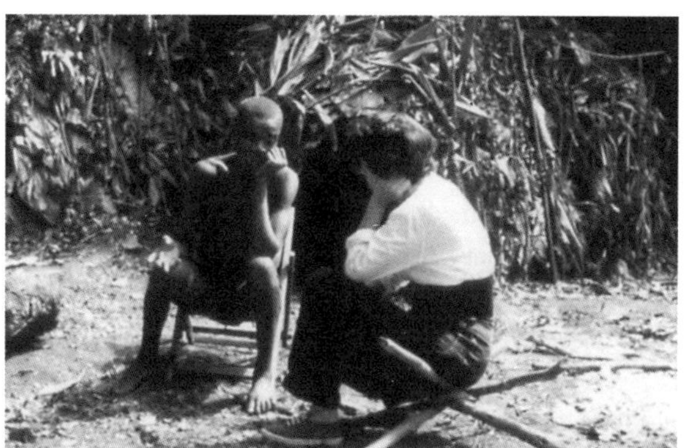

a

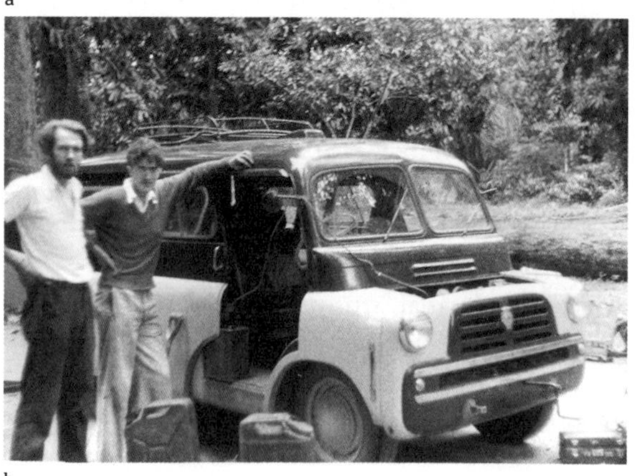

b

Fig. 49a-b
a: Faizi narrating a legend to Anne, c. 1957 (photograph possibly by Colin Turnbull). McDonald archive.
b: Colin Turnbull and Francis Chapman, 1954 (photographer unknown). Anne Eisner Putnam papers, Houghton Library, Harvard University.

She felt that Colin treated her as both old and irrelevant; he probably felt young and frustrated by her. It was an explosive mix.

Some of the underlying tension also came from the worry about de Medina and how things around them could worsen. When de Medina returned from his vacation in early July, the forest immediately became charged with tension once again. Anne thought of him as a very good "third-rate" louse, a villain. She had begun to think it was time to close the hotel for good. To her, it seemed that the okapi station had brought famine because of the increased number of people who had been hired and the concurrent bad crop. Plus, David was building his hotel next door, which could only put even more stress on the area and Anne's guesthouse further into financial ruin. Four trade stores were being built at the roadway, and the minimum wage had gone up five francs a day.

Anne was exhausted from worrying about finances and the hunger among the workmen and the Pygmies. She didn't like the idea of Epulu becoming just another post but could not deny the changes that were upon them. Every one of the workmen had a plantation, and in the past, these plantations provided food for the whole area. The villages of Kapomba, Kopo, and Dar es Salaam were designated by the government to supply the rest, including the necessary rice paddy and peanuts. The economy of these villages depended on Epulu. Since the government had given no warning of any change in Epulu's situation, none of the larger plantations was prepared for the sudden population increase. Moreover, Anne's eviction notice had arrived just at the time of year when new plantations should have been cut. The day she learned that the lease had been renewed, every one of the villagers set about making new plantations, which would take about eighteen months before the first yield, because Epulu would continue as a center. Pygmies were not good agriculturists; they were hunters and gatherers by tradition. Anne felt that some definite provision should have been made for them by the government, given the recent surge in population. It was shocking to discover that newcomers in the region such as de Medina and David were especially favored, while the old inhabitants—the Epulu workmen and Pygmies—found it increasingly difficult to exist. In times of transition, Anne believed, there should have been aid supplied and provisions made for them to be able to stave off the natural imbalance between limited resources and the growing population.

Tensions were high among the people in the village. There hadn't been any violence to date, but Anne did not know how much longer that could continue. She thought the situation was serious and wrote to communicate as much to the new administrator at Mambasa, Mr. Veys. She made clear that the Pygmies had been working at Epulu since its beginning, gathering forest produce and working with tourists, tasks for which they were paid in food and money. Anne herself had been paying five hundred francs a week since the food shortage to save them from starvation. There was hunger all around; people were begging despite the wages and food Anne provided.

In early August, Anne notified de Medina that she had registered an official complaint against him to his superiors. In her letters to the governor of the Oriental Province and to others, she described how he had threatened her with physical violence. She referred back to the by-now-famous champagne scene, but there had been other less overtly violent incidents that nevertheless had her worried about her safety. Anne said that no government employee should threaten a person, "let alone a woman," in this way.

Colin called de Medina "three parts mad" and said that he was "not only unpleasant; he is dangerous." Anne realized how glad she was to have him and Francis there with her at this point. They felt, as Colin put it, that they were "all living on the edge of a landslide."[3]

The hardest choice Anne had ever had to make in her life was upon her: to stay on or to leave Epulu. She reflected and worried. Everything she had worked and fought for would be given up, forever perhaps. How could she abandon these people with whom she had made her home? Had she tested every possible way of keeping the hotel going? How could she give herself permission to leave? And who would she be when she was away from Epulu? How could she rebuild yet again in the loneliness of New York? She loved life out here. It *was* her home.

How could she leave? But under the circumstances, how could she stay?

Anne thought so much that she couldn't think anymore. All she could do was feel. And it felt like everything in her world was cracking, that she was breaking, breaking down after the worst was over, breaking down after she had rebuilt everything (including herself). She had to start all over again, but not here. A new life in her old world. Impossible, it seemed. She wondered if she had the strength.

Farewell to Camp Putnam

Anne finally came to a decision to leave and give up Camp Putnam. She did so well before leaving for New York so that she could deal with as many problems as possible and say her goodbyes. She felt relieved. She had done what she set out to do: work through her grief with the others and restore life to Epulu. Now it was time to go. Many of the European neighbors found it hard to understand why anyone would spend all that time rebuilding and fixing up a place if they were going to leave; it simply didn't make any sense to them as a way to deal with property. But the boys and the Pygmies understood what Anne had been through; they had been through it all together.

Anne started to pack up and close Epulu in earnest. It was a truly awful job and the end of an epoch, not only for Anne but for all the people there. The usual distractions helped to deflect sadness: a flurry of people in and out, white and black people alike, with constant problems to resolve, from the selling of the children's circumcision beads to the stolen bows someone wanted to sell her, from wife money to stolen ivory hammers. Stealing had recently become a serious problem, because the Pygmy children wanted money to buy things in the new stores that had sprung up all along the road. Ugly does it, thought Anne.

As for her babies, Anne knew that they would be well taken care of. All three of them were now back integrated into Pygmy families. Grandma was very protective of W.J. Kokoyou, and his father was paying attention to him now. Every afternoon, they still had their little party together, but Anne was beginning to miss them, and she hadn't even left yet. She was determined to come back; she was going to see them again. Anne promised herself and them that. But she knew it wouldn't be the same. She wondered what they would remember about her later on. She wondered how it would feel to be thousands of miles away, no longer able to hold them in her arms and hear their peals of laughter, their questions about the bugs and anything and everything around them.

Colin and Francis offered to stay over a couple of weeks and help Anne close up. They suggested that she make the transition by going overland with them through Kenya and Uganda and leave with them for Mombasa—the large port on the east coast—then from there to England to spend a week with Colin's family, and finally on to New York.

On Anne's wedding anniversary, she went to Mambasa to visit Pat's grave with Agaranga, Francis, and Colin. They planted flowers and a palm wine tree. Anne had designed a cement block with Pat's name and birth and death dates, but Kempinaire had thought that Pat deserved a monument. He unveiled a huge cement slab in Westminster Abbey style, as Francis remarked, with slightly different proportions. There was a long awkward silence until Kempinaire ventured admiringly: "C'est massif, n'est-ce pas?" ("It's massive, isn't it?"). He seemed so touched by the monument that Anne almost was, too; she actually thought that it was quite awful but did not want to hurt his feelings. The day was not as painful as expected.

Francis and Anne moved out briefly to camp with the Pygmies. Hard to believe that it might be the last camp she would stay in. Anne promised herself that she would make enough money to come back, spend time at Epulu, and do the work she liked without having to worry about running the hotel.

When they returned from camp, Colin also came back with the circumcision children who were to move in within a few days. The medicine man had decided that the children couldn't sleep in their camp, so they went and slept in Colin and Francis's house. Anne did not agree with the idea because anything to do with the circumcised children's rituals had to be burnt afterward, according to Pygmy custom; that was fine in a temporary camp, but she did not want to destroy the guesthouse. So they offered to just leave it at that. It was hardly a "pure" ritual, this circumcision.

The last week in August, Anne informed the boys that she had made the decision to close up for good. It wasn't as difficult as she had expected; most of them had seen it coming. She told the villagers first so that when she gathered the Pygmies, she would have been already able to practice her speech and composure. Several people made very concrete suggestions to call in the medicine man from far off to chase away the evil people and spirits who had gotten hold of the forest. Anne told the Pygmies that her house was to be theirs, and they could move into it and build around it. Faizi—the great elephant hunter featured in the book Anne would soon publish—seemed rather delighted to have such a handsome place.

Anne turned the Camp Putnam village over to the Pygmies. They were rather unbelieving, even as they settled in and built a fire right on top of her carefully nursed gardenia plant. Four families consisting of an unknown number of people moved into her own house. Two more families were in an adjacent house, with others grouped in houses all around. Giving over her house, almost like an exchange for all the time she had spent in their away camps, seemed a rather appropriate way to pass it on, Anne thought.

The *Madami* Manuscript

During 1953, Anne had corresponded with Monroe Stearns and Allan Keller, sending notes and information to them, along with directives about how she wanted the book Keller was ghostwriting with her to be as precise as possible, including a chapter with ethnographic material as an appendix. The line drawings that she proposed of Mbuti and Bira were neither to illustrate the narrative of her story nor to reproduce stereotypes but rather to suggest her own artistic recreation of life among the Pygmies. Throughout 1953, Anne continued to send material and directives.

When Keller's first full draft of the manuscript arrived at Epulu in March, 1954, with the title they had settled on, *Madami: My Eight Years of Adventure with the Congo Pigmies*, Anne sat down and read through it in one sitting. The paragraphs read better than she had expected. But there were far too many stories about killing leopards. Keller was interested in animal adventures. He didn't have the context to understand Anne's need to rebuild Epulu and therefore hadn't included anything about it. The process of healing was now well enough along that Anne herself preferred to express the good part of Epulu rather than her pain. But Epulu's elusive charm had, in fact, eluded Allan quite entirely. Anne thought: *Some people can get this kind of thing into a painting, most can't. Some can get it into writing, most can't.* There were important points that Allan simply couldn't understand, as seen in the following lines he had crafted:

> The firelight danced upon the bronzed, half-chocolate, half-russet red skins of the little men. It was caught and reflected by the deep-set eyes of the women,

sitting beyond the ring of males. Strangely enough I didn't feel out of place. The Pygmies accepted me as a friend and an equal. My color, and their color, made no difference.[4]

Anne reacted in notes: "One is always conscious of color . . . if you forget they remind you. It always enraged Pat to hear them speaking about him as the white man."[5] Anne did feel comfortable, however—but not because of the erasure of differences. She loved the consciousness of color because it always related to her palette. The color terms for the people in Epulu became complicated rather quickly, however, and were more than descriptive of "the way it was" in the patriarchal and colonial hierarchy. If one was of mixed background, and no matter how dark or light, identity depended on who the father was and whether he recognized a child as his. What defined one's status in Epulu—and in the Belgian Congo more broadly—was more than color alone, but how could they possibly cover all of this in the kind of book Keller had set out to craft?

As Christraud M. Geary writes:

Anne intended to write an "authentic" book based on her experiences, challenging many of the stereotypes about the pygmies, about "darkest Africa," and about her own role as a woman in the colonial Congo. Allan Keller and Monroe Stearns, on the other hand, were well aware of that fact that the public was best served by familiar and recognizable story lines about peoples of Africa and women travelers, and that the commercial success of the book depended on its appeal to this readership.[6]

Anne had seen *Dark Rapture*, a 1938 film by Armand Denis and Leila Roosevelt, and she had read Henry Morton Stanley's *In Darkest Africa*, Joseph Conrad's *Heart of Darkness*, and the work of at least one woman writer, Delia Akeley's *Jungle Portraits*; she was aware of the common stereotypes and clichés.

Anne wrote to Stearns, "As for clichés and people liking them you also add that people are interested in my life because it is not a cliché. Therefore I do not understand why the thing shouldn't be consistent all the way through and we can admit that the book doesn't need to have the usual African clichés such as Darkest Africa, steaming jungles."[7] Jokingly trying to sidestep the usual stereotypes of adventure and courage, which she could not espouse, Anne said that she thought it time for a book about a coward.

When no proofs arrived over the summer of 1954, Anne had stewed, worrying about the changes she had requested. She had corrected mistakes in the manuscript that she thought important and had wanted to see put right. They would not be. An advanced copy of the jacket arrived with a photograph featuring a large Anne and a much smaller Pygmy. *Clichés, nothing but clichés!* Here was the paternalistic colonial hierarchy translated into the maternalistic duo of a tall white woman and a small African.

The inside cover of the copy made her stomach do flips:

> From the moment the almost naked pigmies danced out of the jungle shouting "Putnami's back! Putnami's back!" newly married Anne Putnam knew that she was right in coming to Africa.

Anne spat back a letter to Monroe: "I see the word naked appearing two times, which from any point of view except cheapness seems to me to be in poor taste." Here was exoticism at its worst, angling for a sexual innuendo, when the Pygmies were more fully dressed than most of the people on Jones Beach, Martha's Vineyard, or Provincetown—and certainly much more modest in demeanor. If it was odd to think that Anne, of all people (who had often gone swimming at the nude beach on Martha's Vineyard), was shocked by the use of the word "naked," it was because the inaccurate portrayal of Pygmy life deeply concerned her.

Anne balked at Keller's suggestion that she was some kind of scheming wife and protested at "portraying myself" as "blubbering like a baby." How clichéd and Little Mrs. America could you get? Yet she completely let pass and never protested the book's redating of her marriage to before the trip to Africa. Where were Anne's maverick guts to say that she had lived with Pat, yes, *in sin*. Anne did not completely correct Allan's freedom to invent her life as well as that of the Pygmies.

Anne's final corrections did not make it through the mail in time for the printing of the book. When Anne's mother read an advanced copy, she summed up her reaction: "I relived all you have been through, and know how much he [Keller] has eliminated."[8]

As Geary points out, the most original part of *Madami* consisted of the attempt to describe in "her own voice" the Mbuti and Bira as individual people rather than sociological examples or objects of ethnographic study. That Anne's "voice" was voiced over by Keller adds to the problematic depictions both of the context of Epulu and of her as a woman. What did come across was the humanistic portrayal of the people of Epulu at a time when physical anthropology concentrated instead on material data. In this, the book provided a precedent for later anthropological writing in general, which would come to include the voice of the ethnographer only after the 1960s and may have even provided a model (however unacknowledged) for the successful book Colin Turnbull would later write about Mbuti Pygmies.

When all the packing was done, Anne, Colin, and Francis were finally ready to be on their way by mid-September. On the final day, they were just about to leave when Rozos the storekeeper arrived. All the people of Epulu, and more, had come out to send them off, shaking hands all around. A formal, sad moment. With a lot of commotion, Anne piled into the car with Colin and Francis and got as far as Agaranga's house when the car stopped dead. One of the workmen had given Colin a demijohn full of caustic soda, which Colin had poured into the car thinking it was gasoline. Once that snafu had been resolved, they finally made their way out. Simply getting off Epulu territory was so difficult that saying goodbye almost felt like a relief.

They stopped briefly by Pat's grave in Mambasa, said goodbyes, and went on their way, driving through the "Mountains of the Moon," the Rwenzori Mountains, to Ishango in the eastern Belgian Congo, the place where the Semiliki River runs out of the lake and where one sees scads of animals from a safe distance. It was a place Anne had loved, and she had loved being there with Pat. *It is rare to go back to a place and experience it having just as much beauty as one remembers,* she thought; *Ishango was that.* Picnicking on a bluff, they drank to Anne's book with a bottle of warm beer, watching buffalo and different kinds of antelope below.

They arrived at Kampala, Uganda, at the end of September. Colin and Francis stayed at the University of Kampala, Anne at the Imperial Hotel. There she found her hands too clean, too washed from inactivity, and her mind dormant from lack of a challenge.

For the past year or so Anne had often said to herself, *I would be happy if I could just have peace and quiet.* But now she wondered if that was so. She should have liked inner peace, yes, but of the kind that comes only when one is working or loving; such peace is not a static state any more than looking with a painter's eyes. She knew that to retrain her scattered Epulu energies, to focus on the life of painting alone in a studio, was going to be difficult. The Anne who was always looking for a moment by herself at Epulu would certainly feel bereft, for a time, without the world of the Ituri and the people with whom she felt close. She had to let go. An immense sense of relief began to settle over her.

What was going to happen to her now? Anne was tired of worrying. It had been time to stop being responsible for so many people. Responsible only for herself—it didn't seem possible. There were no longer a hundred people dependent on her. How could one have been so laden down with responsibilities one week and without any the next? She felt indebted to everyone who had nursed Pat eighteen to twenty-four hours a day. Some had left, but how could anyone repay the ones who had stayed? And how much she owed Rozos the shopkeeper for having carried her and the people of Epulu for so long, both of them hoping that her ship would come in with the book. Anne vowed to repay him with her first royalties from publication. She vowed, too, to keep making the payments on Epulu. She made good on both later.

In a *cahier,* Anne wrote a letter to the people of Epulu:

> I will do the best I can for you, but you are all too much for me. I pay you off to the best of my ability. I know that you have been good and loyal to my husband for many years and to me for the past seven. We have all been through good times and hell together. But I can't do more. If I stay with you, I can only become a bad screamy person, one you will not like. What should happen if I got

sick? This all takes more money than I have. The neighbors are trying to starve you out. They say bad things. They want to own the forest, but they cannot because they are not apt to gain your love. They do not love you. But my love is empty, you are too many, you are beyond my strength. You need more than I can give you. I can only do you harm.[9]

Pat wanted to be great with his curiosity and energy; Africa was his baby, his canvas. Anne thought her canvas was smaller: *it is silly to try to paint murals when one is an easel painter, though there is no harm in trying*. Sometimes one's limitations were hard to accept. Was one greater or smaller for recognizing them?

Madami Transformed

The *Rhodesia Castle* sailed in early October 1954, from Mombasa, Kenya, taking Colin, Francis, and Anne from Africa to Port Said, to Port Sudan, then to Genoa and Marseilles. From there, they journeyed to Horsham, near Warnham in Sussex, for a stay with the Turnbull family before Anne returned to New York. *Madami* appeared in bookstores in the United States (see fig. 50) just as Anne was arriving in New York City from England. Although the good Pat lived on in the pages of *Madami*, with time, the omission of his illness and death seemed stranger and stranger. To the extent that Anne's life could not be separated from the pall shed over all of Epulu by Pat's worsening state, her book expressed only part of the story; to the extent that the book focused on Anne's positive experiences at Epulu, it created a golden age that never really existed. Mention in passing of Pat's "emphysema" reinforced a form of either utopianism or denial—however one wants to put it—that anyone who had been out to Epulu or had even read Anne's correspondence would have recognized as a survival tool necessary for life there.

The Anne whom readers got to know through *Madami* made public only some of the many identities that she had espoused in Africa: the painter, the wife, the friend and protector of the Pygmies. The narrator "Anne" did not reveal her role as co-wife and sole financial support of Camp Putnam as Pat declined (also not mentioned). Promotional material for the book billed her as a "clever, intrepid and talented personality" who told a "heart-warming human story." While not untrue, it promised a far more cheering and conventional story than what actually happened at Epulu. In the *Madami* version, Pat was from the outset "swimming at the Vineyard . . . convincing me that I should marry him and live in Africa,"[10] as though Anne and Pat had left for Africa "properly" married and had remained so, which is not bad for a rewriting of history. Yet with all the energy Anne had expended bringing the details of Pygmy life into focus, she had only told Allan Keller part of her own story, which gave him free rein to imagine her life as a woman through contemporary stereotypes.

On the other hand, Keller's style communicated assumptions about Anne's nature, such as: "I had moved, woman-like, on instinct alone."[11] But we know that Camp Putnam required more: knowledge and a strong sense of self-preservation, combined with an ability to think on one's feet. And in reality, Anne did not so much resent "housewifely chores" ("which bore me to tears," as Keller has Anne saying in the book)[12] as assume responsibility for delegating them. Whether by design or not, Keller had constructed a portrait of an unwomanly woman for the 1950s. A prime example of Keller's transformation was Anne's presumed lack of maternal instinct, as described at the moment of W.J. Kokoyou's arrival:

> "What in Heaven's name am I to do with this baby?" I stormed at Pat.
> "Why, Anne," he said, "it'll die if we don't care for it. We can't let that happen."
> I nodded dumbly in agreement.[13]

Keller mixed stereotypes to create an odd image of Anne. At one moment, she and Pat looked like the ideal American parents, transposed to Africa, as if in the 1950s television sitcom *The Adventures of Ozzie and Harriet*; at another, Anne was not maternal because she had a profession and as yet no children. Anne did not conform to either model: she was a dedicated painter, now also an ethnologist and writer, who also loved children. Keller's view of how a woman might react under these extraordinary circumstances presented plausible stereotypes to an American audience. That Anne did not fit into these formulas did not deter Keller; that is perhaps why he ignored her request for changes in the narrative after she had read the proofs. His stories of her oscillated between the wacky-housewife version of everyday life in a forest compound and the terrors of deadly ants and man-eating leopards.

Anne agreed with her editor, Monroe Stearns, when he argued that the story was all-important, but the question was, who was telling it? She knew that writing, like painting, cannot reproduce reality—not even an "inner" one. That was one of the reasons she had, at first, resisted Abstract Expressionism. She knew that style and form create truths, working out from an aesthetic tradition. So, too, the tension between autobiography and biography lay at the heart of what was most appealing and yet problematic in this book. Keller had written Anne's biography in the first person, and Anne had collaborated on her autobiography through him as a third party. They had accepted the roles of author and editor, or collaborative writers, even though the two seem never to have discussed the implications of form. Anne only became aware after she saw

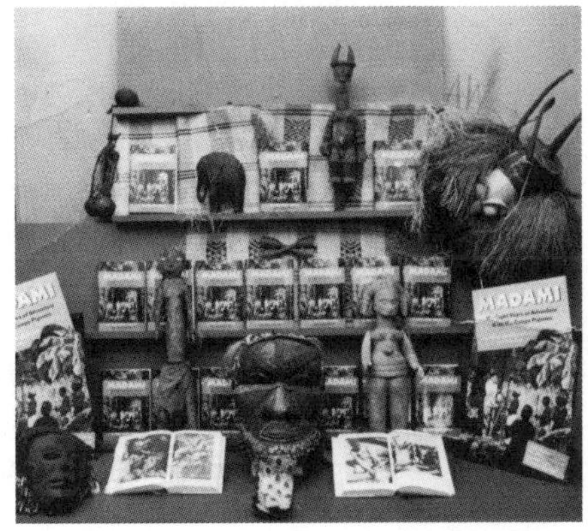

Fig. 50 Madami display, 1954 (location and photographer unknown). Anne Eisner Putnam papers, Houghton Library, Harvard University.

the proofs of how much control she had given up: the possibility of telling her version of life at Epulu. Keller's sense of appeal to the readership of the era, along with his editing skills, made it a popular book. The resulting effect was the creation of an "Anne Eisner Putnam" that Anne could neither totally accept nor renounce. Having co-signed the book, she could hardly distance herself publicly to say, "This isn't who 'I' am."

As soon as *Madami* was published, a slew of favorable reviews appeared in newspapers, from the *New York Times*, the *Herald Tribune*, the *New York Mirror*, and the *New York World-Telegram and Sun* to the *Woodstock News* and the *Belgian Trade*. Sales soared during the fall of 1954. A condensed version of the book appeared in *Reader's Digest*, and with thirteen international (translated) editions of the book itself, it reached more readers than Anne could have imagined. Some reviewers liked the mystery of the forest and the sense of adventure; the headline in the *Kingston Daily Freeman* summed it up: "Darkest Africa Story Is Told in Putnam Book." Others admired the bond between Anne and the Pygmies: "a ray of sunshine in the deluge of dark and stormy books about seething Africa,"[14] wherein "[Anne's] life and the Pygmies' are so intertwined there is no saying just where one ends and the other begins, for they shared many of the same joys, sorrows and fears, which is why her story of this exotic life has a ring of conviction."[15] Goris commented more seriously: "Reading this excellent book, one is forced to revise or at least to question every accepted idea of our economic and social thinking."[16]

A few articles picked up on Anne's importance as an artist (reproducing some of the drawings) and her unique perspective. The then-chairman of the Department of Anthropology at Rutgers University, British-American anthropologist Ashley Montagu, wrote: "Mrs. Putnam is a painter, and her artist's eye is evidently much more interested in the excitements that the fauna has to offer, and especially the human fauna, than anything the flora can produce. Not that all is perfect—man-eating leopards are too frequent for safety and insects too many for comfort and there are poisonous snakes and scorpions. But the country is wonderfully beautiful, and the pygmies help to make it more so."[17] In Montagu's anthropological work, he questioned the term "race" (even contributing to the UNESCO statements on race) and opposed Carlton Coon's stance. He also believed in women's superior advantage. Montagu had just written on *The Natural Superiority of Women* and was clearly sensitive to Anne's approach as a woman, humanist, and artist.[18] Another review, by John Haverstick,[19] reproduced six line drawings by Anne as some of the most fascinating parts of the book. Anne could now consider the reconstruction of her idyllic Epulu complete. If the good Pat lived on in *Madami*, without mention of his tragic decline and death or the complexities of his cross-cultural life, the Anne who lived on through the book presented opportunities and constraints for her life as it continued in New York.

CHAPTER EIGHT

Back in New York On and Off (1955–1959)

Agaranga wrote to Anne regularly in KiNgwana, as he had on each of her prior trips back to New York. Some of the news was heart-wrenching—about hunger, the workmen's inability to earn money, and conflict among those who stayed at Epulu (some of the people had dispersed). He asked if she planned to return. As time went on, he reassured her in subsequent letters that the children were nevertheless well, sent updates on the workmen and the state of the buildings as well as news of births, marriages, and deaths at Epulu. In many letters, he asked to be remembered to her family and the Putnam parents. He also forwarded mail from the bank and from some people who thought Pat was still alive.[1] In return, Anne sent funds—to pay people, to give gifts, and to repair buildings—while also writing him about her health and the success of her book (she promised to send a copy as soon as the French translation came out). She said that she herself felt like a Pygmy, moving from one place to another (New York, Woodstock, Martha's Vineyard). She requested that Agaranga place flowers on Pat's grave in December 1954, one year after his death (her secular way of respecting his memory); Agaranga wrote that he had done so. Anne assured him that she intended to return but could not for some time.[2] Each signed their letters, "It is I" (Agaranga, Anne), but Agaranga expressed the desire for typed letters, as he was having trouble reading her writing and corrected her spelling of his name (Agaranga, not Ageronga).[3] (See fig. 51.)

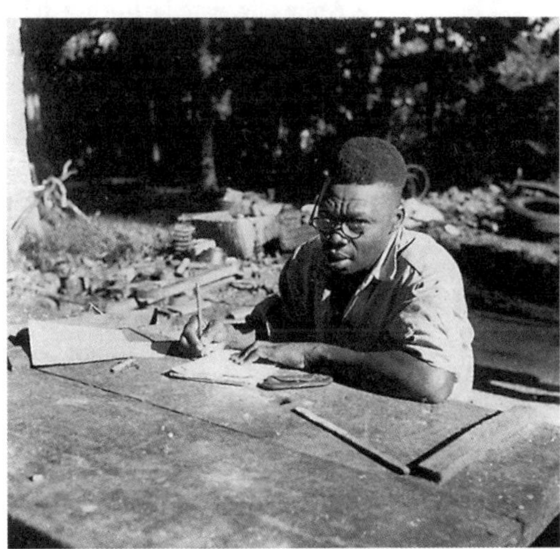

Fig. 51 Agaranga Nunziotika, in Epulu, c. 1954 (photograph possibly by Francis Chapman), Houghton Library, Harvard University.

Anne also received letters from people around the world who had either visited Camp Putnam and wanted to share memories or still wanted to visit (having read the book). During the year following the publication of *Madami* and the condensed version published in *Reader's Digest*, Anne also received fan letters from people who cut through the clichés and seemed to appreciate especially her sense of humanity and empathy. One reader, having discovered that Pat had been ill, nevertheless challenged her silence in the book on the subject, wondering how her account could so differ from reality. Had she simply abandoned her husband in his time of need? Anne responded with the news of Pat's death. These letters—whether comforting or not—were not a replacement for the loss of Anne's active communal life at Epulu, and the isolation of New York made the transition to a life of painting difficult.

This transition was all the more difficult because not long after her arrival in New York, Anne underwent the "ladies' operation"—a euphemism for a hysterectomy. The women around her (her mother, sister, and niece Joan—my sister) were all sympathetic, but no one talked much about illness, as with many other culturally taboo topics. What Anne had called the "curse" had, in fact, truly become one as the "change of life" set in fully. After the operation, hot flashes surged up and engulfed her, drenching her body regularly many times a day. I was by this time coming into adolescence, and I believed that her flushes were due to the tsetse fly bites she had described—that's how informed I was. Anne recovered from her operation slowly; the days alone were long. Back from the hospital in the apartment she had rented on Minetta Street in Greenwich Village, she began working every day with her usual determination, even if it meant only putting stretchers on canvases in preparation to paint. She had to fight the heaviness of mind and body that spells resistance, knowing that long hours alone were the only way to gain back concentration. Soon the training etched in memory began to kick in and provide the mental space necessary for serious work.

Anne alternated painting in her studio with speaking engagements about Epulu and the Pygmies on radio and TV shows (she was interviewed, for example, by Vincent Lopez on his show from the Taft Hotel), in lectures, and on visits to school classes where she introduced bows, arrows, and other objects. Topics varied according to context: Pygmy life and rituals at the American Museum of Natural History, hunting and sports to the men at the Rotary Club of Woodstock, African art to the Pen and Brush Club. And for Ladies' Night at the Adventurers Club, she focused on the "Women's Role in Pygmy Society." Anne spoke about women and cooking, women and their babies: "All African women work hard and the Pygmy about the hardest of any. She chops her wood, gathers her food, cooks. . . . The mothers nurse [the children] until they are three or four years old. Some mothers have up to eight children. They do not have another child before the last is three years old."[4] She also spoke about women and the art of decorating—either on bark cloths or bodies:

> The men make their bark cloths by pounding the bark with ivory hammers, and the women paint them with dye that they get by rubbing two pieces of red wood together. . . . Then if she is in the mood she makes different designs with a twig or her fingers. This is the only artwork the Pygmies do outside of painting their bodies which they do whenever they feel festive.[5]

Anne communicated her interest in the differences between the Pygmies and Westerners (whether European or North American), as well as between the Pygmies and the villagers, with a sense that through the recognition and articulation of differences, people could learn from one another and get along. She described how the Pygmy economy was based on hunting, along with many aspects of their communal lives and rituals, and she took particular pleasure in talking about the experience of women: birth, children, and death. When questioned about birth control and abortion, Anne described the women mixing water with pounded manioc greens to ward off unintended pregnancy. Fertility remained nevertheless the most important value, she stated, and she shared how Pygmy women thought it beautiful that their breasts fell as a sign of parenthood. Anne described in one lecture how—contrary to the way Keller had depicted her reaction to suddenly coming into motherhood—not only had she been overjoyed to receive William J. Kokoyou as an infant but "This foster-motherhood altered the attitudes of all the pigmies [*sic*] toward me. Being a mother is very important to them."[6] She had been welcomed in new ways by motherhood and folded into the community of Epulu in a way not before possible.

In some ways, Anne had passed through many of the same events as her contemporaries—marriage, motherhood, loss—both in New York and at Epulu, though her route had taken her along the margins of each culture. If these events had not all happened so quickly, one might have said that Anne had managed to have it all. But in those ten years, she was also widowed, had to leave her children in the protection of a nurturing community, and returned to a context she thought she had already left forever.

As Anne drafted her lectures, she wished that she "had the talents and total recall of a Proustworld [*sic*]—really be[ing] able to go through trying to live it all again." She realized that even if she were going to return to Epulu as she intended, her life there belonged to an irretrievable past. "Surely my Africa is now a thing of the historic past and for a few of us a nostalgic thing. What are the highlights one remembers, the unimportant details that really made up daily living. . . . The purple flowers on a log across the river in the dry season, the singing of the women and children as they went bathing. The okapi walking back and forth . . . The pygmies flitting back and forth in their bark cloths and carrying their bows and arrows."[7] Her drawings and paintings would hold the memory of that life.

In the Tower of the American Museum of Natural History

When Harry Shapiro contacted Anne in October 1955, he wanted to buy pieces from her collection of African artifacts, which he knew to be important. Shapiro was curator of the Department of Physical Anthropology at the American Museum of Natural History and had kept up with Pat and Anne as they collected artifacts during their trips between 1946 and 1948.

The collection that she had crated up in Epulu took a year and a half to arrive by boat. Anne kept for herself some of the pieces she cared most for, such as "the wife's" Bwaka throwing knife(as opposed to the husband's which had a slightly different shape), and a headrest in the shape of a bird. Anne's living room on Minetta Street, with an array of artifacts from Epulu—a large table made by an Epulu carver, smaller tables, headrests, and other beloved objects—recreated a sense of a life elsewhere. But for the lack of a forest, one might have almost believed oneself to be in some new rondavel at Epulu. At the top of the stairs leading up to Anne's apartment entryway, a pungent odor of linseed oil (used to preserve wood objects in her collection) greeted one at the door. And yet the composition of the room was like no living space at Camp Putnam; it replicated nothing identifiable from the Palais. It was more like the model for a still life yet to be painted, with objects and masks scattered about, and a bark cloth on the wall.

When the rest of the collection finally arrived, she stored some of the works at her parents' barn; they had bought a farm near Woodstock in the early 1950s, when Will retired, to be near the community of the artists associated with the Woodstock Artists Association and Woodstock village. (See fig. 52a-c.) They renovated part of the barn for Anne's African collection to insulate it from creatures and humidity on the ground floor, as well

Fig. 52a-c
a: Anne with William and Florine Eisner, Woodstock, N.Y., c. 1955 (photographer unknown). McDonald archive.
b: Anne in Woodstock, c. 1955 (photographer unknown). McDonald archive.
c: Walker Evans, *Portrait of Anne Eisner*, 1956. Metropolitan Museum of Art, New York.

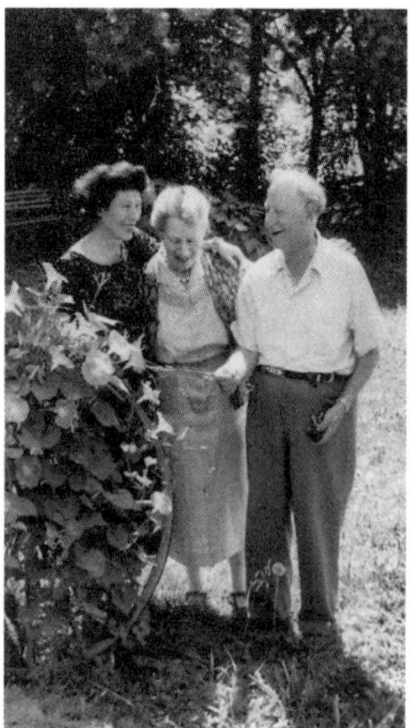

a

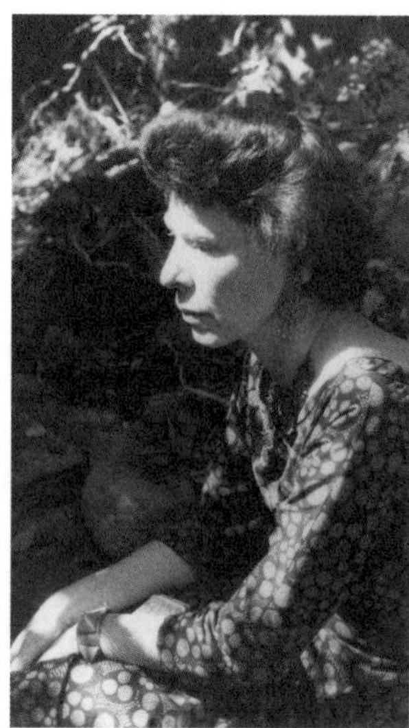

b

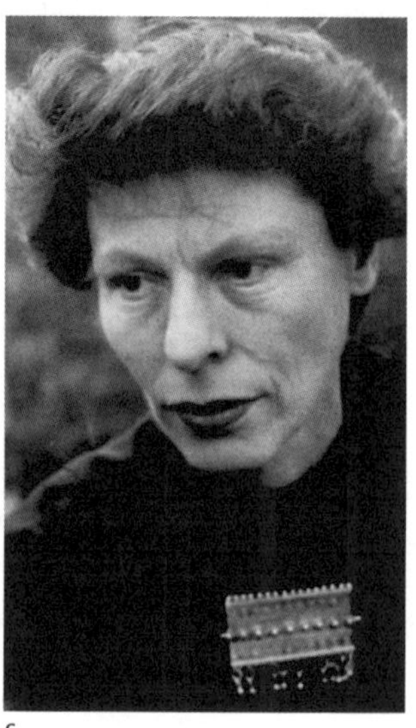

c

as an apartment above for Anne. The Eisners made the rest of the lower part of the barn into studios in which they themselves painted, as they were actively exhibiting.

Ultimately, Anne moved most of the collection to one of the towers of the American Museum of Natural History which Shapiro made available to her. It overlooked Central Park on the southeast side. As the largest private collection ever handled by the museum—containing some one thousand pieces all in all—it was still small compared with the four thousand objects collected during the museum's expedition between 1909 and 1915 by Herbert Lang and James Chapin.

Anne divided the collection for the museum in two: one part in Pat's name with some three hundred pieces, the other in her own with around ninety pieces. This division was a decision that was important to her. She gave Pat the greater notice, even though she had been the one to sensitize him aesthetically to the character of these objects, having chosen and bought many of them. With these collections, she retained something much more important: a part of her relationship to Epulu and therefore to Pat. Caring for the collection was a way of allowing the life she had left to live on: dealing with each piece lovingly, placing it in the museum to be preserved for others to see and study.

Determining Archive Legacies

Anne began cataloging the pieces in the collection, referring to both her notes and Pat's; it required sustained effort, since many of the labels by which they had carefully identified objects had been eaten by termites. Sometimes the sight of a particular piece would set memories in motion; mostly, it was a lot of work. Pat's papers, notes, letters, documents, photos, and maps were fragments without any order. Anne was determined that they should be organized, and she resolved to keep the record of this history.

Anne signaled to Shapiro that Colin Turnbull—now reading anthropology at Oxford—could be the right person to make an assessment of the papers. Anne thought she could trust Colin; he was a link to Epulu, and she looked forward to working with him. Shapiro agreed to the idea, and Anne wrote to Colin.

Colin's very familiar greeting, "Hiya Baby," rebounded excitedly from Magdalen College. "I can't think of anything that would give me greater personal satisfaction than to work on Pat's papers."[8] He wanted to give a "boost to the name of Putnam in the field of Africanists,"[9] he added. "Even if Pat's notes are full of stuff, I certainly hope you will help out on some of the things you know about. . . . It would be fun working together, though no doubt quite exasperating. I think that the ideal would be early in the morning with a bottle of whisky between us and a dozen packets of cigarettes."[10]

Letters flew back and forth during the spring of 1956 while Colin prepared to come to New York. He wrote one series to Anne, another to Shapiro. He wrote Shapiro that he was interested in Pat Putnam's notes because of his own work, speculating that if material were insufficient for publication under Pat's name, he might be able to make use of it in the work he planned to do. Acknowledgment would be made, of course, but he would need some assurance from Shapiro that he could use the information for his own purposes. Colin assumed that the notes belonged to the museum and asked Shapiro, not Anne, about permissions. Shapiro deferred to Anne, but he granted permission to use the material. A gentleman's agreement was therefore contracted before Colin arrived in New York in early August 1956.

Many decisions—not only about the value of Pat's material and what to do with it but also about the history of Epulu that would be written—were riding on this collaboration. The potential for a job at the museum might also be in it for Colin. Was there even a remote possibility that a love affair might happen between Anne and Colin? Was Anne in love with Colin? Was Colin in love with Anne? He was ten years her junior and homosexual, but the relationship between them had always been informed by a process of triangulation. For Colin, Anne was access to the memory of Pat and life at Epulu, and he certainly loved her for that. But Anne had such a strong presence of her own; it intervened, kicked, and bristled. She was "infuriatingly loveable," he wrote me in the 1980s. Infuriation was taking Colin over; he wouldn't be able to accomplish his purpose by staying close to Anne.

By now, Anne knew that Colin would not be Pat's successor for her. Even though it was difficult to resist his youthful charm, she was quickly put off when she felt him taking possession of the project. She expected a collaborative venture, whereas Colin wanted to make it his own. He withdrew from her, distancing himself as he found and drew closer to an authority figure with power like Shapiro.

Things quickly fell apart between them when Colin let someone he met in a bar stay in Anne's apartment without asking her. It felt to Anne like the night Pat had thrown her out of her own house. Couldn't a woman choose where to be, who to be, and who could enter her own personal space? She had opened her home to Colin again and again; why didn't he just graciously accept what she had offered? Anne felt pushed to the limit. Colin was trying to evict her from something; she couldn't yet tell from what, but she had experienced these feelings too many times. Hurting, she held in the anger, for a while.

Then, one evening, they collaborated on a dinner party for some of Colin's relatives from Canada. They had agreed to arrange dinner at her apartment. Colin invited his new friend back to the same space. To Anne, it seemed like a direct provocation. The dinner was fairly amicable until Anne erupted. Colin had been living off her all summer and didn't seem to have any sense of it. She blew up—at the man (a casualty), at Colin, at the whole situation. She confronted him in front of his family; she wanted to hurt him the way he had hurt her. And to seal the deal, she told the young man off at the door. After that, no discussion was possible between them; they would only write again once Colin had left New York. Unaware of any acting out on his part, Colin proclaimed his independence and accused Anne of expecting more from him than he could give. He was right for the wrong reasons. It wasn't about his preference for men; it was about her expectation of him as a friend-turned-colleague, and it was there that he most let her down.

Colin had come for the express purpose of working on Pat's papers and of working with Anne on them. The blowup came at a critical moment. Colin left New York in a fury with Pat's papers in hand. He thought at the time that it was the end of their relationship, as he wrote her upon his return to England: "As for us—I think it better if we both try and forget everything. It is obvious that we can never get on together, so it just isn't worth the effort of trying to patch anything up."[11]

Anne, too, was furious. She had just given away something important: Pat's legacy—and ultimately her own—at Epulu.

Anne and Colin were on very different paths in their lives and in their work, despite their compelling shared bond of Camp Putnam and the memory of it. Anne was separating from her relationship to Pat; Colin was forming his own relationship with Pat's legacy. One of the lessons of life at Camp Putnam had been that relations between people and groups involved human entanglement (ranging from peaceful to violent), and work like Pat's, Anne's, and even Colin's involved just as much complication.

Not one to be defeated by the anguish of disconnection, Anne had always come back each time by focusing on important relationships. First, when Pat had broken their intense love relationship by introducing other wives, Anne made a pact that was inclusive. Then, when Pat did not allow her to care for him during his illness, she looked after the babies. Finally, when she could no long run Camp Putnam and the necessity of letting go seemed imminent, an opening for connection resurfaced in the cataloging of the collection and the return to her art. As for the decisions concerning Pat's material, the blowup provided Colin with a necessary distance from Anne to ensure his sole identification with Pat.

Anne remained troubled about the professional decisions concerning her material and Pat's (although she only voiced concern about Pat's) at this time when she and Colin were in conflict. Monroe Stearns acted as intermediary, writing to Colin:

> Anne Putnam is rather understandably, I think, disturbed over the state of Pat's papers, which you and she worked on last summer. . . . Consequently I am writing you to ask whether you can give me a report on just what you did

> to them, and also whether you think that these papers, providing they were put into proper publishable form, contain sufficient and accurate enough information and data; or whether they would have to be expanded and corrected by a professional anthropologist. . . . Anne feels that a biography of Pat can be extracted from these papers. Do you agree?[12]

Colin replied:

> I spent most of my time sorting them from an incoherent, termite-eaten mess into 150 folders, under various headings. . . . At the best it was a rough sorting, because my primary object was to extract what scientific material there was, and this I think I did. . . . My energies then were directed onto that scientific material to see what could be done with it. . . . Shapiro has seen briefly the typescript I prepared, and Anne has a copy. It is extremely slight and could not stand by itself in published form either as a monograph or even a collection of field-work notes. This would, even if anyone attempted it and succeeded in finding a publisher, only damage Pat's reputation and give him a reputation of superficiality and "dilletanteness" as an anthropologist, and this would be totally unjustified as Pat's knowledge was as wide as it was deep. . . .
>
> As for biography—I told Anne that there was a lot of material there that could be used by a biographer—but it would take a lot of work. The correspondence . . . was revealing not only of the facts of Pat's life . . . but also gave some insight into the man himself.[13]

Then, in early November, Colin wrote to Anne suggesting that—since in his view Pat's material could not be used as it was—he "lump" Pat's material together with hers, putting "the two together as the 'Putnam' material" for his Oxford thesis. "It would be explained how and why this was being done," because between them, as he wrote, damning her contributions with faint praise, "you cover your area pretty well":

> This would simply be an ethnographic work—description of what happens, not a sociological analysis of why it happens. It is in this form that Pat's material and [yours] is of the greatest value—and it is great. It could also include at least some of the legends, and without prejudice I can safely say that it would make all the others together look pretty pale. It would, as I have worked out a tentative plan, form the largest single part of the thesis.
>
> Let me know what you think, Anne. I would like to do it, because in spite of our personal difficulties, and even though I would probably behave the same way again and again, I am still very fond of both you and Pat—and Camp Putnam. But let's leave personal feelings out of this—be they good or bad—and think of it as a worthwhile job.[14]

Colin wrote to Stearns: "I think it would be nice to have Anne and Pat together on this . . . they give a good ethnographic description of the Epulu Pygmies."[15]

When Colin returned to Oxford with the Putnam material after his bitter fight with Anne, the argument ostensibly concerned personal difficulties of getting along. But the larger issue was indeed what would happen with Pat's papers, plus Anne's ethnographic notes and transcribed legends. He acknowledged Anne's and Pat's material in the thesis he would write at Oxford,[16] but when claiming Pat's legacy in later publications, Colin's summary effected a progressive erasure not only of Anne's ethnographic contribution but also of the importance of her presence at Camp Putnam:

> When Putnam died the villagers hoped that I would take his place. We looked somewhat alike, and it was assumed that we were kin, so I was classified as his son. He had become an integral part of the village world . . . [and] was a link between the village world and the colonial world, able to mediate, and thus keep the two worlds apart. When he died, all that died with him. . . .
> Camp Putnam fell into disuse, since his third wife was unable to maintain it (although she gave a good try).[17]

By referring to Anne in relation to Pat as simply "his third wife," Colin blends Anne into a tapestry of anonymity. Giving himself the central position, he finishes what the crisis of 1956 began: his exclusive identification with Pat, whom he had known for only months, and his obliteration of Anne in the history of the place.

Much of the trouble between Anne and Colin arose from the perception of their different positions. Since her introduction to Africa, Anne had been interested in the aesthetics of visual art from African artifacts and art for the purpose of understanding differing cultures. Colin, on the other hand, focused on ethnography and saw art (music being a particular interest) in terms of social institutions.[18] His great talent in comprehending different cultures was the ability to understand the side of the other, often the victim.[19] This ability did not transfer well into his relationship to Anne, who was not other enough for him to empathize with successfully and certainly was not a victim. Both nevertheless had much in common in breaking with the tradition of a scientific paradigm to understand Mbuti life and the larger community of Epulu.

Colin's erasure of Anne going forward in his work on the Mbuti of Epulu was not the end of the story.

The New York Art World, Again

During the years from 1952 to 1955, while Anne was in Africa, the politics and the art world in New York had changed dramatically. Senator Joseph McCarthy's witch-hunt hearings to prove communist infiltration into government, film, and university culture ended in a 1954 Senate censure. The Cold War standoff between the superpowers of the Soviet Union and the United States was ongoing, and Dwight D. Eisenhower's presidency, begun in 1953, had determined the need for a sense of post–World War II unity. Many of the 1930s radicals had since moved to the right, now espousing anti-communist views and capitalism, and some revised memories about positions taken earlier. These changes in position and memory constitute the move from the anti-Stalinists to the New York intellectuals "under the impact of Cold War anticommunist ideology," Alan Wald suggests.[20]

In the years following Anne's departure for Africa, the two main artistic movements had been Abstract Expressionist gestural painting and color-field painting. Her sister, Dorothy, studied with Jack Tworkov for a time, experimenting with abstraction between New York and summers spent in Paradise Valley, Montana. Anne and Dorothy communicated constantly over the years about art; they were going in different directions now. Anne was moving more toward the color-field movement, sharing a concern with depth and surface on the canvas and looking beyond figuration to transform color into content. Emotion had become a strong ingredient, rather than play with form, and she had begun to integrate its effects into her painting from 1951 on, in paintings that flattened perspective and brought out large areas of yellow and brown, green and blue, even a surprising pink in her work during the 1950s.

Anne wrote to her friend and fellow artist Eliena Krylenko Eastman, who was dying of cancer in 1955, that she wanted to help care for her. Painter to painter, she expressed the concern that although she had felt herself in the avant-garde when she left for Africa, she now thought of herself as being in the ranks of conservatives. Anne knew from her mother's letters received while she had been away that many older painters (from Woodstock in particular) agonized about whether to change the way they painted during the sea changes taking place in the art world. Eliena turned down Anne's offer of help on the Vineyard, encouraging her instead to paint individually and work on the collection of African objects; Anne should continue to do what was important to her, as Eliena no longer could.[21]

During these years, Anne lived the malaise of repatriation to New York all the more acutely because she thought it to be temporary. In this in-between period and expecting that she would return to Epulu, Anne came into one of the most creative periods in her painting.

Resisting the Institutional Gaze

One of the photographs that Anne framed and kept with her was a "class photograph" of Camp Putnam that I eventually inherited (see fig. 53). Perhaps taken in 1953, the photo was almost certainly choreographed by Pat, who sits on a chair looking straight at the camera, with Agaranga also front and center, hunched down, and Anne next to him looking toward a child to her right. The villagers and Pygmies are gathered around, as a class or team might have been.[22] Only here the context is not a school; it is a community, in which Pat figures as the equivalent of the teacher or captain of the team. Anne's body language seems to resist the pose of the group as she turns her face to the side; another version of the photograph from the left-hand side shows her smiling in her off-side position.[23] At this time in her life at Camp Putnam, Anne had worried about what it meant to obey or disobey a presumed authority during the times of crisis with Pat (how no one had dared to really challenge him even in his most illogical requests), just as she had thought about her own situation in the colonialist structure. What did Anne remember of this moment? We cannot know.

What we do know is that during 1956, Anne had some of the two hundred Mbuti legends—which she had transcribed into English as of way of giving voice to the Pygmies—typed up. Also important, she worked on a series of

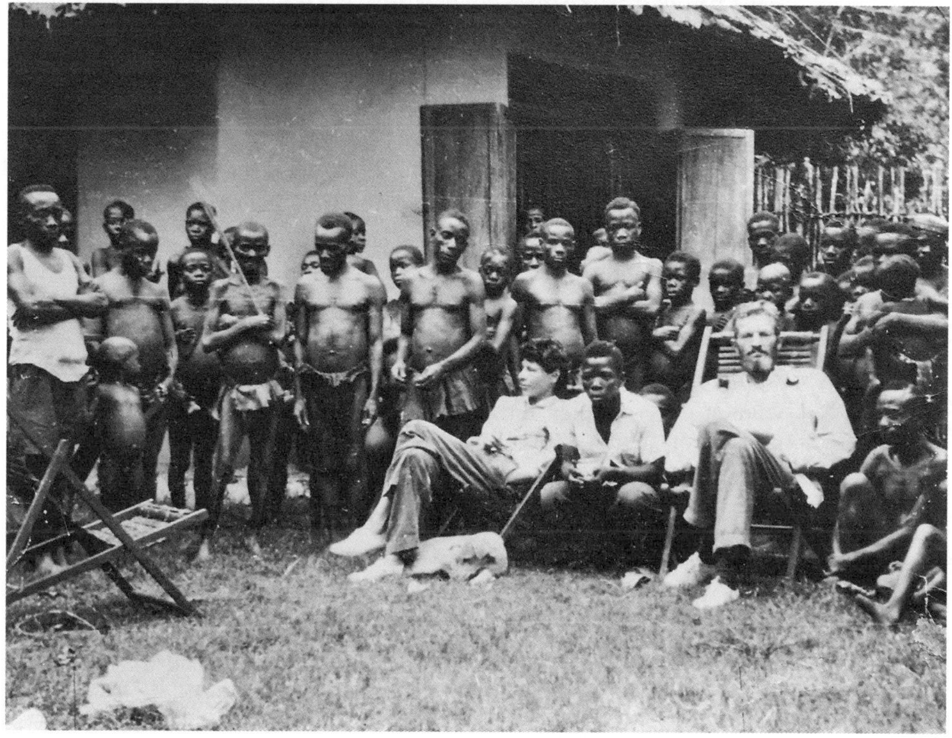

Fig. 53 Anne Eisner, Agaranga Nunziotika, Patrick Putnam, and people from Camp Putnam, c. 1953 (photographer unknown). McDonald archive.

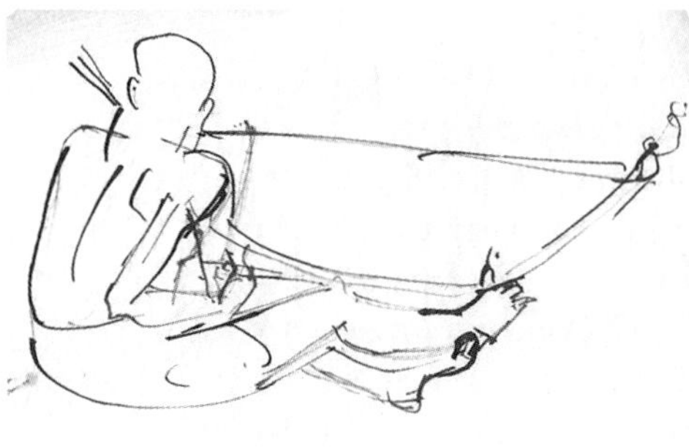

Fig. 54
Anne Eisner, *Musical Bow*, 8½ x 11 in., ink on paper. McDonald collection.

gouaches, very stressed and obsessive, featuring Pygmy figures playing an instrument made from a bow (see pl. 9).

She was clearly inspired by the musical bow instrument (see fig. 54), where players held one end of the string in their mouth and the other with their toe, using the bow with one hand as the other hand hit the string with a small stick. The instrument sounded like a Jew's harp, only louder, and it must have reminded Anne of the times when she had discovered the *elima*—the young women's puberty and premarital ceremony—and heard remarkable music.

In this series, Anne struck out in a new direction technically, inspired by Marthe Guillain's painting where disproportionate parts of the body coalesce into a figure. Anne focused on the relationship of one part to another, giving foot and toes a large and sassy—or let's say resistant—position (with regard to representation at the very least) in the composition. The experimentation in the series signaled a more radical break with representation, as a way to suggest the struggle against submission by individual artist-musicians within a hierarchy. It brought forth a sense of defiance and challenge that put Anne back on track in her work.

Women Crossing Boundaries

During 1956 and 1957, Anne worked feverishly around the clock through several "painting jags." Her paintings and watercolors flattened the spaces of the world and saturated them with color. The subject, however, was not color itself. In one series of paintings and watercolors, she concentrated almost exclusively on everyday activity. She evoked the strong, elegant frames of Bira villager women and the more delicate outlines of Pygmy women. What they all have in common is being women: women at work, women at rest, women with their children. The shapes of these remarkable figures radiate beauty through color and design (see pls. 10, 11, 12). Painting the women with their children, cooking, sitting in doorways—playing with space and color and planes, letting memories resettle in the composition of the canvas. Anne could now paint their bodies and their clothes in her own way, freed from outside constraints—framed and distanced but no less a part of "life" than when she was there. In her experimentation, Anne gave herself back something of the Epulu that had never been there before. Reconstructing her own identity as a woman became possible through this artistic breakthrough.

The colors have an emotional effect, one that—as Joan Miller pointed out—[24]is similar to what the Expressionists were exploring at the time of Anne's artistic activity. But these works bring out something else, too: the universalized particular of women in their everyday lives. To look at these paintings is to sense a joyous limpidity of purpose, bringing emotion through color in the foregrounding of women as her subject. There in New York, surrounded by fragments of life from Epulu—her tables and stools and bark cloths—Anne abstracted her memory of Epulu with strong colors and shapes and told a story that was indeed hers even though it was not "about" her. Anne created a schematized biography of the African woman, not so much as an idealized other but rather as one caring for another in solidarity. The agency granted to these women through Anne's aesthetic was something that Pygmy women exercised through body painting and the decoration of bark cloth. It allowed Anne to reconnect with the expressive side of her work developed early on and to incorporate the history of a time and place in her own particular way. The story is one of connection and reconnection.

In *Beauty Salon* (pl. 10), Anne foregrounds two women in one of a series of women fixing each other's hair. The woman on the right is braiding the hair of the woman on the left. Their clothes resemble the kind of European textiles that many women wore in the village (see fig. 47 in chapter 7), but the dress of the woman on the right echoes the kind of configurations that the Pygmy women painted on bark clothes. The woman on the left is depicted in solid colors. Are they from different worlds, here taking care of each other? We don't know, but both women straddle the line (suggesting the forest) running from left to right. In *Two Women Working* (pl. 11), bark-cloth designs figure on the women's dresses again as they prepare food from both village and Pygmy culture; they seem to exist between the green background suggesting the forest and the yellow of village sunlight. In many of her works from this period, Anne brings the women together at the same time that they cross between an abstractly figured inside and outside of a building or between the forest and the village. Women were able to bridge the agricultural and hunter-gatherer life, inside and outside society in each separate society, just as Anne felt herself to be and to have been.

In *Mother with Child II* (pl. 12), there are two figures: a mother wearing a decorated *pagne* and a child sitting next to the mother's leg, which juts out provocatively from her skirt (perhaps a tip of the hat to Paul Gauguin's 1892 painting *Aha oe feii?* [*What! Are You Jealous?*]). The divide between the inside and the outside as well as between the abstract and the nonabstract is marked, but the outdoor landscape is blocked into geometrical lines marked by color. Both the mother's and the child's bodies cross over from one world to the other.[25] In *Mother with Child IV* (pl. 13), the mother holds her infant child, her elegant black silhouette crossing the white frame of the wall behind her.

By bringing to bear her own experience of personal and artistic exile, painting in New York, Anne's art had become an adventure once again through memory. But the transformation through memory of Epulu also nourished her anticipation of reconnection upon her return to Epulu.

The Return Is Never the Same

Anne booked solo passage back to Africa for the end of July 1957, aboard the S.S. *African* bound for Matadi in the Belgian Congo—a port city where Henry Morton Stanley had opened a station and where a railroad had been built to Léopoldville in the early part of the twentieth century. She was excited to be returning to Africa and to Epulu. At each stop—Dakar, Accra, Abidjan, Lagos—she enjoyed noticing changes, some a vast improvement (desegregation of public eating places in Lagos, for example) and others, like Léopoldville's modernization (skyscrapers, air conditioning, freezers), that struck her as an inevitable sign of economic transformation. When she arrived overland in Stanleyville, she found not only American tourists and Belgians but also local people in the stores and the post office who greeted her with a great to-do. Though occupied by attending to the logistics of finding her baggage and happy to hear KiNgwana again, she simply could not wait for the car she had bought to arrive; she instead hitched a ride with the mail truck to Epulu to get there as soon as possible.

Hello, Epulu!

When Anne returned to Epulu in late September 1957, villagers and Pygmies welcomed her back like a heroine with shouts of joy, streaming out of the forest and the buildings to meet her. She expected to find the houses falling down and everything gone, but they had rebuilt her house and remarkably brought back many of the things she had left behind (pots, pans, carpenters' tools, and even lamps that still worked three years later). "We were all so excited," she wrote, "that nobody could talk for a long time, all we could do was grin and smile and say something meaningless then everybody showed me their new children or their new wife, and each one in turn would say, 'You really did come back to us the way you promised you would.'"[26] She wrote: "Camp Putnam at long last and how beautiful it is. Sometimes one dreams of something for months and years . . . and the dream is far better than the reality. I was afraid of that with my return to Camp Putnam but the reality is even more beautiful than the dream and memory. This place is pure poetry and so are the people."[27] From village after village, people came to pay respects with traditional presents of chicken, rice, and peanuts; Anne gave gifts of palm wine and cigarettes. Greetings and exchanges went on hourly and daily, so much so that Anne's hand hurt from shaking hands with people. One of the old-timers, Musifili, came with a delegation from nearby Dar es Salaam (not the port city) and requested that Anne reopen the market every week.

Camp Putnam looked almost the same to Anne, despite some of the trimmed bamboo trees (which would grow back). In an effort to make things look as they had, people had been making pots for flowers, and Agaranga had made a bark cloth (not clear who decorated it) reminiscent of the ones Anne had hung on the wall in the Palais. Everything looked as it had when she left. But Anne was taken aback by the change on the road: six trade stores, a bakery, and Hotêl de Bière (a hotel that sold beer)—an Ituri equivalent of a strip mall. At a spot along the road that Anne had thought most beautiful, there was now a Shell gasoline sign in yellow and red. The sign made Anne giggle and write: "It's funny if you can forget that it's like putting a knife through a Rembrandt [or] El Greco."[28] She noted that the government had designated a place for the Pygmy village and that most were now commonly wearing old European clothes rather than bark cloths; Anne asked them to put on their bark cloths again. When she visited camps, she noticed that whereas in the old days Pygmy women had few goods to carry with them, they now had to lug pots, pans, mirrors, and other items purchased at the store—to her, signs of Western incursion into their lives. De Medina had left the area for a time, and Anne did her best to get along with Mr. David in the interim.

On this trip, Anne had come back with a specific project: to gather material for an article about the Pygmies intended for publication in *National Geographic* magazine. She spent most of that late fall and winter preparing for it by taking notes. As agreed between them, Colin Turnbull arrived at Epulu in October with a friend who was a musician interested in music of the area, Newton Beal. Colin came to do his own ethnographic research and help out with the photography for Anne's article. He had by then finished his thesis for the BLitt degree at Oxford, into which he had incorporated Pat's and Anne's material about the Pygmies. He and Anne now had a better understanding of their friendship, having recovered from their dispute, and they set guidelines about how to manage in the close quarters of the camp so that each could maintain a working space. Colin often stayed for long periods of time in Pygmy camps. They communicated by notes sent through the forest by carrier, and they exchanged local (and some ethnographic) information regularly.

Anne fit back into the routines without difficulty, visiting in the village, playing during the afternoon parties with the children, William J. Kokoyou, Katchelewa, and Ndeku. They had grown taller and shyer, but after some coaxing, they attached themselves to her once again. When she brought the Peugeot she had acquired, she gave everyone a ride to and from the road—Agaranga, the boys, and then all the families. Amboko, whom Pat had trained as a mechanic, was also to serve as a part-time chauffeur. They picked up Katchelewa and W.J. on the first trip, as the children were to spend weekends with Anne. Anne wrote that, since W.J. Kokoyou understood

KiNgwana but only spoke KiBira now, one would have to learn the other's language; in fact, they seemed to have no problem communicating.

Anne intended to continue painting while she was there, and she was studying the women's cloths, a continuing interest from her series of the women painted in New York. She complained in letters that although she could sketch, she was able to do little painting: too many distractions, too much activity, and too many problems to which she was attending. Most productively, perhaps, was that immediately after getting settled, Anne set up what she called the Epulu School of Arts and Crafts. Encouraging the creative energy of Epulu's inhabitants, she found talent that she hadn't previously realized was there: wood-carvers (a table made from one piece of wood was crafted for Anne), mask-makers, blacksmiths. Anne's idea was for the artists to sell what they created. As for the weekly market she reopened (see fig. 55a-b), Anne was thrilled to see spears and knives, drums, and baskets from the old days. "How handsome it is to see all the women draped around with their plantains, or pots of food they are selling, with colorful cloths."[29]

Despite no longer running the hotel and helping with the dispensary, Anne reengaged fully with communal life at Epulu, including visiting Pygmy camps and welcoming a few tourists. She was also dealing with people who had come down with the flu. The 1957 pandemic, first identified in East Asia, spread throughout the world—the second major pandemic of the twentieth century—and it was taking its toll at Epulu and in the region. Anne transported many people to dispensaries (one now being across the street, another nearby in Koki) and tended to those who stayed home. She noted in letters to her family that many had died, often from pneumonia but also from a serious outbreak of dysentery—several due to one of these illnesses in every village around, mostly among small children and old people. She coped with everything that happened: birth (including another orphaned baby named after her whom a family adopted), death, and everything in between. She wrote that each day was "violently eventful."

Fig. 55a-b
a: Anne dancing with children, Epulu, c. 1957 (photograph possibly by Colin Turnbell). **b**: Anne attending market day, Epulu, c. 1957 (photograph possibly by Colin Turnbull). McDonald archive.

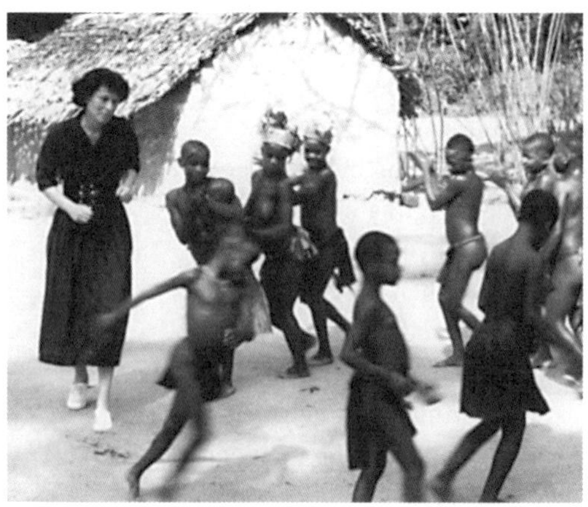

a

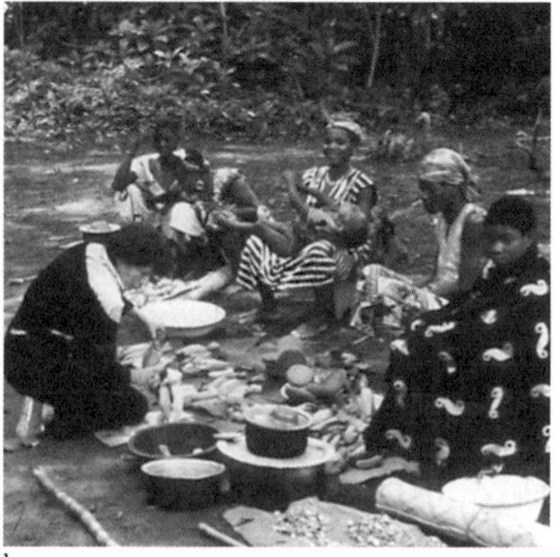

b

Anne continued nevertheless to take copious ethnographic notes, including about the *elima*, the young women's ceremony welcoming them into maturity which she had observed in 1953. She sent long, detailed letters to Monroe Stearns—who was going to be the editor for her *National Geographic* article—and sent Colin her notes as well. She conceived of her article as the narrative of her return to Epulu, going back briefly over the long history with Pat and her own history there (still no mention of the difficulties through which they had lived), then recounting her new life and most recent visits to Pygmy camps, describing their lives and activities. In April 1958, Monroe—who shaped her notes into a narrative—sent Anne a draft of the article, titled "My Life with Africa's Little People."[30] Anne read it, and Colin read it (she was to share the income with him for his excellent photographs). Anne sent back comments and requested modifications, very pleased with Monroe's editing. She said that she wished he could have been the one to work on *Madami* with her. All in all, a positive collaboration.

Reflecting on the different periods of her life as she approached her birthday, Anne wrote: "As I approach my 47th birthday, I realize that 47 has no meaning except that I have lived a number of years, some good, some bad, some wonderful, and some ghastly."[31] She had begun to think she would in fact leave Epulu the following October, which would complete a full year's stay. Did she come to the decision because she had accomplished what she set out to do—gather material on the Pygmies for the *National Geographic* article—and that was done? Or because too much had changed in the area? Possibly because although she could sketch anywhere at any time, she could not concentrate on painting in the way she had hoped and now wanted to get back to her studio in New York. All of these reasons may have contributed to her decision. She was also overwhelmed with the illnesses that were running rampant. Since she was not a health worker and had little backup, she could not hope to deal adequately with the situation on such a scale. This, too, surely figured importantly in her decision. In fact, she seemed quite calm in her letters announcing the decision to leave for good, thinking about her return to New York and encouraging her sister, Dorothy, to meet her in Europe on the way back in the fall to look at paintings together.

Plans Cut Short

On June 22, 1958, Anne telegrammed her family from Léopoldville:

> FELL OFF BICYCLE BROKE LEG, AM IN CAST. FUNDS TEMPORARILY TIED UP. CABLE IMMEDIATELY . . . HOSPITAL FLIGHT EXPENSES AMERICAN CONSULATE GENERAL LEOPOLDVILLE. . . . CONDITION NOT SERIOUS.

About ten days before, on or around June 12, Anne had fallen off her bike (probably riding on a forest path) and was badly injured. The accident had followed a fight with Colin, who was away from Camp Putnam in a Pygmy camp. Amboko the chauffeur was likely the one who drove Anne to Bunia (today the capital city of the Ituri Province, once the Oriental Province, or Province Orientale) about twenty-five kilometers away. She knew the doctor there, Dr. Legrand. His X-ray determined that she had broken her leg (later determined to be a broken hip); he put her in a cast and recommended transportation to a larger center or back to the States. Nine days later, on June 21, Anne was transported on a Pan American World Airways flight from Léopoldville back to Idlewild Airport (now John F. Kennedy International Airport), arriving in New York the following day. Luckily for Anne, Pan Am had just expanded to fly several flights a week to and from Africa. But one can only imagine how difficult the trip must have been for her over many hours; a passenger on board the flight who helped her later wrote that Anne was uncomfortable during the entire trip. Back in New York, doctors operated on her hip, and she stayed in the hospital until July 18. It would take almost a year for Anne to fully recover and walk independently again.

Shortly after the accident happened, Colin wrote a note to Anne at Epulu, saying he had just learned how badly she was injured, not to worry about their blowup, and that he would be glad to keep Camp Putnam running according to her instructions for a short time. The same day, he wrote a letter to the Eisners giving his explanation of the background to the accident:

> Just before the accident, Anne had a big row with me because I was in the forest and in the middle of preserving botanical specimens when I got a note from her saying she thought it would be a good thing if I come in to see a person I had known in Canada, who was now working on a film for Lowell Thomas. My friend wrote and said he was just passing through, and was leaving that morning, but would be back in two weeks and could see me then—that seemed good enough so I sent a note that I'd be glad to see him then, sorry I couldn't get in right away. Poor Anne took that as a terrible slight and flew off the handle and sent me a note saying that I was no longer welcome at Camp Putnam and to clear out. A few hours afterwards she fell from the bicycle and broke her leg.[32]

Colin's relationship with the Eisners felt almost like family—kind of like a brother sometimes being protective, sometimes tattling on or defending his version of events about a sister. Colin seemed to think that his reaction to their row—him claiming a right to stay out in the forest and meanwhile let Anne take care of his friend—was normal and that hers was not. In fact, he had left his friend Newton Beal at Camp Putnam for months at a time while he was away, expecting Anne to host him (and Anne found this difficult until she had a separate living area created for Newton with a small kitchen). In the same letter, Colin told the Eisners that he thought Anne "likes me differently from the way I like her, and she expects more of me—such a situation is never likely to be peaceful for very long!"[33] He did not think to mention his debt to her for the job offer from Harry Shapiro at the American Museum of Natural History—perhaps for him water under the bridge by now. Certainly, Anne's introduction to Shapiro, the transfer of Pat's papers to Colin, and Anne's encouragement and recommendation of him for the job had played a major role in his professional trajectory.

Colin recounted in the letter his and Anne's reconciliation when he arrived in Bunia after a week, where Anne was waiting to be taken to Léopoldville. He assessed Anne's unplanned and painful departure from Epulu because of the accident as "what was needed, though rather drastic. It has had the effect of making the break with Camp Putnam without all the heartache that would have otherwise gone with it. And personally I think Anne will only really begin to feel well again, and be able to paint again, when she gets back and settles down in the States and accepts that this, and it must have been a most wonderful part of her life, is over."[34]

If Colin had a point that the circumstances themselves took away Anne's decision-making about how and when to leave, he woefully underestimated the impact of the injury and misinterpreted her state of mind. Anne herself actually was ready to leave and accept that this part of her life was over, but it is hard to believe that she would have chosen such a physically challenging and difficult way to depart. Before, Anne had gone to great lengths in 1954 to say her goodbyes to all the people of Epulu. Now, under these urgent circumstances, there were no goodbyes to the children, to the workmen (above all, to Agaranga), to the Pygmies, or to everyone to whom she was attached and who was attached to her. How could one think this the best way to end the relationship to Epulu? The heartache would still be there, even though Anne was ready for closure and the return to New York.

Regarding life in the Ituri Forest, Anne's sense of the plural family she found at Epulu was what had made her a good leader. She knew from experience that knowledge was situated in a point of view and that points of view could diverge radically. Her challenge had always been first to understand the context in which people lived and then to try to work out some relationship among the people. If, in the end, she had failed to realize this goal at Epulu, she was not alone. The Belgian Congo was about to explode from within.

Colin enumerated the costs involved with sending everything of Anne's back to New York, and he asked the Eisners if they could help fund him and Newton a little bit beyond reimbursement, as they were broke. Colin then did follow through, taking care of the workers and employing them part-time for a while at Camp Putnam, crating up all of Anne's belongings—including her collection and a roll of paintings—in preparation for transport (the crates would take almost a year to arrive). Colin's detailed and careful attention to these laborious jobs, all the while writing to her consistently, was his gift to Anne and perhaps brought some closure to their conflicted relationship.

Once Anne was back and her surgery was over, she said that whatever her discomfort, it was still much easier than in 1954, when, while recuperating from her hysterectomy, she had gone abruptly through menopause. Now, released from the hospital after more than three weeks, she went to Woodstock to recover with the Eisners on their beautiful farm. She accepted this transition as necessary and showed exceptional patience at her immobilization (reading, sending and receiving correspondence, sketching) for a number of months.

Throughout the following year, 1958, Anne slowly regained her ability to walk—from wheelchair to brace to crutches—and her strength. In a prolonged negotiation that took many months, she gave up her lease on the Epulu land to Mr. David and finally went to spend the summer of 1959 on Cape Cod in the bustle of the art world of Provincetown.

CHAPTER NINE

Changes Political and Personal (the 1960s)

The 1960s were a decade of highs and lows across Anne's two worlds: the United States and the Belgian Congo. John F. Kennedy was sworn in as president of the United States in January 1960 with the iconic request of his inaugural address: "Ask not what your country can do for you—ask what you can do for your country." Shortly after, in June of that same year, Patrice Émery Lumumba—a young man who had worked in the post office in Stanleyville and became a charismatic leader and founder of the Congolese National Movement—addressed the country and the world at a ceremony in the Palais de la Nation in Léopoldville, proclaiming independence from Belgium for the Democratic Republic of Congo. Before Belgium's King Baudouin and dignitaries of both countries, Lumumba challenged the sense that this ceremony and independence accomplished the Belgian "civilizing mission." Instead, he exhorted his contemporaries to revise (by remembering, not forgetting) the dark history of colonialism for their children and grandchildren and to reflect upon the "glorious history of our struggle for freedom." With his ideal of national unity and pan-Africanism, he called upon his countrymen and women to unite in "a sublime struggle, which will lead our country to peace, prosperity and greatness."[1]

John F. Kennedy (born in 1917) was assassinated in 1963; Martin Luther King Jr. (born in 1929) was assassinated in 1968. And Lumumba (born in 1925), the first legally elected prime minister of Congo, had been in office for only two months when he was assassinated in January 1961. The role of the American CIA, the Belgian government, and Lumumba's Congolese enemies in his assassination during the proxy Cold War confrontations between the United States and the Soviet Union is still being debated. After a series of prime ministers in the Republic of Congo, Mobutu Sese Seko (1930–1997)—who had served as secretary of state for national defense with Lumumba and later arrested him—engineered a coup d'état in 1965; he ruled the country, renamed Zaire, for the next thirty-two years, until 1997, when the name reverted back to Democratic Republic of Congo.

In New York, Anne followed the news from Congo with increasing concern for the people at Epulu. In 1959, clashes around the legitimacy of a local election in Stanleyville had resulted in several dozen deaths. Agaranga wrote her in 1959 that workers of Epulu with twenty-five to thirty years of experience were receiving pension contributions from the Belgian government (presumably discontinued during the transition and ensuing tumult). Some of the workers had found jobs away from Epulu, and others (like himself) had not; he was hoping to return to Pawa, northeast of Epulu. The children, he reassured her, were well.

At some point during the turbulent and violent times that followed independence, Mr. David's hotel was bombed, while the mud and thatch buildings of Epulu went untouched and were left to fall into disrepair. It is said that Lumumba—who at the time was a freedom fighter encouraging rebellion in the forest to drive out the Europeans—knew about Camp Putnam (he was from Stanleyville) and had said that the Putnams (only Anne at the time) and a few other Europeans who had become "Africans, and were no longer foreigners,"[2] would have been spared.

By February 1961, Anne was worried and wrote to Agaranga asking after many of the workers by name: Ibrahemu, Émile, Angoli, André the cook, André 2, Alili, Abazinga, Basiani, Hausa, Musifili, Sabani, Faizi, the children, the others, and all the Pygmies. Tired of KiNgwana, she announced that she was studying Swahili in order to be able to write correctly. She informed Agaranga that she had money in a bank in Kisangani (using the name for what before was called Stanleyville) and asked how to get it safely to him. She acknowledged news from another letter (not present in remaining archives of her correspondence), in which he told her that the political situation was not good. She wrote: "Every time I read news from the Congo, I read news of many soldiers fighting there, I think I do not want you to go to Kisangani."[3] Agaranga responded in May that Rozos had been in a car accident, that de Medina had left long ago (he was later poisoned), and that Mr. David was gone; only Congolese were taking care of the animals. The next letter from Agaranga on record is from a year and a half later, in August 1962, in which he says that at long last he received a letter from Colin Turnbull (about whom he had asked a number of times, wanting to know if he would return), letting her know that the children and Pygmies were all "tranquil" and peaceful at Epulu. He requested vegetable seeds and admitted that he was only wearing a *pagne* himself, as he had no money. Agaranga had returned to Pawa but visited from time to time back at Epulu. During 1962, Agaranga wrote to Anne responding about Pat's father Dr. Putnam's death: "I cried and shed tears. Monsieur Putnam died and now his father has also died at Harvard. It is truly too sad a history." By 1963, Agaranga seemed to be painting and sculpting himself now and wondered how to send his work to sell in Europe or the United States (nothing I can find confirms that he was able to do this). He reported that grocery prices had risen astronomically, with little food available: "Nous mourons de faim" ("we are dying of hunger").[4] In his last documented letter, in August 1963 from Pawa, he wrote that he had lost his eyeglasses, asking if she could send him a new pair, as his eyesight was poor. The news was that some Pygmies were now working in Kisangani, while others had married people from another village; Faizi was still at Epulu, along with others. Life was difficult for an elder who had started as a policeman in Penge in the 1930s (from the Bantu Budu tribe), followed Pat to found Camp Putnam, worked closely with Anne for all the years she was there, and was probably now in his sixties. Agaranga was Anne's last connection to what was happening at Epulu.

In 1964, the United States transported Belgian paratroopers and white mercenaries to quell a rebellion in northeastern Congo which had decimated Kisangani/Stanleyville (sixty thousand people were said to have died). Villagers took refuge in the forest, and the Pygmies fought with all sides (the government, peacekeeping troops, and rebels).[5] Even Colin was not able to return to Epulu then, though he had intended to. Instead, he went to northeastern Uganda in 1965–1966, to study the Ik, describing how survival during famine outstripped all morality and goodness —published later in the controversial book *The Mountain People*.[6]

Anne's *National Geographic* article, "My Life with Africa's Little People," had come out in February 1960, just prior to the independence movement, with many photographers credited (but no photographs by Colin). She received laudatory mail from people on several continents, all fascinated by her new telling of the story of her Epulu home, even as the news from the Congo worsened. *Madami* and this article were, for a short time, the primary works of reference for recent Pygmy description.

Differing Views

Then Colin Turnbull's book *The Forest People* was published in 1961. He wrote in his private dedication on Anne's copy : "To Anne and to the memory of Pat, both of you wonderful friends, with sincere thanks for all your help and encouragement. I hope this book will help you recall the days of Happiness at Camp Putnam, and the kindness and understanding that Camp Putnam stood for. With much love, Colin." On John and Dorothy Eisner McDonald's copy, he wrote: "Many thanks to a wonderful family for all their help and encouragement." In the published acknowledgments to the book, however, after thanking his professor, Evans Pritchard, and his colleagues at the American Museum of Natural History (particularly Harry L. Shapiro), he neglected to include Anne's name, instead writing: "But Patrick Putnam deserves special mention, because it was through his friendship and hospitality, and that of his wife, that I first came to know the forest. I only wish he had lived to write this book himself."[7] As Anne had done, but for different reasons, Colin does not include the fact that Pat was no longer alive when he arrived for his second, longer visit to Epulu (from which the material for this book was largely taken), but he only refers to Anne as "his [Pat's] wife." While we do not know exactly how Anne reacted to her own erasure in the acknowledgments (I suspect with anger), we do know that she nevertheless read the book with passionate interest, noting comments in extensive notes and in the margins of her copy. She took particular issue with Colin's assertion that he was the first person to observe the Pygmies away from villagers or Europeans (of which he was one) and his increasing polarization of Pygmies and the forest as "good" and the villagers and outside as "bad." In reaction to an earlier article Colin had written for the journal *Man* (published by the Royal Anthropological Institute of Great Britain), Anne had already written to Colin: "BE CAREFUL? DON'T MAKE TOO POSITIVE A STATEMENT ABOUT WHAT IS PYGMY AND WHAT IS NOT BECAUSE EVEN OUT THERE THE BANTUS AND PYGMIES DON'T."[8]

It was clear from early on—confirmed in the book and by Anne's reaction to it—that one of the major issues that divided Anne and Colin was the question of who was on the inside and who was on the outside. In Colin's moral geography, the Pygmies were good, and the forest was good; the Pygmies were only afraid of what was outside the forest. Colin viewed them as independent spirits who did lip service to the villagers, just as he did lip service to Anne at certain moments. In his view, Anne was identified with villagers as a negative power broker, and he was on the inside as if he was a Pygmy, one of the liberating spirits not to be harnessed. The concept of an "unbridgeable gulf between the two worlds of the two peoples"[9] was indeed solely Colin's view, not Anne's. Her art gave ample testimony to her view that differences between villagers and Pygmies, indeed all people, were not an irreconcilable, dividing force.

In *The Forest People*, there is Pat, there are the Pygmies, and there are also the villagers. However, Anne is nowhere to be found.[10] The book became a huge success and a classic for generations of American students who read it. This vision of an innocent people existing in a far-off a place where for centuries they had lived in a closed community (opposed to what was portrayed as a dismal and bad village) in sync with a protective and beautiful rain forest was surely enticing in a post–World War II, threatening Cold War environment. To the same extent that Colin's book successfully found its place in the anthropological literature and the hearts of readers of the era, so, too, was the reality of Anne's important role and contributions condemned to silence.

Anne was mostly in New York during the early 1960s, returning during the summers to Martha's Vineyard and Provincetown, painting and sketching with fellow painters Sideo Fromboluti and Nora Speyer; now that she was again mobile after surgery, she reconnected with old friends like Aaron Siskind, Max Eastman (with his new wife, Yvette), Herbert Solow, and others. On the Vineyard, Anne had been able to have a good talk with Dr. Putnam before his death, and she continued as she had all along to correspond with Pat's aunt Elsie (always a supporter, now relieved that Anne didn't have to encounter violence in the Congo) and Marley Putnam Castro (Pat's adopted sister, of whom he had been very fond); Marley had written Anne regularly and lovingly from early on in Anne's Congo life. As always, Anne saw a great deal of her sister, Dorothy, and her brother-in-law, John; she kept in close touch with her parents and connected with her nieces Joan McD Miller (1929–2019) and me (I was about to start college).

With little news and little she could do about the life she had left at Epulu, Anne focused her energy on painting, continuing to exhibit, and returning to her studio as a source of pleasure and sustenance.

During the summer of 1962, Anne took a whirlwind trip to Europe, traveling to Paris, where she met up with friends. She returned to the Louvre, the Musée de l'Homme (the anthropological museum, forerunner to the Musée du Quai Branly, where most of its collection is now housed), the Musée de l'Art Moderne, and the Comédie Française (whose building she found to look a little Daumier-like). She spent a few days in Brussels visiting with Marthe, whose time at Epulu with her had been important. Then she moved on to looking at paintings in Florence (which, as she said, "seem to me [to have been] painted by the gods").[11]

Forest Paths

During the years of 1960 to 1963, Anne worked on a series of paintings from memory of the forest, painting "like mad," as she said. Along with group exhibitions to which she contributed, Anne showed the forest paintings together in a solo exhibition, "Congo Rain Forest," at the Kaymar Gallery in 1963. (See pls. 14 and 15.) She extended her lifelong fascination with trees into abstractions of the Ituri Forest that generalized recollections without figures and retained the feel of the forest. From her earliest watercolors, Anne had grouped trees together to show the forest as a pattern of space, as in *Cathedral Woods* from Monhegan Island (see fig. 15 in chapter 1).

Her fascination with light in the Ituri Forest after she arrived at Epulu, and the way in which trees and vines created patterns, culminated in the burst of creativity reworking from memory and abstracting the forest in these late works. In *Entrance to Camp Putnam* (pl. 14), bright yellow recalls the sun-drenched areas of the village, while blues and greens evoke the surrounding forest. Louis Finkelstein commented about this painting: "While the treatment relates to abstract expressionism it is also a very distinctive personal image of a real place, spontaneous and at the same time coherently integrated and readable."[12] This series contrasts strikingly with earlier paintings setting out broad, flat, contrasting colors, while still rendering continuity of color (the blues and greens she had loved in the forest). For the painting *Ituri Forest II*, originally titled *Plantation* (pl. 15)—though clearly a forest and not an agricultural scene—Anne later received a prize from the National Association of Women Artists. The forest had evolved throughout her work and continued in these late paintings as a metaphor for moving through life's complex problems.

Between 1964 and 1966, Anne spent part of each summer on Cranberry Island in Maine, a ferry ride from Mount Desert Island. My family had started to summer there in 1960, renting various houses, because Dorothy's close friends, painters and life partners John (Jack) Heliker and Robert (Bob) Lahotan, had suggested that this would be a good place for her to spend summers and paint. Anne lived either with or in proximity to Dorothy and was in daily contact with other painters on the island: Louis Finkelstein, Mark Samenfeld, and especially Gretna Campbell (married to Finkelstein) and William (Bill) Kienbusch. Martha Campbell, Gretna and Louis's daughter, remembers that Anne and Gretna would go sketching together around the island (as well as in New York) and that Anne was always inclusive of Martha's presence as a child with them. The midmorning mail-boat breaks were a happy routine among some of these artists, as they could discuss their work and plan to see one another's newest paintings. Anne painted a series of works from the woods that surrounded a house overlooking the water where they stayed for two summers. (See fig. 56.)

The reemergence of trees and the forest brought continuity to the breaks and disconnections that Anne had lived through. As Jacques Lipchitz, who had arrived in New York in 1941, put it: "Continuity in an artist's work is analogous to tradition in the broad field of painting and sculpture and just as essential."[13] If continuity is thus to be found in memory—in the memory of one's self and the changes wrought from the encounter with different peoples and cultures—then Anne Eisner kept a tradition going in her work. Anne explored abstract forms during the last period of her work (many landscape watercolors, both abstract and with some figurative of Cranberry Island), and in 1965, she received the Jane C. Stanley Memorial Prize for Watercolor from the National Association of Women Artists. Bill Kienbusch, who had followed her work for decades, wrote to her in 1966 to say that he considered a recent painting of hers (it is not known which one) to be one of her best.

Anne experienced health crises in late 1963, when she underwent a mastectomy for breast cancer, and later, when the cancer metastasized to her lungs. In those days, as Susan Sontag later wrote in *Illness as Metaphor* (1978),[14] the negative effects of myths and attitudes around cancer put the patient in the position of being culpable (in the "fight" or "crusade" against cancer).

People didn't talk about their terminal illness. Perhaps that was why Anne—who did not think of herself as a victim—would not allow anyone to speak about cancer but rather preferred to refer to it as pleurisy, an inflammation of the lung without the dire consequences of lung cancer.

Anne died of cancer in New York City on January 28, 1967, at the age of fifty-five.

Colin Turnbull recognized Anne's ethnographic contribution privately to her family and friends, although it was too late to do so directly to her, in a eulogy during the memorial service held at the New York Society for Ethical Culture:

> Anne had an intensely inquisitive mind and was forever curious about people. It was a totally inoffensive curiosity, without any attitude of judgment. Anne merely observed that people live their lives in many different ways, and she wanted to know why. Once she knew why she accepted that way without further questions as to that person's right to follow it, however much she might disagree with it herself. One of Anne's greatest qualities was her inexhaustible generosity of spirit. . . .

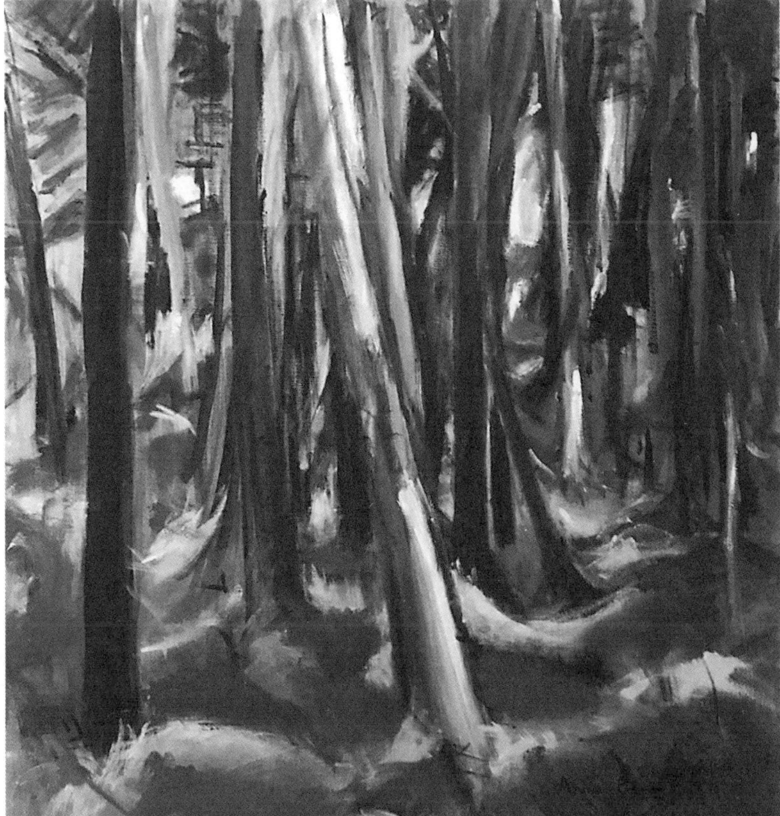

Fig. 55 Anne Eisner, Welcome to Shorelands, 35 x 35 in., oil on canvas, Cranberry Island, 1964. Private collection.

> The pygmies [*sic*], whom Anne loved so much and who loved her so much in return, judge a person's life by the amount of affection with which they are surrounded when they die. A person who dies surrounded by relatives and friends who love her is considered to have the greatest luck, to have lived well and to have died well. By such standards, and they are good standards, Anne has died very well, and according to the pygmies there is no need to mourn. Their philosophy is rather that we should be happy for a life well lived, from which we have all benefitted. It is a lot to ask, but one thing is sure; if we are sad it can only be on our own account, there is no need to be sad for Anne.[15]

The *New York Times* headlined Anne's obituary "Mrs. Patrick Putnam Dies. . .; Artist Painted Pygmies in Congo"[16] and mentioned her studies at the Art Students League and that she had been a member of its board and former secretary of the Federation of Modern Painters and Sculptors; it especially noted her late husband Patrick and how he had taken her to the Belgian Congo as his "bride." Anne was survived by her parents, Mr. and Mrs. William Eisner (Will and Fluff), sister Dorothy, brother-in-law John, niece Joan McD Miller and her husband, Richard Miller, and me. As devastating as it was to her parents to outlive their daughter, Fluff must have felt deep down that what she had said about her own mother (Anna) and grandmother (Julia)—that they lived on in her when she thought about them, and thus carried on—was also true of Anne. "Living on" in the Jewish sense comes through connection. Anne had sought such forms of connection in her art. So today, Anne lives on not only through family and friends (many themselves gone now) but also and especially through her art.

Anne explored the interior and coastal beauty of Cranberry Island in her last paintings and watercolors (see fig. 56) and experimented with both figural and abstract works. In *Still Life with a Bottle* (see pl. 16), she explored, for example, how "strong, simple abstract color shapes" connect "all the shapes and background shades with the physical edge of the picture," as Louis Finkelstein put it.[17] In these late works, she was sometimes bouncing off the works of Hans Hoffman, Pollock, de Kooning, or Kline and in dialogue with her friends and her sister Dorothy's work. Based on long experience, she was also performing her own freedom of expression. Anne had not finished her artistic explorations when her life came to an end. But enjoyment in the act of creating, of working with oils, watercolors, or gouache, marked this last period, as Finkelstein concluded, as "daring, and loose, and animated and spontaneous."[18] Her art is a tribute to a life fully lived with courage, love, and spontaneity.

Epilogue

As I was gathering material for this book in the late 1980s and the 1990s, I interviewed and communicated with a great many people connected either directly or indirectly with life at Epulu. In 1994, I hosted an "Epulu Fest" in the country house my husband, Michael, and I have in Vermont, inviting Leslie Morris, who had just been appointed curator at Houghton Library, along with friends and family. Of the two people who had known Anne well at Epulu, only Francis Chapman was able to come; I had talked with Schuyler Jones in Oxford, and he continues to send me photographs and information. Francis (who came with his wife, Penny) had been at Epulu in 1954 with Colin Turnbull. During our gathering in 1994, he showed the film he had shot of a Mbuti Pygmy *nkumbi* (circumcision) ritual four decades earlier, in 1954. I had interviewed Francis quite extensively in 1991 on what he remembered. He had a clear memory of how Colin's privileging of Pygmies over villagers split the community. At the film screening during the "Epulu Fest," Francis was quite surprised by a voiceover of the film made by Colin in the 1980s, where he speaks of the antagonisms between the groups.

The beauty of this day spent together, along with other friends and neighbors, was to bring alive a sense of the vibrant past surrounding a place (Epulu) and time (the 1940s and 1950s) where so much subsequent anthropological research had also been done.[1] I displayed Anne's paintings and watercolors around my living room and realized that her art performs that same function as well.

John and Terese Hart, American zoologists and conservationists who had built a research station at Epulu during the 1980s, also joined us; they were raising their family in a home built on the site of Le Palais, the building where Anne and Pat had lived decades ago. Their research had concluded that the Mbuti Pygmies were engaged in long-standing relationships with the indigenous farmers, countering other theories contending that they were completely self-reliant in the forest. This finding confirmed the social philosophy to which Anne herself had been committed at Epulu: seeking connection in relations among the different members of the community. The Harts were able to tell me that Anne's youngest adopted child, Ndeku, had died at an early age but that William J. Kokoyou and Katchelewa had grown up integrated into their families and the community at Epulu—and both remembered Anne. John and Terese moved out to Kinshasa when violence came to the Epulu area starting in 1996. Since that time, they have continued research in the Ituri Forest, tracking okapis and helping to establish the Okapi Wildlife Reserve in 1992. The Okapi Wildlife Reserve is now a World Heritage Site covering one-fifth of the Ituri Forest to protect flora and threatened fauna, including okapis, elephants, leopards, chimpanzees, and crocodiles. Mbuti Pygmies, among others, were included in the management of the Reserve. Terese Hart wrote to me in 2004: "In anarchy everything goes . . . arms are everywhere . . . park limits no longer exist. . . . The Mbuti have no land rights, and this seems the one option to assure a continued possibility of that forest-based life."[2] The main threats to the people of this area continue to be deforestation and devastating armed conflict; violence and atrocities near Epulu and more broadly in eastern Congo over the two last decades have decimated or forced migration of the population. During and after the First and Second Congo Wars, the Harts continued conservation work.[3]

Today, when looking at the objects from Anne's time in Africa and her art, I see how fragments of her life live on in what remains in my own collection and in public collections (among others, the American Museum of Natural History, Houghton Library, Musée du Quai Branly, Peabody Museum).

Anne influenced me directly and indirectly. I loved French the minute I started learning the language in high school, seeing it as a gateway to other cultures. And it was Anne who lent me her car in college so that I would be independent and free to roam. I understood from her that there is not just one way to look at a problem, a people, a culture, or even a leaf in the forest; there are many perspectives that can enrich our own. I have also learned through following Anne's struggles that we do not have within us only one voice: not just the painter, the writer, the ethnographer, but a brave woman (which she was) and a woman who enables herself as she enables others. We, too, in a sense are all made of many (sometimes quite different) parts. That is one of the reasons, I believe, that while Anne worked against stereotypes and expectations throughout her life, she looked to find crossovers and intersections—where others perceived separation and opposition—as ways to adapt and solve problems.

Let me end with a few comments about objectivity and accuracy. The condition for writing this book, as with every biography, was my identification with Anne, and in this sense, it cannot at some level be strictly objective. A good way to propel a project, it turns out, is through initial (if not sustained) anger—in this case, first against Anne's beloved Pat, who betrayed her trust by not telling her, until just before their arrival at Camp Putnam, about the co-wives she would not only meet but have to live with there. I came to understand that although Anne felt betrayed and rejected, she worked through her feelings to find her own place within the Epulu community that she came to love, and her art served always as a beacon of optimism. Second, I found myself shocked at how Colin Turnbull, whose *The Forest People* became an iconic work, progressively erased Anne and her significant contributions to Epulu and to his own ethnographic work. In 1990, I had an exchange of letters with Colin in which he encouraged me to publish Anne's letters (my project at the time), giving me permission to quote from his and use any photographs he had taken. He also reminisced about Anne's relationship with Pat, identifying (unsurprisingly) with Pat while he was dying—when Colin had not actually been present. I give this example to say that perhaps we all rewrite history to a lesser or greater extent in our own lives and the lives of others. At the same time, we hope as professionals to do due diligence. Anne and Colin (and their parents) treated each other like family. And like family, not everyone remembers personal history the same way. What can be said, objectively, is that Anne did remain friendly with Colin and his life partner, anthropologist Joseph Towles. A painting that Anne gave them of the Ituri Forest resides, as do some of her notes, in the Towles archival collection at Avery Research Center for African American History and Culture, College of Charleston. I have overcome my own disbelief at Colin's erasure of Anne by writing her story as found in the archive, her writing, and her art and in the way my memory helps me to imagine her struggles and successes.

Accuracy is also an interesting concept in the context of Anne's work and life. As she took notes on and wrote about the Mbuti Pygmies, she was extremely concerned about remaining precise and factual. But when it came to describing herself and her own life, she allowed some quite extraordinary deviation from fact. Was she blinded to her own situation or projecting an image? A little of both, I believe, and the results were self-protective, to be sure. Anne concentrated on those around her as always more important than she was. I think about the ways in which throughout her life, Anne's drawings, watercolors, and paintings tell a most poignant story about observation and what can be expressed. Even in her more abstracted works, her art is "accurate" if one understands accuracy as a complex relationship between the subject and the eye of a painter, who is never absent from the scene. I am particularly struck when I look at Anne's last series of oil paintings from the 1960s, which are forest abstractions. They suggest to me that the forest for Anne as an artist constituted both a treasured aspect of nature and a metaphor for working through life's problems, no matter how tangled and difficult the path.

NOTES

Chapter One. The Early Years (1911–1944)

1. See Joshua Zeitz, *Flapper: A Madcap Story of Sex, Style, Celebrity, and the Women Who Made America Modern* (New York: Crown, 2006), 107.
2. Tess Slesinger to Dorothy Eisner, c. October 15, 1930. Peter Davis archive.
3. All quotations here are from Anne Eisner, notebook, 1927. Anne Eisner Putnam papers, Houghton Library, Harvard University (hereafter AEP papers).
4. In the manner of Thomas Hart Benton and John Sloan, influenced by the work of Kenneth Hayes Miller, Adolf Dehn, Philip Evergood.
5. I thank Katherine Mintie for her comments on Shahn's photography and finding his photograph of Klein's at the Harvard Art Museums.
6. Robert Karen, "The Lost Art of Sarah McPherson," *New York Magazine*, August 17, 1981, 52–53.
7. Matthew Baigell, *The American Scene: American Painting of the 1930s* (New York: Praeger, 1974), 13–18, 23, 38, 46.
8. George Biddle, *An American Artist's Story* (Boston: Little, Brown, 1934), 268, cited in Baigell, *The American Scene*, 46.
9. "Rockefeller Row Splits Art Groups: Salons of America Assail Independents for Shunning Show at Center," *New York Times*, March 23, 1934, 25.
10. See Christie McDonald, "Dorothy Eisner's 'American Album,'" in Christie McDonald, ed., *Painting My World* (Suffolk: ACC Editions, 2009), 12–16.
11. See *Woodstock's Art Heritage: The Permanent Collection of the Woodstock Artists Association, with a Historical Survey by Tom Wolf* (Woodstock: Overlook Press, 1987).
12. Edward Alden Jewell, "Social Comment of the Usual Sort, Naïve Effort and Some Sound Painting in the Independents' Nineteenth Exhibition," *Independent*, n.d., 1934.
13. The last sentence of this comment is quoted in Emily Genauer, "'Anne' Again," in "Gurr Paintings Show Maturity," *World Telegram*, c. September–October 1943.
14. See James Johnson Sweeney, ed., *African Negro Art* (New York: Museum of Modern Art, 1935).
15. Virginia-Lee Webb, ed., *Perfect Documents: Walker Evans and African Art, 1935* (New York: Metropolitan Museum of Art, 2000), 13.
16. Sweeney, *African Negro Art*, 13.
17. In Sweeney, *African Negro Art*, 15.
18. I would like to thank Jay Bochner, author of *An American Lens: Scenes from Alfred Stieglitz's New York Secession* (Cambridge, Mass.: MIT Press, 2005), for conversations about Stieglitz's influence in the early part of the twentieth century .
19. Stewart Cullin, *Primitive Negro Art: Chiefly from the Belgian Congo* (New York: Brooklyn Museum, 1923), n.p., cited in Webb, *Perfect Documents*, 16.
20. Cullin, *Primitive Negro Art*, 17.
21. Sweeney, *African Negro Art*, 11.
22. *Herald Tribune*, March 24, 1935.
23. *New York World-Telegram*, cited in "African Negro Sculpture Confronts America," *Art Digest*, May 1, 1935.
24. Harry Shapiro, "South Seas Primitives for Sophisticates at the Museum of Modern Art," *Art News* 45 (March 1946): 37. Generalizing, Shapiro states: "To the modern artist perhaps one of the most fascinating aspects of primitive art is its freedom from the confinement of absolute realism. Each native tradition, naturally, tends to follow its own particular stylistic or abstract treatment of natural phenomena, including man himself, and to that extent restrains and limits the fancy of the artist. But primitive art, taken in its whole gamut, provides an extraordinarily rich, even bewildering, variety of experimentation in form and design. Realism in an absolute sense with a complete fidelity to every anatomical detail that distinguishes much of European art is almost never the ideal of the primitive artist. A few examples do approach such a standard, but generally naturalistic pieces reveal in some anatomical license the greater concern of the primitive artist for his own conception of balance and symmetry" (68). MOMA revisited Western interest in "tribal" art through the "primitivists" in 1984. See William Rubin, ed., *Primitivism in 20th Century Art: Affinity of the Tribal and the Modern* (New York: Museum of Modern Art, 1984). As earlier, African artifacts were juxtaposed with modernist painting not causally but through a notion of "affinity" and formal qualities. It was a "conceptual" or intellectual notion of the primitive that drew on the writings of Michel Leiris, Georges Bataille, and structuralist anthropologist Claude Lévi-Strauss (Rubin, *Primitivism*, 10). While the exhibit received much praise, some forcefully questioned not only the juxtapositions in display but also the assumptions underlying the

absorption of tribal art by Western artists: the need to look back in history at how a consciously appropriative relation to otherness had been developed by Western artists (to analyze the ethnocentrism of one-way vision, the Westerner looking at primitive art) and also larger ethical issues involved in a power differential. Picasso said that the African objects he collected were more witness than model. Postcolonial literary criticism, in the work of Edward Said, for example, complicated the relationship of power and knowledge in oppositions such as the Occident and the Orient, the West and the other, civilization and the primitive.

25. See Salka Viertel, *The Kindness of Strangers* (New York: New York Review of Books, 2019).
26. Anne Eisner to William and Florine Eisner, July 5, 1937, Portland, Oregon, AEP papers.
27. I am grateful to Debra Bach, curator of decorative arts at the New York Historical Society and Museum, for her comments on this work about women shopping.
28. John McDonald to Alan Wald, November 18, 1974, John McDonald papers, Beinecke Library, Yale University.
29. John McDonald, n.d., notes for a project on Detroit, "revolution," John McDonald papers, Beinecke Library, Yale University.
30. McDonald, "revolution" notes. Alan Wald has also analyzed the way in which many on the left after the Cold War revised the memories of their political positions from the 1930s. He has written me that the concern with fascism was certainly major but that John McDonald and Herbert Solow "opposed the Popular Front, which argued that liberal capitalism should be defended as a bulwark against fascism." Alan Wald to Christie McDonald, email, February 2, 2020.
31. John McDonald to Alan Wald, November 1974 (?), John McDonald papers, Beinecke Library, Yale University.
32. Burnham De Silver interview, box 1, folder 10, notes, Dorothy Gallagher papers, Tamiment Library, New York University.
33. See Christie McDonald, "Brushes with History," *Harvard Review* 30 (Spring 2006): 142–149.
34. A documentary film about Daniel Bell, Nathan Glazer, Irving Kristol, and Irving Howe is thus named. *Arguing the World*, written and directed by Joseph Dorman (New York: First Run Features, 1998).
35. For a history of this period and how it evolved, see Alan Wald, *The New York Intellectuals: The Rise and Decline of the Anti-Stalinist Left from the 1930s to the 1980s* (Chapel Hill: University of North Carolina Press, 1987).
36. Quoted in Alan Wald, "Herbert Solow: Portrait of a New York Intellectual," *Prospects* 3 (October 1978): 42.
37. Quoted in Matthew Baigell and Julia Williams, *Artists against War and Fascism: Papers of the First American Artists' Congress* (New Brunswick: Rutgers University Press, 1986), 65.
38. See Baigell and Williams, *Artists against War and Fascism*, 14.
39. Douglas Gilbert, "Independents' Art Show Is No Place for Those Easily Startled," *New York World-Telegram*, April 25, 1936. A reproduction of the painting was published as well.
40. See Andrew Hemingway, *Artists on the Left: American Artists and the Communist Movement, 1926–1956* (New Haven and London: Yale University Press), 123.
41. Baigell and Williams, *Artists against War and Fascism*, 48.
42. Aaron Douglas, "The Negro in American Culture," in Baigell and Williams, *Artists against War and Fascism*, 84.
43. *Constitution of the Federation of Modern Painters and Sculptors, Inc.*, Article I: Name and Object, 1. Dorothy Eisner papers, Beinecke Library, Yale University.
44. Max Eastman, "Troublemaker," *New Yorker*, September 8, 1934, 31.
45. See Dorothy Gallagher, *All the Right Enemies: The Life and Murder of Carlo Tresca* (New Brunswick: Rutgers University Press, 1988); and Nunzio Pernicone, *Carlo Tresca: Portrait of a Rebel* (New York: Palgrave Macmillan, 2005).
46. Pernicone, *Carlo Tresca*, 246.
47. John Dos Passos to Jack Diggins, April 21, 1966, box 1, folder 15, Gallagher archive, Tamiment Library, New York University.
48. Eleanor Clark Warren to Alan Wald, August 13, 1974, John McDonald papers.
49. Margaret De Silver to Lev Trotsky, October 13, 1937, Leon Trotsky exile papers, Houghton Library, Harvard University.
50. Lev Trotsky to Margaret De Silver, March 31, 1938, Susan De Silver archive.
51. See Pernicone, *Carlo Tresca*, 265–289.
52. Margaret's statement was published below the reproduction of the portrait: "I want to thank you for your very fine editorial on the anniversary of the assassination of Carlo Tresca. Incidentally, neither of the other liberal weeklies took note of this tragic day." *New Leader*, January 29, 1944.

53. Carlo Tresca to Leon Trotsky, August 12, 1939, Leon Trotsky exile papers, Houghton Library, Harvard University.
54. See McDonald, *Painting My World*.
55. Leon Kroll, *New York Evening Post*, December 19, 1931.
56. Emil Holzhauer, "Portraits of Young People," *New York Herald Tribune*, April 15, 1934.
57. See Freda Utley's memoir, *Odyssey of a Liberal* (Washington, D.C.: Washington National Press, 1970), http://fredautley.com/odesayofaliberal.
58. Max Eastman, *Love and Revolution: My Journey through an Epoch* (New York: Random House, 1964), 552.
59. *New York Times*, January 23, 1944.
60. Louis Finkelstein, interview by Christie McDonald, June 8, 1992, McDonald papers, Harvard Archives, Harvard University.
61. See April Kingsley, *The Turning Point: The Abstract Expressionists and the Transformation of American Art* (New York: Simon & Schuster, 1992).
62. Emily Genauer, "Some Really Exciting Paintings in Independents' Jubilee Show," *World Telegram*, April 19, 1941.

Chapter Two.
Take Me Away, Baby (1945–1946)

1. Louis Finkelstein, interview by Christie McDonald, June 1992, McDonald papers, Harvard Archives, Harvard University.
2. Rosanna Warren, "Drawing on the Forest: Anne Eisner at Epulu," in Christie McDonald, ed., *Images of Congo: Anne Eisner's Art and Ethnography, 1946–1958* (Milan: 5 Continents Editions, 2005), 33–41.
3. Joan Mark, *The King of the World in the Land of the Pygmies* (Lincoln: University of Nebraska Press, 1995), 22.
4. Mark, *The King of the World*, 24.
5. See the Patrick Putnam papers, Houghton Library, Harvard University (hereafter PP papers).
6. Adam Hochschild, *King Leopold's Ghost: A Story of Greed, Terror, and Heroism in Colonial Africa* (Boston: Houghton Mifflin, 1998).
7. Mark, *The King of the World*, 152.
8. Colin Turnbull, "The Mbuti Pygmies: An Ethnographic Survey," *Anthropological Papers of the American Museum of Natural History* 50, part 3 (1965): 158.
9. See Mark, *The King of the World*, 63–68.
10. PP papers.
11. PP papers.
12. PP papers.
13. Marcia Graham Synnott, *The Half-Opened Door: Discrimination and Admissions at Harvard, Yale and Princeton, 1900–1970*, Contributions in American History no. 80 (Westport, Conn.: Greenwood Press, 1979), 63.
14. Harry Starr, "The Affaire at Harvard," *Menorah Journal* 8, no. 5 (1922): 266.
15. Synnott, *The Half-Opened Door*, 79.
16. PP papers.
17. Earnest Hooton, "Progress in the Study of Race Mixtures with Special Reference to Work Carried on at Harvard University," *Proceedings of the American Philosophical Society* 65 (1926): 316.
18. Earnest Hooton, "An Anthropological Appraisal of the Jewish People," May 15, 1938, special collections, Harvard University Library.
19. Hooton, "An Anthropological Appraisal," 16.
20. Earnest Hooton, "Why the Jew Grows Stronger," *Colliers Weekly*, May 6, 1939.
21. Hooton, "An Anthropological Appraisal," 21.
22. See Pat Shipman, *The Evolution of Racism: Human Differences and the Use and Abuse of Science* (Cambridge, Mass.: Harvard University Press, 1994).
23. PP papers.
24. Patrick Putnam to Dr. Putnam, May 12, 1942, PP papers.
25. PP papers.
26. PP papers.
27. PP papers.
28. Patrick Putnam to Mr. Orts, January 1, 1932, notes for articles on "Territorial Administration, Colonialism, Feelings of Nit Wits," PP papers.
29. Georges Nzongola-Ntalaja writes: "Although this violence did not meet the definition of genocide in international law as 'acts committed with intent to destroy in whole or in part, a national, ethnic, racial or religious group,' it resulted in a death toll of holocaust proportions that is estimated to be as high as 10 million people." *The Congo from Leopold to Kabila: A People's History* (London and New York: Zed Books, 2002), 22. See also Hochschild, *King Leopold's Ghost*, 231–232.
30. PP papers.
31. PP papers.
32. Ben Wolf, "The Dirty Palette," *Art Digest*, April 15, 1946.
33. *Cahier* notes, July–August 1946, Anne Eisner Putnam papers, Houghton Library, Harvard University.

Chapter Three.
The Voyage to Africa (1946–1950)

1. Anne Eisner to Allan Keller, c. 1954, Anne Eisner Putnam Papers, Houghton Library, Harvard University (hereafter

AEP papers).

2. Patrick Putnam to H. A. Mack, October 17, 1948, Patrick Putnam papers, Houghton Library, Harvard University (hereafter PP papers). My translation from French.
3. Georges Nzongola-Ntalaja, *The Congo from Leopold to Kabila: A People's History* (London and New York: Zed Books, 2002), 40.
4. Anne Eisner, *cahier*, early 1946, AEP papers.
5. Anne Eisner to William and Florine Eisner, January 12, 1947, AEP papers.
6. Anne Eisner to Allan Keller, c. 1954, AEP papers.
7. Anne Eisner to Will and Florine Eisner, January–February 1947, AEP papers.
8. See Joan Mark, *The King of the World in the Land of the Pygmies* (Lincoln: University of Nebraska Press, 1995).
9. Anne Eisner, notes from Libenge, 1947, AEP papers.
10. Anne Eisner to William and Florine Eisner, August 25, 1947, AEP papers.
11. Patrick Putnam to Anne Eisner, 1947, PP papers.
12. Anne Eisner to William and Florine Eisner (?),April 18, 1948, AEP papers.
13. Anne Eisner to William and Florine Eisner (?), February 14, 1948, AEP papers.
14. Anne Eisner to William and Florine Eisner (?),February 16, 1948, AEP papers.
15. Anne Eisner to William and Florine Eisner (?),February 14, 1948, AEP papers.
16. Patrick Putnam to Anne Eisner, February 19, 1948, AEP papers.
17. Anne Eisner to Patrick Putnam, March 1948, AEP papers.
18. Patrick Putnam to Anne Eisner, April 24, 1948, AEP papers.
19. See Mark, *The King of the World*, 59, 107, 138, 141, 142, 144, 180, 206.
20. Anne Eisner to Patrick Putnam, May 2 and 6, 1948, AEP papers.
21. Patrick Putnam to Anne Eisner, May 29, 1948, PP papers.
22. Patrick Putnam to Emily Hahn, January 21, 1938, PP papers.
23. Mark, *The King of the World*, 119.
24. Patrick Putnam to Charles Putnam, February 8, 1948, PP papers.
25. Patrick Putnam to Anne Eisner, March 16, 1948, AEP papers.
26. Patrick Putnam to Agnes (?),1948, PP papers.
27. Patrick Putnam to H. A. Mack, October 17, 1948, box 1 of 16, PP papers. My translation from French.
28. Agaranga to Anne Eisner Putnam, September 28, 1948, AEP papers.
29. Enid Schildkrout, "Modernism and Ethnology in the Ituri: Anne Eisner, Colin Turbull, and the Mbuti," in Christie McDonald, ed., *Images of Congo: Anne Eisner's Art and Ethnography, 1946–1958* (Milan: 5 Continents Editions, 2005), 153–157.
30. Anne Eisner Putnam, *cahier*, 1948, AEP papers.
31. April Kingsley, *The Turning Point: The Abstract Expressionists and the Transformation of American Art* (New York: Simon & Schuster, l992), 16.
32. Anne Eisner Putnam to Will and Florine Eisner, August 30, 1947, AEP papers.
33. Kingsley, *The Turning Point*, 16–21.
34. Dr. Putnam's, niece Anna Lowell Tomlinson, told me this in a conversation with some misgivings, when I visited her on Martha's Vineyard.

Chapter Four. Back at the Epulu Ranch (1950–1951)

1. All quotes from Patrick Putnam to Anne Eisner Putnam, April 22, 1950, Anne Eisner Putnam papers, Houghton Library, Harvard University (hereafter AEP papers).
2. Patrick Putnam to Frank Lambrecht, c. 1950, AEP papers. For more on FFor more on Frank Lambrecht, see his *In the Shade of an Acacia Tree: Memoirs of a Health Officer in Africa, 1945–1959* (Philadelphia: American Philosophical Society, 1991).
3. Agaranga Nunziotika to Anne Eisner Putnam, May 1 and June 5, 1950, AEP papers.
4. Patrick Putnam to Anne Eisner Putnam, July 3, 1950, AEP papers.
5. Written c. 1945, AEP papers. A notes upon her departure from US, July, l946
6. Patrick Putnam to Anne Eisner Putnam, February 1951, AEP papers.
7. While the Belgian government had given Patrick Putnam a position to capture okapis to export, Jean de Medina, a retired Belgian officer, set up and became director of a capture station across the road near Epulu from 1948 to the 1960s. See Susan Lyndaker Lindsey and Mary Neel Green, eds., *The Okapi: Mysterious Animal of Congo-Zaire* (Austin: University of Texas Press, 1999), 55.
8. The BaNgwana were descendants of those who "aided and abetted the slave-traders." Colin Turnbull, *The Forest People* (New York: Simon & Schuster, 1961), 282.
9. Colin Turnbull translates *bakpara* as "master." See Turnbull, *The Forest People*, 281.

10. Hamadi Koki to Patrick Putnam, February 14, 1951, AEP papers.
11. Richard Grinker, among others, confirms this taboo in his book, *In the Arms of Africa: The Life of Colin M. Turnbull* (Chicago: University of Chicago Press, 2001), 81. See Emily Hahn's novel *With Naked Foot* (London: Transworld, 1952, 1959) about the plight of African wives or housekeepers who lived with white men. See also her expurgated book *Congo Solo* (New York: Bobbs-Merrill, 1933) and her article "Stewart," in the *New Yorker*, October 22, 1966, in which Pat—with whom she stayed at Epulu in the 1930s—is depicted through camouflaged names "Den" and "Stewart," respectively.
12. Florine Eisner to Anne Eisner, July 17, 1951, AEP papers.
13. Anne Eisner to Will and Florine Eisner, November 25, 1951, AEP papers.

Chapter Five. Grim Days (1952)

1. Anne Eisner Putnam, *cahier*, 1952–1953, Anne Eisner Putnam papers, Houghton Library, Harvard University (hereafter AEP papers).
2. See Joan Mark, *The King of the World in the Land of the Pygmies* (Lincoln: University of Nebraska Press, 1995), 58. See also Ken Cuthbertson, *Nobody Said Not to Go* (Boston and London: Faber and Faber, 1998), 108.
3. Anne Eisner Putnam to William and Florine Eisner, February 1949, AEP papers.
4. See Suzanne Preston Blier, "Mapping the Ituri: Mbuti Bark-Cloth Paintings and the Canvases of Anne Eisner," and Enid Schildkrout, "Modernism and Ethnology in the Ituri: Anne Eisner, Colin Turnbull, and the Mbuti," both in Christie McDonald, ed., *Images of Congo: Anne Eisner's Art and Ethnography, 1946–1958* (Milan: 5 Continents Editions, 2005), 105–123, 153–157.
5. See Christie McDonald, Kevin Tervala, and Suzanne Blier, "La forêt des sens: art, communauté, durabilité," *Cahier du GHFF Forêt, Environnement et Société 27* (2017): 90–96.
6. Many of these abstract representations were decoded decades later by Robert Farris Thompson and Serge Bahuchet, *Pygmées* (Paris: Musée Dapper, 1991), 94–95, 97, 100–101, 104.
7. Eisner Putnam-Gould manuscript, 1950, AEP papers.
8. Herbert Solow had decided to take a long view about the history of the Congo—its peoples, resources, and political structures. Far from naive about the complexities of the history, Solow nevertheless saw it as a promising time for all concerned. Once the article came out, a jury for colonial journalism of the International Fair of Ghent awarded him its prize
9. "History of Polio," Wikipedia, https://en.wikipedia.org/wiki/History_of_polio. Dr. Hilary Koprowski conducted the first clinical trials of an oral vaccine in the late 1950s by administering it to 250,000 children in the Belgian Congo and Ruanda-Urundi, among other places. "Hilary Koprowski," Encyclopaedia Britannica, https://www.britannica.com/biography/Hilary-Koprowski. It was ultimately not approved in the United States. Albert Sabin developed another oral vaccine, which became available in 1961.
10. Mark, *The King of the World*, 62.
11. AEP papers.
12. Michel Lechat, "Graham Green at the Leproserie," *London Review of Books* 29, no. 15 (August, 2007), https://www.lrb.co.uk/the-paper/v29/n15/michel-lechat/diary.
13. Monroe Stearns to Anne Eisner Putnam, August/September 1952, cited by Anne Eisner Putnam in letter to family, September 13, 1952, AEP papers.
14. Anne Eisner Putnam to Monroe Stearns, August 18, 1952, AEP papers.
15. See Christraud Geary, *In and Out of Focus: Images from Central Africa, 1885–1960* (Washington, D.C.: Smithsonian National Museum, 2003).
16. Patrick Putnam to Anne Eisner Putnam, October 8, 1952, AEP papers.
17. Anne Eisner Putnam, *cahier*, November 1952, AEP papers.
18. Francis Chapman, interview with Christie McDonald, December 1991, McDonald archive. Interview with Francis, p. 9
19. Anne Eisner Putnam, *cahier*, 1952, AEP papers.

Chapter Six. Life Is Difficult (1953)

1. Patrick Putnam to Charles Putnam, copies to others, December 30, 1952, Anne Eisner Putnam papers (hereafter AEP papers). Pat to Dr. Putnam, copies to others, 12/30/52
2. R. Sale to Anne Eisner, December 28, 1952. Translated into French by Grodya Dhechuvi.
3. See Frank Lambrecht, *In the Shade of an Acacia Tree: Memoirs of a Health Officer in Africa, 1945–1959* (Philadelphia: American Philosophical Society, 1991).
4. 1947, AEP papers.

5. For the history of Coon's work in anthropology and the controversies it raised about racism, see Pat Shipman, *The Evolution of Racism: Human Differences and the Use and Abuse of Science* (Cambridge, Mass.: Harvard University Press, 1994).
6. AEP papers.
7. Anne Eisner, Leilo [*sic*] *cahier,* 1953, AEP papers.
8. Anne Eisner, Leilo [*sic*] *cahier,* 1953, AEP papers.
9. Anne Eisner, Leilo [*sic*] *cahier,* 1953, AEP papers.
10. Anne Eisner Putnam to Allan Keller, November 1953, AEP papers.
11. Anne Eisner, Leilo [*sic*] *Cahier,* 1953, 93, AEP papers.
12. Notes, fall 1953, Patrick Putnam papers.
13. Anne Eisner, Alima *cahier,* Leilo [*sic*] camp, *cahier* 3, November 11, 1953, AEP papers.
14. Anne Eisner, Alima *cahier,* Leilo [*sic*] camp, November 24, 1953, AEP papers.
15. Patrick Putnam to Rozos, December 10, 1953, AEP papers. My translation from French.

Chapter Seven. Sisyphus's Sister (1954)

1. "Les expositions en cours," *La Métropole-Anvers,* December 11, 1954; Charles Bernard, *Nation Belge,* December 1954; cited in Philippe Roberts-Jones, ed., *Marthe Guillain Rétrospective* (Brussels: Musées Royaux des Beaux-Arts de Belgique, 1954).
2. Tay and Lowell Thomas Jr., *Our Flight to Adventure* (New York: Doubleday, 1956), 113, 115.
3. Colin Turnbull to William and Florine Eisner, August 5, 1954, Anne Eisner papers, Houghton Library, Harvard University (hereafter AEP papers). Colin to Eisners,8/5/54
4. Manuscript, Anne Eisner Putnam, *Madami: My Eight Years of Adventure with the Congo Pigmies,* 1954, AEP papers, 41.
5. Notes on manuscript, Putnam, *Madami,* 8.
6. Christraud Geary, "Pygmy Images and the Making of *Madami,* a Memoir by Anne Eisner Putnam and Allan Keller," in Christie McDonald, ed., *Images of Congo: Anne Eisner's Art and Ethnography, 1946–1958* (Milan: 5 Continents Editions, 2005), 124.
7. Anne Eisner to Monroe Stearns, August 21, 1954, AEP papers.
8. Florine Eisner to Anne Eisner, August 23, 1954, AEP papers.
9. *Cahier,* fall 1954, AEP papers.
10. Anne Eisner Putnam, with Allan Keller, *Madami: My Eight Years of Adventure with the Congo Pigmies* (New York: Prentice-Hall, 1954), 107.
11. Putnam, *Madami,* 59.
12. Putnam, *Madami,* 113.
13. Putnam, *Madami,* 116.
14. Sterling North, "Book Review," *New York World-Telegram and Sun,* 1954.
15. Margaret Carson Hubbard, "She Kept a Hotel among Pygmies in the African Congo," *New York Herald Tribune,* October 31, 1954.
16. Jan Albert Goris, *Belgian Trade Review,* November 1954.
17. Ashley Montagu, "The Little People," *New York Times Book Review,* October 17, 1954.
18. Ashley Montagu, *The Natural Superiority of Women* (Walnut Creek, Calif.: AltaMira Press, 1953). See also Ashley Montagu, *Man's Most Dangerous Myth: The Fallacy of Race* (Walnut Creek, Calif.: AltaMira Press, 1942).
19. John Haverstick, "Life with the Pygmies," *Saturday Review,* c. October 1954.

Chapter Eight. Back in New York On and Off (1955–1959)

1. Agaranga Nunziotika to Anne Eisner Putnam, November 5 and 15, 1954; December 7 and 22, 1954; throughout 1955, including January 9, January 14, February 20, June 26 and 28, July 8, October 4, November 11. Translations from KiNgwana into French by Grodya Dhechuvi. Anne Eisner Putnam papers, Houghton Library, Harvard University (hereafter AEP papers).
2. Anne Eisner Putnam to Agaranga Nunziotika, April 1, 1955; September 28, 1955. Translations from KiNgwana into French by Grodya Dhechuvi, AEP papers.
3. In *Images of Congo,* we spelled Ageranga's name incorrectly as Ageronga; I have corrected the spelling in this book.
4. Lecture, c. 1956, AEP papers.
5. Lecture, c. 1956, AEP papers.
6. Lecture, c. 1956, AEP papers.
7. Undated typewritten page, AEP papers.
8. Colin Turnbull to Anne Eisner, May 17, 1956; April 4, 1956, AEP papers.
9. Turnbull to Eisner, April 24, 1956, AEP papers.
10. Turnbull to Eisner, May 17, 1956, AEP papers.
11. Turnbull to Eisner, May 21, 1956, AEP papers.
12. Monroe Stearns to Colin Turnbull, November 7, 1956, AEP papers.
13. Turnbull to Stearns, November 12, 1956, AEP papers.
14. Turnbull to Eisner, November 8, 1956, AEP papers.
15. Turnbull to Stearns, December 12, 1956, AEP papers.
16. Colin's survey was originally written as a thesis for the Institute of Social

Anthropology at Oxford University and submitted in 1956 for the degree of bachelor of letters (BLitt). Colin Turnbull, "The Mbuti Pygmies: An Ethnographic Survey," *Anthropological Papers of the American Museum of Natural History* 50, part 3 (1965): 145–236.

17. Colin Turnbull, *The Mbuti Pygmies: Change and Adaptation* (New York: Hold, Rinehart and Winston, 1983), 74.
18. See Enid Schildkrout, "Modernism and Ethnology in the Ituri: Anne Eisner, Colin Turnbull, and the Mbuti," in Christie McDonald, ed., *Images of Congo: Anne Eisner's Art and Ethnography, 1946–1958* (Milan: 5 Continents Editions, 2005), 53–71.
19. See Christie McDonald, "Ethnography, Literature and Art: Making Sense of Colonial Life in the Ituri Forest," in McDonald, *Images of Congo*, 41–53.
20. Alan Wald, *The New York Intellectuals* (Chapel Hill: University of North Carolina Press, 1987), 276; see 267–310 for the impact of McCarthyism.
21. Eliena Krylenko Eastman died on October 9, 1956. Her papers reside at the Lilly Library, Indiana University.
22. The importance of the vernacular class photo, with its inclusions and exclusions, has recently been brilliantly analyzed by Marianne Hirsch and Leo Spitzer in *Class Photos in Liquid Time* (Seattle: University of Washington Press, 2020). An exhibition at the Hood Museum curated by the authors, "The Afterlives of Class Photos," features archives and work by contemporary artists across time and geographies. It presents a critical look at how this vernacular genre supported both assimilation and exclusionary ideologies and could "inspire social and political change."
23. See McDonald, *Images of Congo*, 20.
24. See Joan Miller, "Anne Eisner: Notes from a Painter's Point of View," in McDonald, *Images of Congo*, 149–152.
25. For a more extensive analysis of this and other paintings in the context of debate with Colin Turnbull about the relationships of villagers to Pygmies, see Christie McDonald, "Ethnographies, Literature, Art," in McDonald, *Images of Congo*, 41–53.
26. Anne Eisner to Will and Florine Eisner, September 18, 1957, AEP papers.
27. Anne Eisner to William and Florine Eisner, September 18, 1957, AEP papers.
28. Anne Eisner to William and Florine Eisner, September 18, 1957, AEP papers.
29. Anne Eisner to William and Florine Eisner, October 25, 1957, AEP papers.
30. The article would be published two years later. Anne Eisner Putnam, "My Life with Africa's Little People," *National Geographic* 117, no. 2 (February 1960): 279–302.
31. Anne Eisner Putnam to Will and Florine Eisner, April 21, 1958, AEP papers.
32. Colin Turnbull to Will and Florine Eisner, June 17, 1958, AEP papers.
33. Turnbull to William and Florine Eisner, June 17, 1958, AEP papers.
34. Turnbull to William and Florine Eisner, June 17, 1958, AEP papers.

Chapter Nine. Changes Political and Personal (the 1960s)

1. Patrice Lumumba, "Independence Day Speech (English subtitles)," Palais de la Nation, Léopoldville, June 30, 1960, https://www.youtube.com/watch?v=Xh9c62PRwqo, 6:48.
2. Colin Turnbull, *The Mbuti Pygmies: Change and Adaptation* (New York: Holt, Rinehart and Winston, 1983), 77. See Joan Mark, *The King of the World in the Land of the Pygmies* (Lincoln: University of Nebraska Press, 1998), 167. She recounts how in a bar in Stanleyville, Colin had run into Lumumba, who knew of Camp Putnam and who as a postal worker (the amount of mail back and forth being considerable) apparently expressed respect for Putnam.
3. Anne Eisner to Agaranga Nuziotika, 20 February 1961, Anne Eisner Putnam papers, Houghton Library, Harvard University. Translated from KiNgwana to French by Grodya Dhechuvi. My translation into English.
4. Agaranga Nunziotika to Anne Eisner, March 26, 1963, Anne Eisner Putnam papers, Houghton Library, Harvard University (hereafter AEP papers). Translated from KiNgwana to French by Grodya Dhechuvi. My translation into English.
5. See Mark, *The King of the World*, 214.
6. Colin Turnbull, *The Mountain People* (New York: Simon & Schuster, 1972). The exploration of cruelty, desperation, and evil in the culture of the Ugandan Ik, as opposed to the goodness of the Mbuti, was applauded by some and condemned by others as unethical.

7. Colin Turnbull, *The Forest People* (New York: Simon & Schuster, 1961), 8.
8. Anne Eisner Putnam to Colin Turnbull, c. 1955, AEP papers.
9. Turnbull, *The Forest People*, 143.
10. By the 1980s, when Colin published *The Mbuti Pygmies*, appropriately subtitled *Change and Adaptation*, he had completely rewritten the history of Pat's legacy residing solely with him, as his adopted son, attributing the disuse of Camp Putnam to "his third wife," with no acknowledgment of Pat's death before Colin's own longest stays at Epulu (in 1954 and 1957–1958); the complete erasure of Anne's welcome and hospitality which enabled his ethnography is baffling. (See chapter 8 here.)
11. Anne Eisner Putnam to Will and Florine Eisner, July 15, 1962, AEP papers.
12. Louis Finkelstein, interview by Christie McDonald, June 8, 1992. McDonald archive.
13. Jacques Lipchitz, "Eleven Europeans in America," *Modern Museum of Art Bulletin* 13, nos. 4–5 (1946): 27.
14. Susan Sontag, *Illness as Metaphor* (New York: Vintage Books, 1978).
15. Colin Turnbull, "For Anne, and Her Parents," eulogy, early February 1967, AEP papers.
16. Obituary, *New York Times*, January 31, 1967.
17. Finkelstein, interview by Christie McDonald, June 8, 1992. McDonald archive.
18. Finkelstein interview by Christie McDonald, June 8–9, 1992. McDonald archive.

Epilogue

1. Colin Turnbull returned to Epulu in 1970, as did later Dr. Joseph A. Towles, the African American anthropologist who became Turnbull's life partner. The Towles Archival Collection, which includes Turnbull's papers, is conserved at the Avery Research Center for African American History and Culture at the College of Charleston. Joe Towles died of AIDS in 1988; Turnbull died, also of AIDS, in July 1994. Researchers from Kyoto University (in particular the late Professor Reizo Harako) studied Mbuti and Efe hunters beginning in the 1970s for twenty years. Professors Irven DeVore and Robert Bailey co-directed the "Ituri Project," from 1980 on, about the nearby Efe Pygmies and Lese villagers. Richard Grinker was among those who did field research in the area. Robert Farris Thompson studied the bark cloths of the Mbuti women.
2. Terese Hart to Christie McDonald, email, July 15, 2004.
3. For information about the Harts' work in the Congo, see "Learning by Hart: Exploration and Conservation in the Congo Basin," Rainforest Trust, October 2016, https://www.rainforesttrust.org/learning-hart-exploration-conservation-congo-basin.

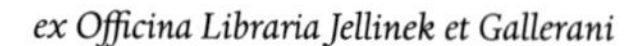

ex Officina Libraria Jellinek et Gallerani